MUSHROOMS

THE ILLUSTRATED BOOK OF MUSHROOMS

Text by
Mirko Svrček

Illustrated by
Bohumil Vančura

CAXTON EDITIONS

CONTENTS

Text by Mirko Svrček
Translated by Marie Hejlová
Illustrated by Bohumil Vančura

Designed and produced by Aventinum Publishing House,
Prague, Czech Republic
This English edition published in 1998
by CAXTON EDITIONS
16 Connaught Street
Marble Arch, London W2 2AF

ISBN 1-84067-047-9

Printed in the Czech Republic by Polygrafia, a.s., Prague

3/13/22/51-01

The Morphology of Fungi

Fungi are thallophytes that have no green-plant pigment (chlorophyll), their cells possess a true nucleus, and they reproduce by spores. Being incapable of the photosynthetic assimilation usual in green plants, they derive organic substances from the bodies of other organisms, living or dead; this way of obtaining nourishment is described as heterotrophic. The fungal body (thallus) is either a single cell or a threadlike structure (hypha). A large number of branching hyphae together constitute the mycelium which gives rise to usually multiform spore-producing cells. Spores are either uni- or multicellular. In most types of fungi, spore-producing cells (basidia, asci, conidiophores) form a part of a special structure made up of hyphal tissue and called the fruit body (sporocarp). Although the fruit bodies are given to extraordinary variation in shape, size and colouring, these do remain fairly constant in individual fungus groups, and so are useful distinguishing characteristics. The same applies to spores. It is exactly the internal and external morphology of fruit bodies, the morphology of spores and the way in which the latter are reproduced that provide the principles underlying the systematic classification of fungi. In this book fungus fruit bodies are classified according to their similarities as well as according to features considered as a manifestation of their affinity.

The simplest types of fungi possess a unicellular,

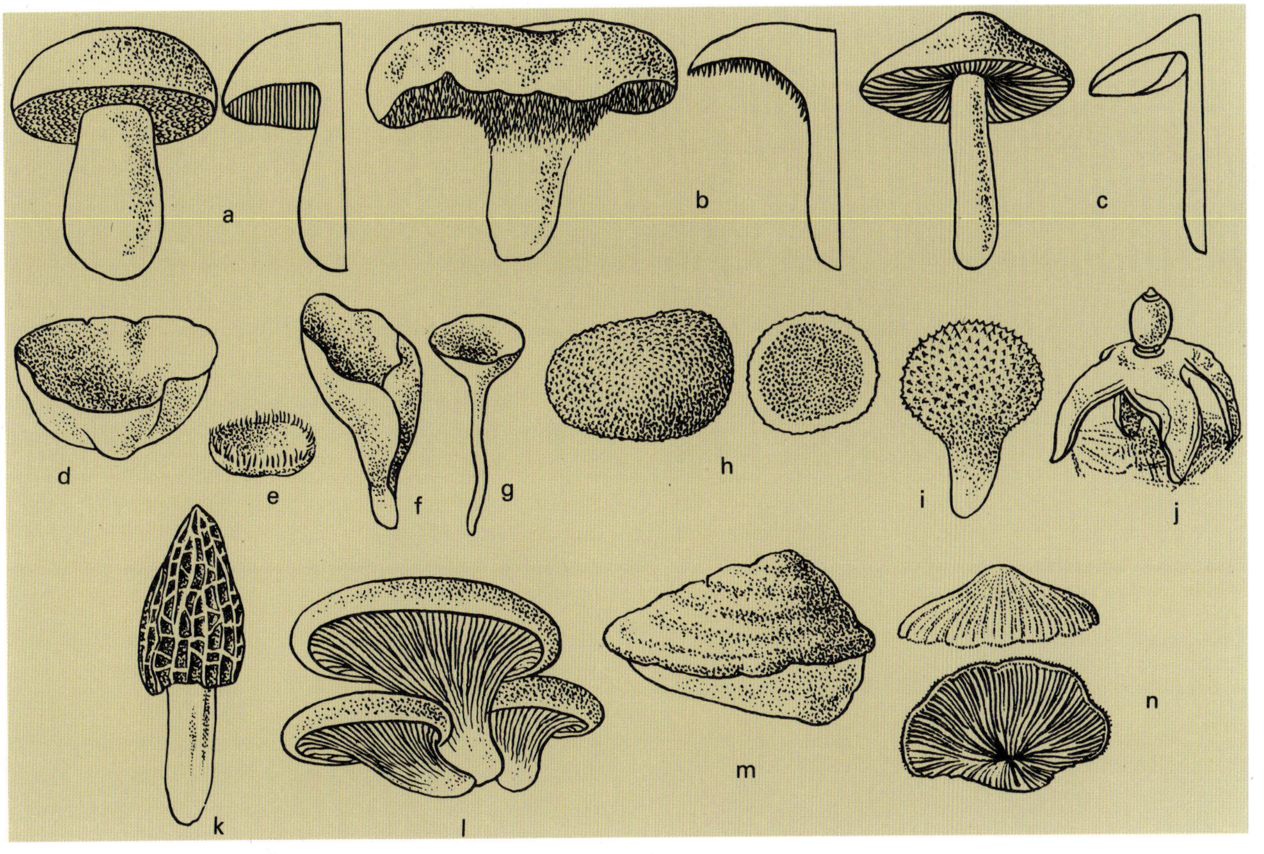

1) Various shapes of fruit bodies:
a – fruit body of Boletaceae differentiated into a cap and a stipe; **b** – fruit body of Hydnaceae with a spiny hymenophore on the underside of the cap; **c** – fruit body of gill fungi with gills on the underside of the cap; **d** – patelliform fruit body (apothecium) of *Peziza*; **e** – patelliform fruit body ciliate (hirsute) in the margin and on the outer surface (genus *Scutellinia*); **f** – upright apothecium in *Otidea*, open on one side; **g** – cup-shaped apothecium of *Microstoma* possessing a long stem; **h** – tuberous fruit body of *Elaphomyces*, its cross section on the right; **i** – fruit body of a puffball (*Lycoperdon*); **j** – fruit body of an earthstar (*Geastrum*); **k** – fruit body of a morel (*Morchella*); **1** – fruit body of a gill fungus with a lateral stipe (*Pleurotus*); **m** – fruit body of a stipeless polypore, laterally attached to the substrate; **n** – cap-shaped, stipeless fruit body with a gilled hymenophore (*Schizophyllum*), viewed from above and from below.

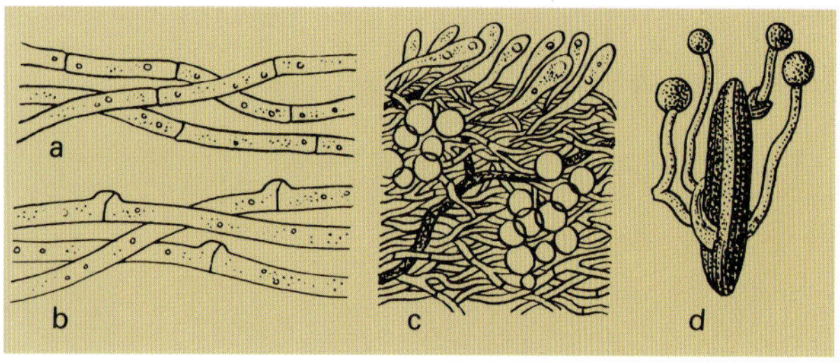

2) **a** – Septate hyphae without clamp connections, **b** – hyphae with clamp connections, **c** – part of fruit-body tissue from the stipe surface of a russula; clavate dermatocystidia in the upper part, globose spherocystidia lower down, lactifers scattered among normal cylindrical hyphae are dark-coloured, **d** – sclerotium of *Claviceps purpurea,* giving rise to pedicellate stromata. Perithecia protruding above the surface only by their verruciform ostioles are embedded in their stilbeous terminal part.

filamentous, branching thallus whose cytoplasm contains a great number of nuclei with no partitions (septa) to divide them; this is the type of thallus encountered in true molds (Phycomycetes). Characteristic of more developed fungi is the presence of septa dividing the mycelial hyphae into a multitude of segments.

Under specific conditions the fungi produce sporiferous cells. In primitive types these sporiferous cells may arise directly from the mycelium. In other fungi, fruit bodies are the first to develop and subsequently to originate spore-bearing cells.

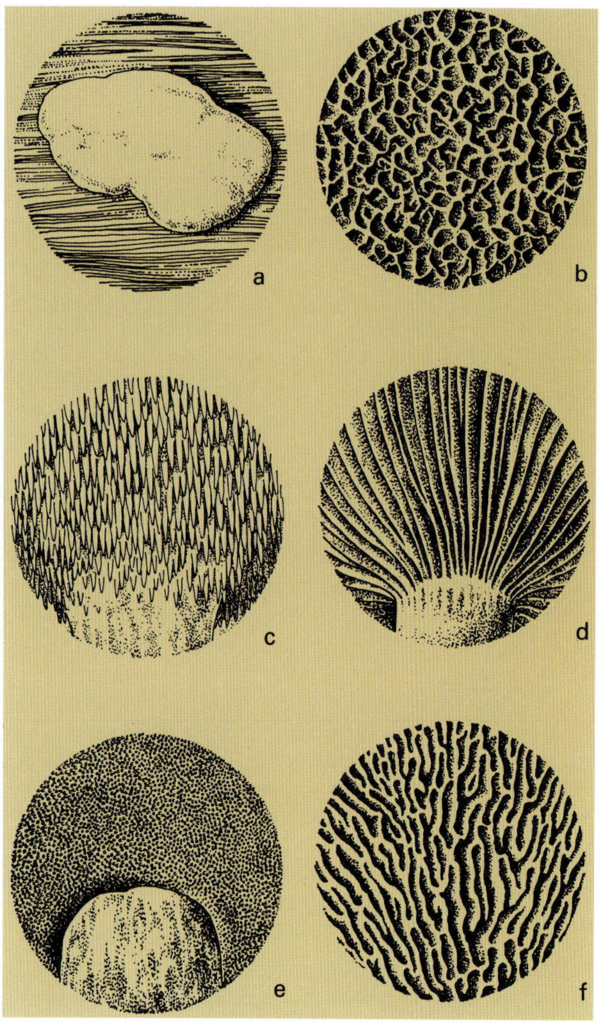

3) Various forms of the hymenophore:
a – smooth (resupinate); **b** – irregularly reticulate, lacunar to faveolate; **c** – spiniform; **d** – gilled (attachment of gills to the stipe); **e** – tubiform (view of tube pores in the vicinity of the stipe); **f** – in the form of irregular, wavy, richly anastomosed gill folds.

The fruit body is an extraordinarily multiform structure in its dimensions (ranging from microscopic sizes up to the size of several tens of centimetres) and also in its shape and colouring. The fruit body of simpler forms may be nothing but a little ball of hyphae entwining the asci. In Ascomycetes the fruit body is either globular, permanently closed (in which case it is known as the cleistothecium – e.g. in mildew, Erysiphales), or it opens either through a regular pore (as does the perithecium of flask fungi – Deuteromycetes) or irregularly. Finally the apothecium, the fruit body characteristic of the Discomycetes, is a more or less open, cup-shaped or discoid fruit body.

In view of the aim and limited scope of this book we shall deal only with the morphology of fruit bodies of higher fungi (Macromycetes). Here we meet with two basic fruit-body types determined by the location of the spore-bearing tissue. In the first case the spore-bearing tissue is situated inside the fruit body which is often globular in shape, as for example in the stomach fungi (Gasteromycetes); such a fruit body is described as being angiocarpous. In the second case the sporiferous part of the fruit body is laid out either over its entire surface or only over a limited part of it; this is a gymnocarpous fruit body encountered in all the other Basidiomycetes. In gill fungi (Agaricales) and boleti (Boletales), as well as in non-gilled fungi (Aphyllophorales) and some disc fungi (Discomycetes) we may come across two types of gymnocarpous fruit bodies:

1. Resupinate fruit bodies are produced, for example, by *Tomentella* and numerous non-gilled fungi, such as *Peniophora.* They form more or less conspicuous layers with either indistinct or sharply delimited margins, of various consistency (floccose, felted, cobwebby, membranous, coriaceous), usually very thin but in some cases several millimetres thick. Basidia, as a rule, are arranged into a hymenium covering the entire upper surface of the fruit body; on the substrate it is often turned downwards, to the ground. Resupinate fruit bodies may be found on the underside of dropped branches and uprooted trunks. Sometimes a tendency to produce lateral caps or forms with a partially recurved or elevated margin can be observed.

2. Upright fruit bodies occur both in the

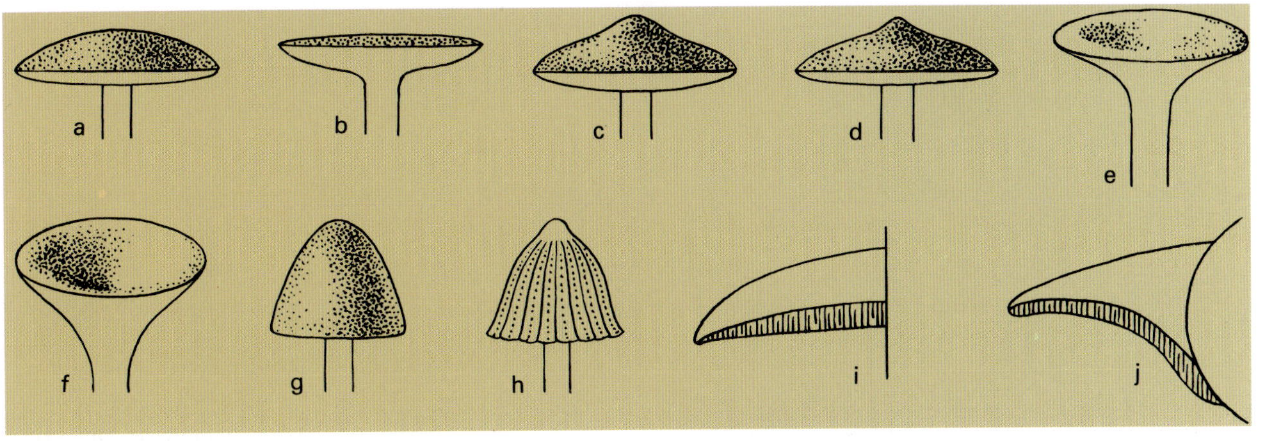

4) Various shapes of the cap:
a – slightly convex; **b** – flatly expanded (applanate); **c** – obtusely umbonate at the centre; **d** – acutely mucronate (tipped with a sharp wart); **e** – depressed; **f** – deeply infundibuliform; **g** – conical; **h** – campanulate (bell-shaped), radially striate up to the centre; **i** – laterally attached polypore cap in cross-section; **j** – section through a semiresupinate cap (in some polypores).

Basidiomycetes and in some Discomycetes. The hymenium covers either the entire external surface or only its upper part (for example in the Clavariaceae). The most developed type is a fruit body differentiated into a stem or stipe (stipes) and a cap (pileus). Most gill fungi and boleti, as well as some tooth-fungi belong to this group. The hymenophore, i.e. the part of the fruit body bearing the hymenium, is usually confined to the underside of the cap. Stipeless fruit bodies, attached to the substrate either dorsally or laterally, occur in some genera of gill fungi (for example *Crepidotus*) and in a great many polypore species (Polyporaceae, Poriaceae).

The hymenophore takes different forms: it is either completely smooth or variously corrugated (veined, wrinkled), or assumes the shape of spines, gills or tubes. All of these forms occur in all the types of fruit bodies referred to above.

The cap and the stipe are also multiform. The cap often changes its shape in the course of the gradual development of the fruit body from youth to old age, and is, moreover, subjected to intraspecific variability, i.e. the caps of single fungi belonging to the same species are not exactly the same. Gills (lamellae) play an important part in classifying and identifying fungi. The manner of their attachment to the stipe is of importance. This characteristic appears most clearly in the longitudinal section through the fresh fruit body, preferably a young and undamaged one – in older specimens it is not always possible to discover how the gills are attached. Of no less significance is the colouring of the gills which changes with the aging of

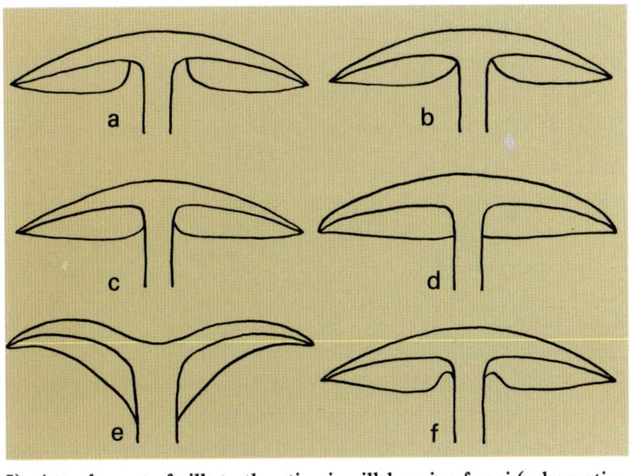

5) Attachment of gills to the stipe in gill-bearing fungi (schematic sections through the cap):
a – remote; **b** – free; **c** – adnexed; **d** – adnate; **e** – deeply decurrent or arcuate-decurrent; **f** – sinuate and attached by a tooth (or decurrent by a tooth).

6) Various shapes of the basal part of the stipe in gill fungi:
a – bearing annular stripes; **b** – with a ring in the upper part of the bulbous basal portion; **c** – with a fusoid extension radicating in the ground; **d** – globularly enlarged; **e** – thickened and tapering to a beet-like extension; **f** – with a high coriaceous or membranous sheath; **g** – with a circumscissile or marginate-depressed bulb.

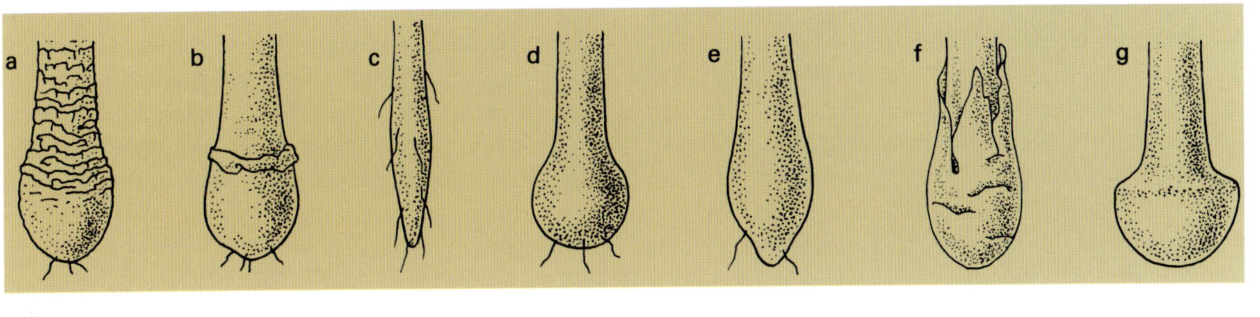

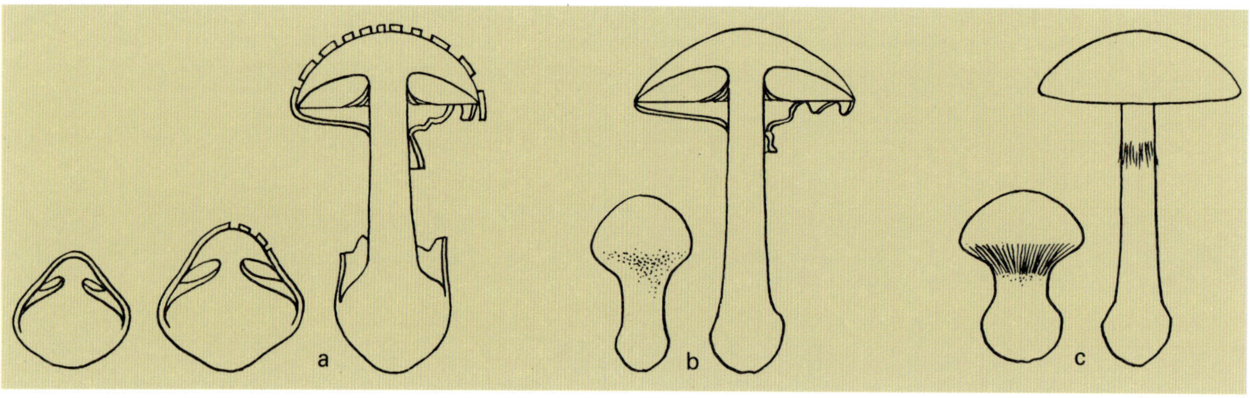

7) Veils of gill-fungi fruit bodies:
a – development of the sheath and warts from the universal veil (*velum universale*) and of the ring on the stipe from the partial veil (*velum partiale*) in amanitas (two young fruit bodies, one mature fruit body); **b** – one young and one mature fruit body with a developed partial veil leaving a ring on the stipe; **c** – partial veil developed only as a fibrous cobweb (*cortina*); in the youngest fruit bodies it connects the cap margin with the stipe surface and covers the gills, later on it remains in the upper part of the stipe as a fibrous ring or as single filaments.

the fruit body. As it matures the fruit body's colouring is affected by the colour of the spores ripening on the basidia which are sometimes produced in quantities so large that they cover the entire gill surface as a white or variously coloured powder. The same applies to the tubes of Boletales and to hymenophores of other fungi. Although nowadays the colouring of the spore print is no longer considered a principal classification criterium of higher fungi, it continues to be of major importance in determining the species.

The cap cuticle provides a great number of important and constant characteristics. Its properties: separability, sliminess, viscosity, dryness, fibrousness, scaliness, etc. are determined by its microscopic structure. More detailed information is given in the chapter dealing with fungi under the microscope. The most conspicuous feature is the colouring of the cuticle – it is the first to attract attention. However, the specification of colours is a highly subjective matter. A certain degree of objectivity may be reached by comparing the colours of the fruit body with printed colour tables (known as chromotaxes) where the colours are arranged according to a certain system and numbered, and eventually named. Several such chromotaxes have been worked out – most of them, however, are inaccessible to non-specialists. For example, one of the most accomplished ones, repeatedly cited in all fundamental mycological works, is Ridgeway R., *Colour Standards and Colour Nomenclature,* published in 1912. In other chromotaxes exactly those hues are often lacking which most frequently appear on fungus fruit bodies, i.e. brown, yellow and red. In most cases, the colour table attached to Moser's key *Die Röhrlinge und Blätterpilze,* 1978, may adequately be used, though to a limited extent.

In gill fungi and boleti, quite young fruit bodies are often enclosed in a cover called a velum. This cover is of two types: the universal veil (*velum universale* or *velum generale*), and the partial veil (cobwebby veil or cortina – *velum partiale*). The former deposits scabby remains on the surface of the cap and a volva on the stipe base of a fully developed fruit body, while the latter connects the cap margin with the stipe and its remnants may be found both in the marginal zone of the cap and in the basal portion of the stipe; also the ring encircling the upper part of the stipe belongs to them. The heterogeneous character of the velum, ranging from fine filaments to a hard membranous cover, makes it essential to examine both quite young and fully developed fruit bodies in identifying some genera (for example *Cortinarius*).

The flesh is of various consistency – it may be very friable, pomaceously brittle, fleshy, watery, succulent, dry, fibrillose, coriaceous, tough or woody. When cut or broken, a number of significant features may be seen of which the most relevant is the colour change which may sometimes be different in the cap and in the stipe, while in the stipe differences may in turn prevail in the colouring of the basal portion and of the other parts. Sometimes the context exudes latex, a colourless or milky liquid whose colouring is either persistent or changes on exposure to air. No less important is the taste of the context (tasting belongs to the indispensable diagnostic procedures in identifying fungi). A discussion of smells and odours emitted by fruit bodies could fill a chapter by itself. There are many of them, and they are often compared to the well-known, as well as to the less usual, smells characteristic of other organisms, plants, animals, or chemical compounds. Their evaluation is often largely subjective, yet the smells are so specific in the individual species that a good expert is in a position to identify a fungus even from small fragments of the fruit body on the basis of their characteristic smell only. Some fungi (e. g. the tooth fungi) maintain their specific smell even as exsiccations (dried specimens).

Fungi under the Microscope

In identifying and studying fungi we cannot do without a high-quality microscope equipped with an immersion lens. Of course we can distinguish several hundred fungus species by the naked eye, but this has its limitations and in a great many cases the identification remains questionable without confirmation by microscopic analysis. Consequently, the confirmed enthusiast should consider whether to invest time and money in the use of a microscope. If so, the fascinating world of the microcosm, lavishly abounding in extraordinary and aesthetically impressive forms, opens before us. As well as the current set of eyepieces and lenses, an ocular micrometer is also indispensable for measuring the size of spores, hyphae, hymenial and other elements.

The mycelium (the actual fungus body) is a relatively uniform structure composed of long cylindrical, septate, colourless or coloured hyphae, sometimes provided with clamp connections. The hyphal walls are smooth, and may be thin or thick, and sometimes encrusted.

The differentiation of individual organs of the fungus body becomes plain only in fruit bodies. The most important organ is the hymenophore, whose internal structure remains constant in the individual genera. It is best observed on the tangential section across the gills, obtained manually with the help of a razor blade. With a little feeling and patience we are sure to succeed in selecting from among a larger number of available sections at least one sufficiently thin to enable us to observe the structure of the trama in a microscopic mount. The trama assumes four basic forms: regular, irregular, bilateral and inverse. The details clearly appear in Fig. 8.

The hymenium is a spore-producing layer composed either of fertile basidia only, or of basidia and sterile, multiform cells. These are cystidia of various types which are longer than basidia, of various shapes, with a bare or encrusted surface, thin- or thick-walled, often growing out of the deeper layers of the gill tissue. The cystidia situated on the gill edge, the so-called cheilocystidia, are frequently arranged into continuous rows, sometimes different in colour from the gill face; such an edge, if observed with a lens, is finely lacerate or ciliate. In some cases the cheilocystidia are filled with coloured pigment. The cystidia present at the gill face are termed pleurocystidia and may be different from cheilocystidia in shape. Gloeocystidia (occurring more frequently in Aphyllophorales) are characterized by a granular or light-refracting content, somewhat oily in appearance. Basidioles (sterile cells similar to basidia in both shape and size) are sometimes present among them; if their shape is different, they are termed cystidioles. While in Agaricales and Boletales the shape of the basidia is, in the main, uniform (usually clavate), in Aphyllophorales it is considerably diversified and plays an important part in their taxonomic classification.

At the basidial apex there are usually four apicules (sterigmata) each of which bears a single spore; basidia with two sterigmata are relatively common, while those having only one or alternatively having more than four sterigmata are rather rare. Developmentally lower types of Basidiomycetes have septate basidia (divided either by transverse walls or lengthwise, by two walls perpendicular to each other), or basidia separating into two branches. Siderophilous basidia are typical of some genera of

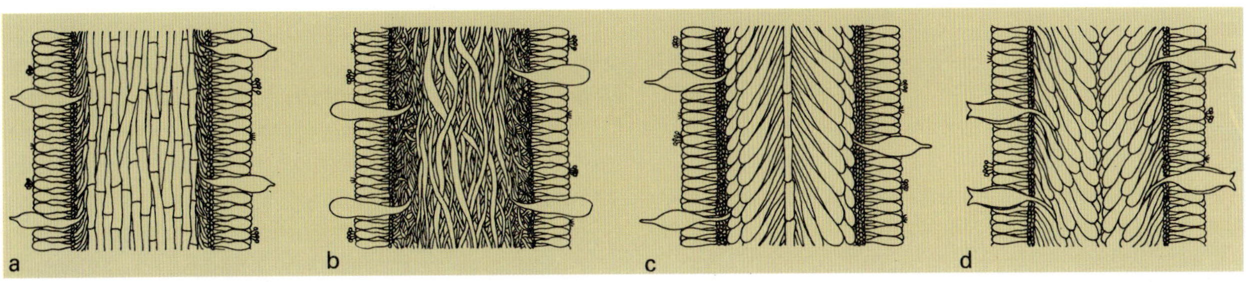

8) Gill-trama types (tangential section):
a – regular; **b** irregular; **c** – bilateral; **d** – inverse; the layer of smaller cells below the basidia (forming a continuous layer – the hymenium) is termed subhymenium; cystidia are protruding among the basidia.

9) Tangential section through a part of gills in a russula: the hymenium contains infertile clavate basidia (basidioles) on the one hand, fertile basidia with four sterigmata and warty spores at their apices on the other hand, and, moreover, cystidia exceeding the basidia in length. The gill tissue is composed of relatively large subglobose cells (spherocystidia), cylindrical hyphae and densely granular, long lactifers extending in some places as far as the hymenium.

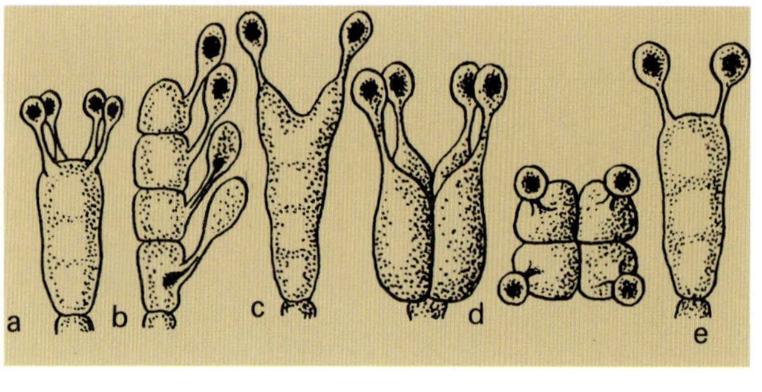

10) Various types of basidia:
a – unicellular basidium (holobasidium) with four sterigmata at the apex; **b** – basidium with three transverse septa (phragmobasidium), a single sterigma grows out at the side of each of its cells;
c – basidium forked at the top into two branches terminating in a sterigma; **d** – basidium divided by four longitudinal walls down to the base (side and top views); **e** – bisporous holobasidium with two sterigmata.

Tricholomataceae – *Lyophyllum, Tephrocybe,* etc.; their plasma contains granules staining black when exposed to ferric acetocarmine.

Trama in the broader sense of the word is the tissue of the entire fruit body, whereas in the narrower sense it implies the gills, cap and stipe but excluding the surface tissues. The context itself, the fruit-body trama, is formed by a system of hyphae of the following three types: generative, binding and skeletal. Most common are fruit bodies consisting of generative (so-called basic) hyphae only; they are ramified, septate, and with or without clamp connections – this is known as the monomitic system. If, besides these, another type of hyphae is present – either binding hyphae (which are more or less thick-walled, strongly fruticose, aseptate and lacking clamp connections), or skeletal hyphae (these are thick-walled, unbranched, long, aseptate) – this is known as the dimitic system. If all the three hyphal types are present in the tissue, they constitute the trimitic system. The fruit-body tissue of some fungus genera contains lactiferous tubes. These are very long, sinuous, usually aseptate hyphae filled with thick plasma of a frequently lacteal character, such as latex in the *Lactarius* species.

The context of fungi of the genera *Lactarius* and *Russula* contains – besides threadlike filaments and lactiferous tubes – clusters of globular cells, the so-called spherocystidia, conditioning the peculiar pomaceous brittleness of the flesh of these fungi. Of particular importance among the surface tissues is the cap cuticle which consists of one or more layers. The outermost layer of a multistratous cuticle is the epicutis, the layer between the epicutis and the cap context is known as the hypoderm or subcutis. If the cuticle is made up of clavate to globose cells, it is known as the hymeniform cuticle.

The colouring of fruit bodies depends upon physical processes taking place within the fruit bodies on the one hand, and upon the presence of pigments (whose distribution also has taxonomic significance) on the other. Intracellular pigments are present either in the plasma or in vacuoles, pigments are also in hyphal walls and in intercellular spaces. The white colour is caused by the air filling intercellular spaces; if these are filled with water, the white colour becomes glassy and colourless (hyaline).

Spores are taxonomically the most relevant and constant characteristics. They are extremely multiform, uni- or multicellular, colourless or exhibiting a whole scale of colours, up to black. To be examined in detail, spores should always be observed under an immersion lens, at first in a colourless medium in water, in a 10-per cent solution of potash lye (KOH), in ammonia, etc.; another mount is coloured by Melzer's reagent, cotton blue, or another colouring matter. Details not always clearly discernible in a cursory inspection of a microscopic mount are subjected to thorough examination: spore-wall thickness, presence of the apicule, shape and size of the germ pore, ornamentation of the spore wall, presence of the suprahilar disc or depression. One of the most significant discoveries that helped clarify the inter-relationships among gill fungi as well as among other fungus groups was the ascertainment of spore-wall amyloidity. Amyloidity is determined by Melzer's reagent with the aid of which the walls of spores or hyphae change either to some shade of blue (amyloid reaction), or to yellow-brown, red-brown or purple-brown hues (dextrinoid reaction). A more recent discovery is cyanophilia: here the spore or hyphal walls turn blue when touched with cotton-blue solution.

Only a brief mention will be made here of the disc fungi, whose larger representatives can often be come across by a mushroom-picker. The spore-bearing layer of their fruit body (apothecium) is composed of asci and paraphyses. The asci are cylindrical or clavate in shape and, as a rule, contain eight spores (ascospores) which are released either through a pore in the tip of the ascus, or by the opening of a lid. In some genera the ascus walls are amyloid. Paraphyses, i.e. sterile filaments occurring among the asci, are often pigmented and consequently affect the colouring of the thecium (hymenium). In general, what has been said about spores of the basidiomycetes applies also to ascospores. The context of the apothecium – which is either directly attached to the substrate or seated on a sterile stem or stipe – has a relatively simple structure and its external layer bears various growths, such as bristles or hairs.

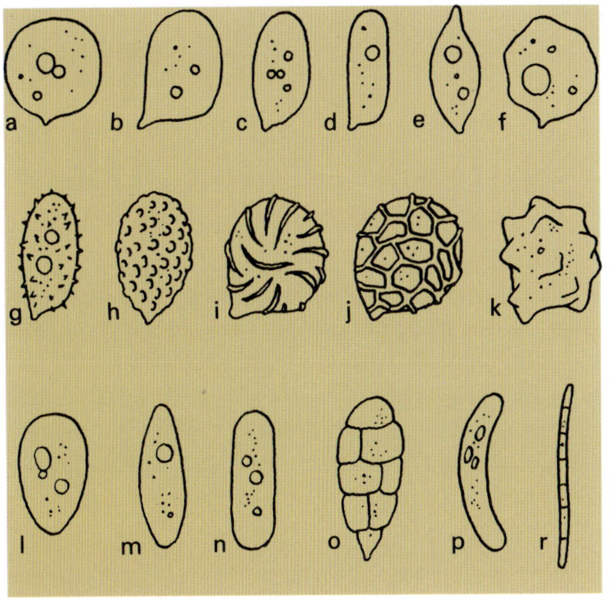

11) Various types of spores and ornamentation:
a – globose; **b** – subglobose, obliquely extending into an apiculus at the base; **c** – ellipsoid; **d** – cylindrical; **e** – fusiform; **f** – angular; **g** – echinulate; **h** – verrucose; **i** – with a pectinate ornamentation; **j** – with a reticulate ornamentation; **k** – tuberculate: **l** – ovoid without an apiculum; **m** – obtusely fusiform; **n** – cylindrical; **o** – divided by transverse and longitudinal septa (so-called muriform); **p** – allantoid; **r** – filiform with transverse septa.

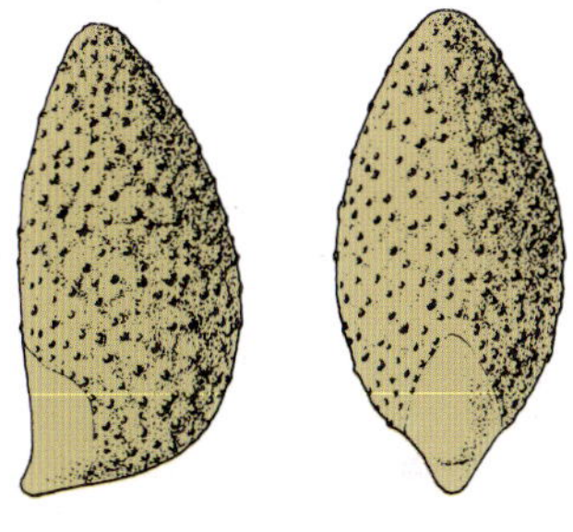

12) A spore of *Galerina* with a verrucose ornamentation and a suprahilar plage in the vicinity of the apiculus; on the left, the side view of the spore (with a discernible depression just above the hilar appendage), and its front view.

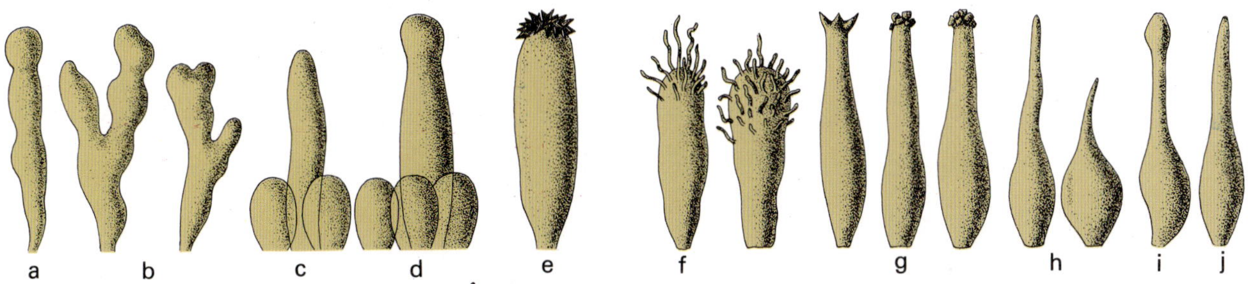

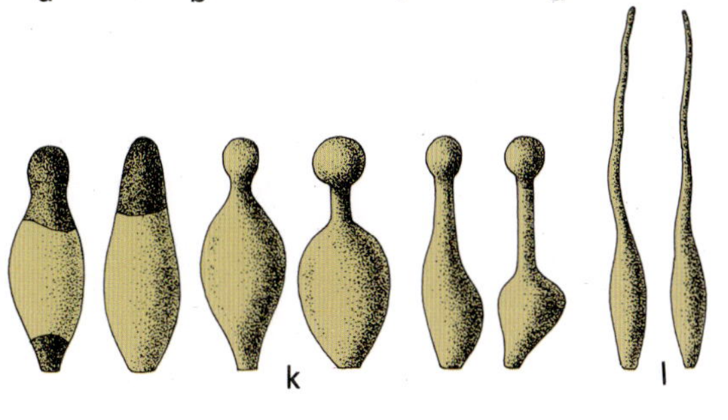

13) Various types of cystidia in gill fungi:
a – irregularly constricted; **b** – ramified; **c** – cylindrical; **d** – with a clavate or stilbeous ending; **e** – with a crystal encrustation at the top; **f** – so-called penicillate; **g** – lageniform with various endings at the top, e. g. tridentate, or crowned by an encrustation in the form of a cap; **h** – pointed; **i** – beaked; **j** – elongated and capitate at the apex; **k** – lecythiform; **l** – filiform (staminiform) with a fusiform extension at the base.

Reproduction of Fungi

Fungi reproduce in two ways: sexually and asexually. Both of them are commonly encountered. Sexual reproduction is generally regarded as a union of two sexually differentiated nuclei, e. g. in spores. The germinating spores form a unisexual mycelium (primary mycelium), consisting of hyphae with uninucleate cells. Each of these cells contains a nucleus with a certain number of chromosomes. The primary mycelium may go on growing for a very long time without forming any sex organs. If two uninucleate, sexually differentiated mycelia meet, the plasmas of the conjugating cells unite into a single binucleate cell – the dicaryon. The dicaryon grows into hyphae made up of binucleate cells, into the secondary mycelium. Even this mycelium can take a very long time to grow; under suitable external conditions, however, it gives rise to fruit bodies. Hence it follows that fruit bodies are composed of hyphae with binucleate cells.

The fusion of the two dicaryotic nuclei takes place only at the hyphal end, in terminal cells transformed into basidia or asci. The single nucleus arisen through the association of two dicaryotic nuclei has a double number of chromosomes (2n), that is, a double amount of nuclear matter and thus of hereditary information. It is only through the subsequent reduction division that the number of chromosomes is lowered to the original state (n). These nuclei give rise to spores – basidiospores on basidia, ascospores in asci. Even though, of course, there are exceptions to this scheme, it is sufficient for a basic understanding of the principle of sexual reproduction in fungi.

Asexual reproduction is never preceded by a fusion of the nuclei of two cells. Its simplest form involves the decomposition of the mycelium into simple fragments termed arthrospores. Another form is the abstriction of independent germ spores (conidia) from specialized hyphae (conidiophores). The conidia vary in shape, size and colouring; they may be unicellular or multicellular. Chlamydospores are thick-walled spores developed from mycelial cells. Their function is that of resting cells capable of surviving long-lasting unfavourable living conditions. Cells giving rise to asexual spores are generally designated as conidiogenous. In classifying the conidial stages of fungi, a great many of which occur independently and are included in the subsidiary class of imperfect fungi (Deuteromycetes, formerly also *Fungi imperfecti*), particular importance is attributed to the manner in which asexual spores are formed.

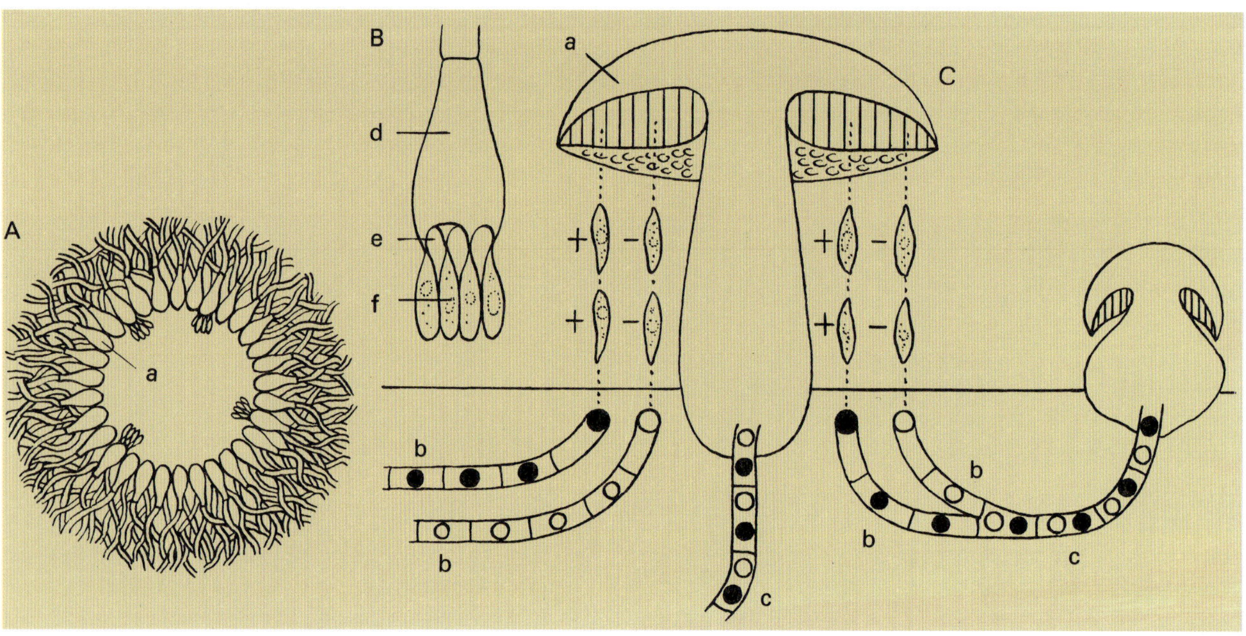

14) Reproduction in Basidiomycetes:
A – cross section through a tube of a bolete; **B** – formation of spores on a basidium; **C** – development of a fruit body from the mycelium; **a** – hymenium; **b** – primary mycelium; **c** – secondary mycelium; **d** – basidium; **e** – sterigma; **f** – sexually differentiated spores.

Spores originating in any of these ways are produced by fungi in such enormous quantities that they not only populate the whole biosphere of our planet but can be found even in the atmosphere. As spores the fungi are omnipresent, and most of them seem to be endowed with the capacity to withstand unfavourable influences and to remain in a latent stage without losing their viability. This overproduction of spores is a necessary precondition for the survival of the species.

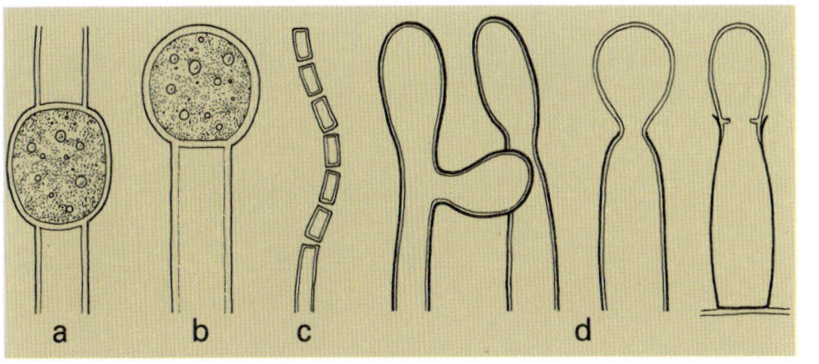

15) Development of asexual spores:
a, b – thick-walled chlamydospores (**a** – intercalary, **b** – terminal); **c** – hypha subjected to chain-like disintegration into immobile spores; **d** – various ways of the development of conidia.

Some Points of Interest in the Life of Fungi

The life of fungi belongs to the most interesting chapters of mycology. Heterotrophic nourishment, which represents the principal characteristic of this huge group of organisms nowadays considered as an independent kingdom besides green plants and animals, has called forth a number of divergent phenomena and properties. Saprophytism and parasitism, two large categories differing in their relation to the environment from which fungi obtain organic substances necessary for building up their fruit bodies, assert themselves in a characteristic manner in the development of fungi; in the remote past, they gave rise to innumerable fungus forms differing not only in shape but also physiologically and genetically. Their classification is a task to be coped with by mycological taxonomy.

Saprophytic fungi, including the greater part of the so-called large fungi (Macromycetes), as well as a good many other fungi, live in their mycelial form in an environment composed of dead plant and animal remains at different stages of decomposition. Their hyphae penetrate through the soil, humus and detritus, through the wood of decaying tree trunks, stumps and branches, or live in the network of withering leaves, needles, herb stems, grass stalks, etc. Many saprophytic fungi are bound by their way of life to a specific and often limited environment.

A generally widespread phenomenon is the symbiosis (co-existence) of fungi with the roots of higher vascular plants, less frequently with ferns and bryophytes; it is termed mycorrhiza. The mycelium either clothes the roots only externally (ectotrophic mycorrhiza), or penetrates inside the root tissue (endotrophic mycorrhiza). The ectotrophic mycorrhiza is easily discernible by the naked eye: the little roots are usually short but thick and often forked so that they may resemble corals in appearance. The mycelial hyphae envelop the roots like a continuous covering with protruding short surface excrescences. The endotrophic mycorrhiza, on the other hand, does not appear on the outside because the hyphae pervade the intercellular spaces of the root network. This type of mycorrhiza is more common than the former. The fungi living in mycorrhizal dependence upon the roots of live trees are not easily raised in pure cultures in a laboratory, and it is only rarely that they may be compelled to form fruit bodies. The cultivation of other saprophytic fungi – particularly lignicolous ones – presents no great problems.

The relationship between the two organisms, the green plant and the fungus, has been and continues to be subjected to a great many studies because of the considerable practical importance of the problem area concerned. Fungi of most various systematic groups live in mycorrhizal association. Mycorrhiza is particularly frequent in Basidiomycetes, but also exists in other groups (e.g. in moulds and ascomycetes). A single tree may be found to live in this kind of

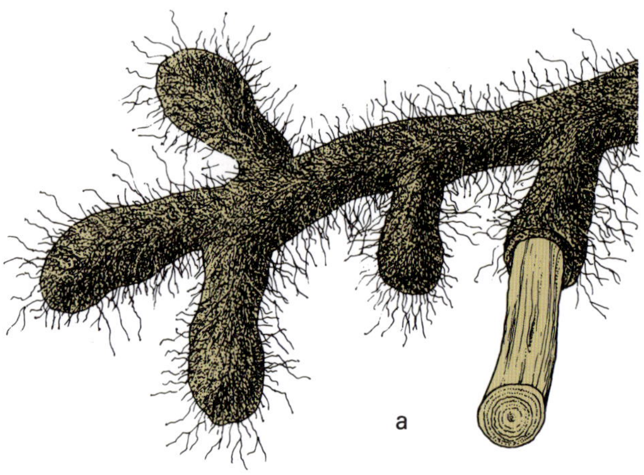

a

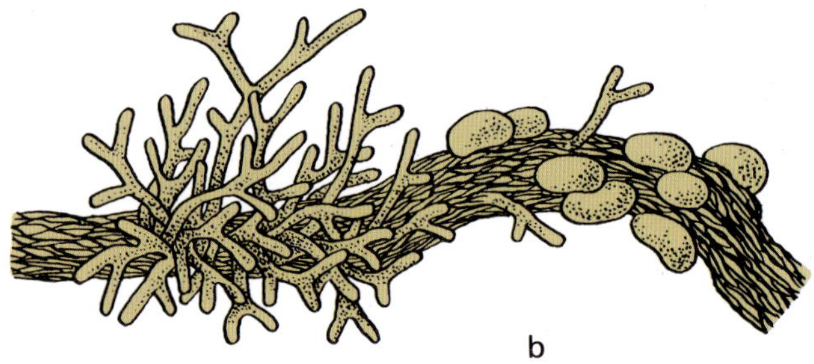

b

16) **a** – ectotrophic mycorrhiza; **b** – fruticose and bulbous mycorrhiza on a pine-tree root.

symbiotic relationship with several fungus species simultaneously – as a rule, however, only one of them produces fruit bodies (often only after the tree has attained a certain age). This gives rise to the heterogeneity and variegation of the mycoflora of forest growths, whose specific structure changes with the age of the forest. Mycorrhizal fungi are indispensable for the life of some plants, e.g. for the seedlings of numerous orchids growing in free nature.

Another remarkable phenomenon is the symbiosis of fungi with animals. Termites (Isoptera) establish and grow in their nests cultures of fungi whose mycelium produces spherical bodies serving the termites as food. Various termite species grow various species of fungi as, for instance, fungi of the genus *Termitomyces* belonging to the Tricholomataceae family, whose large fruit bodies growing out of termite nests are collected by the local inhabitants for culinary purposes. Microscopic fungi are cultivated as foodstuffs by ants inhabiting trunks and stumps; the same is done by bark-beetle larvae (Ipidae) growing the mycelium of the so-called ambrosial fungi in their galleries. An independent group of the microscopic fungi Laboulbeniomycetes lives on the body surface of most various beetles, especially of those inhabiting a relatively damp environment. They do not seem to do any harm to their hosts.

In the remote past, a close co-existence of fungal hyphae and algae gave rise to complex organisms called lichens (Lichenes). Owing to the fact that the fungal component of the lichenous thallus is most frequently represented by an ascomycete, this group of lichens is called Ascolichenes (also lichenized Ascomycetes); as fruit bodies they develop apothecia or perithecia. A much smaller part of the hyphae involved here belongs to the Basidiomycetes – this group of lichens is called Basidiolichenes (or lichenized Basidiomycetes). Some mycologists now regard various gill-fungi species as lichenized Basidiomycetes, although their fruit bodies differ from those of other gill fungi in nothing but the presence of algae in the tissue of some part of the thallus.

After exhausting the nutritional substances in one place, the mycelium of some fungi starts spreading in stripes or in more or less regular circles into the neighbourhood, and its growth in a particular direction manifests itself also by the development of fruit bodies. This is most conspicuous in the so-called 'fairy rings' formed by fungi of the genera *Ramaria, Hydnum, Clitocybe, Tricholoma, Marasmius.* The shape of the rings depends not only on the nutrient content of the soil but also on the layout of tree roots, and it may also be affected by the pattern of water dropping from tree crowns. The radial growth of the mycelium can also be seen in the fungi raised in pure cultures on agar soils.

To a considerable extent, saprophytic fungi participate in the decomposition of cellulose in the wood pervaded by the mycelium which not infrequently causes its characteristic disintegration (for example, cubiform red rot, fibrous white rot, etc.). Some saprophytic wood-destroying fungi also pass over to weakened but still living trees, speeding up their death; consequently they appear as occasional facultative parasites and are called saproparasites. They enter the trunks either through frost cracks or through scars left by broken-off branches, eventually by injuries connected with wood production. The wood infested with fungi sometimes acquires a specific colour. For example, the beautifully green-coloured wood of beeches or other deciduous trees is pervaded by the mycelium of the minute disc fungus *Chlorosplenium aeruginosum* secreting xylochloric acid insoluble in water. Another well-known feature is the phosphorescence of wood created – besides by bacteria – by the mycelium of the Honey Fungus (*Armillaria mellea*). Fungi whose fruit bodies give off a bluish sheen visible by night are widespread in the tropics. The species *Omphalotus olearius* with fluorescent gills, growing in southern Europe, belongs to this group.

Other saprophytic fungi have become specialized on ecologically narrowly confined environments and are never found elsewhere. Anthracophilous fungi live exclusively on burned-over soils or in old fireplaces, in fact wherever wood was burned and where, for some time at least, a suitable microclimate (soil humidity, shade) exists. In such an environment, the gradual succession of individual species can best be examined. As a rule, one of the pioneer species is the disc fungus *Pyronema confluens,* which is minute but still conspicuous due to its proliferation; it may often be seen covering the burned soil with extensive, pink-red layers of its innumerable apothecia. Somewhat later it is replaced by other representatives of disc fungi (*Geopyxis carbonaria*) and various cup fungi (*Peziza subviolacea, P. echinospora*). The last ones to grow here, when the burned-over areas are already overgrowing with mosses or liverworts, are the gill fungi *Pholiota carbonaria, Tephrocybe carbonaria,* and others.

A characteristic fungus community grows on excrements of various animals. These fungi, termed coprophilous, occur in great abundance and probably come from all fungus groups. The most conspicuous among them are members of the genus *Coprinus* whose short-lived, quickly developing fruit bodies are very common indeed. Coprophilous fungi can be successfully cultivated and studied in laboratory conditions on excrements collected in nature and kept in a moist but airy environment. They are therefore often raised as models for physiological and genetic experiments.

Some fungi are parasites, obtaining their nourishment from the bodies of other living organisms, while the host upon which they live is at a disadvantage, being more or less damaged or gradually completely destroyed by the fungus. Most of them are microscopic fungi surpassing the saprophytes in the number of species. Rusts (Uredinales) and smuts (Ustilaginales) are large groups of exclusively parasitic fungi; their economic relevance is due to the serious damage many of them cause in the tissues of cultivated plants. Rusts either develop on a single host, or change their hosts in which they successively produce various stages. Other fungi live inside their host's tissue as endoparasites, while ectoparasites live on its surface, sending within only their mycelium. There are many parasites among the Ascomycetes (e.g. mildew – Erysiphales) and Pyrenomycetes. The proportion of parasites among higher fungi is substantially lower, but cases of a large fungus parasitizing another large fungus are known. By way of example let us mention *Xerocomus parasiticus* living on *Scleroderma citrinum,* or *Volvariella surrecta* parasitizing the fruit bodies of *Lepista nebularis.* Species belonging to the genus *Nyctalis* are commonly found growing on *Russula; Cordyceps ophioglossoides* lives on the subterranean fruit bodies of *Elaphomyces.* Other numerous representatives of the genus *Cordyceps* are widespread, especially in the tropics, and parasitize insects.

There also exist huge numbers of microscopic fungi parasitizing other fungi. In autumn the fruit bodies of some boleti are covered with conspicuous golden-yellow, farinaceous layers of the hyphomycete *Sepedonium chrysospermum:* this is the conidial stage of *Apiocrea chrysosperma.* Fine moulds of the genus *Spinellus* often live as parasites on the caps of fungi of the genus *Mycena,* and brown, matted-tomentose covers of the mould *Sporodinia* occur on the caps of various other gill fungi. However, parasites also have their parasites – for example, the rust *Puccinia* is attacked by the coelomycete *Darluca filum.*

An ecologically specific group are fungi confined to an aquatic environment. Most abundant are the representatives of water moulds (Blastocladiales, Saprolegniales, etc.) living on decaying organic matter submerged in water. Some of them even parasitize aquatic animals. Still smaller aquatic moulds live as parasites on pollen grains fallen into the water, or within the cells of water algae. Rotten leaves lying in shallow and clear water currents are inhabited by a whole community of microscopic Hyphomycetes producing conidia of extraordinary shapes. Larger fungi growing on decaying wood logs and branches submerged in water include representatives of Pyrenomycetes as well as some Discomycetes. A quite specialized group consists of some Pyrenomycetes growing on wood submerged in sea water.

Both parasitic and saprophytic fungi trigger off various chemical changes in the substrate or in their host's body through the operation of their enzymes (ferments). The most important of these, which are most utilized by man, are enzymes evoking alcoholic fermentation. Also amylolytic (disstatic) ferments transforming starch into sugar are generally applied.

Developmentally a very old group of organisms, fungi are at home almost all over the Earth, and their spores are practically omnipresent in the atmosphere.

17) Fruit bodies of numerous gill-fungi species – e.g. *Clitocybe, Marasmius, Calocybe* and *Tricholoma* – grow in 'fairy rings'.

This of course does not imply that the distribution of all the species is worldwide (cosmopolitan). Many species of fungi have an extensive range of distribution, but far more species are confined to specific, often considerably restricted, localities. The occurrence of such fungi is conditioned not only by the presence of an adequate substrate or host, but also by climatic factors, by the underlying geological stratum and its chemical composition, etc. Furthermore, the structure of the mycoflora of each region is the result of a long-lasting developmental process. While the genera and species of fungi growing in many European countries are almost the same, in North America, where the number of species is considerably higher, only about one third of the total corresponds to European species. One reason for this is the specific abundance of woody plants and herbs in North America which have affected the structure of fungus species in the course of their long-term development. While the temperate belts of both hemispheres are characterized by a predominance of saprophytic fungi, in the tropical regions there is an exceeding abundance of microscopic parasitic fungi. It should be emphasized that not all the parasites closely dependent on their host are present in every locality inhabited by that host: their occurrence is often substantially restricted, or they are known from isolated finds only; they may also pass over to substitute hosts. As regards the elevation above the sea level, in comparison with other vascular plants no striking differences appear in the fungi; yet a great many species occur exclusively in high mountains (even above the timberline), others again grow at lower elevations only.

Adventive fungus species are brought from their original homes to remote regions, e. g. by the action of man. A classical example is the transfer of some stinkhorns (Phallaceae) from North America and Australia to Europe.

The Importance of Fungi for Man and the Living Environment

In nature we come across fungi at every step, without being aware of it. They are omnipresent just like bacteria or viruses, but are usually invisible since the spores, wherein genetic information specific for every species is coded, do not exceed microscopic dimensions. They move about in the atmosphere just like the other aeroplankton, being particularly abundant in its low-lying strata and in environments where, under certain conditions, they are capable of reproducing and renewing their vitality. Most people are acquainted with fungi only in the form of their fruit bodies which have always aroused interest of the observers of nature by their general appearance, so different from other plants. Yet these conspicuous fruit bodies are formed only by a small proportion of fungi. The other fungi are too minute in size to be discernible without an optical instrument. In nature, both large and microscopic fungi occupy a significant position irreplaceable by any other organisms. An evaluation based on human criteria, primarily on sanitary and economic grounds, shows them to include organisms either useful or detrimental to man. The first group comprises fungi of practical use in food industries – for example, the entire fermenting industry depends on the capacity of yeast to transform sugar into alcohol and carbon dioxide. Yeast is used not only in the production of alcoholic beverages but also in the brewing, baking and dairy industries. Cultivated strains not only of yeast but also of other fungi (e. g. species of the genus *Penicillium* in cheese production) have many valuable uses. The discovery of substances with an antibiotic effect resulted in a breakthrough in the therapy of a number of diseases of both man and animals – let us only mention penicillin, a product of one strain of the mould *Penicillium notatum*. In the course of the last decades, numerous other fungi have been subjected to research and further antibiotics have successfully been isolated from some of them.

The tradition of mushroom picking, i. e. of collecting large mushrooms for table use, has developed in many countries of the world. This collector's relation to fungi has given rise to a sporting hobby which brings people into the wood for a certain purpose, and consequently has a recreational significance. A drawback of this hobby, however, is the risk to one's life as shown by the growing number of cases of poisoning by toxic fungus species in connection with the increasing popularization of the collection of edible mushrooms. In some countries, the rising demand for mushrooms is compensated, to a certain extent, by an intensive hotbed production of cultivated Common Field Agarics, as well as by the search for other cultivable species, of which particularly the Oyster Fungus (*Pleurotus ostreatus*) and *Stropharia rugosoannulata* seem to be promising.

Fungi are of invaluable help to anyone capable of benefiting from their biological properties. On the other hand, some of them present themselves as enemies: they infest living organisms, plants, animals, and even Man himself. Fungi parasitizing the human body give rise to mycoses, i. e. often chronic and dangerous diseases of the skin, hair, but also of the whole body. These are usually caused by hyphomycetes, yeast fungi and true moulds. Mycoses show a rising tendency in the recent past, and a long-termed application of antibiotics to combat them leads in turn to the danger of yeast infections. Also the spores of some Hyphomycetes can occasionally penetrate into the respiratory organs and cause health troubles.

A whole plant-protection branch – phytopathology – is concerned with plant diseases caused by parasitic fungi attacking cultivated vegetables, flowers and crops, as well as fruit-bearing, ornamental and forest trees and shrubs. Let us mention, by way of example, rusts and smuts parasitizing corn, *Phytophthora infestans* causing potato murrain, *Synchytrium endobioticum* causing potato cancer, *Plasmodiophora brassicae* living on the roots of brassicas, mildews *Plasmopara viticola* and *Sphaerotheca humuli,* and also polyporoses, i.e. diseases in wood caused by pore fungi. In some regions, considerable stretches of forest growths are infested by *Heterobasidion annosus* and by the Honey Fungus (*Armillaria mellea*); the Dry Rot Fungus (*Serpula lacrymans*) can destroy everything made of wood inside houses.

However, the basic importance of fungi rests in their intensive participation in all decomposing processes and other chemical reactions. The decay and putrefaction of organic substances, which are in fact the most important agents in maintaining the natural balance, ensue from the cooperation of bacteria and particularly fungi which, as reductants, turn the accumulated organic compounds into newly utilizable inorganic compounds. Fungi play a role of major importance in the soil. Their mycelium and spores permeate the forest humus, while mycorrhiza often enables woody plants to grow in places where, without the fungi, they could not vegetate. Fungi are present in all ecosystems, both within and outside the forests. They are enormously old organisms that were in existence – together with *Cyanophyta* and algae – as early as the Precambrian era hundreds of millions of years ago. In the course of this tremendously long period they have undergone an unimaginable development about which the recent fungus species, being the last link of a long chain, present an often complexly enciphered evidence. Mycologists, who make painstaking efforts to decode them, observe with anxiety the phenomenon which, in our time, is assuming an almost catastrophic form: the extinction of organisms due to the tempestuous development of industrialization and unmerciful destruction of nature in the name of civilization. Whatever holds for the ever-increasing speed with which plant and animal species are nearing their extinction, applies in the same measure to fungi. The number of hitherto recognized and described species is estimated to exceed 100,000; according to recent opinion, however, the number of actually existing species is probably 250,000 to 300,000, i. e. approximately the same as that of seed plants. If 40–50 per cent of seed-plant species are to die out by the end of the 20th century, as some scientists assume, it is highly probable that the same number of fungus species will simultaneously disappear from the surface of this planet for ever, since most of them are dependent on the endangered plants. They will disappear – many of them without ever having been discovered, identified, and perhaps also utilized for the benefit of mankind. Thus a deep contradiction has arisen between the law of ethics and the coarsely exploiting interests of Man. A change should be brought about while there is still some grounds for hope.

Poisonous Fungi and the Symptoms of Poisoning

Numerous fungus species contain substances detrimental to human beings. In the past most fungi were considered poisonous or at least viewed with suspicion, and people preferred to shun them without thinking of using them for food. Later on, however, hand in hand with a more thorough acquaintance with species and progressing mycological knowledge, the assortment of edible and consumable species started to expand. Mushrooming was ardently indulged in several European countries. The popularization of mushrooming was sometimes so inordinate that almost all fungi were declared edible. It was only the growing incidence of cases of poisoning, which frequently proved fatal, that provided a warning signal and again called for increased caution. Nowadays, a responsible evaluation of the edibility or toxicity of many fungus species is often problematic, since it comes to light that species formerly currently collected and eaten are less innocent than was previously assumed. Involved here are not only the toxic principles representing the direct cause of poisoning, but also other, largely still unknown toxins which can accumulate in the human body after repeated ingestion of some mushrooms and unfavourably interfere with the activity of various organs, mainly of those belonging to the digestive system.

According to the symptoms or types of toxins concerned, poisoning can roughly be divided into several categories. In each of these we shall confine ourselves to those species of poisonous fungi which come into account as the most frequent cause of poisoning.

1. **Poisoning that damages the liver** is also termed phalloid poisoning. This name is derived from the specific name of the Death Cap – *Amanita phalloides* – which is the most frequent cause of this type of poisoning. The fruit body of the Death Cap contains two groups of poisonous substances (toxins) present in high concentration, namely amatoxins and phallotoxins. Both groups of toxins are also present in the closely related species of the so-called poisonous white amanitas, in *A. verna* and *A. virosa* (Destroying Angel), in concentrations still higher than in the Death Cap. Moreover, they were found in some small *Lepiota* species (*L. helveola, L. scobinella*) as well as in some species of *Galerina*. Phallotoxins are responsible for 80–95 per cent of cases of fatal mushroom poisoning and belong to the most insidious poisons as the first symptoms of poisoning appear after a long lapse of time.

Anybody intending to collect edible mushrooms and not willing to confine himself to gathering boleti and chanterelles must inevitably be acquainted with the Death Cap. Although the Death Cap is greatly variable in colour, some of its characteristics are so conspicuous that it can readily be recognized even in case of an atypical colouring. Its toxicity manifests itself after the ingestion of quite a small amount of food prepared of it. One fully developed fruit body was found capable of causing the death of two persons. The first symptoms appear after a relatively long interval (the so-called period of latency), six hours after the ingestion at the earliest (earlier after consuming a raw toadstool), usually in 8–24 hours; sometimes the period of latency is still longer. The first symptoms of poisoning appear as an irritation of the digestive system – intensive vomiting and diarrhoea. These symptoms may last for 48 hours in the course of which the patient suffers great losses of body fluids and mineral substances followed by extreme exhaustion. Cramps in the legs subsequently set in, accompanied by urination disorders which may result in a total stoppage of urine secretion and general apathy, since the organism suffers from poisoning by waste materials it fails to get rid of. The disappearance of diarrhoea and vomiting signals the onset of a short but extremely dangerous period of alleviation which, however, only precedes a further phase characterized by liver-tissue impairment. This period is critical. If sufficiently effective help has not been secured in time, or if the afflicted person has eaten a greater number of fruit bodies, he becomes unconscious and dies on the fifth or sixth day with symptoms of liver failure and sometimes of brain tumescence.

Thirty years ago, up to 80 per cent of those poisoned died after having eaten the Death Cap. Nowadays, when new therapeutic methods are continuously being applied in departments of intensive care, the death rate has considerably fallen and does not exceed 15 per cent. At any rate, phalloid poisoning always seriously endangers life. The therapeutic success attained is due to all who have ventured the long way leading to the identification of toxins contained in the Death Cap and to the discovery and enforcement of new therapeutic procedures.

The first experiments with the Death Cap were carried out as early as 1793 on dogs, but it was not before the 19th century that it was found to contain substances with a hemolytic effect (i.e. causing the lysis of red blood cells); also other toxins were discovered in it later on. Thus both the principal toxins, amanitin and phalloidin, were distinguished. In the thirties of the present century, further relevant knowledge was obtained with the aid of chromatographic methods. The formula of phalloidin was published in 1940, the formula of amanitin one year later. Further partial compounds were discovered in the course of the following years. At present two toxin complexes are distinguished: phallotoxins and amatoxins, differing in chemical composition. Phallotoxins include phalloidin, phalloin, phallisin, phallacin and phallacidin. Amatoxins are marked with Greek letters from alpha to omega; also amanin and the ineffective amanulin belong to them. Most of these substances have also been artificially prepared and some of them are produced synthetically for experiments with laboratory animals. During the experiments a substance was discovered which was called antamanid and is capable of neutralizing the effect of amanitins. 100 g of fresh fungus were found to contain, on the average, 10 mg phalloidin, 8 mg of alpha-amanitin and 5 mg of beta-amanitin, 0.5 mg of gamma-amanitin; all the other toxins and antamanid are present in traces only.

The treatment of poisoning caused by the Death Cap is aimed at the quickest possible elimination of poisonous substances from the blood (still present there 24–36 hours after the ingestion); first of all, however, a stomach rinse is necessary, as well as repeated rinses of intestines, in order to eliminate the extremely toxic spores from the folds of mucous membranes. Then the fluids and mineral substances missing from the patient's body should be supplied, eventually an infusion of sorbite solutions containing large doses of vitamins B and C. In accordance with the values obtained from laboratory tests, large doses of tioctic acid (300, 500 mg or even more per day) are supplied by continuous infusions. In cases of more serious poisoning, when the patient lapses into insensibility or when the poisoning has been diagnosed too late, further treatment in the intensive-care department of the nearest hospital is absolutely essential.

It is often difficult to tell with certainty that the poisoning has actually been caused by the Death Cap; such a diagnosis is conclusive only when fruit-body remnants are found in the organism. Sometimes also the pieces of mushrooms not used in preparing the meal may be helpful. According to T. Wieland and Palysa, the presence of amanitins in any fungus can be ascertained in the following way: a drop of juice is pressed out of the fresh fruit body on a piece of newspaper or on sawdust, or the fungus is cut apart and the section is applied to a piece of paper so that the juice is sucked in. After the spot has been left to dry, hydrochloric acid is dropped on it. If it turns blue, the fungus contains amanitins and hence is deadly poisonous.

Anyone suspected of being poisoned by the Death Cap or other related species must be taken to hospital as quickly as possible – at best to a large hospital equipped with resuscitative aids. Any delay is dangerous. If vomiting, the patient must be given large quantities of liquids to drink (no alcohol or milk!), the best being unsweetened mineral or other water.

Phalloid poisoning may also be caused by some small *Lepiota* species related to *L. helveola* whose toxins are identical to those of the Death Cap. The course of poisoning and its treatment are also the same. (This concerns thermophilic *Lepiota* species which appear more commonly only in some central European regions and in southern Europe.)

Poisoning caused by some *Galerina* species was neglected for a long time, although the first cases were reported as early as 1912 from North America, after the ingestion of *G. autumnalis*. Later on, this and several other – mostly North American – species were found to contain amanitin, but it was not until the early 1960s that conclusive evidence of poisoning by the European species *G. marginata* was reported from Russia. Chemical analysis revealed the presence of alpha-amanitin amounting to about 40 per cent of its content in the Death Cap. The cause of poisoning is ignorance resulting in the confusion of *G. marginata* with the similar but edible *Kuehneromyces mutabilis*. It is therefore necessary to beware of gathering not only *G. marginata* but also all other similar lignicolous *Galerina* species – the short-stipitate *G. badipes* and the unicolorous *G. unicolor*. Amanitin was also discovered in several other species of *Galerina*, mostly in those growing in moss.

In its clinical course, paraphalloid poisoning resembles phalloid poisoning, though the presence of phallotoxins has not been proved. It involves rare cases of poisoning after the ingestion of larger cup fungi, usually *Gyromitra esculenta*, and occasionally also the Sulphur Tuft (*Hypholoma fasciculare*). Poisoning caused by *G. esculenta* is rather puzzling, as many people gather and eat this fungus without any negative consequences whatsoever. Nausea, headache and abdominal pain appear in 5–10 hours after the ingestion, together with repeated vomiting which does not last so long as in phalloid poisoning. Often blood-circulation failure and brain tumescence set in, regularly accompanied by jaundice. The patient may sometimes succumb to a hepatic coma. This poisoning has long been attributed to the effects of helvellic acid; only recently have scientists proved the non-existence of such an acid, pointing out that a mixture of several non-toxic substances is involved. Simultaneously, however, a new effective principle was isolated and called gyromitrin, which quickly decomposes into the strongly poisonous methylhydrazine. However, both the mentioned substances are extremely volatile and disappear almost completely after 10 minutes' cooking. After a normal heat-preparation of fresh *G. esculenta* for table use, neither gyromitrin, nor methylhydrazine can be regarded as the cause of poisoning. In this fungus further four substances related to gyromitrin have been discovered; of these, hemolysin initiating the lysis of red blood cells is also destroyed by cooking. The most plausible explanation is that some old and infected fruit bodies of *G. esculenta* become poisonous only secondarily.

Occasional cases of poisoning after eating some other larger Discomycetes – *Gyromitra gigas, G. infula, Sarcosphaera crassa,* etc. – take the same course as poisoning by *G. esculenta.* Both gyromitrin and methylhydrazine were found in some of them.

Cases of poisoning by the Sulphur Tuft have repeatedly been reported from Russia as well as from some central and southern European countries. Their course was typically phalloid. Japanese mycological literature states that the Sulphur Tuft belongs to poisonous fungi responsible for the greatest amount of poisoning in Japan. This is almost incomprehensible in view of the fact that the Sulphur Tuft has an offensively bitter taste which remains unaffected by cooking.

2. **Muscarine poisoning.** Its name is derived from the specific name of the Fly Agaric – *Amanita muscaria.* In the past, fruit bodies of the Fly Agaric were steeped in milk used for poisoning flies. It has been discovered only in the present century that both the Fly Agaric and the Panther Cap (*A. pantherina*) contain but a small amount of muscarine, and that their toxicity is due to another toxic principle. On the other hand, muscarine was found in large quantities in other species, particularly in those of the genus *Inocybe* and in some white species of *Clitocybe.*

Muscarine poisoning sometimes manifests itself while the meal is still being eaten – as a rule, however, within two hours after it. The symptoms are conspicuous perspiration, salivation, lacrimation, vomiting and diarrhoea, fall of blood pressure, slowing down of the pulse and shivering. A remarkable symptom is the contraction of pupils accompanied by sight disorders. A reliable antidote is atropine; this, however, must not be applied in poisoning caused by the Fly Agaric and Panther Cap. In the whole of Europe, muscarine poisoning is mostly caused by *Inocybe patouillardii* containing approximately 500 times more muscarine than the Fly Agaric. A fatal dose is contained in 100–150 g of a fresh fungus. Also other *Inocybe* species contain relatively large quantities of muscarine – e.g. *I. lacera, I. geophylla, I. argillacea,* and it is only in some species of this genus that no presence of muscarine has been proved (e.g. in *I. jurana*). Also several white *Clitocybe* species contain large quantities of muscarine – namely *C. dealbata* and the closely related (or perhaps identical) *C. rivulosa, C. phyllophila,* and *C. cerussata.* A small amount of muscarine was discovered in some *Hebeloma* species, e.g. in *H. crustuliniforme* and *H. sinapizans,* but also in *Armillaria mellea* and *Omphalotus olearius.* Slight symptoms of muscarine poisoning appear after their ingestion. Moreover, *O. olearius,* abundant in southern Europe, causes symptoms showing the presence of another content principle, hitherto unknown. According to some authors the true *O. olearius* occurs only in southernmost Europe, while the fungus growing further northwards (e.g. in the Czech Republic) belongs to a different species, probably related to some poisonous *Omphalotus* species from North America, containing the toxins illudin S and M. Also the type of poisoning caused by *Mycena rosea* bears some resemblance to muscarine poisoning; its content principle has not yet been discovered.

3. **Psychotropic poisoning** involves serious cases characterized by the irritation of brain tissue. For a long time the intoxication caused by the Fly Agaric was the only form of mushroom poisoning accompanied by psychic disturbances. It was not before the 1950s that other so-called cult fungi, formerly used in religious ceremonies and rites, were identified; their ingestion leads to different manifestations of psychic disturbance. Two types of psychotropic poisoning are distinguished: psychotonic poisoning caused by the so-called mycoatropine, and psychodysleptic poisoning caused by psilocybine.

In Europe, poisoning by mycoatropine is caused by three *Amanita* species. Most common are cases of poisoning after eating the Panther Cap, less frequent are those caused by the Fly Agaric, and practically unknown is poisoning by *A. regalis.* The poisonous content principles of these amanitas have not yet been exactly identified, and this is why the designation 'mycoatropine poisoning', though inadequate, is still used nowadays.

The course of poisoning caused by all the three species is substantially the same: nausea is experienced between half an hour and three hours after consumption, accompanied by vomiting, headache, quickened heartbeat, and a persistent dilatation of pupils occasionally leading to vision disturbances. Often the condition of the affected person resembles alcoholic intoxication: the patient becomes talkative, shouts obscenities, sometimes laughs or weeps, strikes himself and keeps on running to and fro. These states of excitement may be dangerous for the sick person and must therefore be mitigated. Subsequently the patient faints, recovers from time to time, hallucinates, screams, defends himself against invisible danger, etc. but finally falls into a profound sleep from which he usually awakens into a normal state, without remembering his previous behaviour. This poisoning comes to its fortunate end on the second or third day. First aid consists in the stimulation of vomiting and in taking the patient to hospital; he must be given neither milk nor alcohol. The treatment starts with a stomach rinse, the excitement is controlled by remedies of the chlorpromazine type, physostigmine (never atropine!) is administered as an antidote against mycoatropine.

Psilocybine poisoning occurs after consuming some species of the genus *Psilocybe,* or fungi belonging to related genera about which, nowadays, abundant literature is available. These fungi are distributed mostly in Mexico and in some Central American countries. They contain so-called hallucinogenic substances thanks to which they had long been used in religious rituals and were kept secret until the twentieth century. Their research is due to the efforts of the American ethnographers Mr. and Mrs. Wasson who succeeded in acquiring hallucinogenous fungi, which they studied and identified with the help of mycologists. Chemical analyses of these fungi were carried out, and it was even possible to cultivate some of them. The effective substance was finally produced artificially, whereby its experimental testing on volunteers and its application for therapeutic purposes was made possible.

Fungi containing hallucinogenic substances generally produce small, inconspicuous fruit bodies growing on dung or excrements. They belong to the genera *Psilocybe, Panaeolus, Panaeolina* and *Stropharia.* The amount of effective substances in the fruit bodies is variable, particularly in the European representatives of the mentioned genera whose effect is substantially smaller in comparison with the Mexican species.

The psychic symptoms following the ingestion of hallucinogenic fungi are extremely varied. In some individuals they manifest themselves as euphoria, in others as sight disorders and hallucinations; sometimes they assume the form of the kaleidoscopic effect involving the duplication of objects in inappropriate colours; still other persons, on the contrary, feel anxiety and fear, suffer from terrifying delusions, and these states may lead to delirium and suicide attempts. Thanks to a lower content of effective substances, the European fungi evoke much milder symptoms.

Hallucinogenic fungi contain four active substances; psilocybine, psilocine, baeocystine, and norbaeocystine. Psilocine is considered the main bearer of hallucinogenic properties. However, poisoning by these fungi is exceptional, and there is no danger of misusing European hallucinogenic fungi for intentional intoxication.

4. **Orellanin poisoning caused by *Cortinarius.*** The first mass poisoning by *Cortinarius orellanus,* reported from Poland in 1962, attracted the attention of all mycologists. Since that time, powerful toxic substances have been proved to exist in a number of *Cortinarius* species originally considered harmless, and evidence of their presence in other species is recorded annually.

A characteristic of orellanin poisoning is the relatively long time interval between the ingestion of fruit bodies and the first symptoms of poisoning. It is the longest latency period in mushroom poisoning which may take up to 17 days; hence it follows that, as a rule, the first symptoms of poisoning are not at first connected with the consumed food. This type of poisoning manifests itself as acute or chronic kidney damage: urine secretion is overabundant at first, but slows down later and ultimately stops altogether; stomach pains appear, accompanied by vomiting, a feeling of dryness in the mouth, and thirst. The sick person dies, showing symptoms of kidney failure.

The toxin – which is the effective substance here – is called orellanin and was first isolated from *C. orellanus.* It is more powerful than the toxins present in the Death Cap. A mixture of about ten compounds is involved here, the most important of which is grzymalin (named after the author of the discovery). The treatment of orellanin poisoning is possible only in specialized large-hospital departments where the patient may be supplied with an artificial kidney. Similar poisoning was observed after the ingestion of *C. speciosissimus* and *C. gentilis;* the opinion is justified that other *Cortinarius* species of this group are equally poisonous; this applies e.g. to *C. phoeniceus, C. turmalis* and *C. bolaris.* Therefore, mushroom pickers should avoid collecting absolutely any member of the genus *Cortinarius.*

5. **Poisoning called forth by the ingestion of various other fungi.** We shall confine ourselves to several common species about which the reader should be informed. Of particular interest is *Paxillus involutus* which, until recently, had been considered edible. Up to now it has not been found to contain any toxins. The poisoning involved assumes the form of allergy: in individuals who have been eating this mushroom for years without any difficulties whatsoever, its further ingestion may cause nausea, abdominal pains, diarrhoea, sometimes very high temperatures, red urine, and an acute kidney insufficiency. The symptoms may set in gradually, the kidney damage may turn chronic. It is nowadays considered poisonous and to be avoided.

Characteristic of southern Europe is the occasional incidence of poisoning by *Tricholoma pardinum* manifesting itself half an hour to two hours after ingestion by vomiting and diarrhoea (i.e. loss of fluids and mineral substances), possibly resulting in kidney damage. The same symptoms may be observed in poisoning by *Entoloma lividum,* eventually by other poisonous *Entoloma* species – such as *E. rhodopolium* and *E. nidorosum.* Poisoning caused by *Nolanea verna* is accompanied by an intensive diarrhoea lasting for several days and by the consequent exhaustion of the organism. Here the first symptoms of poisoning appear in 2–4 hours, maybe also in 24 hours. In some countries there have been cases of poisoning by *Agaricus xanthoderma,* because of its confusion with edible agarics of a similar appearance. It is only after eating a large amount of fruit bodies that this type of poisoning manifests itself by persistent vomiting which may last for several hours. Also after consuming large amounts of fruit bodies of fungi sometimes used as spices, digestion disorders may turn up – for example in case of *Lactarius helvus, Collybia fusipes, Scleroderma citrinum* and *S. verrucosum.* In the case of *S. verrucosum* symptoms of poisoning appear very quickly after eating this mushroom fried on fat.

In specialized literature, data concerning the edibility or inedibility of many fungus species are often contradictory. In general, increasing knowledge tends to increase the number of species considered inedible or poisonous, rather than the other way round. Hence it is urgently recommended that the collection of mushrooms for table use should be confined to the narrower assortment of well-tried species to avoid running any risk. The rule of distinguishing edible species of *Russula* and *Lactarius* according to the taste of the flesh of fresh fruit bodies helps to exclude all the hot-tasting fungi belonging to these genera as inedible, although some of them are suitable for eating if subjected to a special preparation (this actually happens in some countries). Hot-tasting *Russula* and *Lactarius* species (e.g. *Lactarius turpis* and *L. torminosus*) may cause poisoning which manifests itself by stomach and intestinal troubles. This is caused by substances of a still unknown chemical composition characterized by thermolability. This is why in some countries, particularly in the north, these mushrooms are collected, cooked and preserved in salt or fermented. However, in southern and central Europe the very same species are considered inedible or poisonous.

In conclusion let us briefly refer to mushrooms currently collected as edible whose ingestion, however, sometimes calls forth unpleasant troubles or individual intolerance. Cases of this kind have so far not been explained, and naturally the content principles causing them are still unknown. For example, poisoning by the Honey Fungus whose symptoms appear after eating not only raw or inadequately prepared mushrooms but also well-prepared ones is completely unaccountable. It is assumed that a poisonous species may exist as one of the complex of so-called microspecies (the Honey Fungus represents exactly such a complex) which have not yet been satisfactorily distinguished. Also the brown-coloured *Tricholoma* species, especially those growing in coniferous forests (mostly under pine trees) on the lower slopes of mountains, include suspect species calling forth symptoms of poisoning. Some yellow or greenish species of *Tricholoma,* often bitterish to burning in taste, are mistaken for *T. flavovirens* and cause gastric troubles. The separate species of the genus *Ramaria,* abundantly collected in many regions, are not distinguished by practical mushroom gatherers; they contain the laxative emodin, concentrated in the branch tips of their fruit bodies. It is therefore necessary to use them with care. Allergenic properties may be observed in many dozens of other fungus species described in books as being edible, and are mostly eaten without ill-effects.

It is a generally known fact that no alcoholic drinks must be taken after eating meals prepared with certain mushroom species, otherwise symptoms of poisoning might appear. Best known in this respect is *Coprinus atramentarius.* In most cases, poisoning makes itself felt soon after ingestion; its symptoms include reddening of the skin, intense heart palpitation, asthmatic troubles, vomiting, diarrhoea and feelings of anxiety. They disappear within two hours but can re-emerge after drinking some more alcohol. The same holds for some other mushrooms as well.

Edible Mushrooms, Their Collection and Use

The definition of 'edible mushroom' is extremely difficult. The findings obtained in the course of the last decades reveal the necessity to be reserved and evaluate individual fungus species on the basis of much stricter criteria. In the present conception, a fungus species is considered edible if eating it causes no health disorders, provided it has been properly cooked (boiling, frying, baking). The basic amount is a 100–200 g portion of mushrooms prepared. It is recommended to refrain from eating any raw fungi whatsoever. The ingestion of even small portions of raw fruit bodies of certain current mushroom species, which may be eaten quite safely after cooking, can cause grave nausea (e. g. the Honey Fungus). The time needed for cooking varies from species to species, since it depends on the consistency of the flesh: in fruit bodies with soft flesh it takes about 10 minutes, for tougher flesh at least 20 minutes are necessary. Only faultless, young or recently developed fruit bodies should be gathered for the table; they must be neither overripe and flaccid, nor infested with microorganisms, mould or insect larvae. Fruit bodies covered with a slimy and viscid cuticle, such as is usual e. g. in the *Suillus* species, must be cleaned and deprived of their pellicle in the very place where they have been found: this saves us a lot of extra work when cleaning them at home. It is also advisable to avoid collecting flabby, large caps of some *Leccinum* species unable to withstand transport. The collected mushrooms are put into a wicker basket. Plastic bags are absolutely inappropriate for the purpose, as the fruit bodies deposited therein get crushed and overheated. At home it is best to keep the mushrooms in a refrigerator at a temperature of 5–8 °C; here they remain in a good condition for 24 hours, but desiccate more rapidly.

The dish prepared with mushrooms should be eaten at once if possible, its further preservation (in the refrigerator of course) and reheating reduces its goodness and substantially affects its edibility. Mushrooms should be prepared for the table according to well-tried recipes, or it is possible to enrich the diet by using some species to prepare special dishes accentuating their taste qualities. For example, Saffron Milk Cap (*Lactarius deliciosus*) is best when pickled in vinegar, prepared as goulash or roasted on butter; puffballs are appetizing in soups; caps of *Lactarius volemus* and of the Parasol Mushroom taste excellently when roasted on fat, etc.

If we refuse to risk poisoning and the often ensuing serious damage to health, we must observe the basic rule – namely, that only the species we are quite reliably acquainted with should be collected. If, in spite of everything, we are keen on enlarging our assortment and knowledge by further species, it is best to contact some specialist who will identify the mushrooms for us or confirm the correctness of our identification. It is also expedient to visit mycological advice bureaus functioning in certain cities, or else it is possible to attend special lectures and courses organized by mycological associations or clubs. The identification based exclusively on comparison with coloured plates is often rather unreliable (in view of the great colour and shape variability characterizing many species, of a possibly inaccurate reproduction of colours, etc.). It is always only a detailed, exhaustive description that can be conclusive and decisive.

The digestibility of mushrooms is directly related to the cellular structure of their bodies. Mushrooms are less digestible than other plants due to the fact that their cell walls are largely composed of the polysaccharide chitin resistant to the action of digestive fluids in the human organism. The cellular plasma contains 70–95 per cent of water and only a negligible amount of sugars and fats which represent the substantial proportion of nutritional substances. The mushroom flesh contains about 3–9 per cent of proteins, their compounds being amino acids and peptides. Altogether, about 20 various amino acids were found in mushrooms; their content varies even in individual specimens of the same species. Sugars represent 1–6 per cent of the content, for the most part in the form of polymers, but there is also glycogen, mannitol, traces of sorbitol, arabitol, and others. Mushrooms further include 0.5–3.5 per cent of fats, mostly glycerides and glycolipides, less frequently phospholipides (e.g. lecithin), often in the form of oil droplets within spores or in the tissue. Also vitamins are present in mushrooms, especially the provitamin carotene, vitamins of the vitamin-B group, vitamin D, E and K in small quantities, and traces of vitamin C. Mushrooms also contain various enzymes and substances with antibiotic effects. The mineral substances contained in mushrooms are first of all potassium (K), phosphorus

(P), calcium (C) and iron (Fe). The capacity of fungi to accumulate from the soil these mineral substances (trace elements), which are so important for the enzymatic processes taking place in the human organism, presumably exceeds that of green plants. The concentration of trace elements in fungus fruit bodies depends on the habitat.

Recommendations as to which edible mushrooms should be collected are always a problematic matter, connected with various circumstances among which tradition, conservatism, individual taste, etc. play a major role. In general it can be said that in countries where wild edible mushrooms are not habitually collected, preference is given to artificially produced field agarics. Among the mushrooms gathered in their natural state, high value is attached to those belonging to the Boletaceae family: in most cases they are easily recognized and endowed with a pleasant smell, taste and consistency. The most popular and generally known bolete is of course the Edible Boletus or Cèpe (*Boletus edulis*). Otherwise it is recommended to eat mushrooms in mixtures in which the specific taste qualities, consistency and smell of the single species come to the fore. Species with a less distinct taste are added to strongly aromatic or more acridly tasting species. An adequate preparation in the kitchen renders the mushrooms more palatable and more digestible. Tougher species are cut into thin slices, dried mushrooms ground into powder can be used as spices, many species can be preserved in salt or pickled in various solutions. The trimmings added to mushroom dishes should be easily digestible – e. g. potatoes and vegetable salads. Special literature brings a great number of recipes for everybody to choose according to his individual taste.

Inedible Fungi

In popular mushroom manuals and mycological exhibitions, the described, illustrated and exhibited species are usually divided into poisonous, edible and inedible ones. The category of inedible fungi is one which is most problematic and most difficult to define. For the most part, this designation covers fungi which are neither edible nor poisonous, or whose edibility is still open to doubt due to a lack of exact information. As a rule, they possess qualities making them unsuitable for table use: too small fruit bodies, unpleasant smell and taste, excessively tough flesh, and sometimes they inspire distaste by their appearance or place of occurrence (e. g. coprophilic fungi). Most of these features, however, can be purely subjective. With the spreading of knowledge of individual fungus species, some of them are gradually being reclassed from the category of inedible fungi into that of poisonous fungi. In future it might be expedient to omit the category of inedible fungi altogether, and to distinguish only mushrooms suitable for table use and safely verified as regards their harmlessness to health, and fungi detrimental to the human organism – i. e. poisonous.

Where and When to Go Mushrooming

There is a difference between those who gather mushrooms exclusively for practical purposes, i. e. for enriching their diet, and those who regard fungi as an object of scientific interest. However, both kinds of mushrooming can be pursued as a hobby.

The practical mushroom picker's attention is usually focussed on a limited number of fungus species which he can safely recognize and which he prefers. Only if he fails to find his favourite species, or on the recommendation of other collectors, will he also take other edible mushrooms. The mushroom picker's actual season is relatively short: in European conditions, it is concentrated at the end of summer and the beginning of autumn, i. e. from August to October, when mushrooms grow most abundantly. It is also necessary to take account of the weather, as the most favourable conditions for mushrooming arive after heavy rainfalls followed by warm weather. Mushrooms like neither wind nor excessive temperature variations. However, edible mushrooms may be found even in spring, if the weather is both moist and warm. This is the time when large-sized spring Discomycetes appear – morels (*Morchella*) and members of the genera *Discina* and *Gyromitra*; of the gill fungi it is *Hygrophorus marzuolus, Strobilurus* species growing on cones, later on St. George's Mushroom (*Calocybe gambosa*) and *Entoloma clypeatum.* Mushroom pickers prefer sunny places sheltered from wind, such as southward-facing woodland margins, lawns (even in city parks), gardens, forest clearings, etc. It is advisable to look for light deciduous or mixed forests, while in extensive, monotonous conifer forests no mushrooms are usually found in springtime. In summer, if the weather is exceedingly dry, situations on shady slopes facing northwards or in river and brook valleys should be looked for.

Some edible mushrooms may be gathered from spring till autumn on tree stumps or trunks, e. g. *Kuehneromyces mutabilis.* In the period of the most intensive vegetation of fungi we may find mushrooms almost in every forest, but not all forest growths are equally rich in mushrooms. Sometimes you will roam large spaces without success before striking on a woodland locality where a number of species grow side by side. There are mushroom pickers who mark the trees in whose vicinity they have found, for example, various boleti. Such a place often remains fertile for a number of years, since these mushrooms live in mycorrhizal dependence on a particular woody plant and regularly form fruit bodies there at a certain time. A knowledge of woody plants helps in the search for mycorrhizal mushrooms (a number of boleti grow exclusively under aspens, birches and poplars). Wherever the countryside is richer in its natural aspect, particularly as concerns the structure and specific variety of woody plants, its mycoflora also displays a greater abundance of species. Geophilous fungi growing in the humus, fallen foliage or needles prefer forests without any herbal or shrubby undergrowth. Where the wood is excessively overgrown with grass and a buoyant, dense herbal vegetation, or where the soil is covered with a continuous layer of branches left behind after wood sifting or wood production, geophilous fungi are usually scarce.

Edible mushrooms are also gathered outside the wood, e. g. in meadows, fields and pastures. Whole swarms of champignons (*Agaricus*) often appear there after summer rainfalls. After the height of the season, which is usually in September, several lignicolous species may be found growing on stumps and decaying tree trunks in the cool season – perhaps also during a mild winter. This applies to the Winter Fungus or Velvet Shank (*Flammulina velutipes*) and the Oyster Fungus (*Pleurotus ostreatus*).

Anybody whose concern for fungi is primarily based on his scientific interest can pursue his hobby on a substantially larger scale: he may collect and study fungi almost all the year round, depending only on the group he selects. Leaving aside all the microscopic fungi wherein scarcely any amateur mycologist takes interest nowadays, there still remains a number of interesting and often little-known species (sometimes even unknown ones, hitherto not described) whose seeking in nature, microscopic examination and identification yield much satisfaction to anybody whose attention they have aroused by their various shapes and way of life. They can be collected from spring to winter in most various habitats within and outside the forest. During our excursion we proceed as slowly as possible, focussing our attention both on the ground and on stumps, dead branches either scattered about or jutting out, trunks of uprooted trees, but also on the remnants of herbs and grasses, decaying leaves, needles, animal excrements, burned-over areas, roadside edges overgrown with low moss, and ditch banks or old walls. Good results follow from a systematic inspection of some selected small ecotypes (e.g. areas around springs, alder coppices), examined in regular intervals throughout the year or for several years, while all findings are recorded and documented and a detailed description of the ecology of individual species is supplied. A mycological herbarium composed of exsiccati (dried fungi) is an inseparable part of descriptions and notes made in connection with these observations: it serves not only as a documentary material but also as a valuable comparative material for further study.

How to Collect and Identify Fungi

With regard to the aim of this book, the present chapter will again deal exclusively with higher fungi which are the most conspicuous ones in nature, and consequently are the first to attract attention. The major part of the higher fungi consists of so-called pileate fungi, whose fruit bodies are usually differentiated into a stipe and a cap. The pileate fungi moreover include fruit bodies of stomach fungi (Gasteromycetes) – puffballs (*Lycoperdon*), members of the genera *Bovista* and *Scleroderma,* but also other species whose fruit bodies are conspicuous in shape, e.g. stinkhorns (*Phallus*) and earth stars (*Geastrum*). Some species of larger cup fungi (Discomycetes), flask fungi (Pyrenomycetes) and non-gilled fungi (Aphyllophorales) belong here as well. The fungi included here predominantly belong to the Basidiomycetes, while the representation of the Ascomycetes is relatively small.

All the fungi whose fruit bodies are collected in the open air for the purposes of study and identification should immediately be deposited with care, one by one, in metal or plastic boxes of various size. Non-gilled lignicolous fungi are cut off together with a part of the substrate and wrapped into a piece of newspaper or put into a paper bag. We must not forget to put down the name of the host or, rather better, to enclose a fragment of the plant whereon the fungus has been found; in lignicolous fungi either a fresh or a dry leaf of the woody plant in question will do. It has proved useful to add to the fresh small and fragile gill-fungi fruit bodies a fresh leaf of any green plant which, by evaporating water, keeps the air in the box humid and thus prevents the fungus from desiccating. After our return from the expedition, we put down on the margin of the paper in which the separate finds are wrapped the data concerning the locality, habitat or substrate, and the date of collection. After processing the material the notes are clipped out and deposited together with the collected specimens first into the drier and then into a herbarium envelope. They are crucial for writing the herbarium label. In lignicolous fungi, particularly in those having resupinate fruit bodies, the quickest possible desiccation of the collected material is necessary: only in this way is it possible perfectly to preserve on the exsiccations the qualities of the hymenium (especially the shape of basidia) which are of primary importance for the identification.

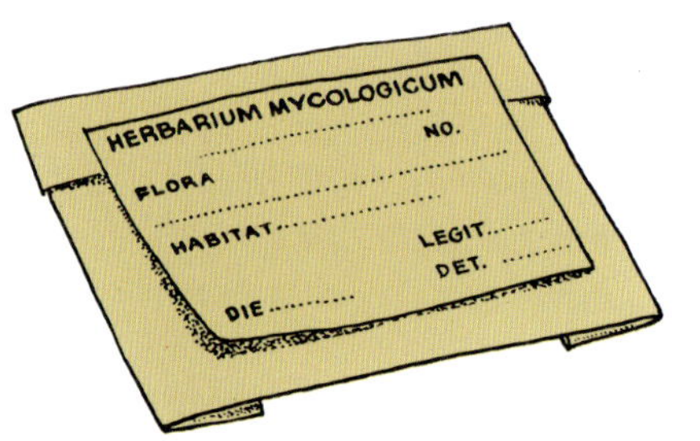

18) A herbarium envelope of strong paper for keeping exsiccations and a label containing the necessary data (the name of the identified fungus, its locality, habitat, substrate, the date of the find, the name of the collector and that of the identifier) to be glued on the herbarium envelope.

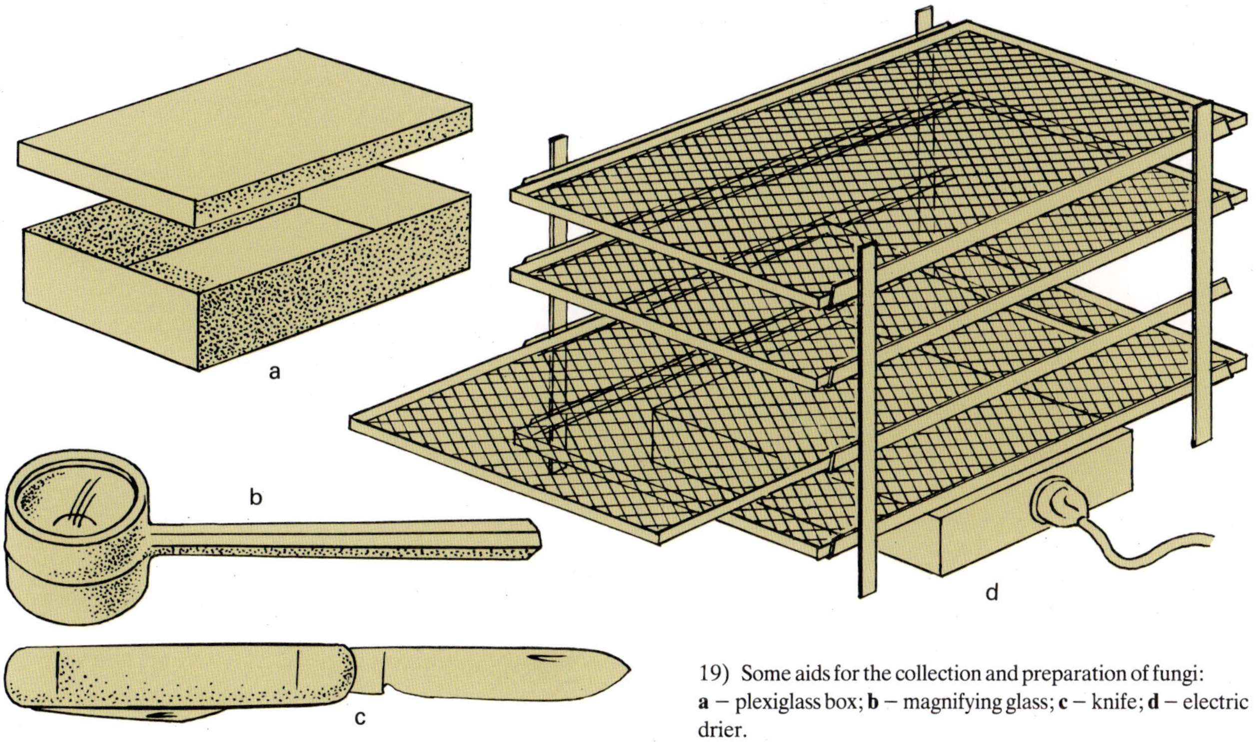

19) Some aids for the collection and preparation of fungi: **a** – plexiglass box; **b** – magnifying glass; **c** – knife; **d** – electric drier.

The present classification of gill fungi is predominantly based on microcharacteristics observable only under the microscope (shape, size, ornamentation of spores, fruit-body tissue, structure of the gill trama, cuticle of the cap and stipe, etc.). Notwithstanding, it is of extraordinary importance to work out a detailed description, or at least notes, concerning all the perceivable characteristics involved (colour, taste, smell, chemical reaction of the context): these characteristics usually disappear in the desiccated fruit body, or change so much that they can no more be reliably ascertained. The spores and the fruit-body structure can of course be most easily studied on fresh fruit bodies, yet they can also be examined on well dried exsiccations at any later time. Fruit bodies are usually dried as a whole, only large specimens are cut lengthwise into two or more parts. They are dried in moderate (40–60 °C) but permanent temperatures, without interruption, until they become bone-hard or fragile. Then they are placed for a few hours into a plastic bag containing a piece of paper or cotton wool dipped in water. The fruit bodies absorb a small amount of moisture, which makes them pliable. Only then do we put them into herbarium envelopes of tough, strong paper, and slightly press them by hand. This will prevent the fruit body from breaking when further handled. The collection of exsiccati must be kept dry and disinfected at least once a year (carbon-disulphide fumes being the best disinfectant), and protected against insects by chemical agents.

An important distinguishing feature of fungi is the colour of the spore print. The spore print is obtained by cutting off the cap of a fresh, ripe fruit body from the stipe and placing it flat, gills downwards, on a piece of white paper (eventually on a black one, if a white spore print is expected). The cap together with the paper are either inserted into a plastic bag, enclosed in a tin or covered with a bowl. As a rule, the spore print appears on the paper in a few hours. When using a microscope, we jot down and draw the shape and size of spores (these are measured, just like other micro-elements, by an ocular micrometer), as well as the ornamentation of the spore wall, ascertained with the aid of an oil immersion lens after applying Melzer's reagent or cotton blue to obtain the required colour reaction. Further, sections are cut through the gills and the cuticle of both the cap and the stipe. Minute parts of tissue from the fruit-body surface are cut off with a razor blade and turned into so-called crush mounts; these are far less elaborate and usually prove sufficient for identification. A tiny piece of tissue, perhaps a fraction of a gill, is mounted in a droplet of water on a microscope slide, and a small glass cover slip is placed over and slightly pressed. Microscopic mounts of fresh fruit bodies are prepared in water, those of exsiccations in an aqueous ammonia solution, in a 10-per cent potassium hydroxide (KOH) or lactophenol.

Every observation is recorded and sketched on a separate sheet of paper. On principle, each finding and herbarium item is kept separately. This method has turned out to be the best: it allows an easy manipulation and a large number of descriptions can easily be classified according to a certain system, or alphabetically, and can quickly be looked up again. Descriptions may be complemented with coloured

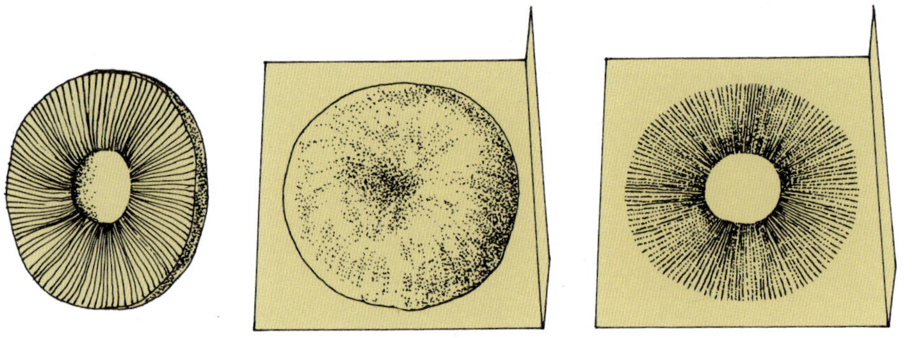

20) The spore print of gill fungi is obtained by cutting off the cap and placing it on a piece of white (eventually black) paper.

sketches or photographs. Everybody who takes a serious interest in mycology must become acquainted with the fundamentals of working with a microscope, for nowadays it has become absolutely impossible to do without a good microscope in pursuing this branch of study. Anybody who can draw well is on the winning side, because no microphotograph, and frequently not even a macrophotograph, good as it may be, can fully replace an exact and readily made sketch of the fruit bodies under examination.

Today the identification of fungi is aided by an extensive literature – from general keys up to monographic elaborations of genera or whole families. It is advisable to use the most modern versions and continuously to compare them with older works. The best solution for a beginner is to contact a specialist in the respective fungus group who will help him to overcome the first and most difficult obstacles.

Steps in the Description of Macro- and Microcharacteristics of Gill Fungi

Mode of developement

Cap: size, shape (in youth, at maturity, in old age), margin, centre, cuticle and its colouring, presence or absence of the velum, consistency.

Stipe: size (length and thickness), shape, attachment to the cap, surface, mycelium at the base, presence or absence of the velum, consistency, properties of the context in the longitudinal section.

Gills: attachment to the stipe, distance, breadth, colouring, edge, surface, colour change on injury.

Tissue: original colouring and eventual changes on the cut, presence or absence of latex (and its changes), smell, taste, consistency.

Spore print: colouring.

Microchemical reactions (on the cap cuticle, stipe surface, gills, context where broken): the most frequently used media are green-vitriol solutions, phenol, sulphovanillin, guaic tincture, ammonia, potash and soda lye, phormol, hydrochloric, nitric and sulphuric acid, argent nitrate, sulphorormol, benzidine.

Microcharacteristics: basidia, cystidia and other hymenial elements, spores (size, shape, apiculus, germ pore, wall-thickness, ornamentation, colouring, amyloidity, cyanophilia), trama;
structure of the cap and stipe cuticle, mycelium at the stipe base;
hyphae in the fruit body (presence or absence of clamp connections, pigmentation, etc.)

Ecological data about the habitat

Locality

Date of collection

Total amount of fruit bodies used for the description

Illustration of the material described (drawing, photograph)

Registration of the exsiccatus (number in the herbarium, in the list of finds)

Classification of Fungi – A Brief Survey

Views about the classification of fungi are far from uniform: the evaluation and sometimes even the content of higher and lower categories differ according to individual authors. What one regards as a class represents a phylum for another, not to speak of the differences in the lower categories (orders, families, subfamilies, etc.) and their classification in the system. The present chapter has been restricted to merely a basic survey of the orders constituting the two principal groups of the so-called true fungi (Eumycophyta) – i. e. Ascomycetes and Basidiomycetes. Within each order, the families included in this book are referred to and, for the most part, briefly described. This will enable the reader to acquire a good picture of the systematic classification of the fungus species presented here. Mycetozoans (Myxomycota), nowadays generally regarded as fungi, and also moulds (Phycomycetes) remain outside the sphere of our interest. Imperfect fungi (Deuteromycetes) are briefly referred to, owing to their relevance in studying 'large' fungi (Macromycetes).

Fungi

Phylum: true fungi – Eumycophyta
- Class: Ascomycetes
  - Subclass: Protoascomycetidae
    - Order: Eurotiales
    - Order: Microascales
    - Order: Onygenales
    - Order: Laboulbeniales
  - Subclass: Ascohymenomycetidae
    - Order: Erysiphales
    - Order: Pezizales
    - Order: Tuberales
    - Order: Helotiales
    - Order: Phacidiales
    - Order: Xylariales
    - Order: Hypocreales
  - Subclass: Ascoloculomycetidae
- Class: Basidiomycetes
  - Subclass: Heterobasidiomycetidae
    - Order: Protoclavariales
    - Order: Auriculariales
    - Order: Tremellales
    - Order: Uredinales
  - Subclass: Holobasidiomycetidae
    - Order: Aphyllophorales
    - Order: Polyporales
    - Order: Boletales
    - Order: Agaricales
    - Order: Russulales
- Class: Gasteromycetes
- Auxiliary class: Deuteromycetes

Ascomycetes

Ascomycetes are usually regarded – together with Basidiomycetes – as 'higher fungi'. The common feature of all Ascomycetes is the production of spores in spore sacs (asci), most often eight to an ascus. The mycelium is always septate, and the septa are furnished with a simple minute opening facilitating the passage of plasma and nuclei. The principal constituent of mycelial walls, as well as of all hyphal walls in the fruit body, is chitin. The greater part of Ascomycetes produce fruit bodies on their mycelium which basically assume two forms substantiating the division of these fungi into two main groups. In the first group the fruit body is usually globular, closed, opening at maturity either by rupture (the cleistothecium), or by a small pore at the apex (the perithecium or pseudothecium). In the second group the fruit body is freely open, either from the very beginning or at least in the later stages (the apothecium). Together with the asci, sterile filaments (paraphyses) also develop within the fruit body. Many species also form asexual (conidial) stages to which the designation anamorphs is nowadays applied, while the ascus stages are termed teleomorphs.

The classification and identification of Ascomycetes is based exclusively on the ascus stage. This large group of fungi, including about 40,000 hitherto described species, is predominantly composed of inconspicuous fungi with fruit bodies usually no more than 1 mm in size, occurring in nature on most various substrates. They are commonly divided into Pyrenomycetes and Discomycetes, but in fact both these groups represent several independent developmental lines whose delimitation is not uniform. In principle, three groups exist which are attributed the value of subclasses: Protoascomycetidae, Ascohymenomycetidae and Ascoloculomycetidae.

Fungi of the subclass **Protoascomycetidae** have globular asci with a thin, simple wall provided with no opening apparatus; it becomes slimy and desintegrates at maturity. Four orders of almost exclusively microscopic fungi are included here:

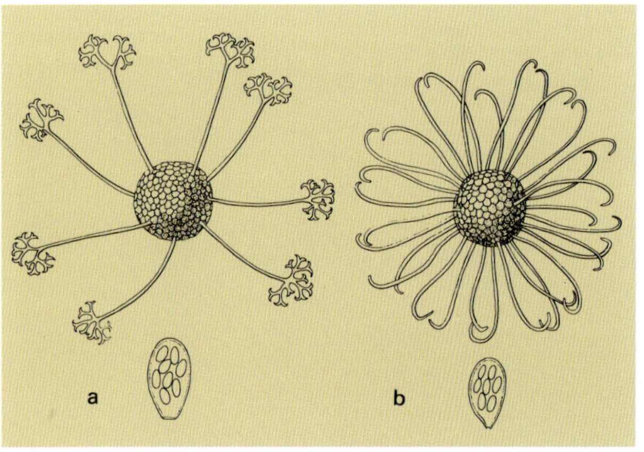

21) Examples of mildews: cleistothecia with appendages, asci with spores; **a** – *Microsphaera* sp., **b** – *Uncinula* sp.

Fungi of the order **Eurotiales** are saprophytes currently distributed in soil and humus where they decompose organic remains. The so-called moulds of the genera *Penicillium* and *Aspergillus* belong here – of course both these names relate only to the conidial stages, valid names for the much rarer ascus stage of the genus *Penicillium* being *Talaromyces,* for *Aspergillus, Eurotium.* This order, however, also includes some larger fungi with globular fruit bodies up to several centimetres in size. They are represented in our forests by the genus *Elaphomyces.*

The order **Microascales** has become notorious particularly by its microscopic member *Ceratocystis ulmi* whose mass occurrence has led to the extermination of most European elms. The disease caused by this fungus is called Dutch elm disease.

Fungi of the order **Onygenales** have small, stipitate, globular fruit bodies growing on the horny tissue of claws, hoofs, horns, but also on the feathers of dead birds. These ceratophilous fungi are represented by the genus *Onygena.*

Fungi of the order **Laboulbeniales** are sometimes regarded as an independent class of Ascomycetes and their position in the system is still ambiguous. They are narrowly specialized parasites of insects (especially beetles) and spiders to which, however, they do not seem to cause much harm. Their minute, fusiform fruit bodies are fastened to the surface of the host's body by a 'foot'.

Fungi of the subclass **Ascohymenomycetidae** have asci whose length usually exceeds their breadth. Their apex is equipped with an opening apparatus or a lid for discharging ascospores. The ascus wall is thin, and does not turn slimy when mature. They are usually divided into seven orders:

The order **Erysiphales** (mildews) includes the most common and also most conspicuous parasites of vascular plants. Their surface mycelium often forms extensive coatings, particularly on the leaves, which are either white, farinaceous (family Erysiphaceae), or brown to blackish (Meliolaceae, currently distributed almost exclusively in the tropics or subtropics). Minute, globular, closed fruit bodies (cleistothecia), often provided with variously shaped filaments, appear to the naked eye as dark little dots. Numerous pests of cultivated plants belong to this group, for example *Uncinula necator,* grapevine mildew (known especially in its conidial stage as *Oidium tuckeri*), further *Podosphaera leucotricha* on apple-trees, *Microsphaera quercina* on oaks, etc. Traditionally the order Erysiphales was classed with the subclass Protoascomycetidae referred to above; at present, however, it has been reclassified as a member of the subclass Ascohymenomycetidae, with respect to its asci opening through a lid.

The following four orders are currently referred to as cup fungi (Discomycetes).

The fruit body of **Pezizales** is a typical apothecium, globularly closed only in youth; soon it opens into its definitive shape which is semiglobular, patelliform or discoid, often flatly expanded or even convex. The inner surface, known as the disc (thecium), bears asci and paraphyses arranged in palisade-like structures.

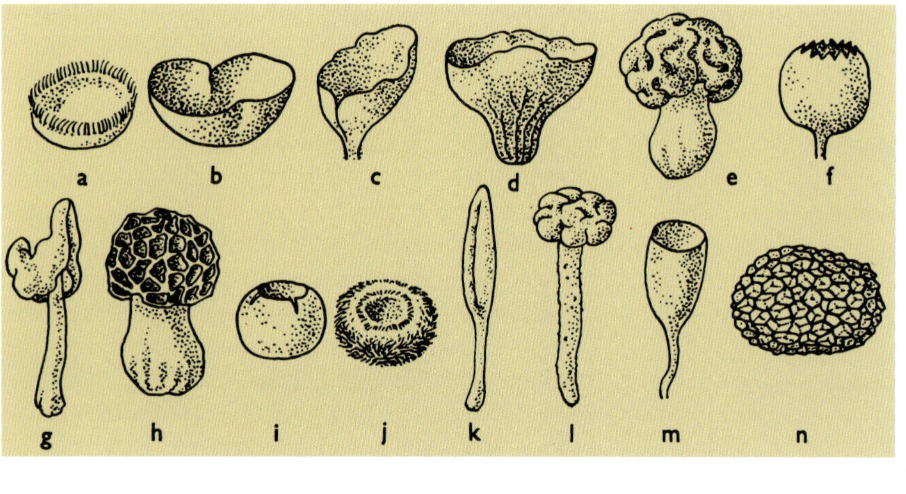

22) Examples of fruit bodies in Ascomycetes: **a** – *Scutellinia*; **b** – *Peziza*; **c** – *Otidea*; **d** – *Helvella*; **e** – *Gyromitra*; **f** – *Tarzetta*; **g** – *Helvella elastica*; **h** – *Morchella esculenta*; **i** – *Peziza vesiculosa*; **j** – *Mycolachnea hemisphaerica*; **k** – *Geoglossum*; **1** – *Leotia lubrica*; **m** – *Urnula craterium*; **n** – *Tuber aestivum*.

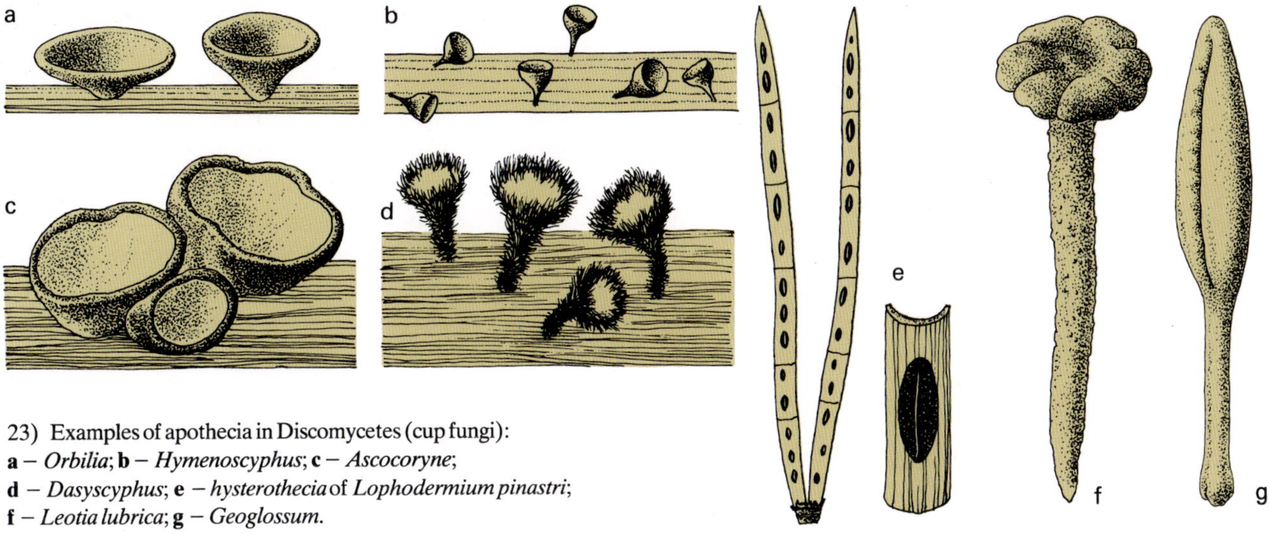

23) Examples of apothecia in Discomycetes (cup fungi):
a – *Orbilia*; **b** – *Hymenoscyphus*; **c** – *Ascocoryne*;
d – *Dasyscyphus*; **e** – *hysterothecia* of *Lophodermium pinastri*;
f – *Leotia lubrica*; **g** – *Geoglossum*.

Fruit bodies in the most developed forms, Helvellaceae and Morchellaceae, are differentiated into a stipe and a cap. Asci open by a lid and ascospores are shot out. In some genera the ascus membranes are markedly amyloid. As well as numerous representatives of minute size, Pezizales also include the largest and hence the most conspicuous species of Discomycetes. Some of them show remarkable colours, especially red, orange and yellow. They grow almost exclusively as saprophytes on bare ground, in moss, on putrescent wood or on other plant remnants, many of them on excrements, dung and on burned-over soils. They are generally divided into six families. An important identifying feature is – besides other characteristics – the ornamentation of their ascospores. This book deals with species of the families Humariaceae, Otideaceae, Pezizaceae, Helvellaceae and Morchellaceae.

The order **Tuberales** consists of hypogeous fungi. The tuberiform fruit body remains closed, the incidence of spore-bearing locules opening on its surface is rather rare. Asci usually cover the walls of galleries and cavities inside the fruit body. Spores are often large, ornamented; unlike the preceding species, they are not ejected out of the asci but get free through the decomposition of the entire fruit body. The Tuberales are mycorrhizal fungi distributed mainly in warm regions, in deciduous forests, and on calcareous soils. They include the families Tuberaceae and Terfeziaceae.

The order **Helotiales** is the largest group of cup fungi. Their lidless asci open at the apex by a ring-shaped apparatus through the centre of which the spores are violently discharged. Their fruit bodies are typical apothecia, mostly minute in size (1 mm and less in diameter), sessile or stipitate, smooth or hairy, bristly and felted, in some genera embedded in the substrate at first and pushing their way to the surface; more advanced types have upright fruit bodies with long stipes, cylindrical or pileate (e. g. in the family Geoglossaceae). They grow predominantly as saprophytes, rarely as parasites, on plant stems, leaves, wood or rind.

The fruit body of fungi belonging to the order **Phacidiales** is called the pseudoapothecium; this is embedded in the tissue of the host plant and covered with a black stromatic layer which bursts open at maturity, disclosing the disc. The disc is covered up in dry conditions. The fruit body opening through a longitudinal slit is called the hysterothecium and is characteristic of the family Hypodermataceae. This includes for example the genus *Lophodermium;* some of its species live as needle parasites, causing a disease known as needle cast. Other typical representatives of this order are the genus *Rhytisma* whose conidial stage causes black spottiness on maple leaves, and *Colpoma* with the species *C. quercinum,* commonly found on dead oak branches.

The last-named two orders have been given the common designation Pyrenomycetes (flask fungi). These include also the subclass Ascoloculomycetidae (with the exception of the order **Lecanorales**). Here the fruit body is a typical perithecium containing asci which, in the orders **Xylariales** and **Hypocreales,** are unitunicate, opening at the apex by an amyloid pore or by an opening apparatus of another kind. The globular or lageniform perithecium has its own wall made up of pseudoparenchyma, even when it is embedded in the stroma. It ordinarily opens through a minute circular opening at the apex, often terminating in a neck-like extension (ostiole) whose channel is lined with hyphae (periphyses).

The order **Xylariales** is a group extraordinarily rich in species; it is divided into a number of families sometimes considered as independent orders. They live predominantly as saprophytes on branches and trunks of trees or shrubs and on herbal stems; many species are coprophilous. Larger and more conspicuous Pyrenomycetes belong for the most part to the family Xylariaceae; some of them are commonly found on dead wood logs, trunks and stumps.

Fungi of the order **Hypocreales** are distinguished from the preceding species by their colouring – their perithecia or stromata are mostly bright red or yellow. They include a large number of genera and species distributed predominantly in the tropics. In the north temperate zone they are represented by the genus *Nectria. N. cinnabarina* is a lignicolous pyrenomycete whose conidial stage, known under the name *Tubercularia vulgaris,* is one of the commonest small fungi living on dead branches of various woody plants. Also the well-known ergot belongs here; it is the sclerotium of *Claviceps purpurea,* nowadays cultivated and industrially processed for medicinal purposes.

The subclass **Ascoloculomycetidae** includes on the one hand three orders of Pyrenomycetes, and on the other hand lichenized fungi – i. e. the greater part of lichens subjected to research by an independent scientific branch, lichenology. A characteristic feature of this subclass are bitunicate asci whose walls consist of two layers. After the spores have attained maturity, the outer layer bursts open at the apex, while the inner layer juts out of the newly created opening and the ascospores are discharged. The small fruit bodies resemble the perithecium but are regarded as a special structure termed the ascocarp (also pseudothecium or ascostroma). It is in fact a stroma consisting of one or more locules with no special wall dividing them from each other. This group comprises a vast amount of genera and species of both parasites and saprophytes inhabiting most various parts of plants. No uniform classification of orders and families has so far been worked out.

Basidiomycetes

This is the developmentally most advanced class of fungi, including at least 20,000 species. The characteristic feature common to all fungi of this group lies in the origin of spores (basidiospores): they develop on specialized cells called basidia. A young basidium has two nuclei coalescing into a single nucleus. A twofold reduction division gives rise to four haploid daughter nuclei entering by apical or lateral pedicels (sterigmata) into the basidiospores borne at the tips of sterigmata. Basidiomycetes of a less advanced type usually possess divided or septate basidia. The shape of basidia remains constant and is considered of paramount taxonomic significance in determining mutual relationships. Basidiospores are unicellular and are constant in shape and size in the individual taxons. Another important distinguishing feature is their wall, often ornamented with various excrescences, and amyloid in many species or genera. Basidia are usually aggregated in a continuous layer (hymenium), wherein special sterile cells (paraphyses, cystidia) are often present. The mycelium consists of simple or branched hyphae penetrating through the substrate; sometimes they are quite conspicuous. Mycelial hyphae are septate, consisting mostly of chitin. Each septum is furnished with a 'dolipore' (an opening in the central, bilaterally thickened part of the septum covered by a semiglobular membrane). In the primitive types, the fruit body itself is reduced to a layer of hyphae bearing the hymenium or single basidia only; they usually assume the form of coatings or membranes which are termed resupinate fruit bodies. More highly developed forms usually possess an upright fruit body differentiated into the pileate part (cap, pileus) and the stipitate part (stem, stipes). The hymenium, which in the simpler forms covers the entire outer surface of the fruit body, is confined in the more advanced forms to a specific, exactly delimited part, the so-called hymenophore, situated usually on the underside of the cap. The surface of the hymenophore is often enlarged by various excrescences, tubes or gills. The fruit body either has no apparent cover (a gymnocarpous fruit body) or is enclosed – at least in the initial stages of development – in a special covering (veil, velum). The spore-producing tissue sometimes develops within the fruit body, as for instance in the Gasteromycetes.

Basidiomycetes usually live as saprophytes on decaying plant remains, on the forest floor or in humus and duff; many of them form symbiotic relationships with roots of green plants (mycorrhiza). Most species are confined to the forest environment: here they play a significant role and their fruit bodies represent a remarkable phenomenon especially in the summer and autumnal aspect of plant communities. Their principal function consists in their contribution to humus formation, to the decomposition of wood – nor is it possible to overlook their role as a means of sustenance.

The shape of basidia underlies their division into two subclasses – Heterobasidiomycetidae and Holobasidiomycetidae.

The subclass **Heterobasidiomycetidae** includes Basidiomycetes with either simple or – most frequently – septate (i. e. multicellular) or more or less deeply divided basidia. It is formed by the following four orders:

Fungi of the order **Protoclavariales** have basidia consisting of a globular or cylindrical part (hypobasidia) to which inflated or elongate epibasidia are attached, bearing sterigmata with spores. The fruit bodies are often remarkably gelatinous or elastic. These small fungi usually live as saprophytes on dead wood. They are classed into two families, Tulasnellaceae and Dacrymycetaceae; a common representative of the last-mentioned family, *Calocera,* is dealt with in this book.

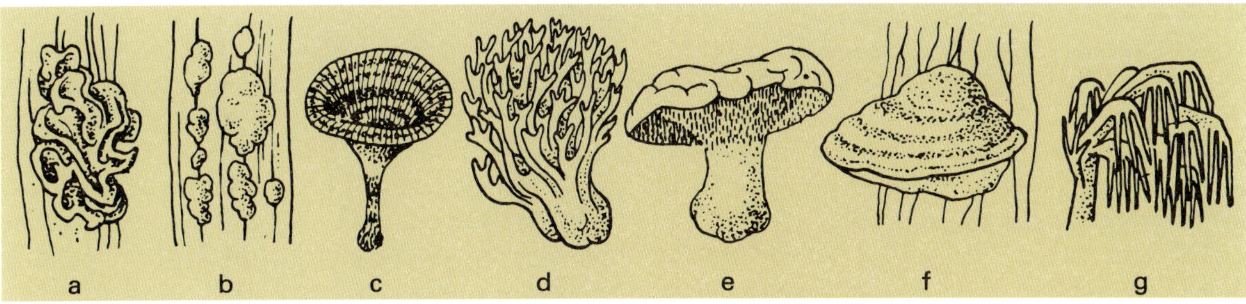

24) Examples of fruit bodies in Aphyllophorales and Tremellales: **a** – *Exidia*; **b** – *Darcymyces*; **c** – *Coltricia perennis*; **d** – *Ramaria*; **e** – *Hydnum repandum*; **f** – *Fomes*; **g** – *Hèricium coralloides*.

Fungi of the order **Auriculariales** have cylindrical or clavate basidia divided into several cells by transverse septae. A single sterigma ending in a spore develops from each of these cells. The family Auriculariaceae has been included here.

Fungi of the order **Tremellales** produce almost globular, cruciately septate basidia, divided by one or two longitudinal septae perpendicular to each other into two or four parts. The fruit bodies are mostly gelatinous and are of various shapes. This order includes predominantly wood saprophytes, of the larger ones particularly various species of the genus *Tremella* and *Pseudohydnum* belonging to the family Tremellaceae.

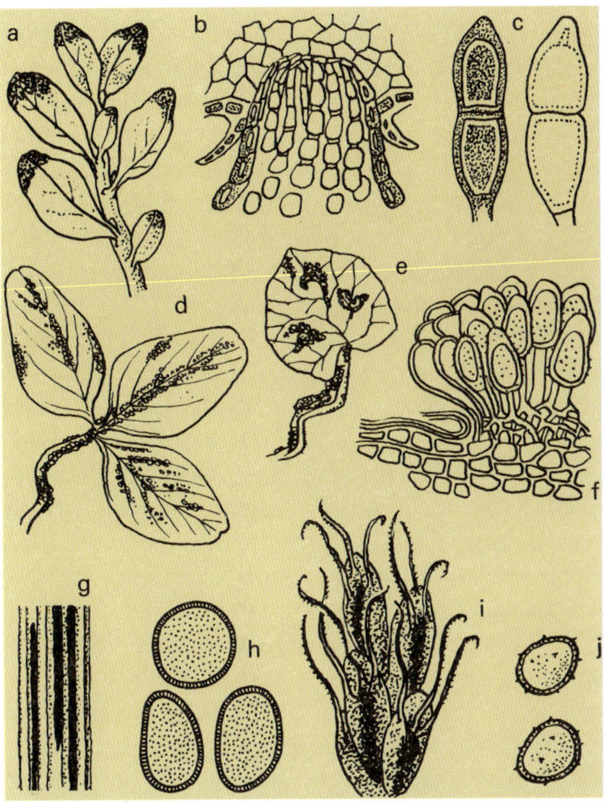

25) Examples of some parasitic rusts and smuts: **a** – *Exobasidium vaccinii* on Cowberry leaves; **b** – cross section through a rust aecium; **c** – teliospores of the rust *Puccinia*; **d** – deposits of the rust *Uromyces trifolii* on clover leaves; **e** – telia of the rust *Uromyces ficariae* on the Lesser Celandine; **f** – teliospores of *Uromyces ficariae;* **g** – deposits of the smut *Ustilago longissima* on *Glyceria* leaves; **h** spores of the smut *Ustilago longissima*; **i** – cereal grains attacked by the smut *Ustilago segetum*; **j** – spores of *Ustilago segetum.*

The order **Uredinales** (rusts) includes micromycetes parasitizing green plants in which they cause the so-called rustiness: the attacked plant is covered with minute rusty, orange, brown to black-coloured deposits in the form of tubercles or other structures. The tissue of the infested plants often withers, in other cases rusts may cause hypertrophic growth. Rusts that attack cultivated plants, especially cereals, are of considerable importance. Numerous rust species produce four types of spores: aeciospores (spring) in cupulate aecia, urediospores (summer) in uredia, teliospores (winter) in telia; teliospores germinate into the promycelium from which sporidia arise (the fourth type of spores). A characteristic of the rusts is an alternation of sexual and asexual generations; in some of them there is also an alternation of hosts on the one hand, and a narrow specialization on a certain (often a single) type of host on the other. The substantial part of species is concentrated in the genera *Puccinia* and *Uromyces.*

In the past, smuts (Ustilaginales) used to be introduced here as the following order. Today they are included in the class Endomycetes which represents the transition between moulds (Phycomycophytina) and primitive Ascomycetes. Other authors, however, join smuts and rusts into the independent class Teliomycetes. Smuts, like rusts, parasitize vascular plants.

The subclass **Holobasidiomycetidae** is the developmentally most advanced group of Basidiomycetes. Fungi belonging to this subclass have unicellular basidia usually bearing four sterigmate spores at their apex. The hymenium is either freely expanded or enclosed in the fruit-body tissue. The subclass is divided into six orders. The first five are the so-called Hymenomycetes in which the hymenium is freely opened before the spores have reached maturity and covers either the entire fruit-body surface or some of its parts. The spores are actively discharged from the basidia, forming the deposited spore mass. The sixth order, **Gasterales,** includes fungi with closed fruit bodies within which spores are formed; these, however, are not actively discharged from the basidia and fail to form any spore deposit.

The Gasterales do not form a developmentally homogeneous group – in fact it is an extremely heterogeneous grouping. Perhaps they represent the termination of several developmental lines of different origin. Different views are therefore supported in their classification, manifesting themselves in the unequal evaluation of the individual groups. Many mycologists regard the group discussed here as an order (Gasterales), others (including the author) as a higher category – a class (Gasteromycetes).

The order **Aphyllophorales** (non-gilled fungi) have either a resupinate fruit body spreading out loosely on the surface, or one of a definite shape. Resupinate species are most frequently found on the underside of uprooted tree trunks and fallen branches, on putrescent wood logs, in stump cavities, etc. So far a definitive classification of this large order has not been worked out; several families including a great number of genera are distinguished.

The following survey again presents families included in this book:

Stereaceae are lignicolous fungi having tough, resupinate to pileate fruit bodies usually surviving for several years, often densely arranged one above the other.

Thelephoraceae have brown-coloured, mostly angular, echinulate or verrucose spores. This holds for the genera *Tomentella* and *Thelephora,* as well as for the pileate fruit bodies of Hydnaceae – such as the genera *Hydnellum, Sarcodon* and *Phellodon.*

A characteristic of lignicolous fungi of the family Ganodermataceae are also brown-coloured spores, but these are truncate and ornamented. The fruit bodies of Ganodermataceae are tough to ligneous.

The family Coniophoraceae has relatively large, coloured, smooth spores – e. g. genera *Serpula* and *Coniophora.*

Clavariaceae and Sparassidaceae have erect, cylindrical or clavate, simple or ramose fruit bodies. The hymenium covers most of the outer surface of the fruit body. There are a large number of genera including *Clavaria, Ramaria* and *Sparassis.*

Hydnaceae and Auriscalpiaceae are fungi with an echinate (spiny) hymenophore – for example *Auriscalpium, Hericium, Hydnum.*

The family Poriaceae includes the greater part of polypores whose tubular hymenophore is inseparable from the tough context to which it is firmly accreted. Besides many true polypores (e.g. *Albatrellus, Fomes, Laetiporus, Trametes, Piptoporus*) the genus *Fistulina* also belongs here, though it is often classed with the independent family Fistulinaceae. A part of the polypores (the genus *Polyporus*) has been transferred as the family Polyporaceae into the order Polyporales, together with several genera bearing a lamellate hymenophore but similar in anatomical structure.

Cantharellaceae and Lentinellaceae are fungi with a distinctly developed fruit body whose underside is covered by the hymenium; this surface is either smooth or augmented by blunt, shallow, often anastomosing ridges, gill-folds or gills. From the well-known genera belonging to this group, which are collected for table use, let us mention the Chanterelle (*Cantharellus*), *Craterellus* and *Gomphus,* sometimes classed into the independent family Gomphaceae.

The hymenophore in the Schizophyllaceae is formed by pseudogills splitting in two along the edge.

The order **Polyporales** includes fungi having a lamellate or porous hymenophore. The fruit bodies are mostly annual, fleshy when alive, often tough in dry weather, resilient or almost hard as wood, and with a central, eccentric or lateral stipe. The hyphae are relatively thick-walled. The spore print is white, cream-coloured or lilac (greyish violet). They are mostly lignicolous fungi. The families Polyporaceae and Pleurotaceae belong to this group.

As a general rule, fungi of the order **Boletales** have a tubular hymenophore covering the lower surface of the cap as a continuous layer, quite easily separable from the cap context. The fruit bodies are fleshy in most cases, often with a developed covering (velum), usually with a central stipe. They grow on the ground, most frequently in mycorrhizal association with woody plants. The following three families are included in this book:

In the true Boletaceae the velum is either present or absent, the cap cuticle is either viscid or dry, smooth or matted-tomentose. The pores are white, yellow, olive-hued, pink or red, sometimes staining blue, green or red when bruised. The spores are ellipsoid to elongate-fusiform, mostly smooth. They are mycorrhizal fungi. Best known are the genera *Boletus, Tylopilus, Suillus, Xerocomus* and *Krombholzia.*

Paxillaceae are closely related to the foregoing family. Their hymenophore bears gills which are sometimes anastomosed or forked, relatively narrow, decurrent, yellow, orange or brown. The cap has an involute margin. The spore sprint is whitish, cream-coloured, yellow or brown; the spores are ellipsoid, ovoid, cyanophilous, nonamyloid. The genera *Paxillus, Hygrophoropsis* and *Omphalotus* belong here.

Gomphidiaceae have thick, decurrent, distant gills, fleshy fruit bodies with a dry to markedly glutinous cap, a black or olive-black spore print, and fusiform, smooth, cyanophilous, nonamyloid spores. Cystidia are developed. The genus *Gomphidius* is sometimes divided into two genera – *Chroogomphus* and *Leucogomphidius.*

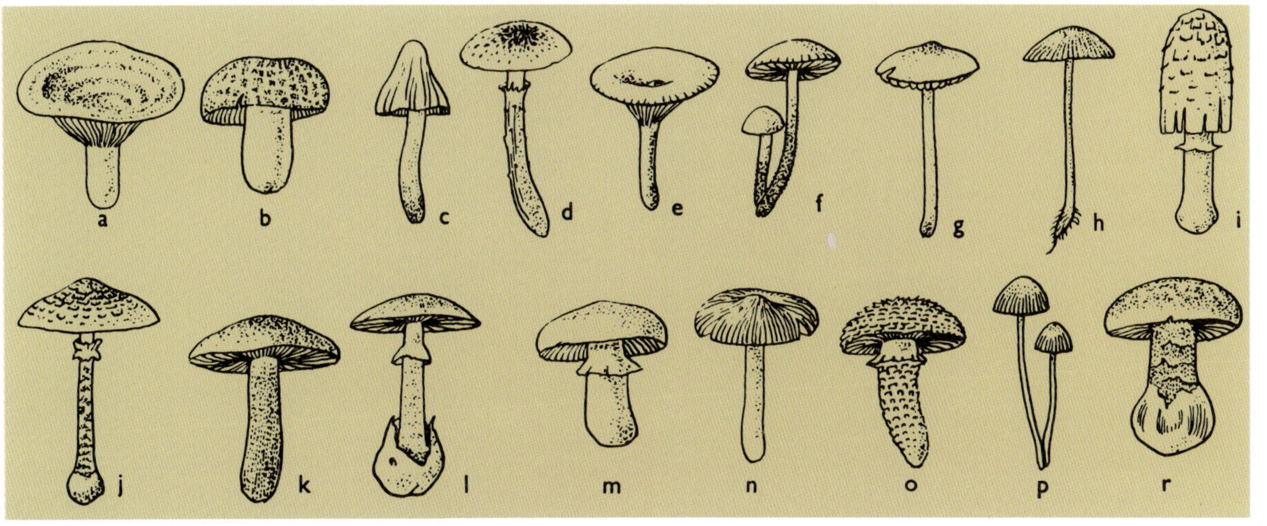

26) Examples of gill-fungi fruit bodies: **a** – *Lactarius*: **b** – *Russula*; **c** – *Hygrocybe*; **d** – *Armillaria mellea*; **e** – *Clitocybe*; **f** – *Collybia*; **g+h** – *Mycena*; **i** – *Coprinus*; **j** – *Lepiota*; **k** – *Tricholoma*; **l** – *Amanita*; **m** – *Agaricus*; **n** – *Inocybe*; **o** – *Pholiota*; **p** – *Psathyrella*; **r** – *Cortinarius*.

The order **Agaricales** – gill fungi – has juicy or tough-fleshed fruit bodies, usually differentiated into a cap and a stipe, which may sometimes be reduced so that the fruit body is directly attached to the substrate. The hymenophore bears gills that are exceptionally narrow, veiny or ribbed, or the hymenophore is entirely smooth. The spore print varies in colour; the spores are colourless or coloured, sometimes dextrinoid or amyloid, smooth or ornamented. When young the fruit body is sometimes encased in a veil, leaving remnants of various kind on its surface (patches on the cap, filaments or scales on the stipe, a volva at the stipe base, etc.). The gill fungi are usually divided into ten families:

Hygrophoraceae have soft, juicy or waxy fruit bodies often covered with slime, light to variegated in colour, with or without a fugacious veil, thick and distant gills, markedly long and narrow basidia, and colourless and smooth spores.

The family Tricholomataceae is one of the largest gill-fungi families. It includes fungi of various size, with or without a velum, with a fleshy to fibrillose context, with a central or lateral stipe, and with adnate to deeply decurrent gills. The spore print is white or yellowish, exceptionally it may be pale pink or violet. The spores are often amyloid, rarely cyanophilous, and smooth or ornamented. With a view to the vast amount of genera not even their selection is introduced here, and the reader is referred to the illustrated section of this book where he will find a number of representatives of this family.

Similar to the above family in appearance are the Entolomataceae. They also include fungi of various size and colouring, with a central or lateral stipe or maybe entirely stipeless. They differ from the Tricholomataceae in having a pale to vivid pink spore print. The spores are mostly angular, elongate, nonamyloid. The basic genus is *Entoloma*. This name is nowadays used by some mycologists as the only generic designation covering all the species which, in the original conception, represented altogether five independent genera: *Entoloma, Nolanea, Leptonia, Eccilia* and *Claudopus*. On the other hand, French mycologists apply the collective designation *Rhodophyllus* to the genera referred to above.

Pluteaceae are fleshy fungi with a central stipe, with thin, broad, crowded, free to remote gills formed by an inverse trama. In some species, a volva is developed at the stipe base. The spore print is pale pink, spores are smooth, without any germ pore, nonamyloid, and cyanophilous. The Pluteaceae often grow on wood. The genera *Volvariella* and *Pluteus* are included here.

Amanitaceae are characterized by fleshy fruit bodies; the stipe can easily be removed from the context of the cap. When young the fruit bodies are enveloped in a velum, leaving warts or patches on the cap cuticle and an annulus on the stipe. A sheath (volva) is often developed at the stipe base; it assumes various forms and is sometimes reduced to mere flocci. The gills are free, broad, the gill trama is bilateral, the spore print is white, rarely tinged with green, the spores are colourless, mostly smooth, sometimes amyloid. The very plentiful genus *Amanita* is classed with this family, as well as the small genus *Limacella* formerly regarded as one of the *Lepiota* species.

Agaricaceae have fleshy fruit bodies with a central stipe which can easily be disconnected from the cap context and bears an annulus. The gills are crowded, free, broad, thin. The cap cuticle is often squamulose or floccose; the gill trama may be regular or irregular;

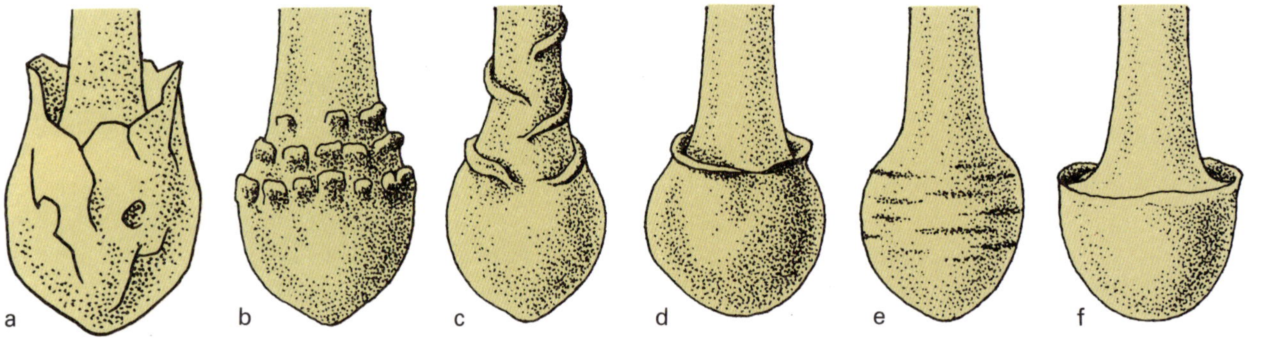

27) Examples of the basal end of the stipe in some species of *Amanita*: **a** – *Amanita phalloides*; **b** – *A. muscaria*; **c** – *A. pantherina*; **d** – *A. gemmata*; **e** – *A. rubescens*; **f** – *A. citrina*.

the spore print is white, greenish, pink, reddish brown, rusty or purple-brown; the spores are smooth, rarely verrucose, often thick-walled. The fruit bodies grow on the ground, on dung and humus. Of the principal genera included, *Agaricus, Lepiota, Macrolepiota,* and *Cystoderma* should be mentioned.

The fleshy fruit bodies of the Coprinaceae have a central stipe and thin, free or adnate gills; their trama is regular. In the genus *Coprinus,* fruit bodies develop extraordinarily quickly and, as the spores ripen, at first the gills and ultimately the whole fruit body start dissolving into a pulpy mass (autolysis). This process does not take place in the genera *Panaeolus, Panaeolina* and *Psathyrella.* The spore print is dark brown, purple-brown to black, the spores are smooth or ornamented, mostly possessing a discernible germ pore. Coprinaceae grow on the ground, on dung, excrements, wood, and on the remains of herbs or grasses.

Bolbitiaceae are smaller-sized and often thin-fleshed fungi with a central stipe. The gills are thin, broad, adnate, the gill trama is regular, the spore print is rusty brown, rusty ochre to umber-brown, the spores are smooth, with a germ pore. The cap cuticle is composed of globular to pyriform cells; cheilocystidia of a characteristic shape are often developed. Bolbitiaceae grow on excrements, on the ground, on wood and other plant remains. Important genera are *Conocybe, Bolbitius,* and *Agrocybe.*

Variously sized fleshy fungi with a central stipe belong to the family Strophariaceae. The cap cuticle consists of long hyphae, the sometimes distinctly developed velum leaves a ring or other remnants on the stipe. The spore print is pale violet or tinged with various shades of brown. The spores are smooth, mostly furnished with a germ pore. Cheilocystidia and also pleurocystidia are developed, some genera have chrysocystidia. Strophariaceae grow on the ground, often on decaying wood or on other plant remains, sometimes also on excrements. The main genera belonging here are *Stropharia, Hypholoma, Psilocybe* and *Pholiota.*

Cortinariaceae greatly resemble Tricholomataceae and represent the second largest family of gill fungi. The characteristic feature common to all Cortinariaceae is the colour of the spore print which, as a rule, is brown or rust-coloured; it is white only exceptionally. The spores are often ornamented, verrucose, and usually lack a distinct germ pore; the cap cuticle is composed of radially arranged hyphae; the gill trama is regular.The universal veil (*velum generale*) is either developed or absent; the partial veil is usually present in the form of a cortina. Cystidia are often present. Cortinariaceae grow on humus, wood and moss, and many species form ectotrophic mycorrhizae. The name of the family is derived from that of the most plentiful genus of gill-bearing fungi, *Cortinarius,* comprising approximately 500 species and divided into several subgenera which were once considered to be independent genera. Of the other large genera belonging to this family, let us mention *Inocybe, Hebeloma* and *Galerina.*

The order **Russulales**. Originally the Russulales were regarded as a family of the order Agaricales; at present, however, they are taken to be an independent order. A characteristic feature here is the structure of the fruit-body context containing – besides long, cylindrical hyphae – groups of globular cells (spherocysts) nidulariaceously arranged in its tissue. It is the spherocysts that cause the characteristic friability, that is the pomaceous brittleness of the broken context. Lactifers are also present in the context. In the *Lactarius* species they are filled with latex, i.e. a milky-white juice oozing from bruised places in fresh fruit bodies. The cap cuticle is often variegated; the spore print is white to bright yellow; spores are broad, subglobose, and broadly ovoid or ellipsoid, with a conspicuous strongly amyloid ornamentation on the surface. Cystidia are present in the hymenium. The order has a single family – the Russulaceae, including the genera *Russula* and *Lactarius* represented in the European forests by a large number of species. For the most part, they are mushrooms living in ectotrophic mycorrhiza with woody forest plants.

The class of **Gasteromycetes** (stomach fungi) includes fungi with an angiocarpous, predominantly globular fruit body which is either permanently closed or opens only in connection with the maturation of basidiospores. The fruit body consists of an external cover (peridium) and the part enclosed within (the gleba) containing the spore-bearing tissue. The gleba is often composed of cavities whose walls are partly formed by thick-walled hyphae; in the mature fruit body, these hyphae are transformed into the capillitium, while the other hyphae of the gleba disintegrate simultaneously with the basidia. The basidia are distributed throughout the fruit body either evenly or like birds' nests; sometimes they line the inner walls of the chambers or cavities in palisades. The development of the gleba is typical of individual families and genera of the Gasteromycetes. Ripe spores are not actively discharged (as for instance in the gill fungi).

Phallaceae are conspicuous and sometimes very ornamental fungi. The young fruit body is egg-shaped. The peridium is often composed of three layers, the middle layer being thick and gelatinous. At maturity it is pierced through at the apex by the receptaculum (i.e. the infertile part of the gleba). The receptaculum carries the fertile part upward, while the rest of the peridium remains at the base in the form of a cup (volva). At maturity the fertile part of the gleba covering the surface of the receptaculum decomposes into a pulpy matter emitting an unpleasant odour. This odour attracts insects and these subsequently disperse the basidiospores contained in this matter. A number of tropical genera belong here, the genera indigenous to Europe are *Phallus* and *Mutinus*. The genera *Clathrus, Anthurus, Lysurus* and *Dictyophora* are sometimes classed with the independent family Clathraceae.

Hysterangiaceae have hypogeous, tuberiform or subglobular fruit bodies often overgrown with mycelial threads, and a cartilaginous or gelatinous gleba composed of a tissue radially developing from the infertile base or from a gelatinous columella. The spores are smooth, ellipsoid or cylindrical, and are almost colourless. The genus *Hysterangium* belongs to this family.

Earth stars (Geastraceae) are terrestrial, and in the tropics even lignicolous fungi. When young, the globular or pyriform fruit bodies are usually embedded in the ground. In mature fruit bodies the outer peridium bursts and lifts the fruit bodies above the ground. The outer peridium splits into rays, in the centre of which the inner peridium with a globular gleba is seated. The gleba contains the capillitium and spores. The Geastraceae often remain in their spot for a long time.

Lycoperdaceae are mostly epigeous (at least at maturity). They are globular, pyriform or clavate in shape; the gleba fills the whole interior of the fruit body or passes over into a sterile tissue in its basal portion. The peridium consists of a thin and readily decomposing outer layer (exoperidium), and a usually thin, papery layer (endoperidium) opening by a small peristome or irregularly decomposing. In the members of the genus *Geastrum* it splits to form regular rays, the endoperidium is either attached to the exoperidium or is borne on a pedicel; the peristome is situated at the apex of the endoperidium. The capillitium is usually developed. Spores are globular, small, and coloured. The main genera include *Lycoperdon, Bovista, Calvatia, Langermannia,* and *Geastrum. Langermannia gigantea,* whose fruit bodies grow up to 50 cm in diameter, are among the largest of fungi.

Sclerodermataceae have tuberiform, fleshy, sometimes stipitate fruit bodies developing on or under the surface of the ground. The peridium either opens by an apical pore or bursts irregularly. At maturity the gleba is reduced to powder – either directly, or following an intermediate disintegration into pip-like

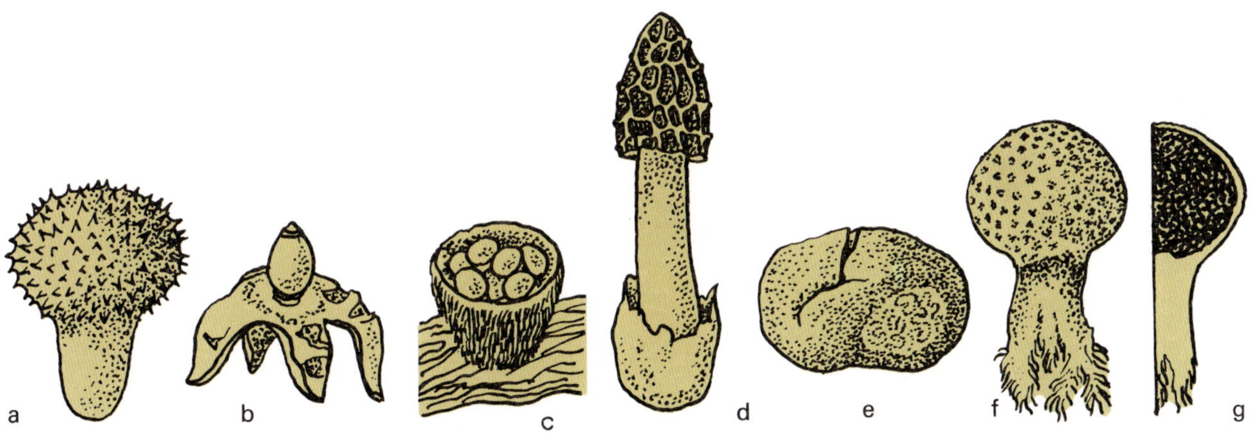

28) Examples of some Gasteromycetes fruit bodies: **a** – *Lycoperdon*; **b** – *Geastrum*; **c** – *Crucibulum laeve*; **d** – *Phallus impudicus*; **e** – *Rhizopogon*; **f+g** – *Scleroderma verrucosum*.

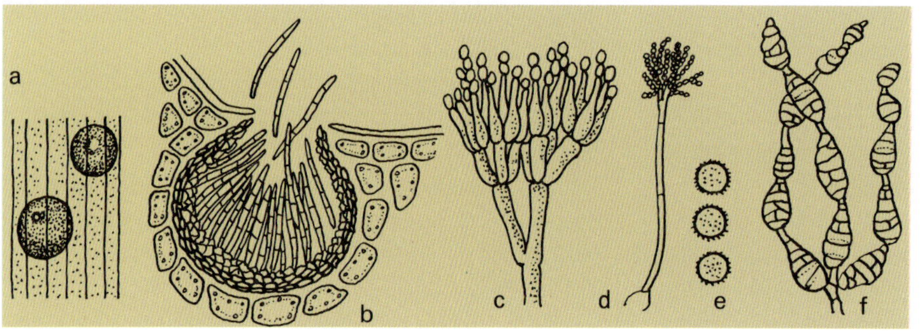

29) Examples of some microscopic fungi of the group Deuteromycetes: **a** – pycnidia of *Phoma* sp.; **b** – section through the pycnidium of *Septoria* sp. with conidia; **c** – conidiophore of *Penicillium* sp. with conidia; **d** – conidiophore of *Aspergillus niger* with conidia; **e** – conidia of *Aspergillus* sp.; **f** – conidiophore of *Alternaria tenuis* with conidial chains.

structures. The basidia are either regularly distributed in the gleba, or form nidi, or fill in the cavities. Spores are globular, ornamented, and coloured. The best-known genera of this family are *Scleroderma* and *Pisolithus.*

Closely related to the Sclerodermataceae are Astreaceae, even though, in appearance, they markedly resemble members of the genus *Geastrum* to which they are not linked.

Nidulariaceae have globular or cup-like, sessile fruit bodies with a chambered gleba disintegrating into single peridioles. These either remain attached to the inner wall of the peridium, or are discharged. The basidia form the hymenium covering the walls of the peridioles, or assemble into nest-like structures situated within the gleba. Spores are ellipsoid, smooth, and colourless. The Nidulariaceae thrive on decaying plant remains or on old dung. On the whole, they are small fungi interesting both in appearance and in biology.

Deuteromycetes
(*Fungi imperfecti*)

This vast group includes all fungi characterized by purely asexual reproduction (without any foregoing nuclear association either by the decomposition of hyphae, or by the formation of special spores, known as conidia). They are known only in this form (nowadays termed anamorph), or demonstrably belong to other fungus groups – mostly to Ascomycetes – as their particular developmental stage. They mostly involve minute organisms which, for the most part, can be distinguished only under the lens, and only a first-rate microscope makes possible their identification and study. They occur practically everywhere, as saprophytes or parasites. Approximately 20,000 species have been described hitherto. They are divided into two main groups – Coelomycetes and Hyphomycetes. In the Coelomycetes, conidia are borne on conidiophores or arise directly from conidiogenous cells growing out of the sterile hyphal tissue which forms closed or open fruit bodies. Several hundred genera including many thousand species belong to this group.

In the Hyphomycetes, conidia arise either directly from the mycelium or, most frequently, they originate on conidiophores from specific, so-called conidiogenous cells. Conidiophores grow freely on the substrate as fibrillose, hirsute or matted-tomentose layers. These so-called pseudomoulds are of considerable importance in phytopathology, technical mycology, veterinary science and medicine as organisms causing various diseases in plants, animals and man. The colouring of conidiophores substantiates their division into colourless ones (Moniliales or Moniliaceae) and dark-coloured ones (Dematiales or Dematiaceae). Of the most important genera at least the following should be referred to: *Aspergillus, Penicillium, Botrytis, Monilia, Cladosporium* and *Fusarium.* Also the Hyphomycetes include a great number of genera and species.

The designation Blastomycetes covers a group of microscopic fungi which are explicitly gemmiparous. This is also why they are termed 'asporogenous (anascosporogenous) yeasts'. The genera included here are *Candida* and *Cryptococcus;* some of them cause skin and other diseases in Man.

Glossary of Basic Mycological Terms

acyanophilous – not staining blue when touched with cotton blue.

aethalium – a pulvinate or semiglobular fruit body of some slime moulds arising from the association of a large number of sporangia.

allantoid spores – curved cylindrical spores, sometimes also referred to as sausage-shaped.

amyloid – spore walls or hyphae staining blue in solutions containing iodine. In mycology, Melzer's reagent is used for testing amyloidity; the colouration appears in various shades of blue (from bluish grey over deep blue or bluish green to black).

anamorph – a stage of the fungal thallus which is either sterile (e.g. sclerotium, rhizomorph), or producing asexual spores (conidia, chlamydospores). Most of the conidial stages in fungi are anamorphs.

annulus – ring; in general it is a remnant of the veil (*velum partiale*) on the fruit-body stipe, usually in the form of a membranous collar.

anthracophilous – inhabiting burned-over soil or growing directly on burned wood.

apical – at the apex.

apiculus – a minute projection at the basal end of the spore by which the spore is attached to the sterigma.

apothecium – the fruit body of the Discomycetes with an open thecium.

ascocarp – the pseudoperithecium of some Pyrenomycetes.

ascospore – a spore of the Ascomycetes borne in an ascus.

ascus – a saclike, cylindrical or claviform structure in the Ascomycetes where, after nuclear association and a subsequent reduction division, spores (ascospores) develop.

asexual reproduction – vegetative reproduction; in general, this implies reproduction through elements arisen without any foregoing fusion of the plasmatic and nuclear contents of two sexually different cells.

assimilative pigment – photosynthetic pigment (particularly chlorophyll in green plants).

autotropic nutrition – the capacity of the plants to transform absorbed inorganic substances into organic ones.

basidiole – a sterile basidium (without sterigmata) or other sterile hymenial cells resembling the basidia in both shape and size.

basidiospore – a spore of the Basidiomycetes separated from the basidium by a sterigma (pedicel).

basidium – a cell mostly clavate or cylindrical in shape, bearing pedicellate (sterigmate) spores (basidiospores) developing subsequent to nuclear association and the reduction division following thereon. It is characteristic of the Basidiomycetes.

bilateral gill trama – see trama.

binding hyphae – mostly thick-walled, richly branched fruticose hyphae with a short basic pedicel, aseptate, lacking clamp connections.

bitunicate ascus – a double-walled ascus.

capillitium – sterile fibres mixed with the spores within the fruit bodies of some Gasteromycetes or Myxomycetes.

carminophilous basidia – see siderophilous basidia.

caulocystidium – a cystidium developed on the stipe cuticle.

cheilocystidium – a cystidium occurring on the edge of a gill.

chemical reagents – are used in identifying fungi as well as in preparing microscopic mounts. The most common ones are a 3–10 per cent aqueous solution of ammonia, a 2–5 per cent solution of potassium hydroxide (KOH), lactophenol, lactic acid, Melzer's reagent, cotton blue, acetocarmine. Colour reactions of the context in fresh fruit bodies are tested e.g. by an aqueous green-vitriol solution, phenol, sulphovanillin, benzidine, etc.

chlamydospore – a thick-walled vegetative spore developed from a hyphal cell.

chrysocystidium – a claviform cystidium in gill-bearing fungi filled with an amorphous, often yellow-coloured matter.

clamp connection – a protuberance arching over the hyphal septum in numerous Basidiomycetes.

cleistothecium – a closed globular fruit body of the Ascomycetes opening by rupture.

collarium – a collar-like arrangement of gills about the apex of the stipe.

columella – a sterile part of the sporangium or fruit body, usually leading from the apex of the stipe or from the base into the spore-bearing part (in slime fungi, moulds and some Gasteromycetes).

conidiogenous cell – a cell bearing conidia.

conidiophore – a specialized independent hypha, either simple or branched, bearing conidiogenous cells and conidia.

conidium – an asexually (vegetatively) produced spore on a hypha or conidiophore.

coprophilous – inhabiting excrements or dung.

copulation – the fusion of two sexual cells, or of the contents of sexually different cells.

cortina (cobweb) – a membranous veil covering the hymenium only, eventually a part of the epicutis of the cap.

cotton blue (CB) – dissolved in lactic acid, it is used to colour hyphae, spore walls, and particularly the spore ornamentation, mostly in the Discomycetes.

cyanophilous – readily turning blue to violet in a cotton-blue solution; the opposite is acyanophilous.

cystidiole – a sterile cell in the hymenium situated between the basidia, arising from the same hymenial level as the basidium but differing from it in shape.

cystidium – a sterile cell in the hymenium of the Basidiomycetes; it is larger, different in shape from the basidium, and usually more deeply embedded in the hymenium.

dendrophysis – much branched, often dendriform cell found in the hymenium or in the cap cuticle.

dermatocystidium – a cystidium growing from the cuticle of the fruit body; the pileocystidium develops on the pileus cuticle, the caulocystidium on the stipe cuticle.

detritus – a layer of decomposed remains of organic matter (mostly of plant origin) lying on the surface of the ground.

dextrinoid – staining yellowish to reddish brown or vinaceous (purplish) brown in Melzer's reagent; it means the same as pseudoamyloid.

diploid – having a twofold number of nuclear chromosomes, as e.g. in the zygote.

eccentric stipe – attached to the pileus extracentrally but not laterally.

epicutis – the outermost layer of the multistratal cuticle covering the pileus of gill fungi; it differs from the other layers in structure.

epigeous – developing above the surface of the ground.

excipulum – the external tissue forming the apothecium.

fimicolous– growing on dung or excrements.

fructification – the stage or period when the fungus produces fruit bodies.

fruit body – a part of the thallus differentiated in shape, consisting of hyphae and reproductive spore-producing cells.

gametangium – an organ producing gametes, i.e. sexual-reproduction cells.

generative hyphae – basic ramified, thin-walled, septate (partitioned) hyphae with or without clamp connections, filled with plasma (see hyphal systems).

germ pore – a usually flattened spot in the thinned part of the spore wall through which the spore germinates.

gill folds – the hymenophore assumes the form of thick and narrow ribs covered with a continuous hymenial layer.

gleba – the fruit-body tissue of the Gasteromycetes producing basidia.

gloeocystidium – a thin-walled cystidium generally having a refractive or granular (often oily) content. It is elongate, claviform or cylindrical, usually deeply anchored in the hymenium, sometimes also in the trama or cap cuticle.

haploid – having half the number of chromosomes in the nuclei of germ cells (gametes).

heterotrophic organisms – having no assimilative pigments, they derive organic substances directly from the living or dead tissues of autotrophic organisms (green plants) or animals.

hilar depression – a slightly depressed spot on the ventral spore wall right above the apiculus.

host – a plant or animal with which either the entire life cycle of a parasite or saprophyte, or at least a part of it is connected.

hydnoid – having a spinulose hymenophore.

hygrophanous – the cap in gill fungi is darker-coloured when damp than after drying out. With the moisture disappearing it fades in colour and is often divided into two contrasting colour zones (the apical and the marginal), or is radially striped with darker and lighter colour shades.

hymeniderm – the structure of the hymenidermal cuticle of the cap is similar to that of the hymenium (all cells are arranged on the same level).

hymeniform – a layer of globular, pyriform, shortly cylindrical or claviform cells arranged in a palisade (e.g. the cap cuticle in some gill fungi).

hymenium – a layer of basidia arranged palisade-like.

hymenophore – part of the fruit body bearing the hymenium.

hypha – filament; the basic structural unit of the fungus body, usually divided by septae into longer and shorter cells; hyphae constitute the mycelium and the major part of the fruit body.

hyphal systems – the fruit body can be composed of one, two or three types of hyphae: the monomitic system consists exclusively of basic (generative) ramose hyphae with or without clamp connections; the dimitic system is made up of generative and skeletal, or generative and binding hyphae; the trimitic system has generative, skeletal and binding hyphae.

hypogeous – growing underground.

hypothallus – also subiculum; a mass of intertwined surface hyphae forming a felted or cobweb-like layer from which fruit bodies arise.

hypothecium – a layer of tissue immediately beneath the thecium of the Discomycetes.

hysterothecium – the usually elongate fruit body of Ascomycetes or lichens with a narrow longitudinal slit in the middle.

incrustation – the surface of hyphal walls is coated with a hard crust, granules or small crystals of frequently refractive colourless matter (incrusted hyphae).

irpicoid – the hymenophore assumes the shape of irregular, flattened (foliated) teeth or short lamellae.

irregular – see (gill) trama.

jellification – coagulation into jelly; the walls of jellified hyphae are coated with a layer of usually colourless jelly.

lactifers (laticifers) – long, nonseptate hyphae bearing thick, granular plasma or latex (milky-coloured juice).

lamellae – gill-like structures of the hymenophore radially spreading out from the stipe to the cap margin.

lamellules – short gills beginning in the cap margin but not reaching the stipe.

lamprocystidium – a thick-walled cystidium in gill fungi.

lateral stipe – attached to one side of the cap.

lignicolous – growing on wood.

macromycetes – an auxiliary term applied to large fungi whose fruit bodies are visible with the naked eye (they usually exceed 0.5 cm in size).

margo – marginal edge of the apothecium.

meiosis – one of the two successive nuclear divisions of a diploid nucleus is reductional, the result being four daughter nuclei having a haploid (n) number of chromosomes.

Melzer's reagent – the solution of chloral hydrate in water with an admixture of potassium iodide (KI) and iodine (I) used for testing amyloidity (KI, 1.5 g; I, 0.5 g; distilled water, 20 cc; chloral hydrate, 22 g). It was discovered and used for the first time by the Czech mycologist V. Melzer and is one of the most generally applied and most important reagents in taxonomic study and in identifying fungi.

metachromatic – a layer of cells or hyphae changes colour through the application of a given colouring agent, yet the newly acquired colour differs from that originally borne by the colouring agent – e.g. cresylic blue discolours to red.

metuloid – a thick-walled cystidium with a strongly incrusted surface arising in the deep layers of the hymenophore tissue.

micromycetes – an artificial grouping of fungi of predominantly microscopic dimensions whose fruit bodies usually do not surpass the limit of discernibility with the unaided eye. This group includes all imperfect fungi, rusts, smuts, moulds, and the greater part of Ascomycetes.

micron – 1 µm = one thousandth of a millimetre. In mycology, all microelements subjected to microscopic study are indicated in microns.

monomitic – see hyphal systems.

mycelium – the vegetative part of the fungal thallus obtaining nutritional substances from the substrate.

mycology – the science of fungi.

mycorrhiza – a symbiotic association of fungus hyphae with the roots of green plants.

nonamyloid – failing to turn blue in Melzer's reagent.

ocrea – partly membranous remnants of the universal veil (*velum generale*), attached to the base of the stipe like a sheath, having a distinct upper margin. They are typical of the *Cortinarius* species belonging to the subgenus *Telamonia.*

oidium – a thin-walled cell arising from the disintegration of a vegetative hypha.

oogonium – a female sexual organ.

oosphere – an egg cell.

oospore – a thick-walled spore formed as the result of fertilization of the oosphere.

ornamentation of spores – the spore-wall surface is sculptured with various excrescences (warts, spinules, ridges, reticulation).

ostiole (ostiolum) – a part of the perithecium narrowing down into a neck-shaped extension provided with a canal lined with hyphae and opening by a pore.

palisade tissue – more or less parallel claviform or cylindrical elements usually situated on the pileus surface or composing the hymenium.

paraphyses – sterile filaments filling up the space between asci (see ascus).

parasite – an organism living or growing upon other living organisms from which it derives nourishment and, in doing so, damages or destroys them.

peridium – the cover enveloping the fruit body in Gasteromycetes; outer peridium = exoperidium, inner peridium = endoperidium.

perithecium – a closed, usually more or less rounded fruit body characteristic of the Pyrenomycetes, provided with a wall which, as a rule, opens at the apex by an ostiole.

phialide – a specific cell on the conidiophore, giving rise to conidia.

pileocystidia – cystidia situated on the pileus surface.

plage – suprahilar disc; a more or less circumscribed, smooth spot on the spore wall immediately above the apiculus.

plasmodiocarp – the extending, sessile and ramose fruit body of slime moulds.

plasmodium – a body of plurinucleated, naked protoplasm in Myxomycetes exhibiting slow motion and ultimately changing into fruit bodies.

pleurocystidium – a cystidium occurring on the face of gills.

pore – an opening at the apex of the ascus, or an opening in the ostiole of the perithecium.

poroid – a hymenophore consisting of tubes.

pseudoamyloid – see dextrinoid.

pseudoparaphyses – paraphysoid filaments; sterile threads in some Pyrenomycetes separating the single asci contained in the pseudothecium.

pseudoparenchyma – fungous tissue composed of globular or subglobular cells.

pseudothecium – the perithecium-like fruit body of some Pyrenomycetes; developmentally, however, it is a stroma containing bitunicate asci and pseudoparaphyses – i.e. remnants of the inner tissue.

pycnidium – a closed, mostly ball-shaped fruit body producing nothing but conidia.

radial – spreading out radially from the centre to the margin (for example, fibres on the pileus surface).

receptaculum – an alternative designation for the apothecium or for its greater part; also the bearer in Phallales.

resupinate – reclining over the surface and mostly attached to the substrate (fruit bodies of numerous Aphyllophorales).

rhizoid – a rootlike or strandlike mycelium at the base of the fruit body.

rhizomorph – mycelial strands with a thickened (sclerotized) outer layer.

ring – see annulus.

saprophyte – living on dead organisms, their remains, and on organic matter or mineral soils.

sclerotium – a tuberiform, lenticular or irregular structure composed of firmly intertwined hyphae; it is a resting stage from which, under certain conditions, fruit bodies or hyphae may develop.

sections through the gills – the tangential section is made across the gills in the marginal part of the cap;
– the longitudinal (radial) section is cut through the centre of the cap so that it mostly passes between the gills or longitudinally bisects them;
– the cross (transverse) section is cut horizontally to the surface of the ground (in fruit bodies growing on the ground).

septum – partition; a transverse or longitudinal wall in fungus hyphae and spores.

seta – a thick-walled, tough, usually dark-coloured cystidium tapering upward, or a structure similar to it.

sexual reproduction – fusion of the plasmatic and nuclear content of two sexually differentiated cells, and the subsequent development of spores.

spherocystidium – a globular cell in the tissue of Basidiomycetes (e.g. in the genus *Russula*).

siderophilous basidia – their plasma contains a large quantity of granules turning dark in ferric acetocarmine; the same as carminophilous basidia.

skeletal hyphae – thick-walled, unbranched, long, nonseptate hyphae; see also hyphal systems.

sporangiophore – a hyphal branch bearing the sporangium.

sporangium – an asexually produced cell bearing one or more spores (e.g. mycetozoan fruit bodies).

spore – the reproductive monocellular or multicellular body functionally corresponding to the seed in higher plants but lacking an embryo.

sterigma – the minute pedicel on the surface of the basidium upon which a spore is borne.

stroma – a rigid structure composed of hyphae wherein fruit bodies or cavities containing asci or conidiophores are embedded (mostly in Pyrenomycetes).

subhymenium – a layer of tissue under the hymenium

(its structure is sometimes different from that of the trama).

subiculum – see hypothallus.

substratum – the nutritive base (e.g. earth, soil, plant remains, wood, excrements).

suprahilar disc – see plage.

terrestrial – growing on the ground.

thecium – the uppermost part of the Discomycetes fruit body with the hymenium; the latter consists of asci and paraphyses arranged in a palisade.

thallus – a simple plant- or fungus body undifferentiated in roots, stalks or leaves (gills).

trama – the tissue supporting the hymenium in Basidiomycetes; in gill fungi, the following four types of gills are distinguished: regular trama (the hyphae are parallel to each other); irregular trama (some hyphae diverging in various directions are interwoven with the parallel hyphae); bilateral trama (the hyphae are parallel only in the mediostratum of the gills, while in the margins they diverge towards the hymenium in a curve); inverse trama (similar to the bilateral trama but the hyphae are diverging backwards).

trichoderm – the cuticle consisting of densely clustered and erect hairs.

trimitic – see hyphal systems.

tubes (tubules) – vertically arranged tubular structures composing the hymenophore.

vegetative reproduction – see asexual reproduction.

velum (veil) – the cover enveloping the whole fruit body or a part of it; *velum universale* (*generale*), universal veil, enfolds the entire fruit body; *velum partiale,* partial veil, connects the cap margin to the apex of the stipe, covering the hymenophore when young.

volva (*cup, sheath*) – a usually membranous, cup-shaped structure around the base of the stipe (a remnant of the universal veil).

zygospore – a resting spore resulting from the conjugation of the contents of two gametangia or two gametes.

zygote – a cell in which two nuclei of the opposite sex have fused together. It is diploid, having a double number of chromosomes.

COLOUR PLATES

Key to symbols used:

edible

inedible

poisonous

deadly poisonous

Orange Peel Fungus

Aleuria aurantia (Pers. ex Hook.) Fuckel

The cup fungi (Discomycetes) are the second largest group of the Ascomycetes, immediately following the flask fungi (Pyrenomycetes). However, most are small, inconspicuously coloured, and occur in such places that they easily escape the notice of the naked eye. The Orange Peel Fungus is one of the larger-sized species, attracting attention by its colouring. It grows often gregariously on exposed, damp, mostly sandy and clayey ground of woodland tracks and ditches, and does not appear before the end of summer or the beginning of autumn. When viewed from a distance its apothecia, which vary greatly in size, strongly resemble scattered pieces of orange peel. They are saucer-shaped, regular at first, later often irregularly wavy. The beautiful colour of the fruit bodies is due to an orange pigment contained within the tissue, especially within the threadlike paraphyses, in the form of numerous granules and droplets. In Melzer's reagent the paraphyses rapidly change to blue-green but the ascus walls remain colourless. This is the substantial difference between this species and members of the genus *Peziza* where the ascus walls, being amyloid, turn blue in Melzer's reagent. The spore surface in the Orange Peel Fungus is ornamented with a reticulation made up of wide, hexagonal meshes.

The regular consumption of the Orange Peel Fungus is inadvisable, even though it is innocuous and sometimes used for decorating vegetable-salad dishes.

The Scarlet Elf Cup (*Sarcoscypha coccinea*) is similar to the Orange Peel Fungus in appearance, except for its scarlet disc. It grows on rotten branches and trunks of deciduous trees towards the end of winter and early spring.

Spores of *Aleuria aurantia*: 16–24 × 8–10 μm, ellipsoid, colourless, reticulate.

Sarcoscypha coccinea

Aleuria aurantia

Detail of spore ornamentation

Otidea onotica

(Batsch ex S. F. Gray) Fuckel

Like the vast majority of other species belonging to this genus, *Otidea onotica* produces long fruit bodies that grow perpendicularly to the substrate. On one side they split lengthwise down to the base and have incurved margins, their attenuated basal part often tapers downwards into a short stipe. Their colour is ochre, yellow or brown. The flesh is relatively thin and dry. They resemble hares' or rabbits' ears. The distinction between the individual species of the genus *Otidea,* several dozens of which are known, is far from easy because of their remarkable similarity.

Notwithstanding, *O. onotica* is one of the few easily distinguished species, differing from all the others in both size and colouring. On the outside it is cream-yellow to orange; the disc bears a pleasant pinkish hue. The fruit bodies are up to 13 cm high and 1–3 cm wide, which makes *O. onotica* one of the largest species in the family. It appears most frequently in small clusters but also solitarily in humus or in a deep layer of decaying foliage covering the floor of deciduous forests – usually under hazels, hornbeams and oaks, and less often in coniferous forests.

A characteristic of all the species of *Otidea* are paraphyses hooked at the apex and usually provided with a short excrescence, as well as broadly ellipsoid, smooth spores filled with two large droplets. The ascus membrane is nonamyloid.

Owing to their relatively rare occurrence and to the dry, thin flesh, the Otideaceae are of little significance for the practical mushroom gatherer.

2 paraphyses

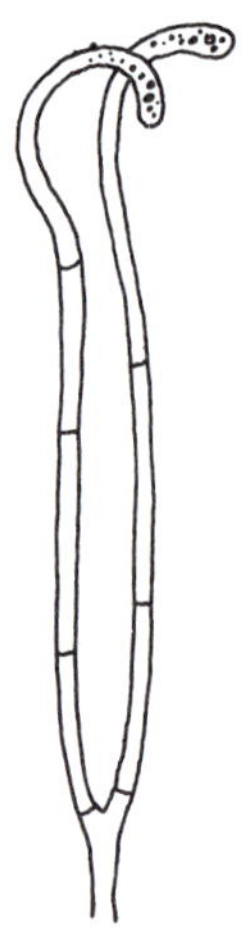

Ascus containing eight spores

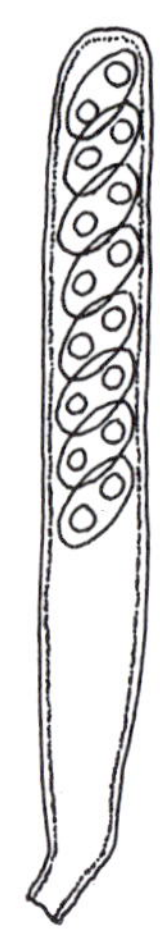

Spore: 15–24 × 8–10 μm, ellipsoid, smooth, colourless

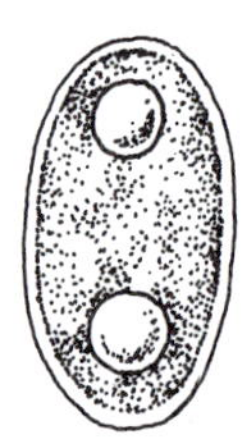

Sarcosphaera crassa
(Santi ex Steudel) Pouz.

Sarcosphaera crassa has a rather unique way of life. The fruit bodies develop under the surface of the ground as whitish, hollow globules sunken in the upper soil layers, thus resembling some hypogeous fungi such as truffles. The fruit bodies, however, soon split open at the apex to form several large, triangular rays, thus forming an ornamental star-shaped structure. At this time the fruit bodies are already exposed to view on the surface of the substrate, wherein only their deeply concave bottom part remains embedded. They attract attention not only by their large size (being 8–25 cm wide), but particularly by their beautiful amethyst-coloured disc, which grows paler with age. Whole groups of these goblet-shaped apothecia can be found growing in a single habitat.

S. crassa has a particular liking for heavy clay soils; its fruit bodies are most often encountered in forests growing on a calcareous substrate. Though it prefers firs, it is also found under pines and spruces. It is poisonous; in the past, cases of poisoning were reported after the ingestion of fresh fruit bodies used for decorating, e.g. in vegetable-salad dishes.

In microscopic features, the genus *Sarcosphaera* is related to the genus *Peziza;* both have markedly amyloid ascus walls (i.e. turning blue with Melzer's reagent). In mycological literature *S. crassa* is often described under wrong names (*S. dargelasii, Pustularia coronaria* and *P. macrocalyx*).

Spore: 11–14 × 5–7 μm,
ellipsoid, smooth, colourless

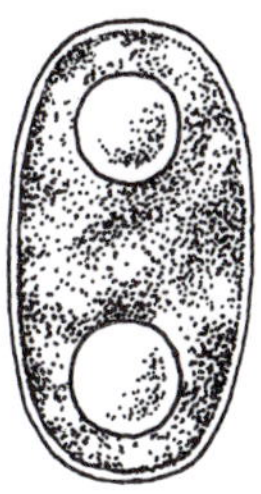

The apical part of the paraphysis

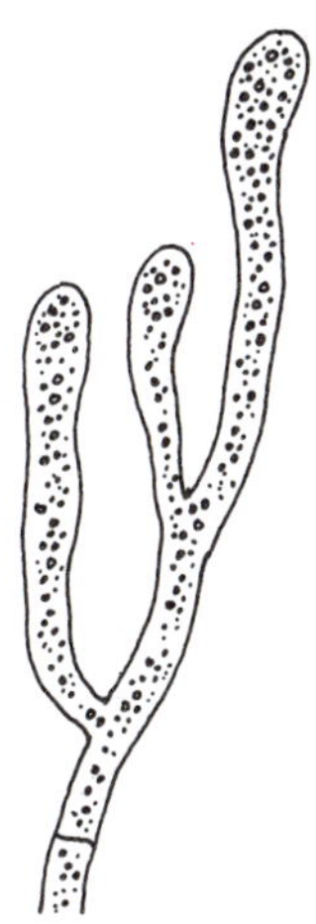

Discina perlata (Fr.) Fr.

This is one of the characteristic species of Discomycetes whose fruit bodies appear soon after the snows melt and the forest soil has warmed up. Its apothecia are usually found on the cut surface or on the roots of spruce stumps overgrown with moss, often in glades and woodland clearings. They often grow gregariously and attract attention both by their patelliform shape and by their chestnut-brown disc with its wavy margin. A short, deeply furrowed white stipe grows on the underside of young fruit bodies, which makes them resemble the former genus *Acetabula* (today united with the genus *Helvella*). They differ from this by having completely different spores. The spores of *Discina perlata* are ornamented with a fine reticulum similar to that on the spores of *Gyromitra gigas*. Since the spores of both species are marked with small warts around each pole, they will be of no help in distinguishing these two fungi. *D. perlata* and *G. gigas* grow in similar habitats, in the same season of the year. Both species are edible and taste excellent.

Rhizina undulata is very similar to *D. perlata* in shape and colour. It can easily be distinguished by its underside from which numerous perpendicular, tough, rootlike structures develop, attaching *R. undulata* to the substrate. It often appears in large quantities in summer and autumn on burned-over forest areas – especially on charred roots of pine-tree stumps, because its mycelium grows in pine wood. It is inedible.

Spore of *Discina perlata*:
35–40 × 12–15 µm,
scaphoid, colourless

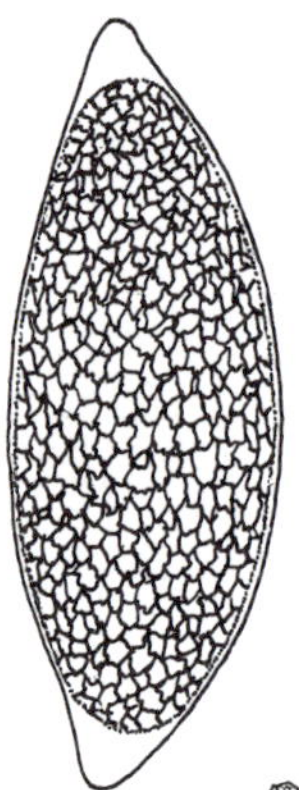

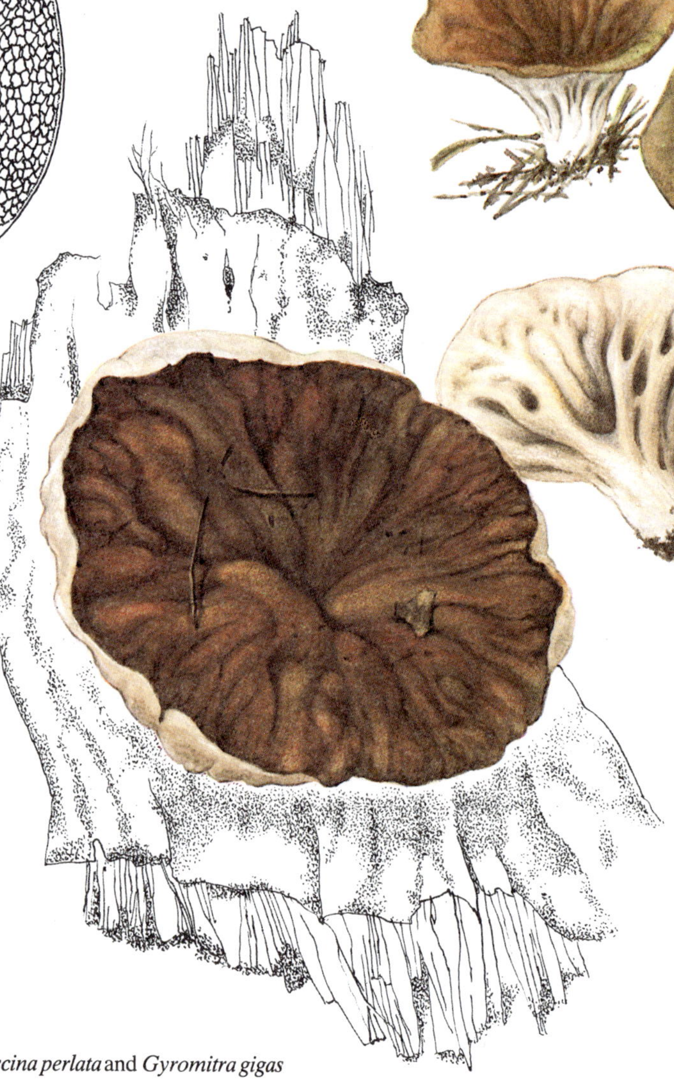

Discina perlata and *Gyromitra gigas*

Rhizina undulata viewed from above and from the side

Rhizina undulata

Lorchel, Turban Fungus

Gyromitra esculenta (Pers. ex Pers.) Fr.

The Lorchel is a typical representative of the vernal mycoflora of coniferous, particularly pine, forests. Here its fruit bodies appear in May and at the beginning of June, usually on bare ground. It prefers open spaces, e.g. woodland clearings, where it can be found near to stumps; sometimes it also thrives directly on these or on their roots. In some areas it is quite common – for example in pine woods growing on sandy substrates.

It is often collected as an edible mushroom, but its edibility or inedibility remain a point of dispute. In most recent specialized literature, the Lorchel is not recommended for eating, or is forthrightly classed among the poisonous fungi. Poisoning by the Lorchel is somewhat puzzling. Although young fruit bodies are edible without any ill-effects, cases of poisoning have been reported – even if rarely – after the ingestion of older fruit bodies. This is why in some countries its sale has been forbidden. The substance causing this poisoning as well as its mechanism have so far eluded explanation.

Gyromitra gigas (*Discina gigas*) is similar to the Lorchel but is more robustly built. Its pale ochre cap bears large, loose lobes, while the cap of *G. esculenta* has smaller and more rounded lobes, and is substantially different microscopically. *G. gigas* is less common than the Lorchel; it grows in the same season of the year mainly on old stumps and roots, or on wood rotting in the soil. It is edible and tasty.

Spore of *Gyromitra esculenta*:
18–22 × 9–12 µm, ellipsoid, colourless, smooth

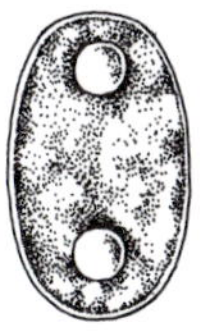

Fruit body of *Gyromitra gigas*

Gyromitra gigas

Gyromitra esculenta

Common White Helvella, False Morel

Helvella crispa (Scop.) ex Fr.

Fungi of the family Helvellaceae belong to the highly developed Discomycetes. Their fruit body is differentiated into a sterile part (in the form of a stem or stipe) and a fertile part, bearing the sporiferous layer made up of asci and paraphyses. The fertile part is saucer-shaped or resembles an irregularly formed cap or saddle. All Helvellaceae have broadly ellipsoid, usually smooth spores with a remarkably large oil droplet in the middle and often several minute droplets around. The saddle fungi grow in summer and autumn in forests, on bare and relatively damp ground, in fallen foliage and in humus.

One of the most abundant species is *Helvella crispa,* which is commonly encountered in both deciduous and coniferous forests. It is easily recognized by its almost white or creamy yellowish fruit body, irregularly lobate cap and deeply grooved stipe. The outer cap surface is finely felted, in contrast to the very similar *H. lacunosa* whose cap has an entirely smooth outer surface. *H. lacunosa* is usually coloured grey, or greyish brown to blackish; there also exist almost white forms, but these are very rare. This species also grows on the ground in shady and rather damp parts of both coniferous and deciduous forests, and under shrub thickets. Both species are edible.

Spore of *Helvella crispa*:
15–18 × 10–12 μm,
ellipsoid, colourless,
with minute droplets on the poles

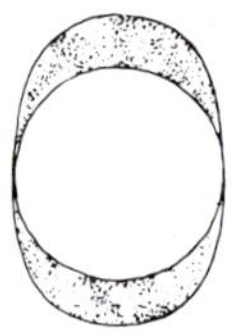

Helvella lacunosa

Helvella crispa

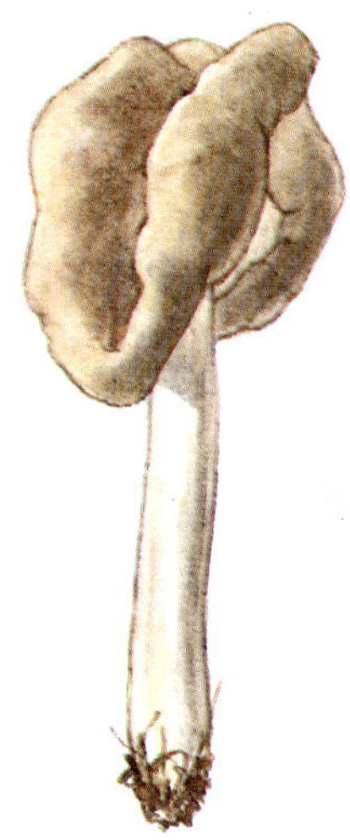

Helvella elastica

Common Morel

Morchella esculenta Pers. ex St. Amans

Morels are the most advanced Discomycetes and, at the same time, the best-known cup fungi to be collected for their excellent taste. Morels are extremely variable in the shape, size and colouring of fruit bodies, and mycologists have not yet arrived at a uniform evaluation of all these variations. The remarkable variability of individual characteristics can be observed even within a single population, when this is represented by large numbers of fruit bodies.

The cap of the Common Morel is attached to the stipe by its lower margin and is marked with longitudinal ridges of irregular shape. The ridges are usually sinuous and are separated by deep intermediate pits (lacunae). These lacunae are rounded to rounded-polygonal in shape, freely opening at the cap margin. In its typical form the Common Morel has an ovoid-ellipsoid to globular, sometimes obtusely conical or even cylindrical cap, usually 4–8 cm high and 4 cm wide, ochre-yellow, brownish or greyish. It grows in April and May in sunny places in forests, but also in lawns, parks, gardens, etc.

Morchella conica is similar to *M. esculenta* in size. Its cap is conical, darker-coloured, with parallel main ridges and intervening tetragonal pits closed at the lower margin of the cap. It is also edible. The fruit bodies of all Morels are hollow and fragile.

Spore of *Morchella esculenta*: 18–22 × 10–14 μm, ellipsoid, colourless, smooth

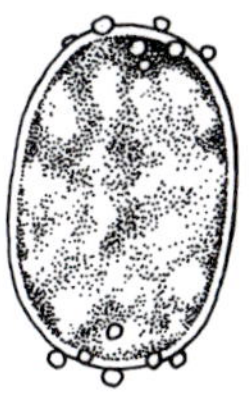

Morchella conica

Morchella esculenta

Morchella elata Fr.

It is one of the largest species of the genus, the fruit bodies being 10–25 cm high and as much as 8 cm wide. It differs from the Common Morel not only in size but also in its elongate-cylindrical, but sometimes only slightly pointed, globular cap whose colour is a shade of brown or more rarely pink to reddish purple. The main ribs of the cap are rather thin and more or less parallel, connected by thin, narrow, transverse and oblique ridges; elongate, tetragonal pits are thus formed between the ribs which are closed at the cap margin. The longitudinally pitted or grooved stipe is usually strongly inflated into a bulbous base as much as 8 cm thick.

Morchella elata grows in April and May, and on higher ground also in June. It is sporadically scattered on the ground of deciduous and coniferous forests, in gardens, in old parks, and very often on rubbish heaps in urban yards. It is edible.

Another large species, the Prague Morel (*M. pragensis*), occurs in places greatly affected by human activity, e.g. in factory yards, building sites, dumps, railway side-tracks, and often in the very centre of large industrial cities. The Prague Morel has a bilaterally compressed cap resembling a ping-pong bat, considerably elongated, and yellow to olive-brown. The size of its fruit bodies varies within the range of 6–28 cm in height and 4–8 cm in width. It is also edible.

Spore: 20–25 × 13–16 μm,
ellipsoid, colourless,
with minute droplets on the poles

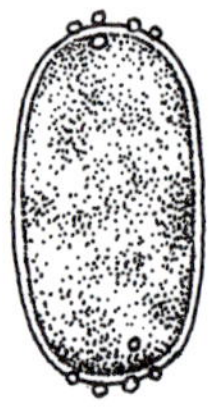

Asci with eight spores

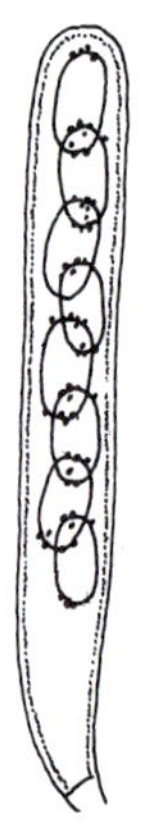

Paraphysis

Early Morel

Verpa bohemica (Krombh.) Schroet.

The Early Morel is another important spring fungus, easily identified by its cylindrical, hollow, slender stipe with a campanulate cap seated at its apex. The cap is attached to it by quite a small area at the very top, otherwise it spreads away from the stipe surface: this is clearly seen on the longitudinal section. The cap surface is uneven and undulate with rounded, longitudinal, ochre or yellow-brown, thick folds. The fruit body reaches up to 15 cm in length; often, however, quite small specimens with a short stipe can be found. The spores which, due to their huge dimensions, belong to the largest among fungi, develop in the asci in twos only.

The Early Morel was described by the Czech mycologist V. J. Krombholz in the vinicity of Prague 150 years ago. It grows from March to the beginning of May on humus-rich soil among fallen leaves in deciduous forests. Although it prefers warm, mainly limestone substrates, it also occurs on relatively acid soils. Often it accompanies either aspens or rowans. It is an edible mushroom with a very good flavour which might perhaps be confused only with *Morchella hybrida*; the latter is also edible.

The cap of *M. hybrida* is attached to the stipe down the entire upper half of its length, while its lower half is free. Also the cap surface is different in shape: it is formed by narrow, thin, longitudinal and transversely interconnected ridges. Its spores are considerably smaller than in the Early Morel, being only 22–25 × 12–15 μm in size. Its favourite habitat are moist forests.

Spores of *Verpa bohemica*:
55–80 × 15–22 μm,
ellipsoid-oblong, yellowish, smooth

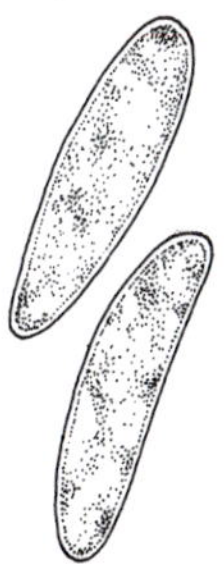

Paraphyses and ascus containing two spores

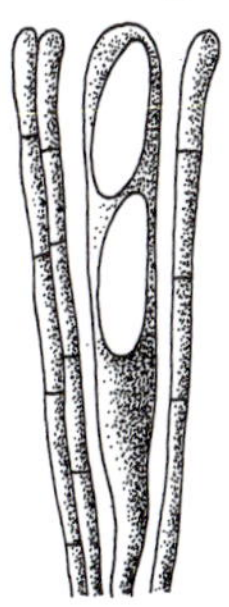

Morchella hybrida

Section through the fruit body

Verpa bohemica

Distribution of *Verpa bohemica* in Europe

Choiromyces venosus

(Fr.) Th. Fries

Many mushroom pickers confuse *Choiromyces venosus* with truffles. Its fruit bodies have an irregular tuber-like shape; they are 5–15 cm in size, very hard and relatively heavy. Their surface is off-white to greyish brown at first, gradually becoming yellow to brown. A cross-section reveals a tough inner matter (the 'gleba') shot through with a multitude of extremely thin, labyrinthine channels discernible as fine veins of unequal width and varying length. The gleba is white, with brown veins at the time when the spores are ripening. The asci arranged in the veins are clavate, bearing 2, 4 or 8 spores.

From the ecological point of view, *C. venosus* belongs to hypogeous fungi, as its fruit bodies start developing under the surface of the ground. It is only later that they partly jut out of it. *C. venosus* grows in summer and autumn in all types of woods, and in both sandy and heavier, clayey soils. It is widespread throughout the temperate zone of the northern hemisphere, even in regions where true truffles (genus *Tuber*) do not occur. It is an edible species but it is not advisable to keep ripe fruit bodies of *C. venosus* in a closed room owing to their penetrating smell which soon saturates the whole space and becomes unbearable. The fungus is used only in small doses as spice to season foods.

Spore: 16–22 μm (including spines), globose, shortly and obtusely echinulate, pale yellow

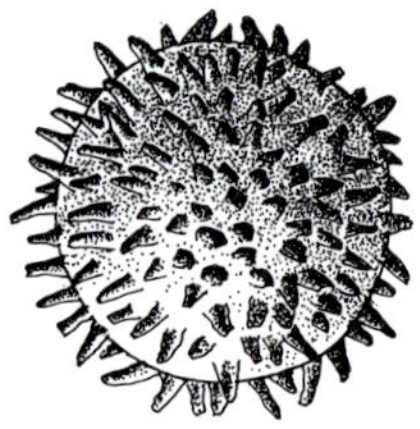

Ascus with eight spores

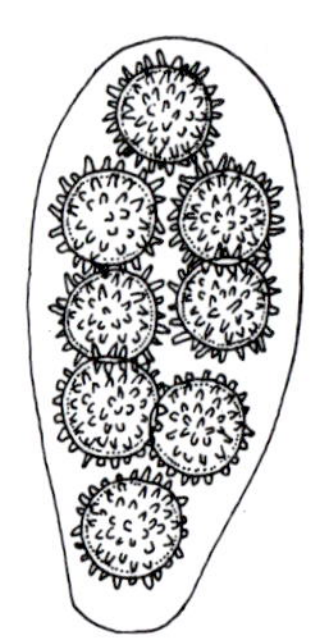

Summer Truffle, Common (English) Truffle
Tuber aestivum Vitt.

True truffles are highly prized aromatic fungi, used since antiquity for culinary purposes – mainly as filling in meat courses and as spice. Since time immemorial they have belonged to the most widely known and most esteemed fungi. They are most common in countries bordering the Mediterranean, and especially in southern France and Italy, yet the Summer Truffle also grows in some warm regions of central Europe, as one of the few large truffle species found in those parts. Being symbiotically associated with the oak, it is ordinarily confined to oak forests. It is usually accompanied by a typically thermophilous flora profusely developing mostly on limestone substrates.

Tuberous fruit bodies, varying in size from 1 cm up to 10 cm, are covered with a continuous coating of almost black conical warts. Their development takes place out of sight, relatively deep underground. Their gleba is whitish or yellowish at first, but ultimately brownish and interwoven with whitish veins; it is strongly aromatic at maturity. One to six spores develop in each globular ascus; their surface is ornamented with a wide-meshed, angular, high reticulum. The fruit bodies grow from late summer until winter. Although the Summer Truffle is not as pleasing to the palate as the Winter Truffle (*Tuber brumale*) or the Périgord Truffle (*T. melanosporum*), it nevertheless belongs among high-quality esculents. Of course, the relatively coarse warts must be removed before their preparation for table use.

Spore: 40–50 × 12–32 μm,
elliptic-globose, yellowish brown, reticulate

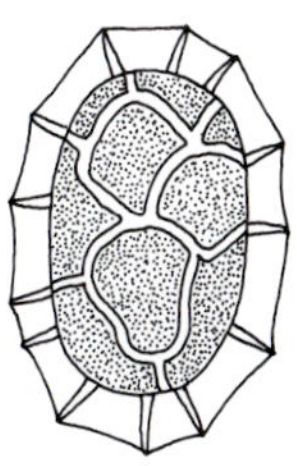

Ascus with two spores

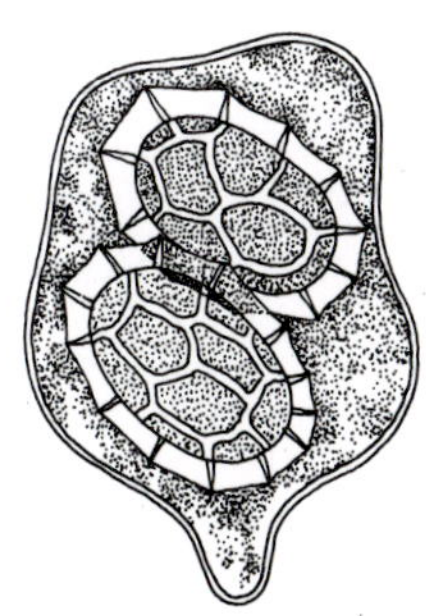

Winter Truffle
Tuber brumale Vitt.

This is one of the 'true' truffles that are highly esteemed from the culinary point of view. Although its aroma is not so intense as in the renowned Périgord Truffle (*T. melanosporum*), it exceeds the Summer Truffle in both aroma and taste. The tuberous fruit bodies of the Winter Truffle, ranging in size from a hazel nut to a human fist, are covered with low and broad, tetragonal to hexagonal, dark warts. The gleba is ashy grey, intertwined with dirty white veins. One to six ripe spores develop in shortly pedicellate, globose to ovoid asci and are densely covered with long spines.

The Winter Truffle is a subterrestrial fungus. It is confined to forest humus and lime-rich soils often overlaid with decaying foliage, particularly in warm oak forests; in some regions, however, it also appears in beech and hornbeam forests. It attains maturity in late autumn or in winter. In the process of ripening, the fragrance of its fruit bodies, pleasant at first, is gradually replaced by a nauseating odour, especially after keeping ripe fruit bodies in an enclosed space for several days. The Winter Truffle, abundantly distributed in some parts of France and Italy, rarely occurs in more northern regions of western Europe.

Spore: 21–42 × 17–28 μm,
ellipsoid, echinulate

Ascus containing three spores

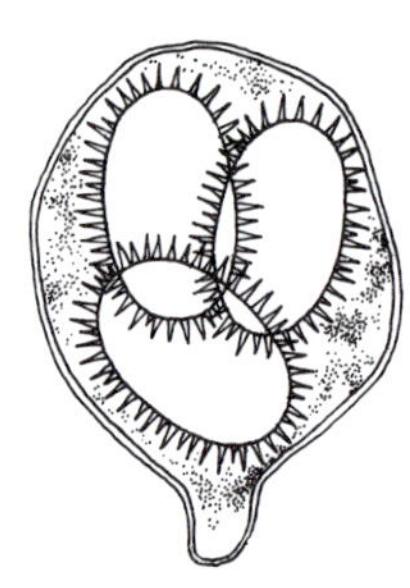

Elaphomyces granulatus Fr.

The globular shape of *Elaphomyces granulatus* and its subterranean growth encourage mushroom pickers to regard it as a truffle. Yet it has nothing else in common with true truffles (*Tuber*), and in fact it is classified as a member of quite a different group.

In nature we usually come across *E. granulatus* in spruce and pine forests. As a rule, we find fruit bodies dug out by animals, or their remnants lying about on the surface of the disturbed forest floor; sometimes we find them growing under uprooted trees. We can try – often with success – to dig them out ourselves, not deep below the surface of the ground, close to the roots of pine trees or near their trunks. Since the fruit bodies are compact and tough in consistency, they are capable of surviving in their habitats for a very long time. One usually finds fruit bodies with an ochre or buff, densely verrucose cortical layer (peridium), enclosing the inner fertile part (gleba). When ripe, the gleba is transformed into a purplish black, powdery matter in which vast multitudes of spores marked with a verrucose ornamentation are distinguishable under the microscope. Young fruit bodies are rarely found; their gleba is solid, whitish, later yellowish, often reddish, without veins.

E. granulatus is attacked by the parasitic pyrenomycete *Cordyceps ophioglossoides* whose sulphur-yellow mycelium forces its way through the fruit body and destroys it. *C. ophioglossoides* rises above the surface of the ground in the form of a clavate-cylindrical stroma in which little globular fruit bodies (perithecia) are submerged. These are visible only under a microscope.

Spores: 28–32 μm, globose, echinulate, blackish brown

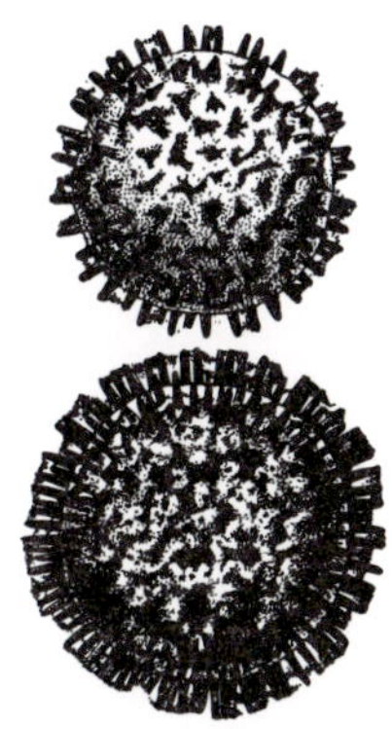

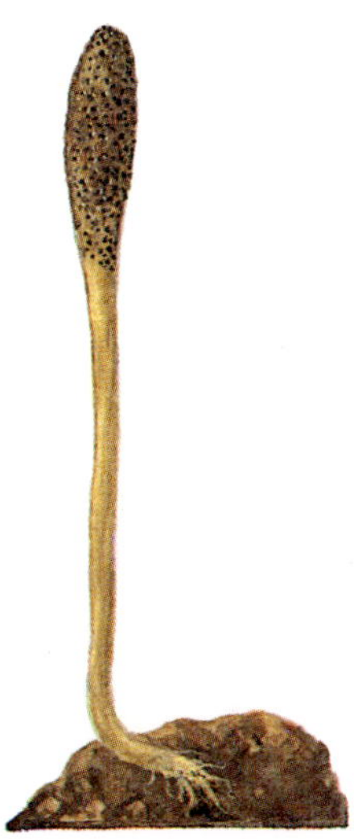

Stroma of *Cordyceps ophioglossoides*

Elaphomyces granulatus

Common Earth-ball
Scleroderma citrinum Pers.

This common inhabitant of forests, particularly sandy pine woods, may sometimes be mistaken for a truffle. However, the Common Earth-ball, together with some other closely related and similar species of *Scleroderma,* represents the class Gasteromycetes (stomach fungi). Their spores arise on basidia and not within asci, as is the case in truffles. The Common Earth-ball has tuberous or subglobular fruit bodies with a typical structure; they are formed by two layers – the outer peridium and the inner gleba. The peridium, cracking into wart-like structures, is tough and distinctly separated from the gleba. The gleba of young fruit bodies consists of a white, firm, minutely chambered context emitting an intense spicy odour. The context soon acquires a rosy hue, gradually passing over into poppyseed-blue, greyish and black. On reaching the final stage of its development, the context disintegrates into a dark green, powdery matter containing spores. These are released through openings at the apex of the irregularly cracking peridium to be dispersed in the neighbourhood.

The Common Earth-ball is a poisonous fungus. Despite this it can be used as a spice, but only in small quantities (the amount of dried powder approximately covering the tip of a rounded knife, or several slices of young fruit bodies). Overdosed foods or those prepared from ripe fruit bodies cause poisoning accompanied by vomiting and heart troubles.

Fairly common along hedgerows and roadsides is *S. verrucosum* with its thin, minutely warty peridium. It often terminates in a stipe-like and furrowed base ending in a cluster of mycelial threads.

Spores of *Scleroderma citrinum*: 7–15 μm, globose, reticulate-spinose, blackish brown

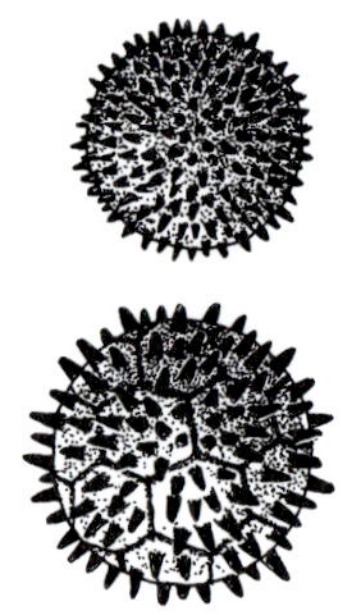

Scleroderma citrinum

Scleroderma verrucosum

Pisolithus arrhizus

(Pers.) Rauschert

This fungus is related to the genus *Scleroderma* from which it differs in the minutely phaseoliform structures composing the gleba, easily discernible on the longitudinal section through a young fruit body. When fresh, the gleba is juicy and pulpy. The peridioles of which it is composed are located in a shiny black case; they are yellow at first and brown when older, and contain basidia with spores. At maturity the whole interior of the fruit body disintegrates into a strongly pulverous, chocolate-brown matter formed by the spore mass from the crumbled peridioles. This is released through the upper part of the peridium which has fallen to pieces. The sterile, thick and branched basal part of the peridium resembles a root. It is sometimes as much as 30 cm long, embedded deep in the ground where it remains long after the disintegration of the fruit body.

Pisolithus arrhizus is most commonly found on sandy soil in pine forests. Here it sometimes grows along tracks or on deep inclines of hollow ways torn down and grooved by rainfalls, overgrown with only a scattering of heather and low seedlings. Young fruit bodies of *P. arrhizus* are edible in small quantities (as is the case in *Scleroderma*). In our opinion, however, very few mushroom pickers would ever think of tasting this fungus.

In older mycological handbooks, *P. arrhizus* is usually referred to wrongly as *P. arenarius*.

Spores: 9–12 μm, globose, echinulate, brown

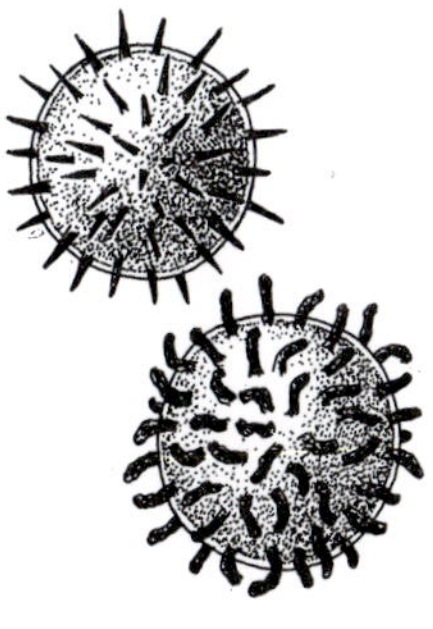

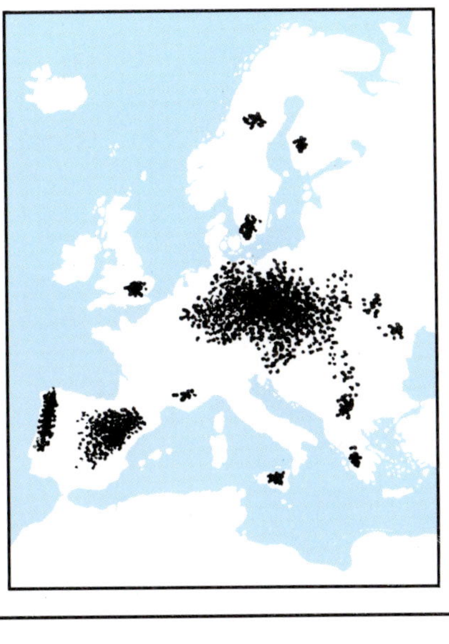

Astraeus hygrometricus

(Pers.) Morg.

Fungi with star-shaped fruit bodies have always attracted the attention not only of laymen but also of mycologists. This is also why *Astraeus hygrometricus* has usually been subjected to study in connection with the order *Geastrales,* though the genus *Astraeus* bears no affinity with Earth Stars (*Geastrum*). *Astraeus* belongs to the independent family of Astraeaceae included in the order Sclerodermatales; this family is more closely related to the genera *Scleroderma, Pisolithus* and *Tulostoma.*

Seated in the centre of the coriaceous outer peridium, which splits at maturity to form regular stellate rays, is the globular inner peridium with an irregular, small peristome at the apex. The rays of the outer peridium tend to curve inward or coil up in dry conditions (so covering the inner peridium), and to expand again in rainy weather. In old fruit bodies the surface of the rays is densely cracked into minute areoles; they are dark grey to black in colour. The fruit bodies remain in their habitat for a very long time – often for many years.

A. hygrometricus grows in colonies on sunny rocks, on stony and rocky slopes overgrown with sparse woods, and in the outskirts of oak or pine forests. It occurs predominantly on more acid substrates (on slate, granite and sands) and avoids lime-rich soils. Fresh fruit bodies are found from autumn till spring, older ones throughout the year. It accompanies almost exclusively oaks and pines, and its distribution is world-wide. It is inedible.

Spores: 8–12 μm, globose, verrucose, brown
Mature spore (a), spore in an optical section (b)

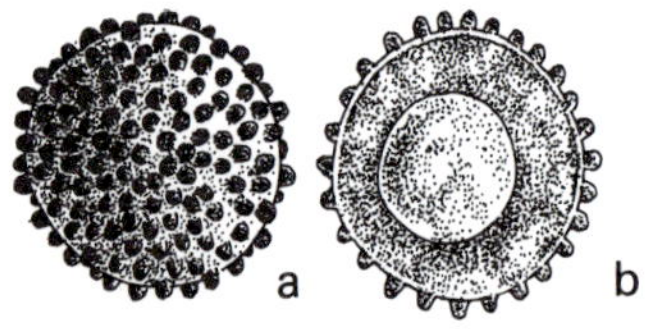

Geastrum quadrifidum

Astraeus hygrometricus

Distribution of *Astraeus hygrometricus* in Europe

Cyathus striatus
(Huds.) ex Pers.

The fruit bodies of this neat little fungus look like small goblets that are grey and elegantly grooved inside; their outer surface is coated with stiff brown hairs. Nothing in their appearance bears resemblance to most of their close relatives, the Gasteromycetes. The fruit bodies are 10–15 mm high and 8–10 mm wide. In quite young fruit bodies, the peridial mouth is covered by a thin white membrane (epiphragm). It is only after its removal that 1.5–2 mm long lenticular pips (peridioles) can be seen at the bottom. These bear reproductive cells (basidia) composing the hymenium contained in the peridioles. Spores develop on the basidia.

Like nearly all the other related genera and species, *C. striatus* is a saprophytic fungus. It colonizes decaying branches, rotten wood logs, and decomposed stumps as well as old herb stems, particularly those lying about in damp and shady places. After summer rains it often appears gregariously.

It can be easily distinguished from *C. olla,* which is almost the same size. Its cup-like fruit bodies are whitish and only felted on the outside; pale grey inside. The cup margins are flaring, sometimes curved backwards. This species prefers manured ground, hence it is more frequently found outside the forest in fields, garden hotbeds, etc.

An even more common species is *Crucibulum laeve;* its fruit bodies are vasiform, ochre and felted on the outside, with yellowish lenticular peridioles inside. They grow on various plant debris, often gregariously.

Spores of *Cyathus striatus*:
16–22 × 8–10 µm, ellipsoid, colourless, smooth

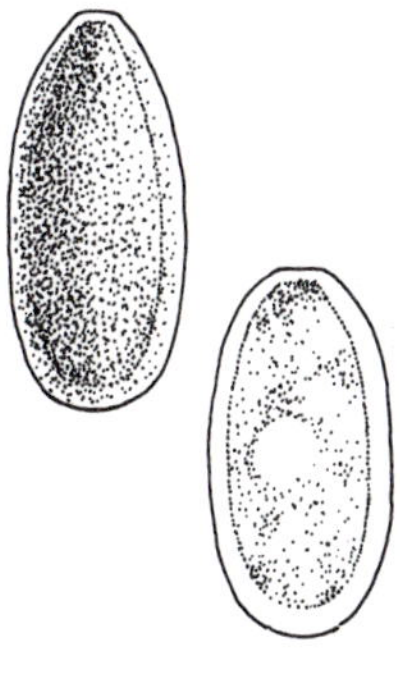

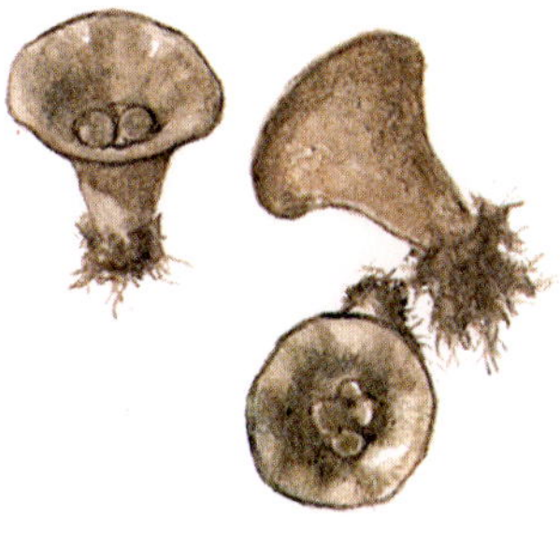

Cyathus olla

Cyathus striatus

Sphaerobolus stellatus
Tode ex Pers.

This is one of the smallest of the Gasteromycetes. When looking for it, one must carefully examine old and decaying plant remains such as stems, branches, pieces of wood and bark, but also old cow dung and excrements from other herbivores. On worked wood exposed to enduring humidity, e.g. in hothouses, hotbeds, etc., *Sphaerobolus stellatus* can even manifest itself as a wood-destroying fungus – otherwise it is of no particular importance.

The development of its fruit bodies is an interesting sight; from the tiny globular fruit bodies, only 1–4 mm in size and white-felted on the outside, an equally globular bright orange pip (peridiole) is released and discharged to a considerable distance under strong pressure. The emptied fruit body has the shape of a deep, semiglobular saucer with a margin split to form 5–8 pointed rays, neatly star-like. Reproduction is effected by the discharged globular peridiole containing basidia with spores.

S. stellatus is most commonly found after summer rains. We can bring its fruit bodies home together with the substrate, and watch the jerking out of the pips stirred up by sudden illumination or another impulse (such as touch).

Spores: 6–10 × 5–6 μm,
irregularly ellipsoid, smooth, colourless

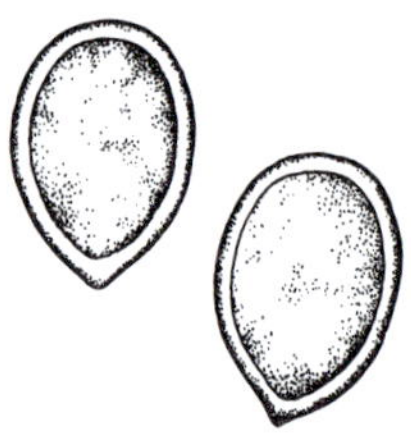

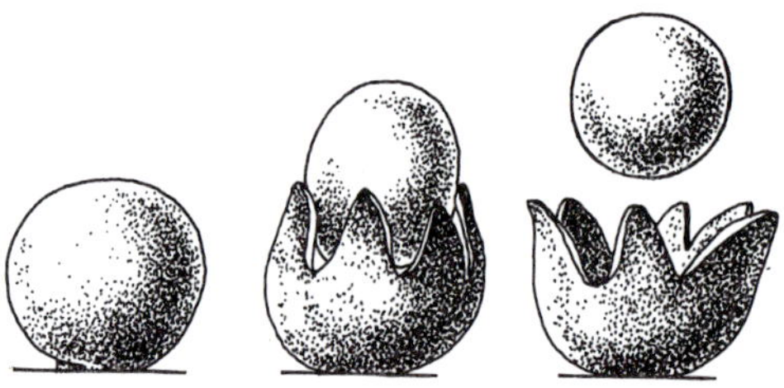

Discharge of the peridiole from the fruit body

Bovista nigrescens

Pers. ex Pers.

Fungi of the genus *Bovista* are sometimes confused with puffballs (*Lycoperdon*). In fact they closely resemble each other – the main difference consists in the structure of the capillitium. In the puffballs the hyphae are simple, usually unbranched, and almost equally thick all along their length; in *Bovista* these are much branched, with a stronger main axis and lateral threads tapering to the apex. Moreover, spores are borne on markedly long pedicels. Without using the microscope, these genera can be distinguished by the presence or absence of the sterile base in the fruit body. In the puffballs this is well-developed and clearly separated from the fertile true gleba by a membranous septum, while in *Bovista* the sterile base is absent altogether. Their peridium consists of two layers: the fragile exoperidium and the firm endoperidium.

Like the other three or four European species, *Bovista nigrescens* grows outside the forest in meadows and pastures, on grassy slopes, along field paths, and also on lawns of urban parks. It is a robust fungus growing up to 5 cm in size; its mature endoperidium ranges in colour from blackish brown to almost black. Closely related is *B. plumbea,* occurring predominantly in lowlands. It is smaller, measuring only 1–3 cm in diameter, its endoperidium is pale grey or bluish grey. Young fruit bodies, still white both on the outside and inside, can be collected for eating.

Spores of *Bovista nigrescens*: 5–6 μm, verrucose, yellowish brown, with 5–8 μm long pedicels

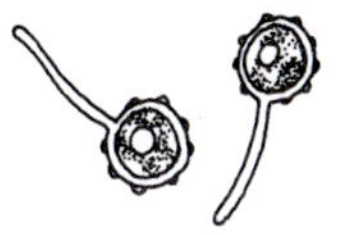

Mature spore, strongly magnified

A branched capillitial thread

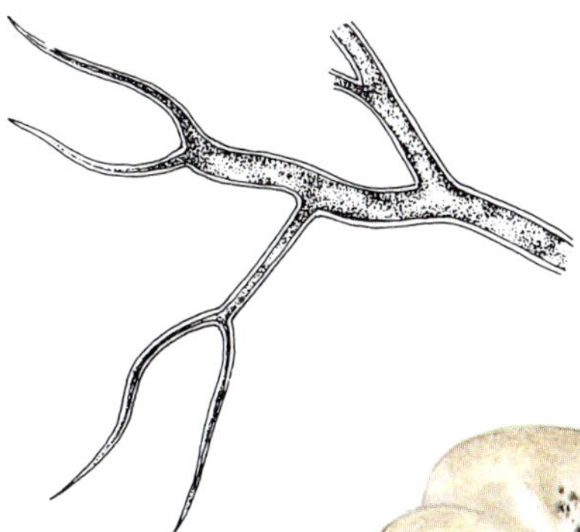

Bovista plumbea

Bovista nigrescens

Common Puffball
Lycoperdon perlatum Pers. ex Pers.

This is one of the most abundant puffballs commonly found in forests of all kinds. Its fruit bodies grow up to 8 cm in height and 5 cm in width; they are pear-shaped or club-shaped, often growing gregariously on the ground among fallen leaves and needles as well as in grass. The young fruit body is entirely white, densely coated with spines and readily detached conical warts leaving characteristic angular patches (areoles). With the ripening of spores, the soft, porous white flesh of the gleba gradually becomes yellowish at first, then greyish green and finally brown, turning into a brown spore powder. This is released through a small pore situated at the apex of the fruit body. The capillitial threads are only sparingly dichotomically branched, 4 mm thick, thin-walled, yellow-brown. The fresh context of the gleba has a pleasant mushroom-like smell and a mild taste.

The collection of quite young, still white fruit bodies of this puffball for table use can be fully recommended: they are suitable for all culinary purposes, particularly for flavouring soups.

Lycoperdon pyriforme, visibly obviously different from the above by the minutely verrucose or, rather, farinaceous surface coating, grows on decaying wood, especially on stumps where its fruit bodies are often aggregated in dense tufts. It grows out of clearly visible white mycelial threads penetrating deep into the rotting wood. Young fruit bodies are also edible.

L. echinatum, which grows in summer and in autumn mainly in beech or mixed submontane forests, is also an edible species.

Spores of *Lycoperdon perlatum*: 3.5–4.5 μm,
globose, slightly rough, pale yellow
Young spore (a)
Ripe spore (b)

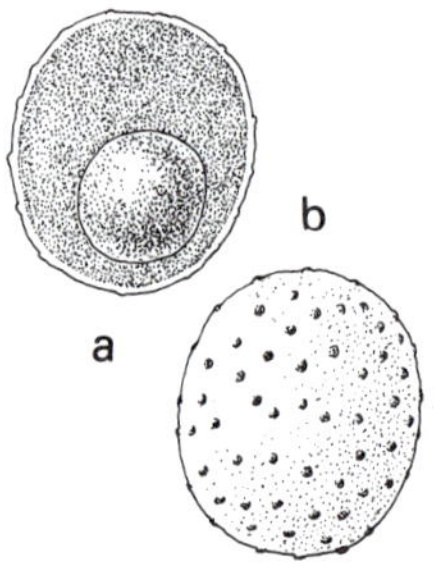

Capillitial thread

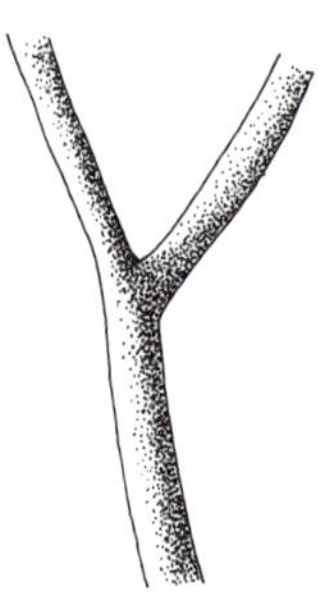

Lycoperdon pyriforme

Lycoperdon perlatum

Lycoperdon echinatum

Giant Puffball

Langermannia gigantea (Batsch ex Pers.) Rostk.

A Giant Puffball is always a notable find – especially where a fruit body of a maximal size and weight is concerned. One of the largest fruit bodies reported hitherto, found in 1955 in northern Bohemia, was 46 cm high, 212 cm round, and weighed 20.80 kg. Hence, it was one of the largest fungi ever found. Of course, fruit bodies of smaller dimensions are usually found – yet thanks to their size, globular shape and dazzling white colour they are showy and visible from a considerable distance. Moreover, they can be found either in human settlements or in their vicinity: in gardens, lawns, meadows, on slopes, and in pastures.

The exoperidium of the Giant Puffball gradually turns yellow and peels off in pieces, while the gleba is transformed into yellowish brown, cottony lumps. Being undifferentiated into a fertile and a sterile part, the whole interior of the fruit body undergoes this change once the spores begin maturing. The fluffy lumps consist of numerous long, septate, sparsely perforated capillitial threads and minute spores with a short stipe.

The Giant Puffball, also known in older mycological literature under the names *Lycoperdon giganteum*, *L. maximum* and *L. bovista*, is widespread all over the world: it grows even in the tropics and in the far north. At an early stage, while the fruit body is still white both on the outside and inside, it is edible – and is probably the most palatable of all puffballs. The best way of preparing it for the table is to make mushroom steaks.

Spores: 3.5–4 μm, globose, smooth, yellowish brown

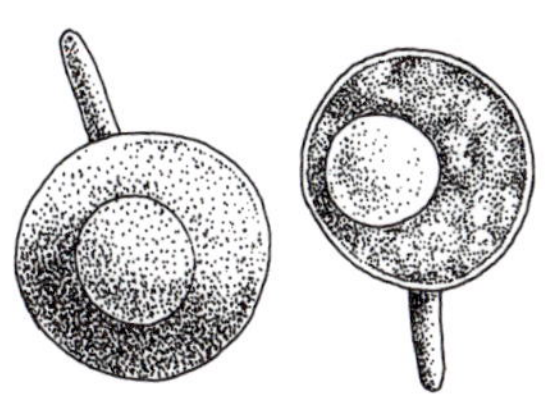

Capillitial thread

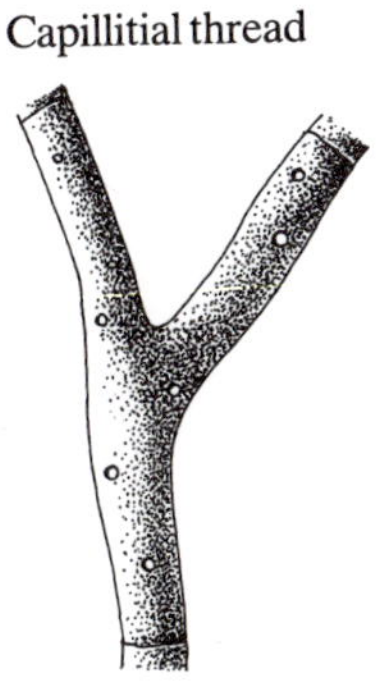

Geastrum triplex Jungh.

There are approximately 30 species of earth stars (*Geastrum*) growing in Europe, and they are among the true gems of nature. They occur very rarely however, and are rapidly disappearing due to mankind's devastation of the countryside.

Geastrum triplex is one of the largest earth-star species. When fresh, it is also one of the most beautiful. It usually forms sparse colonies in humus-rich woods, in gorges, around old stumps, and in shady localities. Though it prefers deciduous forests, it also occurs in unraked and unkept remote parts of old gardens and parks, especially under oaks, ashes, beeches, hornbeams, maples and limes. Sometimes it also makes its appearance in raspberry and nettle growths, and on rubbish heaps in woods. It is rare in coniferous forests, occurring especially under old spruces or firs in various herb-growths. It grows from September till November. Young, still-closed fruit bodies are onion-shaped, ochre-brown to pale pinkish. The exoperidium bursts into 4–7 (mostly 5) pointed, unequal rays; the endoperidium is sessile, with a fibrillose mouth delimited by a clearly discernible circular area. The specific name *triplex* is derived from the apparent division of some fruit bodies into three parts (the endoperidium, the collar arisen from the flaring fleshy part of the cracked exoperidium, and the incurved rays of the exoperidium at the base). *G. triplex* is inedible.

Spore of *Geastrum triplex*: 4–5 μm, globose, shortly spiny, light brown

Geastrum triplex

Geastrum rufescens

Wood Witch, Stinking Polecat, Stinkhorn
Phallus impudicus L. ex Pers.

This conspicuous and well-known fungus has become exceedingly widespread and, in some regions, it is almost becoming a weed fungus. To the detriment of other, evidently more sensitive and less adaptable fungus species, the Wood Witch is flooding the forests in vast multitudes, and attracting attention from afar by the typical vile odour of its ripening fruit bodies. It occurs in woods of all types, but also in gardens and parks. Young stages, the well-known elastic eggs similar to tennis balls, are about 6 cm in size, with a characteristic tough mycelial rhizomorph at the base. Their faint odour is suggestive of radish. At first they are hypogeous but soon develop into a long, upright, cylindrical receptacle of a porous, spongy consistency that is up to 20 cm high and 5 cm wide, terminanting in a bell- or thimble-shaped cap. This is covered with an olive-green slime emitting a nauseous smell (while the strongly diluted slime smells sweetly of honey), which attracts numerous insects, particularly flies, that subsequently help to disseminate its spores.

The range of the Wood Witch covers the entire temperate zone of the Old World; its northernmost limit is in southern Sweden. It is absent from North America where it is represented by the related *P. hadriani* which also grows in Europe.

The young, still tough and closed eggs of the Wood Witch are good when fried, although most people prefer to avoid this fungus or unnecessarily destroy it. This, however, does not seem to curb its further diffusion at all.

Spore: 3.5–5 × 1.5–2 μm, long-ellipsoid, smooth, yellowish

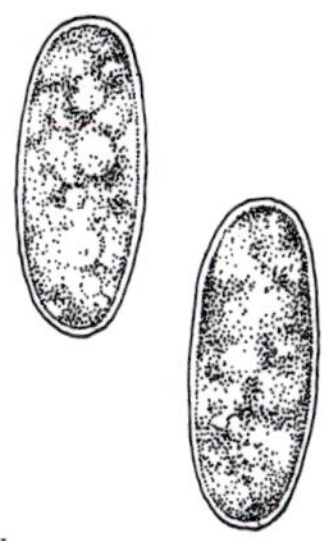

Section through a young fruit body

Hysterangium graveolens Velen.

Hysterangium graveolens is one of the most common representatives of hypogeous gasteromycetes. There exists a large number of such fungi, and their correct identification is a distinct problem for the specialists. This applies in particular to the genera *Hymenogaster, Rhizopogon, Melanogaster* and others, whose discrimination meets with difficulties because the fungi involved are given to extraordinary variation in both macro- and microcharacteristics.

In general, fungi of the genus *Hysterangium* can easily be distinguished by their readily separating peridium. From the tuberous fruit bodies – brown with a whitish, greyish and later reddish tinge, 1–3 cm in size – the peridium sloughs off in large, thick patches, revealing an olive-green, relatively tough and elastic gleba. A section through the gleba clearly reveals both greyish, jellified and dendriform veins branching off from the common central column or columella, and narrow and flexuous veins. Fruit bodies have a white mycelial rhizomorph at the base and grow, for the most part, caespitosely or gregariously right under the surface of the ground, most frequently in spruce forests. At maturity they partially emerge above the surface.

H. graveolens is commonly found along woodland paths. It is an edible fungus but, due to its very small size and relatively rare occurrence, it is of no great importance for mushroom pickers. It is often introduced in literature under the name *H. clathroides* or *H. separabile.*

Spores: 10–17 × 4–6 µm, cylindrical, smooth, almost colourless

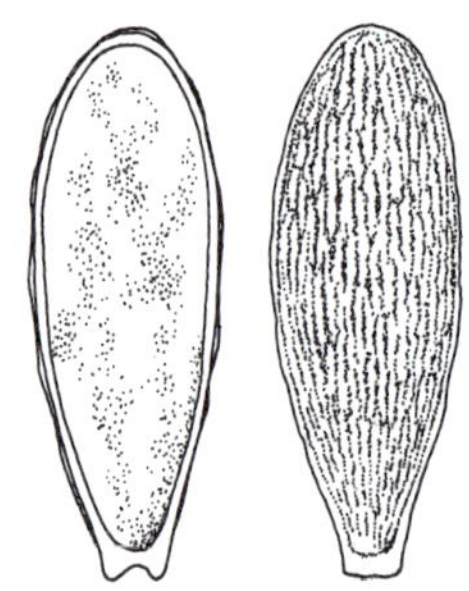

Hysterangium graveolens

Rhizopogon foetens

Anthurus archeri

(Berk.) E. Fischer

During World War I and in the years following it, several exotic fungus species were introduced to Europe; the most vital of these is apparently *Anthurus archeri,* at present reported from many parts of western and central Europe. Its original habitat is probably Australia. It is a remarkable species in both shape and colouring, and it is exactly thanks to its striking appearance that a good many reports about its occurrence and increasing distribution are nowadays available.

The young stage resembles the 'egg' of *Phallus impudicus* but is smaller, being less than 4 cm in diameter, with bluish violet mycelial threads. An upright receptacle, up to 10 cm in height, develops from the egg; it is divided into 5–8 long arms tapering towards the tips which are fused at first but later open out into a star-like form. The arms are extremely brittle, whitish pink on the outside, beautifully orange-red inside, transversely wrinkled, at maturity strewn with islets of olive green slime which, as in *Phallus impudicus,* emits a foul smell.

In Europe, *A. archeri* occurs predominantly in places affected by human activity, for example on old rotting straw, on wood and sawdust, in rubbish dumps, along tracks and roadsides, but sometimes also in the forest under trees where it grows directly from the forest-floor humus.

Another species imported to Europe which, however, occurs much more rarely is another fungus of the order Phallales – *Lysurus gardneri.* It has a cylindrical receptacle bearing on its apex 5–7 erect, lanceolate, pale orange arms whose inner surface is orange, red or pink.

Spores of *Anthurus archeri*:
6–7.5 × 2–2.5 µm, ellipsoid,
smooth, colourless

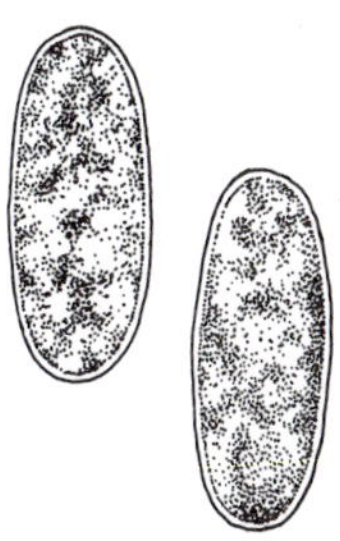

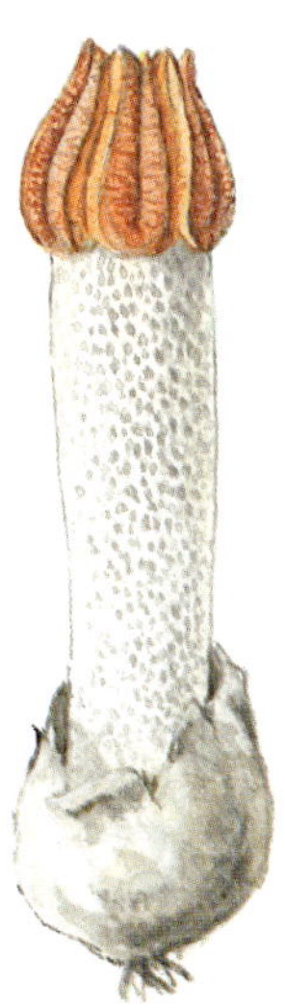

Lysurus gardneri

Anthurus archeri

Blackening Russula

Russula nigricans (Bull. ex Mérat) Fr.

When visiting a forest in springtime, we may frequently encounter groups of old, blackened, as if mummified fruit bodies which are similar in shape to the genus *Russula.* In fact they usually belong to some species of *Russula* from the group of 'nigrescent' russulas (section *Nigricantes*). Most often it is the Blackening Russula. The robust fruit bodies of this fungus are capable of surviving in the forest for a very long time.

The Blackening Russula occurs in summer and autumn in both deciduous and coniferous forests. Its cap grows to be 8–20 cm wide; its stipe is 4–10 cm long and 2–3.5 cm thick.

The gills are very distant, thick and brittle, and the spore print is pure white. When cut or bruised, the flesh of a fresh fruit body turns brick-red, but later it becomes grey and ultimately black. The flesh of the related *Russula adusta,* found most frequently in pine woods, does not turn red but directly brown to black. The difference between the two species clearly appears also in the gills: these are markedly closer in *R. adusta* than in *R. nigricans.*

Both *R. nigricans* and *R. adusta* are edible mushrooms widely collected in some regions, yet they are not so suitable for eating as it is sometimes maintained. Their flesh is relatively tough, and also their earthy smell is a drawback.

The decayed and blackened fruit bodies of russulas of the section *Nigricantes* sometimes serve as hosts for interesting minute fungi of the genus *Nyctalis,* growing in groups or clusters on the surface of the caps. The two species of *Nyctalis* are fleshy, whitish, at most 2 cm wide, often bearing incompletely developed gills on their underside. When young, the fruit bodies of *N. lycoperdioides* resemble small puffballs.

Spore: 6–8 × 6–7 µm, ellipsoid, with very subtle ornamentation

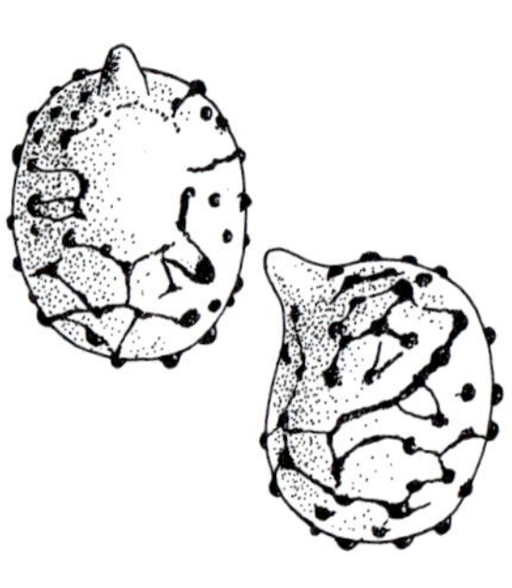

Common Yellow Russula
Russula ochroleuca (Pers.) ex Fr.

In late summer and early autumn, the monotonous spruce-forest floor covered only by needles or a sparse undergrowth is enlivened with yellow fruit bodies of russulas. Relatively damp submontane forests are often crowded with them. The species involved is most usually the Common Yellow Russula. Its 4–11 cm wide cap is coated with a yellow, sometimes almost golden-yellow cuticle, viscid in damp weather, rather shiny when dry, sometimes slightly wrinkled or slightly venose, readily peeling almost to the cap centre. The white or, more rarely, yellowish stipe is 3.5–7 cm long and 1–2.5 cm thick, tough at first, spongy elastic later, cylindrical, occasionally with a clavately expanded base, often covered with minute scales or brownish granules. On aging it gradually turns grey; this is best discernible on fruit bodies saturated with water. The gills, white at first, become cream-coloured with age, sometimes with a lemon-ochre tinge, staining light brown on handling, especially at the edge. The flesh has an inconspicuous, faintly acid, fruity smell and a rather acrid – rarely mild – taste. The spore print is white or cream.

The Common Yellow Russula occurs not only in conifer forests but also, rather more sporadically, in deciduous forests. It grows on acid soils and is widespread all over Europe. In spite of its acrid taste, this species is collected by some mushroom pickers to flavour bland mushroom mixtures.

Spores: 8–10.5 × 6.5–8 μm, subglobose, fairly strongly echinulate, almost reticulate

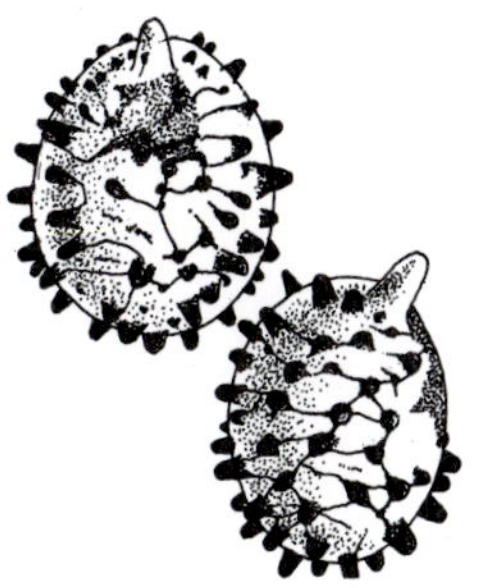

Cracked Green Russula

Russula virescens (Schaeff. ex Zanted.) Fr.

The green colour in gill fungi is invariably regarded as a warning signal by all mushroom pickers who, though not safely acquainted with the individual species and hence incapable of reliable identification, are keen on gathering mushrooms for culinary purposes. This is because the most poisonous fungus, the Death Cap, has a green-coloured cap. Many a mistake with fatal consequences has been caused by the failure to distinguish the Cracked Green Russula or some other similarly coloured species (e.g. the Grass Green Russula) from the Death Cap. However, a more experienced mushroom picker who can make a clean-cut distinction between *Russula* and *Amanita* is in a position to enrich his collection by green *Russula* species as well.

One of these is the Cracked Green Russula, readily distinguished by its verdigris or greyish green cap, fading to pale buff with age, and having a characteristically areolate cuticle. The cap is 5–12 cm wide; the stipe is 3–9 cm high, 2–5 cm thick, cylindrical. The spore print is white or whitish. The whole mushroom is relatively stout and firm-fleshed; its cap tends to remain semiglobular-convex for a long time. The gills, stipe and flesh are white but susceptible to staining rusty. The flesh of a fresh fruit body, when touched with a drop of green-vitriol solution, immediately turns deep red.

This edible and, moreover, delicious russula is abundant in summer and autumn in relatively dry and sparse deciduous and coniferous forests.

This species is also used in industry: it is dried on a large scale for the purposes of mushroom-extract production. It has also proved suitable for flavouring soups and sauces.

Spores: 8–10 × 7–8 μm, subglobose, with a delicate ornamentation

Bare-toothed Russula

Russula vesca Fr.

The Bare-toothed Russula is one of the most savoury mushrooms of this genus. It is currently collected all over Europe, being easily distinguished from other russulas – its confusion with any other species is hardly possible. The whole fruit body has a relatively firm flesh. The cap is 6–11 cm wide, covered with a dingy reddish fleshy cuticle weathering to grey or bleached in places, or on the contrary tinged with pale hazel or lilac grey. In wet conditions the cuticle is sticky, marked with pronounced radial wrinkles or veins, sulcate at the cap margin. The stipe, 3–10 cm in length and 1.5–3 cm in width, is often much shorter than the diameter of the cap. It narrows downwards, with rusty spots on a white surface. The tendency to turn rusty becomes most conspicuous in places nibbled at by slugs or squirrels, or otherwise damaged. This in fact applies to the whole fruit body. Also the edges of the white, relatively narrow gills turn rusty. The cortex of a fresh fruit body soon develops a taste of hazel nuts but is almost inodorous. The spore print is pure white. The reaction of the Bare-toothed Russula to the green-vitriol solution is extraordinarily intense: one drop of the solution instantly colours the stipe surface or the flesh to orange-red or pinkish orange.

The Bare-toothed Russula occurs very abundantly from the end of May throughout the summer in forests of all types. In some regions it is most common in oak forests on non-calcareous substrates.

Spores: 6–8 × 5–6.5 μm, subglobose, very minutely and sparsely verrucose

Reaction to ferrous sulphate

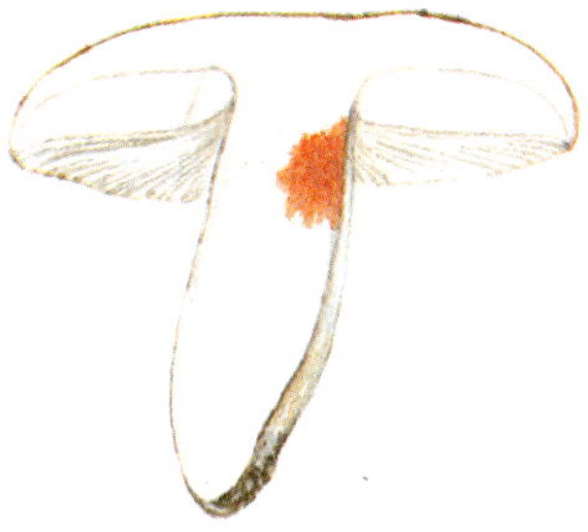

Russula cyanoxantha
(Schaeff. ex Schw.) Fr.

Some *Russula* species show extraordinary variability in the colour of fruit bodies. This applies also to *Russula cyanoxantha.* In some of its forms, the cap cuticle is blurred cloudy violet or bluish purple. Very often, however, specimens are found in which green predominates – the cap centre especially is often dark green; in still other cases the cap may be partly pinkish beige to lilac. But despite these fairly large colour variations, this species can safely be distinguished by one characteristic feature: if we let our fingers pass over the gills, these seem greasy, pliable, and do not break as in other russulas. The relatively short and thick stipe is usually pure white all over (more rarely rosy with a violet tinge), and also the gills are persistently white. If the cap of a fresh fruit body is cut off from the stipe and placed on a sheet of black paper with the gills facing downwards, spores resembling chalky white powder may be found to have dropped on the sheet in the course of several hours. The colour of the spore print is a significant distinguishing feature on the basis of which individual species of *Russula* can be identified. Another essential feature for distinguishing this species is the finely wrinkled cap cuticle and the pleasant, non-acrid taste of the odourless flesh which shows no colour reactions in a 10 per cent green-vitriol solution.

R. cyanoxantha is a good edible mushroom. It appears as early as the end of spring, particularly in deciduous forests but later also in coniferous forests. It is distributed throughout the north temperate zone and in north Africa.

Spores: 7–10 × 7–8 μm,
subglobose, verrucose, colourless

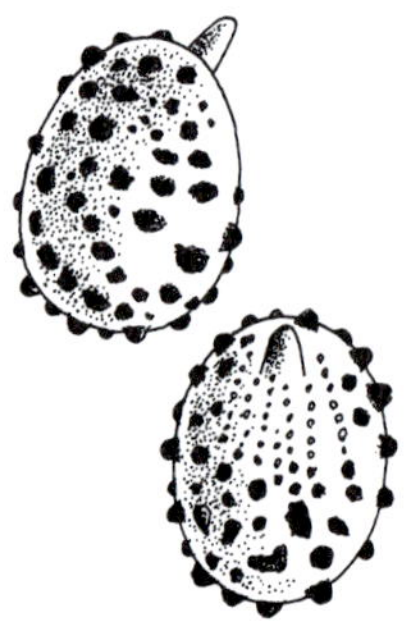

Grass Green Russula

Russula aeruginea Lindbl. in Fr.

The collection of green-coloured Russulas (but not only these) for table use is always risky for anybody who is not reliably acquainted with the basic assortment of poisonous fungi and ignores or underestimates expert opinion. He is permanently exposed to the danger of poisoning by the Death Cap. It is difficult to differentiate between these fungi even after a careful comparison of exact descriptions of both genera in question, *Russula* and *Amanita.*

The Grass Green Russula has a cap up to 10 cm wide, olive-green, sometimes lighter, with vague ochre, brownish or whitish patches so that the green colour is sometimes more or less suppressed. The cap margin is relatively thin, sharp-edged and striate. The glabrous cuticle, tacky when moist, is readily separable almost to the centre. The stipe is 5–8 cm long, 1–2 cm thick, firm-fleshed, cylindrical, often tapered at the base. It is pure white but tends to turn yellow or brown, particularly in its basal portion. The gills are thin and crowded, later subdistant, white, in older fruit bodies tinged slightly cream-yellowish. The originally white flesh becomes rusty on injury or with age, rusty stains appear in all parts of the fruit body. The odourless flesh often has a rather pungent taste.

The Grass Green Russula occurs abundantly not only in spruce and pine forests and under birches (to which it seems to be symbiotically bound), but also in grass along woodland tracks and in parks, predominantly in acid soils. It grows throughout the summer and is edible.

Spores: 6–10 × 4.5–6.5 μm, subglobose, sparsely verrucose

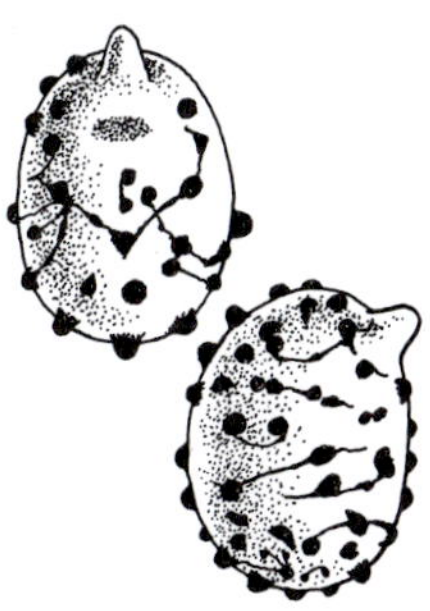

Spore print

Russula olivacea
(Schaeff. ex Secr.) Fr.

This is the most robust russula inhabiting European forests. Its cap grows up to 20 cm in diameter; it is shallowly convex, flat to broadly depressed later, with a dull, almost velvety cuticle separable at the margin only. It is very variable in colour. In some specimens purplish red or violet predominates, in others olive-green tinged with ochre or brown. There is, however, one feature characteristic of this russula: the pigment in the cuticle along the periphery of the cap is distributed in flexuous narrow bands. The 6–10 cm long and 2–5 cm thick stipe is robust, cylindrical, firm at first, later spongy, tinged with purple either all over its surface or at least on one side, slowly turning yellow to brown in the basal part when bruised. The gills are remarkably broad (up to 1.5 cm), distant, thick, brittle, soon completely or partly bright egg-yolk-yellow with red-coloured edges. The flesh is white, rather dry, inodorous, and tastes bland. When touched with a drop of phenolic (carbolic) water it instantly produces a reddish violet stain.

Russula olivacea occurs in the warmest summer months especially in rather dry, sunny forests or in their outskirts. It grows under spruces and pines, but also in beech forests, usually on relatively acid soils. It is edible and tasty although its flesh is much too dry.

Spores: 7.5–12 × 6.5–10 μm, subglobose, thickly covered with spines up to 1.5 μm high

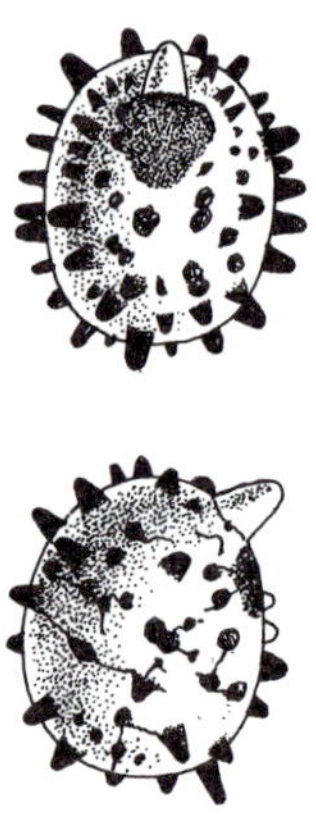

Shed spore print

Russula mustelina Fr.

Russula mustelina is a robust, firm-fleshed species with a hard stipe and mostly brown-coloured cap which may grow as much as 15 cm in diameter. The cap cuticle is smoky ochre-brown or yellowish brown, slightly viscid and shiny when moist, matt when dry, finely radially wrinkled, and detachable at the margin. The stipe is 3–11 cm long, 1.5–4 cm thick, cylindrical, often crooked, white but later slightly yellowish, gradually turning brown or rusty and becoming brown all over when old. The gills are thick, crowded, tough, 10–15 mm broad, white at first, soon becoming cream- or butter-coloured, straw-yellow, marked with ochre-brown or rusty spots in age. The flesh is tough, white, readily turning yellow-brown with age; it is almost odourless and has a mild to sweet taste.

R. mustelina is confined to old coniferous (mostly spruce) forests in submontane and montane regions. It is absent from lower elevations and secondary spruce monocultures. Young fruit bodies show strong resemblance to the Edible Boletus by their semiglobular-convex cap and by its colouring.

R. mustelina is an edible mushroom of good quality. It could be confused only with the inedible Stinking Russula (*R. foetens*) growing in similar places. However, the cap of the Stinking Russula has a deeply grooved margin and is predominantly ochre-yellow in colour. The whole cap is markedly viscous. This russula has a strongly nauseous smell and a rather pungent taste.

Spores of *Russula mustelina*:
7–11 × 5.5–8 µm,
ellipsoid,
with low confluent warts
to shallowly pectinate

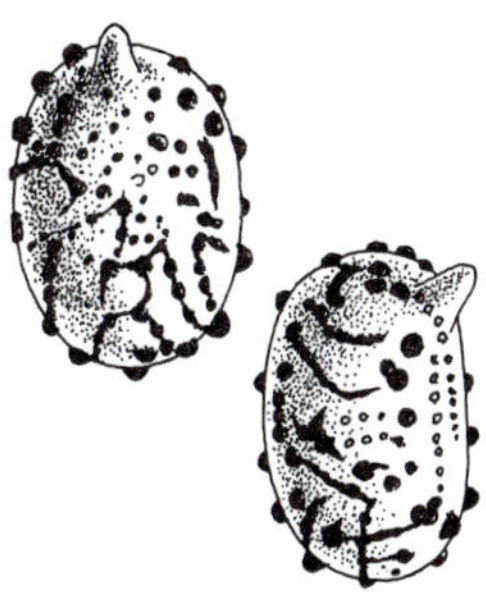

Spore of *Russula foetens*:
8–10 × 8–9 µm,
spiny, colourless

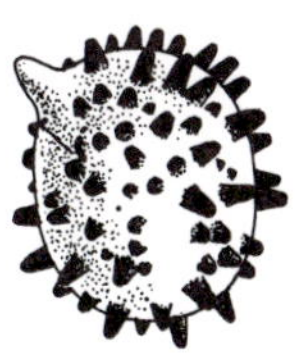

The shed spore print
is pale ochre

Russula foetens

Russula mustelina

Russula xerampelina

(Schaeff) ex. Fr. (s. str.)

Russula xerampelina was once considered to be an independent species principally on the basis of three features. The first is a marked trimethylamine smell (i.e. a smell of pickled herrings or boiled crayfish; another fungus with a similar smell is *Lactarius volemus*). The second distinguishing feature is the tendency of fruit bodies to turn brown on injury, the third is a typical chemical reaction with a 10 per cent green-vitriol solution. When touched with this, the flesh turns green. This is also why the Czech mycologists Melzer and Zvára, who elaborated a modern conception of the genus *Russula* in 1927, treated this species as belonging to the independent section *Viridantinae.*

R. xerampelina is a strongly variable species, and there seems to exist no colour hue absent from its cap cuticle. Furthermore, mycorrhizal relationships have arisen between individual varieties differing in colour and the woody plants upon which they depend. This is why some present-day mycologists regard these deviations as microspecies. The well-known French mycologist H. Romagnesi, a specialist in the genus *Russula,* distinguishes 15 independent species belonging to the section *Viridantinae.*

In the prevailing opinion, the typical form of *R. xerampelina* is a relatively robust russula with a bright reddish purple or carmine cap, sometimes tinged with black in the centre, about 10 cm in width, with a mostly pinkish red stipe, occurring in coniferous forests. This species, like all the others included in this group, has a mild, nonacrid context and is edible.

Spores: 8–11 × 7.5–8.5 μm
subglobose, spiny

Spore print

Russula integra
(L. ex Hook.) Fr.

Russula integra is one of the most common russulas found in summer and in early autumn, even if the weather is dry, in spruce and pine forests on a calcareous substrate. The fruit bodies are medium to large in size. The cap is 5–12 cm in diameter, semiglobular at first, expanded-convex later, slightly depressed at the centre, tough-fleshed when young. Its colour may be dingy dark violet, reddish brown, dirty ochre-brown, dull or violet-red, or chocolate or light brown. At the centre it either fades to shades of yellow or green or, on the contrary, becomes almost black-brown. The margin is blunt and only later densely striate. The cap cuticle is glabrous, remarkably shiny when dry, detachable to one half of its radius. The stipe is up to 7 cm long and 2–3 cm thick, firm, white all along its length, unchanging on injury. The gills are thick and broad, at first white and then pale ochre with a whitish reflex at the edge or tinged with sulphur-yellow. The flesh is white, unchanging, with a mild taste, and has virtually no odour.

This species is so extraordinarily variable in colour that an unambiguous identification of its members – especially in nature – is not always easy. After all, this applies to most *Russula* species which as a rule cannot be exactly identified without detailed microscopic examination. *R. integra* is a tasty edible mushroom.

Spores of *Russula integra*:
9–12 × 8–10 µm, elliptic-globose,
densely covered with long spines
up to 1.8 µm in length

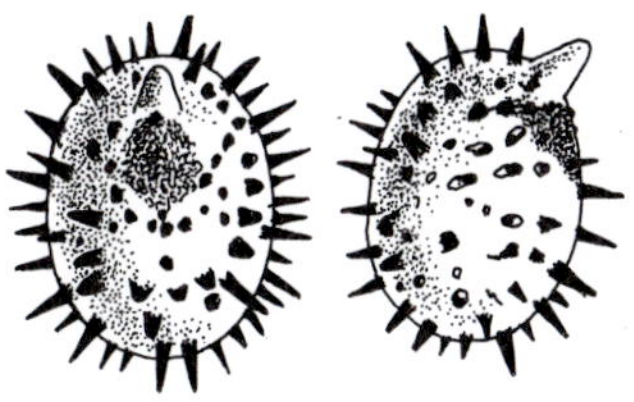

Spore print

Russula puellaris is very similar to *R. integra*
Spore: 8–10 × 7–9 µm, subglobose, spiny

Russula puellaris

Russula integra

Russula paludosa Britz.

A large russula of a lofty build and pleasant red colouring – this is perhaps the most distinctive characteristic of this species. The 6–15 cm wide cap is semiglobular when young, flatly expanded in age, beautifully red-coloured like ripe strawberries or rosehips. This colour often changes to orange or cream-yellow. The cap cuticle is glabrous, moist, shiny when dry, and readily peeling far towards the centre of the cap. The long (6–15 cm) and thick (2–4 cm) cylindrical stipe is white, very often tinged red or rosy on one side. The gills are rather crowded at first, becoming fairly distant later and alternating with numerous lamellules. They are up to 12 mm broad, pale cream-coloured when young, then pale ochre, sometimes with reddish edges (especially near the cap margin). The flesh is relatively firm, permanently white, and has a mild, sometimes penetrating taste.

R. paludosa is a typical species of damp coniferous forests on acid soils, occurring mostly in pine woods and less often in spruce woods. It can often be found growing in moss or sphagnum, and in billberry, red-whortleberry and molinia undergrowths. Under favourable conditions, it appears in large quantities in late summer in foothill and mountain forests. It is among the most tasty of edible russulas and is very popular.

Spores: 9–12 × 8–10 μm, broadly ellipsoid, verrucose to verrucose-echinulate, with 1.3 μm long warts or spines confluent at least in part

Spore print

Sickener

Russula emetica (Schaeff. ex Fr.) S. F. Gray

The Sickener is the most notorious of all the poisonous russulas. It is of medium height, its cap is 4–10 cm wide, slightly convex to flat, with a glabrous, smooth cuticle readily peeling to the very centre of the cap, sticky when moist, and shiny when dry. The cuticle resembles fiery red corn poppies in colour but it soon fades, especially after rain; some fruit bodies even have a pure white cap. The stipe is 5–10 cm long, 1–2 cm thick, persistently white all over, rarely tinged red, brittle and easily broken. The gills are close to subdistant, slightly ventricose, white or with a slightly yellowish reflection. The flesh is brittle, pink or light red under the cap cuticle, otherwise white, sometimes yellowing with age. It has an acid fruity smell and an intensively acrid taste. The spore print is pure white.

The Sickener grows on damp to wet soils on acid substrates overgrown with coniferous forests. It is often found in deep carpets of the mosses *Polytrichum* and *Leucobryum* or of *Sphagnum,* and, as one of the few representatives of its genus, it grows directly on peat.

It is possible to find several very closely related species (or varieties) under deciduous trees but some of these, on the contrary, prefer calcareous soils. All of them are poisonous as is the Sickener. Poisoning manifests itself by disorders of the digestive tract.

Spore: 8–12 × 7–9 μm, subglobose, with confluent warts and spines

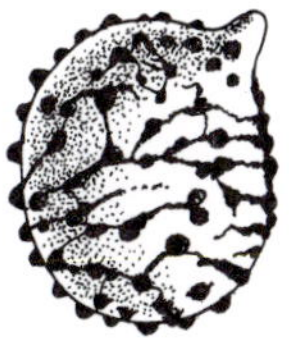

Also the relatively abundant *Russula lepida* belongs among red-coloured *Russula* species

Russula emetica

Russula sanguinea

(Bull. ex St. Amans) Fr.

When strolling through pine woods in late summer or autumn, we may find the beautifully coloured and shapely *Russula sanguinea* growing by moist, grassy forest paths. Its cap grows up to 10 cm in diameter; it is moderately fleshy, soon flat, broadly depressed, narrowing towards the margin, incurved, and often wavy. Its cuticle is blood-red or carmine, eventually rosy, discolouring in places to pale cream or even whitish. In rainy weather the cuticle is somewhat sticky, otherwise it is dry and matt, undetachable. The stipe is relatively short, tapering towards the base, red or pink for the most part, but often marked with lemon-yellow spots; the flesh also shows a tendency to turn yellow. The obviously decurrent gills are whitish when young, later they become dark cream-coloured, sometimes with reddish edges. The flesh is white, pink under the cap cuticle near the margin, with a slightly acrid fruity smell. The taste is usually rather pungent, sometimes bitter, exceptionally almost mild.

The taste of the flesh in many red-coloured russulas is acrid, though to a varying degree. Probably the most acridly tasting russula is *R. badia* whose flesh smells strongly of cedar wood. After tasting it a burning feeling remains on the tongue for a long time, sometimes resulting in a loss of sensitivity. The chemical composition of resinaceous substances which are assumed to cause vomiting and diarrhoea after the ingestion of acrid russulas is still unknown.

Spore: 7.5–10 × 6.5–8 μm, broadly ellipsoid, densely covered with obtusely conical spines up to 1 μm high

Spore print

Lactarius piperatus (Fr.) S. F. Gray

Fleecy Milk Cap *Lactarius vellereus* (Fr.) Fr.

Unusually large white fungi, commonly encountered in summer on the forest floor, mostly belong to two *Lactarius* species. Both occur gregariously, either in groups or in circles. They are also similar in appearance: the 8–18 cm wide cap is soon expanded, centrally depressed or slightly funnel-shaped, the stipe is short. The milk abundantly oozing from the bruised flesh is white, unchanging, and acrid. The only difference between the two species lies in the coating and the distance between the gills. In *Lactarius vellereus* (2), both cap and stipe are softly velvety subtomentose and gills are distant, while in *L. piperatus* (1) cap and stipe are glabrous and gills are dense. *L. piperatus* strongly resembles the closely related *L. glaucescens* whose originally pure white milk changes to greyish green on exposure to air. This is particularly apparent on the gills whose injured edges are beaded with ultimately drying drops of milk in the form of greyish green globules.

White *Lactarius* species can easily be confused with the Milk-white Russula (*R. brevipes*). This, however, has neither latex nor an acrid taste, and the gills often bear a pale bluish collarium where they are attached to the stipe.

All these species occur abundantly in forests of all kind, though *L. piperatus* prefers mixed forests. In spite of its acrid taste it can be prepared for table use by frying it on salted bacon, with onion and pepper. Otherwise it is hardly suitable for eating. The Fleecy Milk Cap and the Milk-white Russula are inedible.

Spores of *Lactarius piperatus*: 8–9.5 × 5.5–7 μm, colourless, indistinctly anastomosing, finely verrucose

Spores of *Lactarius vellereus*: 7.5–9.5 × 6.5–8.5 μm, colourless, subreticulate, finely verrucose

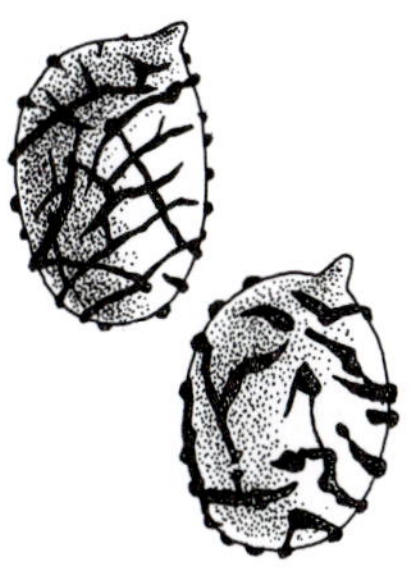

Lactarius piperatus — *Lactarius vellereus* and *Russula brevipes*

Woolly Milk Cap

Lactarius torminosus (Schaeff. ex Fr.) S. F. Gray

Among the large fungi there is a great number of species that are closely associated with the birch. The Woolly Milk Cap, a steady companion of birch woods, is certainly one of them. From July to October, its caps, up to 15 cm wide, slightly convex, deeply depressed at the centre, later almost funnel-shaped, red-hued with dark bands, appear among the fallen foliage or in grass. The Woolly Milk Cap is easily identified by its strongly involute cap margin covered with long, dense, whitish hairs. In young fruit bodies these hairs completely cover the gills, reaching up to the short, thick stipe which is of the same colour as the cap. The gills are crowded, narrow, whitish with a pink flush. Bruised flesh sheds white, unchanging latex with a strongly acrid taste. The spore print is a pale cream. The most recent research proved that the Woolly Milk Cap remains slightly poisonous after cooking. The toxic principle, most probably contained in the acridly tasting milk, causes vomiting and diarrhoea. In some countries this mushroom is boiled in salted water for 20 minutes and then pickled in vinegar to eliminate its negative properties.

The Woolly Milk Cap strongly resembles *L. pubescens,* distinguished by its paler cap lacking the bands. It grows under birches as well, frequently even under solitary trees outside the woods, in grass on pasturelands, in gardens and along roadsides. It is inedible.

Spores of *Lactarius torminosus*:
7–10 × 6–8 μm, broadly ellipsoid, subreticulate

Lactarius torminosus   *Lactarius pubescens*

Saffron Milk Cap

Lactarius deliciosus (L. ex Fr.) S. F. Gray

The best-known group of *Lactarius* consists of species whose fresh fruit bodies shed bright orange or wine-red latex where injured. The best example of this is the Saffron Milk Cap, commonly gathered as a tasty edible mushroom. Its latex is carrot-red when fresh; it does not change colour later – at most it dries to a paler shade. Its light orange-ochre cap turns almost ochre in places, turning green only slightly if at all. The Saffron Milk Cap grows in mycorrhizal association with pines. Its fruit bodies are sturdy, its cap bears distinct concentric stripes and may grow to 20 cm in diameter. The stipe is short and strong, never exceeding the diameter of the cap in length.

The very similar *L. salmonicolor* is more intensely orange and has a wine-red latex. It grows under firs.

However, the true double of the Saffron Milk Cap is *L. deterrimus,* which grows exclusively under spruces. Its slender fruit bodies usually have a long stipe and a green-banded cap; green spots develop also on the gills. After a longer time interval (sometimes as much as 30 minutes) its milk changes colour from the original orange to wine-red.

Several other species are included in the group of *Lactarius* mentioned above, yet their position in the system of fungi has not been definitely elucidated. Different opinions also prevail among mycologists as to the definition of characteristic features of *L. deliciosus* and *L. deterrimus*.

Spores of *Lactarius deliciosus*:
7–9 × 6–7 µm, ellipsoid, partly reticulate

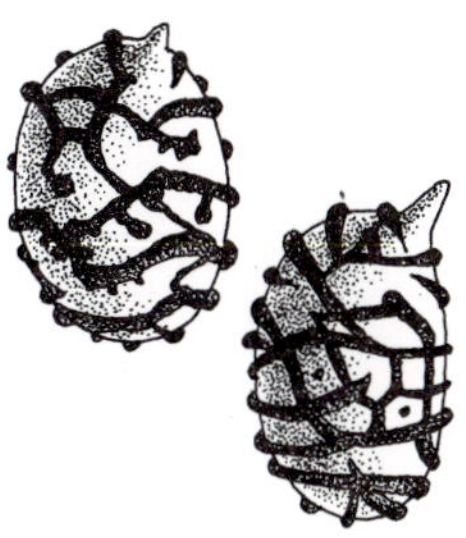

Section through the fruit body of *Lactarius salmonicolor*

Lactarius salmonicolor

Lactarius deliciosus

Lactarius helvus (Fr.) Fr.

In moist coniferous forests overgrown with moss, especially on acid substrates, whole swarms of this ochre-brown *Lactarius* commonly appear in summer and in autumn. It has a particular liking for soils saturated with water and is often found in peat-bogs among live *Sphagnum.* The cap is 5–12 cm in diameter, soon expanded, somewhat depressed in the centre, with relatively thin and brittle flesh, of a leathery buff colour, but sometimes with a reddish flush, matt, densely felted to minutely tomentose-squamulose, with no concentric rings. The stipe is only 1–1.5 cm thick, cylindrical, often rather long, relatively firm, hollow when older, light ochre-brownish. The gills are crowded, shortly decurrent, whitish and later ochre-yellowish. The pale ochre-pinkish or pale ochre flesh has a distinctive specific odour of soup spices and a mild taste. When cut it exudes small quantities of watery, bitterish latex not changing colour on exposure to air. The spore print is whitish.

Older mycological manuals recommend *Lactarius helvus* as spice for seasoning soups and sauces, although it is evidently poisonous. Symptoms of poisoning appear after the ingestion of several fruit bodies, usually accompanied by vomiting.

L. helvus can hardly be confused with any other species. Only *L. quietus* is slightly similar, but this smells of bedbugs, its cap cuticle is entirely glabrous, and injured flesh exudes cream-yellow, unchanging, slightly itchy latex. It is very abundant under oaks and also grows in dry places. It is harmless.

Spores of *Lactarius helvus*:
6.5–9 × 5.5–6.5 μm, broadly ellipsoid, subreticulate, amyloid

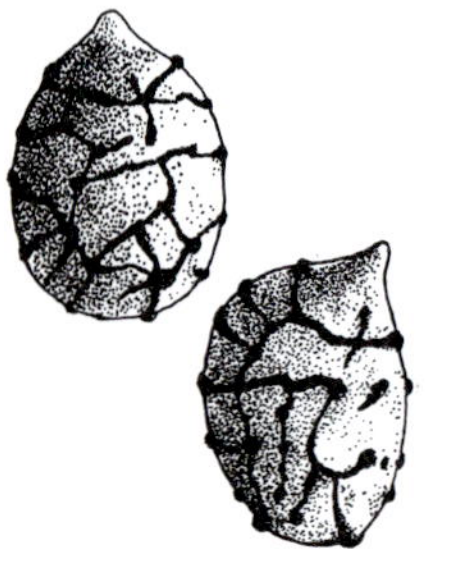

Lactarius helvus

Lactarius quietus

Lactarius volemus (Fr.) Fr.

This attractive fungus, well-known to practical mushroom pickers, grows in dry summer weather when other edible mushrooms are rather scarce. Unfortunately, recently it has been disappearing from European forests – just like a number of other fungi – and there are regions where it has become a rarity, although it used to be quite common there only 30 years ago. One of the reasons of this phenomenon is an ever increasing exploitation of forests accompanied by intensive wood production systematically decimating old forest stands, including pine woods, which are the favourite habitat of *Lactarius volemus.*

It cannot be confused with any other species, as its specific properties make it easily distinguishable: a red-brown to brownish orange cap, 5–15 cm wide, with an entirely glabrous, dry, slightly pruinose cuticle; a large amount of pure white, sweet latex oozing from the injured flesh of fresh fruit bodies. *L. volemus* turns brown with age and on injury, emitting a smell of trimethylamine, aptly compared to the smell of pickled herrings. The same smell may be noticed in *Russula xerampelina,* which also turns brown in age. The flesh of both these species colours green when touched with green-vitriol solution. The entire fruit body of *L. volemus* is hard and thick-fleshed, hence it is mainly the caps that are suitable for eating – either raw or fried on fat, or in mushroom mixtures.

Sometimes *L. volemus* is mistaken for *L. mitissimus,* a small, reddish orange species which, among other things, is distinguished by its acridly tasting latex; its flesh does not turn brown and there is no smell of trimethylamine. It is edible.

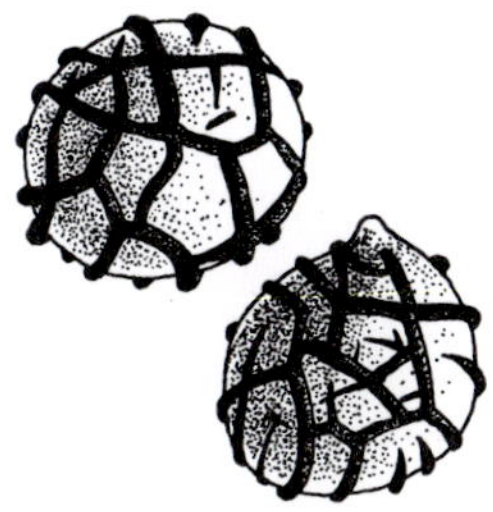

Spores of *Lactarius volemus*:
8–10 μm, globose, finely verrucose, subreticulate

Lactarius mitissimus

Lactarius volemus

Strobilomyces floccopus
(Vahl ex Fr.) P. Karst.

This peculiar bolete evokes a somewhat gloomy impression. Characteristic felt-like scales cover the whole surface of its 5–12 cm wide, umber- or sepia-brown cap. The large recurved scales are blackish at the top and almost erect near the cap margin. The woolly veil covering the tubes at youth leaves appendiculate fragments along the cap margin of fully developed fruit bodies. The whitish tubes as well as their relatively large angular pores gradually turn grey to brown, staining red where bruised. A fluffy annulus is clearly discernible on the cylindrical stipe. The flesh is whitish when young; in fresh fruit bodies it turns pale orange when cut, then dirty violet. Old fruit bodies have a markedly dry, cottony consistency, a mild taste, and an indefinable smell. The spore print is almost black.

Strobilomyces floccopus occurs in coniferous and mixed forests, and only rarely in pure deciduous woods, being most abundant under conifers on noncalcareous soils. As a general rule it grows solitarily, usually in summer and in autumn. In Europe it is the only representative of its genus; it is distributed throughout the temperate zone of the northern hemisphere. *S. floccopus* is edible; however, its general appearance and the excessively dry flesh of older fruit bodies do not contribute to its attractiveness as an edible mushroom.

Spore: 10–15 × 9–12 μm,
subglobose, with a reticulate ornamentation

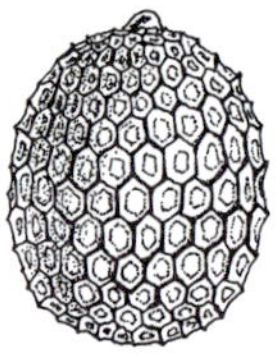

Optical section through the spore

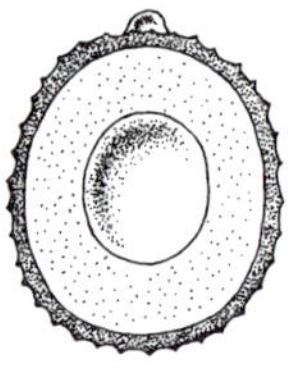

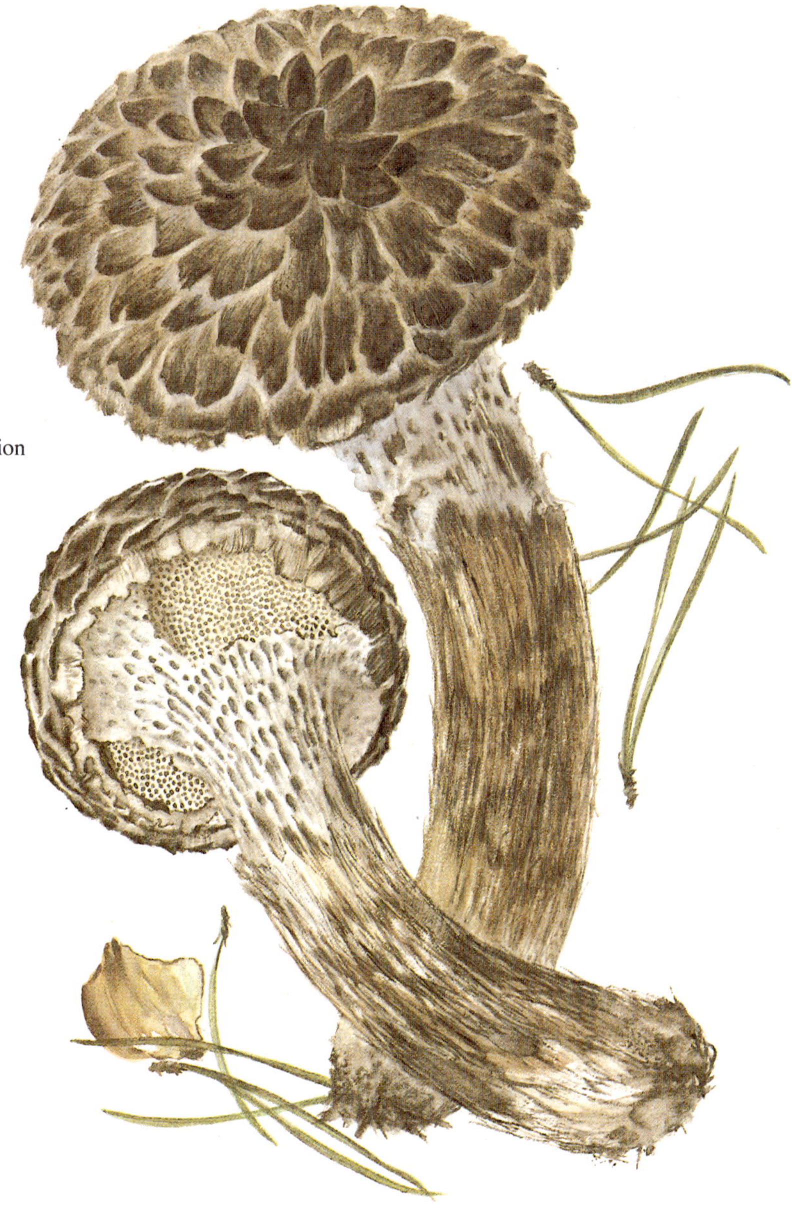

Porphyrellus pseudoscaber
(Secr.) ex Sing.

This single European representative of the genus *Porphyrellus* greatly resembles *Strobilomyces floccopus* in colour, but possesses neither scales (being smooth and glabrous) nor a veil. The spores are also different.

The whole mushroom has a sooty appearance. The 5–16 cm wide cap is pale grey at first, gradually darkening into various shades of olive- to umber-brown, staining almost blackish when handled. Its cuticle is dry, almost felted to velvety, and is not capable of being peeled off. Also the tubes, grey in youth, turn darker on handling, but sometimes they stain slightly bluish or even reddish. Their pores are angular with a denticulate mouth. The surface of the cylindrical or claviform stipe, frequently hooked at the base and of the same colour as the cap surface, is finely felted-punctuate and longitudinally striate. When cut, the pallid flesh stains bluish green or greyish red at first, then brown to black.

Some authors also distinguish *Porphyrellus porphyrosporus* whose flesh does not turn blue and the pores are pallid or greyish from youth. The spore print is red brown.

P. pseudoscaber occurs most abundantly in coniferous and mixed submontane forests, being less common in deciduous forests. In central Europe it belongs to the typical fungus species of submontane to montane spruce forests, as well as of fir-beech forests on acid soils. It is widespread all over the north temperate zone. Though edible, its taste is less appetizing than that of other boletes.

Spores: 14–20 × 6–7 μm,
ellipsoid-fusiform, smooth, brownish

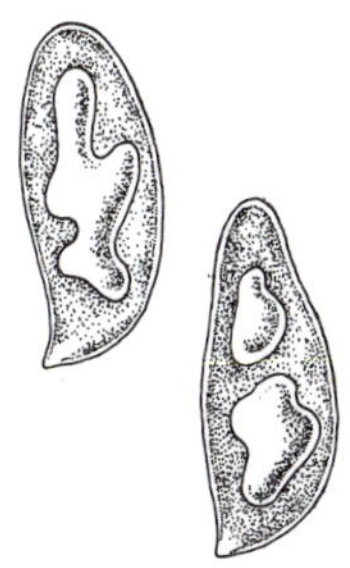

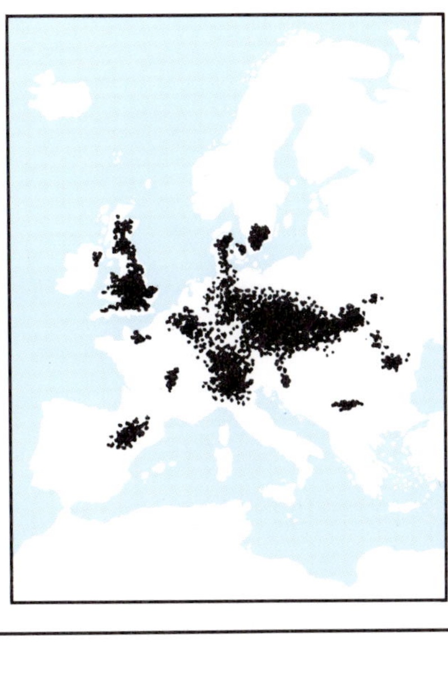

Gyroporus castaneus
(Bull. ex Fr.) Quél.

This neat bolete is by no means a common species. The 3–8 cm wide cap is slightly convex, soon flatly expanded, red-brown to chestnut-brown, with an almost velvety-tomentose surface, dry. The stipe is 8 cm long and 3 cm thick, the same colour as the cap; it is also finely tomentose-velvety, frequently striated and wrinkled, with a surface that often appears crumpled. Its context, white in youth, is soon partitioned into chambers or it becomes hollow altogether. The veil is absent. The tubes are white at first, then cream yellow, almost light lemon-yellow at maturity, often staining brown when handled. The tube pores are relatively minute, and the same colour as the tubes. The mildly tasting flesh is almost without odour. The spore print is pale yellowish.

The favourite habitat of *G. castaneus* are dry, warm and sparse woods on acid soils where it gives preference to open places exposed to sunlight. Sporadically it occurs also outside the forest in ditches, lanes, field margins and pastures. It grows from July to November and is widespread in the warmer regions of the entire north temperate zone. Though edible, its taste is not particularly appetizing.

G. cyanescens, the second European representative of this genus, is characterized by its flesh and tubes staining deep blue when cut or handled, and by a straw-yellow or yellow-brownish cap. It occurs in sandy pine forests or in mountain beech forests. It is also edible.

Spores of *Gyroporus castaneus*:
7–10 × 4.5–6 µm, ellipsoid-fusiform, almost colourless

Gyroporus cyanescens

Gyroporus castaneus

Distribution of *Gyroporus castaneus*

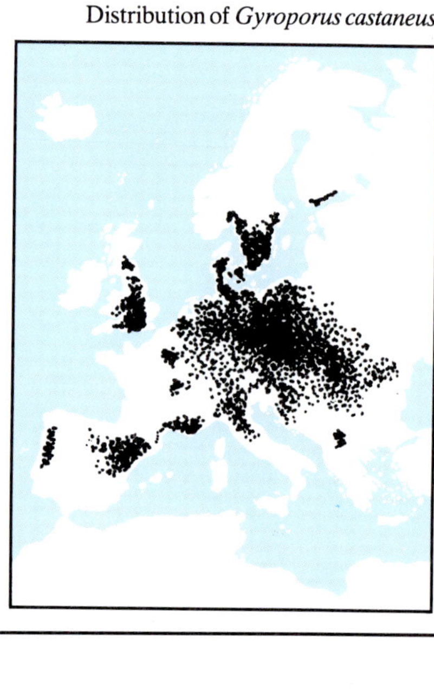

Boletus cavipes
Klotzsch in Fr.

Boletus variegatus
Bow. ex. Fr.

Boletus cavipes (1) is easily recognized by the shape of its fruit bodies on the one hand, and by its habitat on the other: it can usually be found under the larch, to which it is symbiotically bound. It also grows under solitary trees, often where larches are skirting woodland tracks. It occurs from July to October, preferring submontane forests and clayey soils. The colouring of the cap can vary considerably – sometimes it is pale lemon-yellow or orange-yellow, sometimes vivid red-brown. Its most conspicuous feature – besides the tomentose-scaly, soft and elastic cap – is the hollow stipe and large, elongate, radially arranged, decurrent pores, covered in youth with a white veil.

It is an edible mushroom with a relatively good flavour suitable for soups, mixtures, etc. Since meals prepared only of *B. cavipes* have a slightly astringent taste, it is recommended to prepare it in mixtures with other mushrooms, e. g. with some *Suillus* species.

B. variegatus (2) is a typical mushroom of pine woods on an acid substrate, particularly on sands. It grows from August to October, often in large quantities, and there are regions where its collection has become very popular indeed. Especially young fruit bodies are good. Its flesh has a peculiar, fruity-fungus smell reminiscent of *Scleroderma*. The cap surface is velvety to finely scaly, somewhat slimy when wet, the flesh turns blue when bruised.

Spore of *Boletus cavipes*:
8–10 × 3–4 μm,
ellipsoid-fusiform, pale yellow

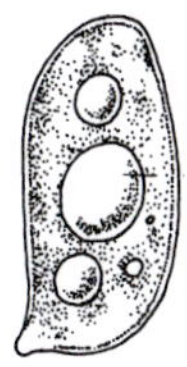

2

1

Spore of *Boletus variegatus*:
8–10 × 3.5–4μm,
ellipsoid-fusiform,
pale green-yellow

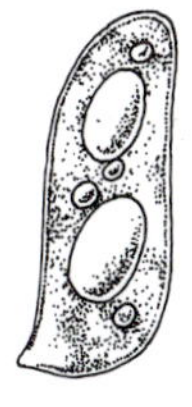

Boletus cavipes | *Boletus variegatus*

Gyrodon lividus
(Bull. ex Fr.) Sacc.

The genus *Gyrodon,* monotypical (i. e. including one species only) in Europe, differs from other boleti by having extraodinarily short tubes. They are only 2–5 mm deep and not easily detachable from the cap context. Their relatively large pores are irregularly sinuous, radially arranged, and clearly decurrent.

Gyrodon lividus has a 4–10 cm wide cap, whitish with an ochre shade, then rusty brown or olive-chestnut, clearly felted, sticky when moist, turning blue under the cuticle. The stipe is usually thin and short (3–12 cm long and 0.5–2.5 cm thick), often curved and eccentric, concolorous with the cap. The tubes and pores are at first lemon- to golden-yellow, then green-yellow and olive-brown, discolouring bluish green or brown when handled. The flesh is pale yellow, brownish at the base of the stipe, deep blue under the tubes, with traces of greyish blue and then of reddish brown in the remaining parts of the fruit body. It is softly spongy, with an indistinctive smell and a somewhat acid taste. The spore print is ochre-brownish.

This interesting member of the family Boletaceae grows on wet, often grassy, ground abounding in sedge tufts, exclusively under alders with which it lives in mycorrhizal association. It prefers calcareous substrates and grows from July to October. Its range covers the whole of Europe, extending eastwards beyond the Urals. It is a rather rare species which, though edible, is of little significance for practical mushroom pickers due to its sporadic occurrence and the excessively soft consistency of the fruit bodies.

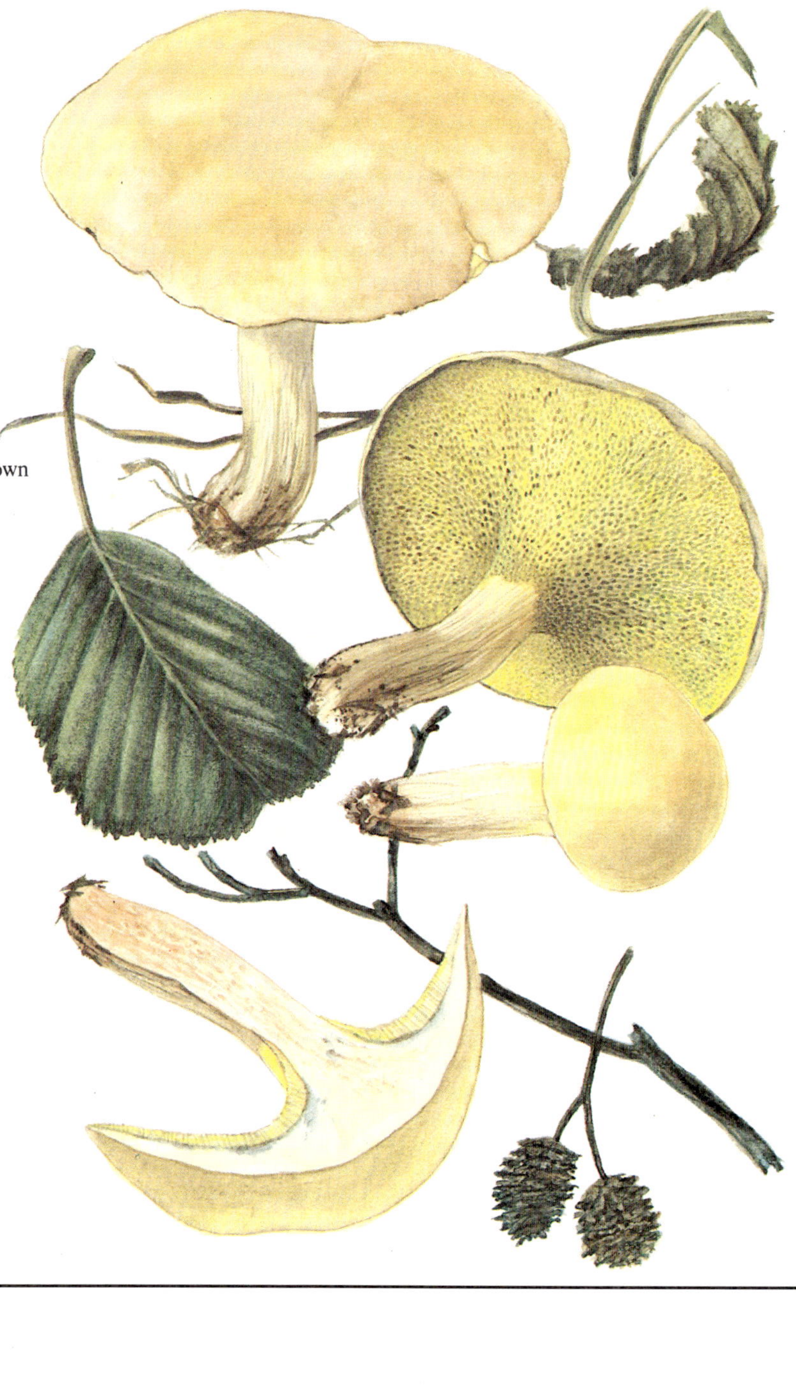

Spores: 5–8 × 3.5–5μm, globose-ellipsoid, pale yellow brown

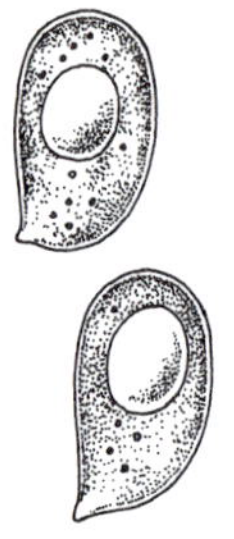

Suillus grevillei

(Klotzsch) Singer

Suillus grevillei occupies a significant position among boleti symbiotically associated (by mycorrhiza) with the larch. It can easily be distinguished by its orange- to lemon-yellow cap, very slimy when moist, with a readily peeling cuticle. The cap is 4–12 cm wide, remaining semiglobular for a long time. The annulus attached to the 5–10 cm long and 0.5–1.5 cm thick stipe is the remnant of a white or yellowish veil covering the lemon- to chromium-yellow tubes of young fruit bodies. The flesh has a pleasant, slightly resinous smell and sometimes stains pale greenish when cut.

In summer and in autumn, when the weather is favourable, this species can be found growing under larches in vast quantities. It is a very delicious edible mushroom. When it is gathered, its cap cuticle should immediately be peeled off: because of its excessive viscidity, anything that comes into contact with it will adhere to it. In young fruit bodies whose pellicle peels off less readily it is advisable at least to wipe off the slime.

S. grevillei is distributed throughout the north temperate zone, from lowlands up to the mountains – practically wherever the larch naturally occurs or is cultivated.

Also *Boletus cavipes* and, less frequently, *Suillus viscidus* may be found growing under the larch. Both these species are edible and tasty.

Spores: 10–12 × 3–4 μm, cylindrical-fusiform, pale yellow

Suillus viscidus Fr.

In older mycological literature *Suillus viscidus* is usually described under the name *Boletus aeruginascens.* Its cap is 4–13 cm in diameter, with a slimy and glossy surface, greyish white, yellow-grey, olive-grey or grey with a reddish flush, sometimes with darker striae, fibrillose-scaly when dry. In young fruit bodies the cap is connected with the stipe by a whitish or yellowish membranous veil whose remnants may be found at the cap margin of mature specimens. The tubes are whitish, then dark grey to brown-grey, with relatively large, angular pores passing over to the stipe apex in a retiform arrangement. The 6–8 cm long and 1.5–2 cm thick stipe is rather thin, yellow-grey, with a transitory ring. The stipe surface under the ring is covered with irregular pits. The flesh is white, later greyish, yellowish or brownish in the stipe, readily turning blue when cut above the tubes. It has an inconspicuous smell and a pleasantly sour, fruity taste.

This species grows in a mycorrhizal relationship with various larch species; in Europe it is the European Larch (*Larix decidua*) which *S. viscidus* accompanies high up into the mountains, to an altitude of 2,300 m. It occurs from May to October, ranging throughout the north temperate zone where it occurs both in established larch stands and under planted and cultivated larches. Although it is edible and relatively savoury, mushroom pickers usually prefer to bypass it due to its rather unattractive colouring.

In the Alps and in the High Tatras, the variety *bresadolae* has been found. It has a darker, red-brown cap and stipe, lilac rosy pores and a lemon-yellow flesh.

Spores: 8–14 × 4–5.5 μm,
ellipsoid-fusiform, pale yellow

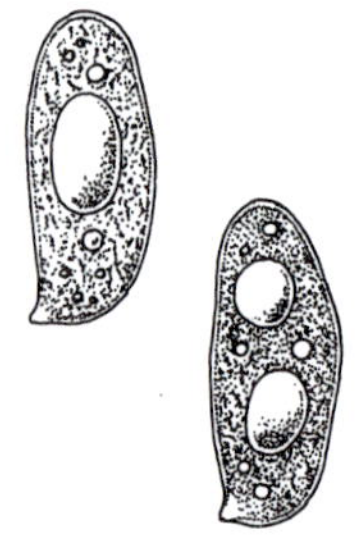

Suillus placidus
(Bonorden) Sing.

All species of *Suillus* are mycorrhizally dependent on conifers, some of them specializing in particular genera or even in particular species. *Suillus placidus* is linked exclusively to pines with needles arranged in whorls of five. Among the European species it is the Cembran Pine (*Pinus cembra*), among the North American species the Weymouth Pine (*Pinus strobus*), much planted and cultivated in woods and parks. It is worth noting that under Weymouth Pines it occurs in almost all situations where there is a number of these trees growing together, while under the Cembran Pine it is substantially less common. As an adventive (introduced) fungus species, this *Suillus* was first described by the German mycologist Bonorden from a Weymouth Pine culture in the Teutoburger Wald in 1861, while in the eastern part of North America (the original habitat of the Weymouth Pine) it was described as late as 1873 by the American mycologist Peck under the name of *Boletus albus*.

The fruit bodies of *S. placidus* appear most often gregariously from June to October. They differ from most of the other species of *Suillus* in their whitish or yellowish white cap, often with a lemon-yellow tinge, which in older fruit bodies sometimes passes over to a shade of violet. They have whitish yellow, later lemon-yellow tubes often exuding white droplets, and a whitish stipe covered with red-violet or brown-red granules. The veil is not developed. The flesh is white, yellowish above the tubes, sometimes tinged violet under the cuticle.

S. placidus is edible.

Spores: 8–10 × 4–5 µm, ellipsoid-fusiform, pale yellowish

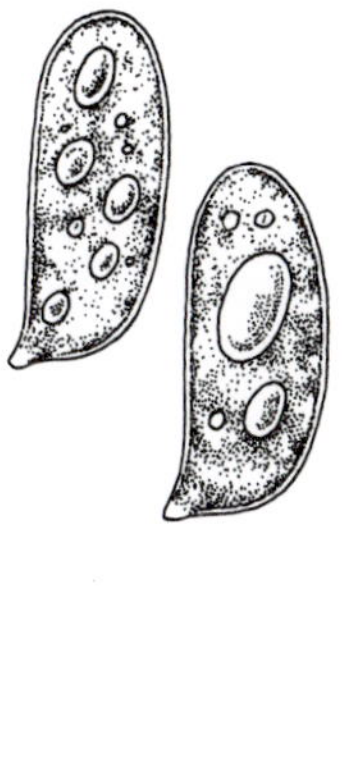

Slippery Jack

Suillus luteus (L. ex Fr.) S. F. Gray

This species grows exclusively under pine species whose needles are arranged in pairs. In Europe this is primarily the Scots Pine and the Mountain Pine (*Pinus mugo mughus* and *P. mugo rotundata*). It is only very rarely that the Slippery Jack appears under the European Black Pine and several alien species kept in parks and gardens. It occurs abundantly within the range of the mentioned pines which it accompanies up to the northernmost limit of their distribution, e. g. to northern Siberia and the Kola Peninsula.

The 4–12 cm wide cap has a chocolate- or yellow-brown, readily peeling cuticle, slimy and glossy when moist, radially fibrillose when dry. The tubes are pale yellow, then lemon- to golden-yellow, with relatively small pores. The stipe is cylindrical, lemon-yellow, strewn with yellow or brown granules above, brownish below, sheathed with a conspicuous tomentose-leathery veil. The flesh is whitish, then lemon-yellowish, with a pleasant fruity taste and smell.

It is the veil, which leaves an annulus on the stipe and sometimes persists at the cap margin in the form of scattered patches, that differentiates the Slippery Jack from the otherwise very similar *S. granulatus.* The latter is an excellent tasting edible mushroom.

S. bovinus has no veil either; it has a light ochre-brown cap with only a partly separable cuticle, the stipe is thin and finely fibrillose. It grows under pines on sandy soils. It is edible but of an inferior quality.

Spores of *Suillus luteus*:
7–10 × 3–3.5 μm, ellipsoid-fusiform, pale yellow

Suillus luteus — *Suillus bovinus*

Suillus fluryi Huijsm

In mycological literature *Suillus fluryi* is usually described under the name *S. collinitus.* This species is somewhat problematic from the taxonomic point of view. It is closely related to *S. granulatus* from which it is not distinguished by some mycologists. Other mycologists, however, believe it to be a ringless form of *S. luteus. S. fluryi* is currently identified as such by mycologists in eastern France, northern Italy and Switzerland, for there it occurs more commonly than in other parts of Europe.

S. fluryi differs from *S. granulatus* by its light ochre-yellow cap cuticle interwoven by numerous radially arranged dark brown fibres, contributing to the general impression of a rusty brown colouring. It has yellow-olivaceous tube pores exuding no latex droplets, and a stipe which is yellow only in its apical part, dotted red to black, and terminating in a pink-coloured base enveloped in often pink mycelial threads. Also the flesh of the stipe is pink in its basal part. The flesh turns violet when touched with potash-lye or soda-lye, and bluish green in green-vitriol solution.

S. fluryi makes its appearance at a later time than *S. granulatus,* from the end of September to November, i.e. at a time when the fruit bodies of *S. granulatus* are already starting to disappear. It grows mainly under the European Black Pine on dry, calcareous soils, i.e. in habitats similar to those of *S. granulatus,* but is much rarer. It is also edible.

Spores: 8–9.5 × 3.5–4.5 μm, ellipsoid-fusiform, pale yellow

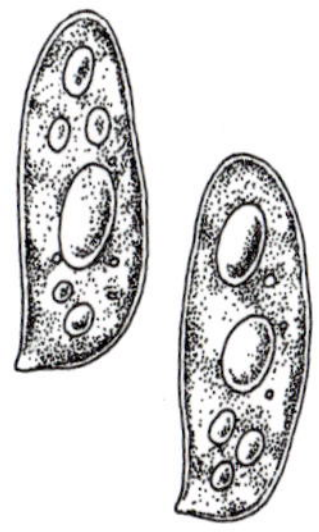

Suillus granulatus

(L. ex Fr.) O. Kuntze

Suillus granulatus has no veil, consequently no ring is present on its stipe. This species strongly resembles *S. placidus* from which it may be distinguished by the absence of the ring as well as by a lighter-coloured cap with always some shade of yellow-red, drying to ochre-yellow. The relatively short tubes are often decurrent, pale yellow or dirty yellow at first, ochre yellow to brownish yellow in age. A conspicuous feature of fresh fruit bodies are plentiful droplets of a milk-coloured liquid oozing from the tube pores. They adhere to the surface of the stipe immediately below the tubes, drying brown and changing into brown or reddish granules. The stipe is yellowish, later brownish, with a white mycelium at the base. The whitish to yellowish context rapidly becomes soft and watery and has a slightly sour, fruity taste and smell.

S. granulatus has developed a mycorrhizal relationship with pines having their needles arranged in pairs – primarily with the Scots Pine, Mountain Pines, and the European Black Pine. It occurs under these trees from lowlands up to the mountains; for example in the Alps it is capable of growing at an altitude of 2,250 m. It is often gregarious in grass along woodland paths or in the outskirts of pine woods and shows a preference for lime-rich soils. It is an excellent edible mushroom.

Sporadically we may also come across ringless forms of *S. luteus* which could easily be mistaken for *S. granulatus*. These forms, however, always differ in the colour of the cap, pores and stipe.

Spores: 8–10 × 4–5 μm, fusiform, yellowish

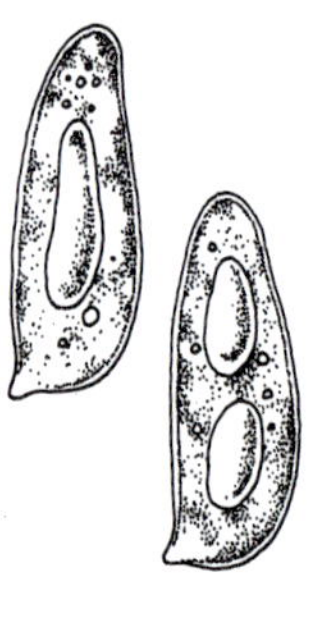

Shed spore print

Phylloporus rhodoxanthus
(Schw.) Bres.

Phylloporus rhodoxanthus is the only European representative of its genus. Originally it was described as a gill fungus under the name *Agaricus pelletieri,* later it was considered to belong to the genera *Clitocybe* or *Paxillus.* Its actual place, however, is among the boleti. The erroneous assumption that this is a gill fungus was substantiated by the peculiar structure of the hymenophore which in fact assumes the shape of thick gills interconnected by numerous transverse ridges of various height, forming variously sized retiform cavities in the basal part of the gills.

The general appearance of its fruit body resembles *Xerocomus subtomentosus,* having the same velvety-tomentose cap surface and a beautifully golden yellow hymenophore. The cap is 3–7 cm wide, olive to purplish brown. The cylindrical stipe is 3–5 cm long, 1–1.5 cm thick, narrowing downwards, often eccentric, reddish or yellow-brown. Also the spores show its close relation to the boleti.

This interesting mushroom grows solitarily in no particular abundance in deciduous, mixed and coniferous forests, most frequently along forest paths, in clearings among grass, on the walls of woodland ditches, etc., favouring places under oaks or pines. It grows from July to October and is widespread in the warmer areas of almost the whole of Europe, with the exception of the northernmost regions. It is edible, yet in view of its rare occurrence it should be protected, not collected.

Spore: 10–14 × 3–5 μm,
oblong- to fusiform-ellipsoid, pale yellowish

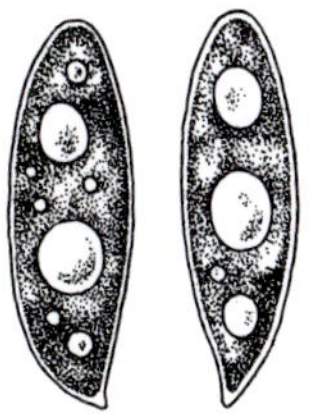

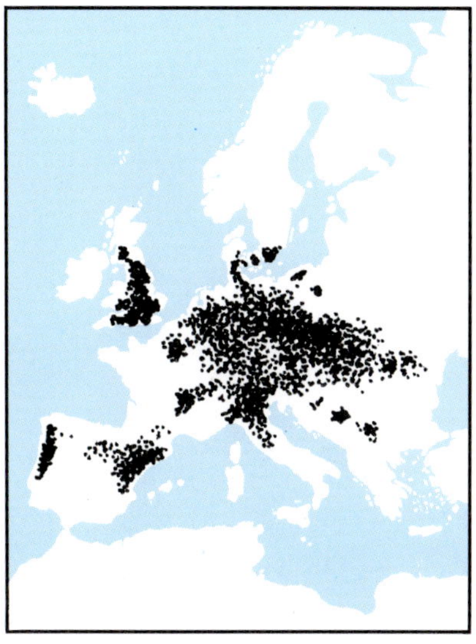

Xerocomus parasiticus

(Bull. ex Fr.) Quél.

Xerocomus parasiticus represents one of the sporadic instances of parasitism among boleti. Furthermore, it is a noteworthy species from the point of view of its ecological and phytogeographical distribution. It parasitizes and partly destroys the fruit bodies of *Scleroderma citrinum* and *S. polyrhizon.* As a rule, the fruit bodies of *X. parasiticus* grow in small clumps out of the basal part of the tuber of *Scleroderma* fruit bodies. Although the host is very common and plentiful, its parasite is rather rare. It has been reported from most European countries and from north Africa. It resembles a small *X. subtomentosus* in size, appearance and colouring. Its cap is 2.5–7 cm wide, subglobular in youth, expanded in age, leathery yellow or yellow-brown, changing to olivaceous, finely felted, slightly cracking round the centre when the weather is dry. The tubes are pale yellow, later lemon-yellow to olive-brown, and adnate. The stipe is cylindrical, rather thin, tapering downwards and hooked, pale yellow, brownish to olive-brown and finely dotted. The light yellow flesh is more deeply coloured in the stipe and above the tubes. Its taste is mild and its smell inconspicuous.

Due to the extreme rarity of its occurrence and the small size of fruit bodies, it is of no significance for practical mushroom pickers – on the contrary, its protection is most important.

Spores: 10–18 × 3.5–5 μm, cylindrical, yellow

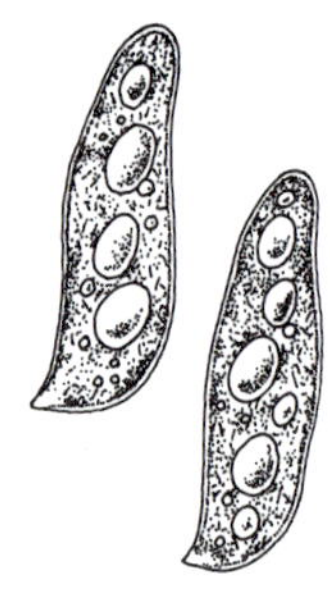

Xerocomus rubellus
(Krombh.) Quél.

In 1836, the Prague physician and mycologist V. J. Krombholz described a bolete found near Prague, greatly resembling the fairly common *X. chrysenteron* but distinguished from it by its conspicuously red-coloured cap. In the course of time, this mushroom was repeatedly described under various names (e. g. *Boletus versicolor* Rostk. 1844) and in various countries of Europe and North America. With a view to the date of description, however, Krombholz's designation is given priority.

In spite of the pronounced distinctive colouring of the cap in *X. rubellus,* its close affinity with *X. chrysenteron* can hardly be denied. This is why some mycologists have regarded it (and continue to do so) as a mere variety or form of the latter. In fact the only demonstrable difference between the two mentioned species lies in the lack of brown pigment in the cap cuticle of *X. rubellus.* This enables the red pigment to gain the upper hand and decisively to assert itself, while in *X. chrysenteron* it remains obscured by the brown pigment. Hence also the tubes and the context of *X. rubellus* are substantially brighter yellow to golden yellow.

X. rubellus grows predominantly under deciduous trees, mostly oaks, limes, hornbeams and beeches, especially at lower elevations, in sunny, warm places, frequently accompanying tree rows along roadsides; its occurrence is typically solitary and rather rare. Otherwise everything applying to *X. chrysenteron* also holds good about this species.

Spores of *Xerocomus rubellus*:
ellipsoid-fusiform, 9–17 × 4–6.5 μm

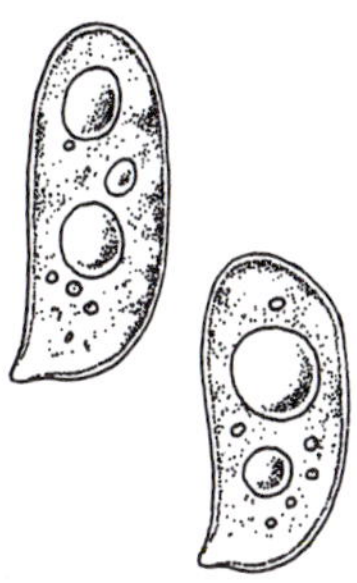

Xerocomus chrysenteron

Xerocomus rubellus

Bay Boletus

Xerocomus badius (Fr.) Gilb.

The Bay Boletus has a chestnut- or chocolate-brown, smooth, 5–12 cm wide cap, slightly sticky in wet weather. The tubes are pallid, later yellowish to yellow-green, turning green after handling, and the whitish flesh turns slightly blue when cut. The cylindrical stipe, frequently hooked and narrowed towards the base, is pale brownish, 3–8 cm long, 1.5–3 cm thick. The flesh has a pleasant mushroom-like smell and taste.

It grows profusely in coniferous forests, mainly in submontane regions, from summer to late autumn. Sometimes it grows directly from the foot of trees or on rotten stumps, not uncommonly also out of decayed spruce cones into which its mycelium has forced its way from the ground. It often appears in woodland margins where its fruit bodies are frequently hidden in low grass. There are regions where it proliferates in spruce and pine forests.

It is gathered as a tasty edible mushroom. The fact that it grows until late autumn and that it is rarely attacked by insect larvae is an advantage. However, the mushroom is a favourite food of rodents, thus it often happens that its fruit bodies bear traces of their teeth. It cannot be confused with any other similar species, perhaps only with the Bitter Boletus which is also abundant in coniferous forests. This, however, has a much lighter-coloured cap and a markedly reticulate stipe, pinkish tubes, and its flesh, not staining blue when cut, is repulsively bitter.

Spores: 12–16 × 4–6 μm, fusiform, pale yellow-brown

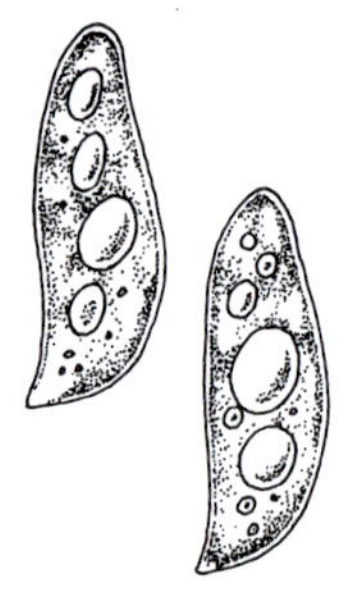

Xerocomus badius

Xerocomus subtomentosus

Red-cracked Boletus
Xerocomus chrysenteron
(Bull. ex St. Amans) Quél.

Xerocomus subtomentosus
(L. ex Fr.) Quél.

These two *Xerocomus* species can frequently be collected, often in large quantities, at times when no true boleti are available. However, their relatively soft flesh (which particularly applies to the Red-cracked Boletus) makes them impossible to transport and, in addition, they are often infested with other fungi covering them with 'mouldy' layers. This is usually the golden yellow coating of the imperfect fungus *Sepedonium chrysospermum,* a conidial stage of the pyrenomycete *Apiocrea chrysosperma.*

X. subtomentosus (2), being tougher than *X. chrysenteron* (1), is more highly appreciated by mushroom pickers. The two species, however, are frequently confused. *X. subtomentosus* has a 4–10 cm wide cap without any cracks, the cortex layer underneath the cuticle does not contain any purplish red pigment, the tubes are of a nicely rich chromium-yellow, the stipe is usually ribbed near the apex and narrowing downwards.

The Red-cracked Boletus, being an extremely variable mushroom, may sometimes be reliably distinguished only by its more or less rimose-areolate cap cuticle in whose cracks the carmine-red pigment is showing through; its presence may be ascertained even in uncracked fruit bodies by carefully scraping off the cuticle with a fingernail. The tubes of this bolete are usually pale yellow, sometimes green-yellow; the stipe is cylindrical, mostly not ribbed, red-tinged in places, ordinarily not attenuated at the base.

Both species grow in summer and autumn in deciduous and coniferous forests of the north temperate zone.

1

Spores of *Xerocomus chrysenteron*:
13–15 × 4–6 μm, fusiform, pale yellow

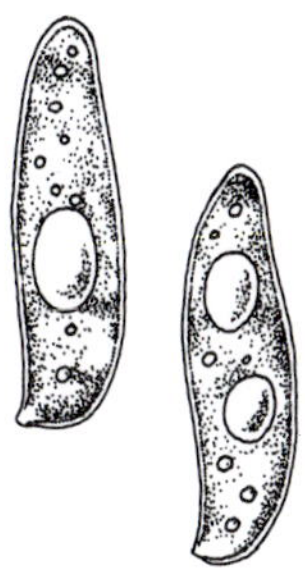

Spores of *Xerocomus subtomentosus*:
12–14 × 5–6 μm, ellipsoid-fusiform, pale yellow

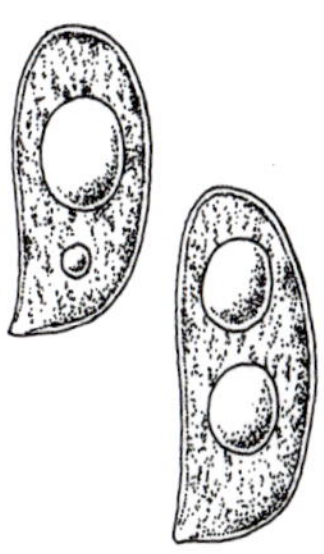

2

Xerocomus chrysenteron   *Xerocomus subtomentosus*

Xerocomus porosporus Imler

Species related to the Red-cracked Boletus also include *X. porosporus*. European mycologists treated it for a long time as *X. truncatus,* irrespective of the fact that *X. truncatus* is a different North American species. The only macroscopic difference between *X. porosporus* and *X. chrysenteron* is that the chinks in the cracked cap cuticle of the former are white or ochre-yellow, and not pink or reddish as is the case in the typical forms of the Red-cracked Boletus. This difference, however, primarily relates to fruit bodies growing in shady conditions. In fruit bodies of the Red-cracked Boletus exposed to stronger sunshine the cracks in the cap cuticle are also white, for they penetrate deep into the cortex; nevertheless, the rosy flush is discernible on at least parts of the cap. The two species can be reliably distinguished under the microscope by the shape of spores. In *X. porosporus* the major part of spores (not all of them) are truncate, while spores of the Red-cracked Boletus are always rounded at the top. There is no difference between the mentioned species in any other characteristic. As *X. porosporus* remained unidentified for a long time, the data about its range of occurrence are still incomplete. It certainly grows in several European countries and in North America, mostly in mixed forests under oaks, hornbeams, aspens, spruces and pines. It is edible.

Spore of *Xerocomus porosporus*:
12–15 × 5–6 µm, fusiform, yellowish brown

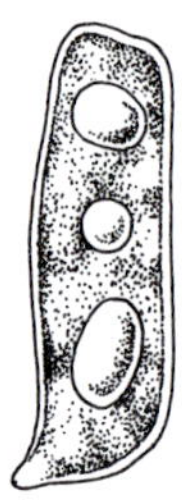

Detail of the cap
of *Xerocomus chrysenteron* sub lente

Xerocomus porosporus

Chalciporus piperatus
(Bull. ex Fr.) Sing.

The genus *Chalciporus* combines the qualities of the genera *Xerocomus* and *Suillus*. Its fruit bodies are small, the cap cuticle is dry or slightly slimy, glossy when dry, the stipe is thin, the flesh and the mycelium are yellow. It forms a mycorrhizal association with both coniferous and deciduous trees. In Europe this small genus is represented by two species.

Chalciporus piperatus has a 2.5–6 cm wide cap, rarely larger, semiglobular at first, then slightly convex, yellow-brown or ochre-brown; the tubes are up to 1 cm deep and are a shade of brown, with pores having a more pronounced red flush. The tough stipe is 3–6 cm long and 0.5–1 cm thick, often curved and narrowing towards the base. It is the same colour as the cap, bright yellow at the base. The flesh is whitish, yellowish to brownish in the cap, yellow in the stipe. It has a hot peppery taste and is almost odourless.

C. piperatus grows from July to November, being most common in pine woods. In deciduous forests it particularly favours beech, oak and hornbeam stands, and is also found under birches.

The variety *amarellus* is treated by some mycologists as an independent species. It is still smaller, with a cap only 2–3 cm across, lighter coloured, with yellowish brown tubes whose mouths are wine-pink or yellowish red. The flesh is slightly bitterish. It occurs very rarely under firs and spruces. Both species are edible only when mixed with other mushrooms.

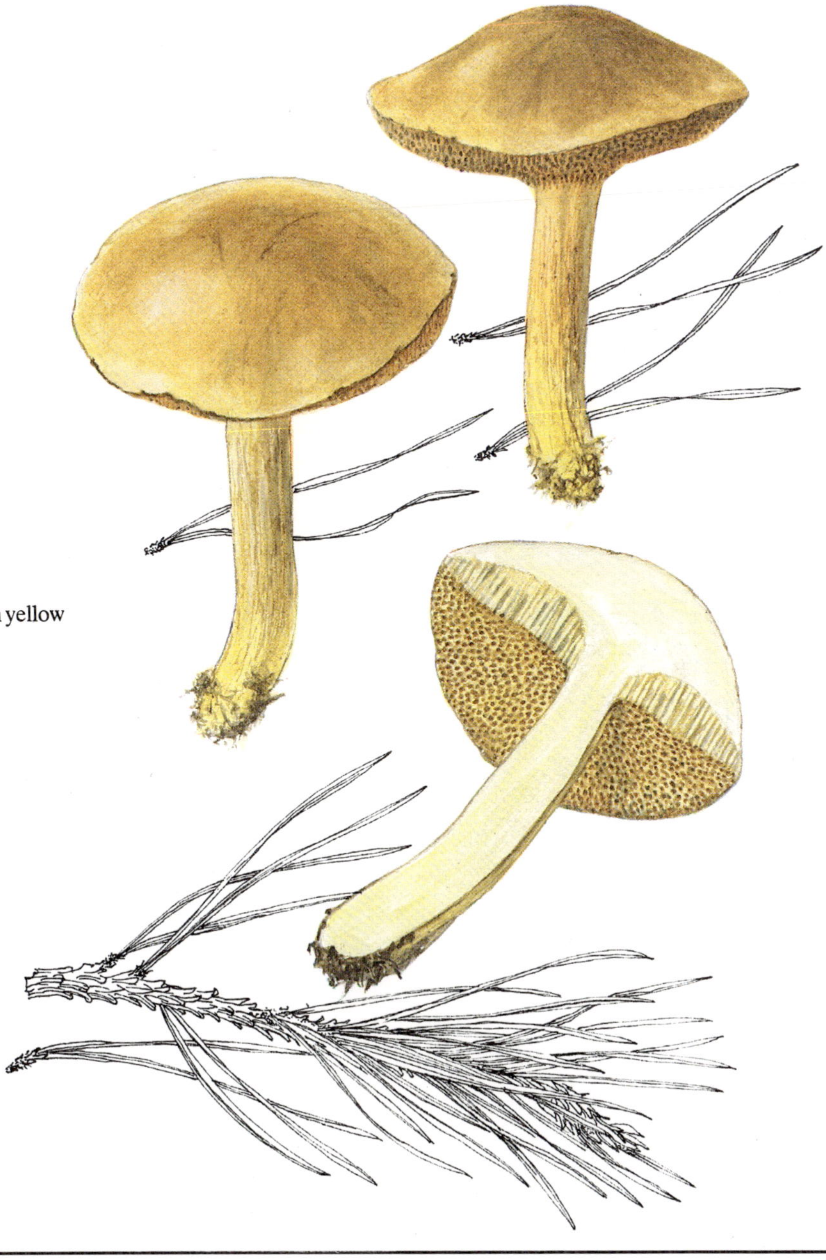

Spores: 8–12 × 3–3.5 μm, oblong-ellipsoid, light brownish yellow

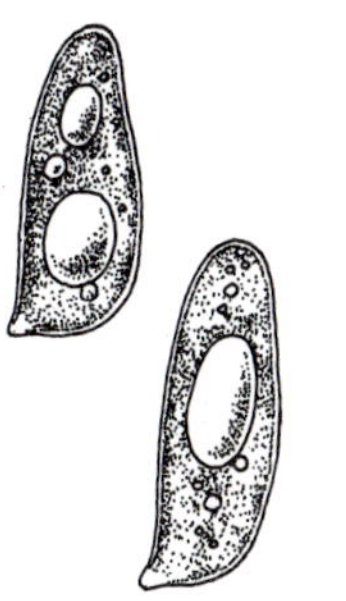

Boletus lupinus Fr. ss. Romagnesi

This is a robust, fleshy bolete with a 6–14 cm wide cap, subglobular when young, then semiglobular to slightly convex, ash-grey to whitish in colour, sometimes with a slight greenish tint, often with pink or red patches, and tinged yellow at the margin. The tubes are yellow, then ochre-yellow, up to 15 cm long, with predominantly carmine or dingy purple-red angular pores staining blue where handled. The shortly cylindrical stipe is pale yellow above, brownish below, sometimes with a reddish flush. For the most part it bears no reticulation, but only occasionally a fine reticulum is present below the apex. The flesh is yellow but pales in older specimens, it is brownish in the stipe base, staining blue throughout the fruit body when cut. It has an acid, rather unpleasant taste and smell, slightly reminiscent of *Lepiota cristata.*

Boletus lupinus is a very rare and hitherto little known species, related to the Devil's Boletus (*B. satanas*) which it greatly resembles. However, the stipe of the Devil's Boletus is marked with a reticulum reaching to its lower half at least, the cap is whitish or pallid brownish, never bearing red patches but often with a greenish tinge. Old fruit bodies of the Devil's Boletus emit a nauseous odour of decomposing flesh.

B. lupinus is most commonly found in the fallen foliage of beech forests in France, Italy, Switzerland, Denmark, Sweden, the Czech Republic and Slovakia. Like the Devil's Boletus, it is poisonous.

Spores: 12–17 × 5–6 μm,
narrowly almond-shaped, smooth, yellow-brown

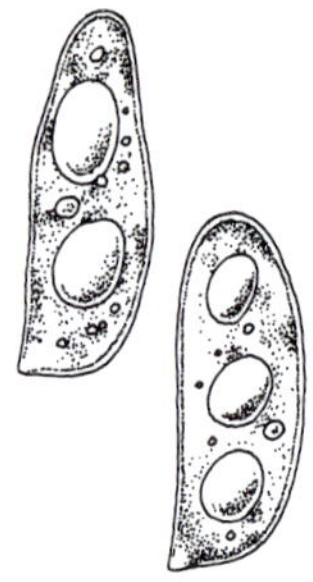

Red-stalked Boletus

Boletus erythropus (Fr. ex Fr.) Krombh.

The Red-stalked Boletus is a typical representative of boleti whose flesh instantly turns dark blue on exposure to air. The bluing of the flesh is best seen in fresh fruit bodies and represents a characteristic common to several species differing in the colour of the cap and stipe surface.

The cap of the Red-stalked Boletus can be 20 cm wide; as a rule, however, it is smaller, most often dark brown, with a felted to velvety and dry cuticle turning almost black in bruised places. The tubes are 2–3 cm deep, yellow-green, with relatively small pores which are yellow only when young; soon they acquire a vermillion to dark blood-red colour weathering to orange in age. The stipe is clavate-cylindrical, 2–4 cm thick, more intensely yellow above, red tomentose-punctate to scaly on a yellowish background in the middle, tinged olive-green at the base. The flesh is deep yellow, quickly changing to deep blue when handled or cut. The same applies to tube pores and to the stipe surface. It has a faint mushroom-like smell and a mild taste.

The Red-stalked Boletus grows mainly in spruce forests, sporadically in beech woods (here mostly on a calcareous substrate), and under firs. It is widespread throughout Europe, especially in submountainous and mountain forests. In the Alps it reaches an altitude of 2,000 m. It is an edible and tasty mushroom. Of course it must be well prepared; the ingestion of raw or insufficiently cooked fruit bodies causes stomach troubles.

Detail of the stipe surface of *Boletus erythropus*

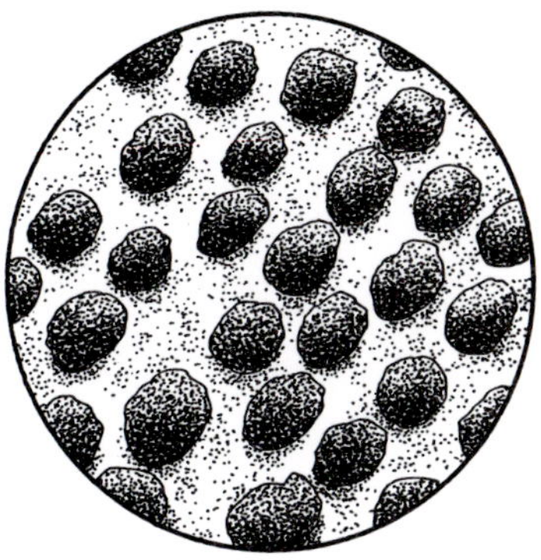

Spores: 13–18 × 5–6.5 μm, elliptical-fusiform, smooth, olive-yellowish

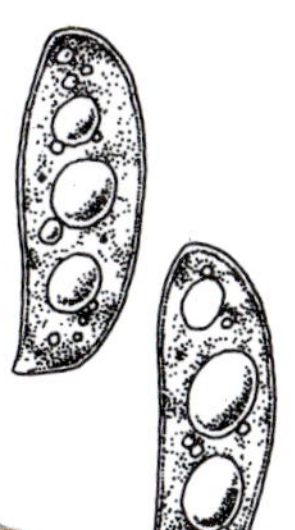

Boletus calopus also belongs among blue boleti. Its flesh, however, does not turn so intensely blue and is offensively bitter

Boletus erythropus

Boletus luridus
Schaeff. ex Fr.

Boletus luridus is the second most widely known and also most commonly found blue bolete. The cap of *B. luridus* attains 5–20 cm in diameter. Its cuticle is relatively pale in various light yellow or olive-yellow to brownish shades, often it is almost yellow or yellow-orange, but may also be pale carmine-red; it is finely felted, staining dark or blue when handled. The tubes are yellow, tinged olive-green or lemon-yellow when young, later yellow-green to dirty olive, with usually orange but also brick-red to blood-red pores. The oblong-clavate, 2–8 cm thick stipe is yellow below the apex, in the middle and lower down the yellow colouring passes into red, near the base it becomes dark wine-red, even blackish brown in places. The stipe surface is covered all along its length by a coarse, red, long-meshed reticulum. The flesh is pale yellow, in the stipe usually wine-red; just like the tubes and the stipe surface, the cut flesh instantly turns ink-blue, while the red-coloured places stain violet. The flesh has a faint mushroom-like taste and smell.

This bolete, characterized by considerable colour variability, occurs predominantly in deciduous forests – mainly under oaks and beeches. It may also appear under conifers, mostly on a calcareous substrate and in warmer regions. It grows from May until the autumn. It is particularly the presence of reticulation on its stipe that constitutes the difference between the Red-stalked Boletus and the species discussed here. It is edible, yet the same applies to it as to the Red-stalked Boletus: the ingestion of raw or insufficiently cooked fruit bodies causes vomiting.

Spores: 10–16 × 5.5–6 μm, spindle-shaped elliptical, smooth, brown-yellow

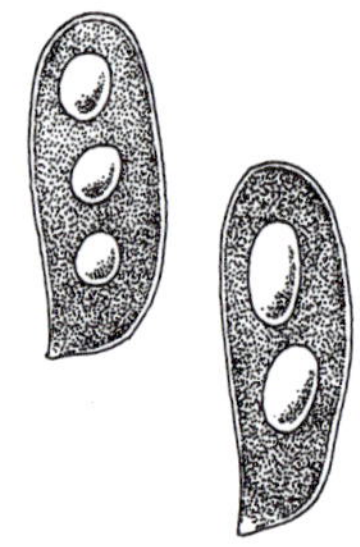

Detail of the stipe surface

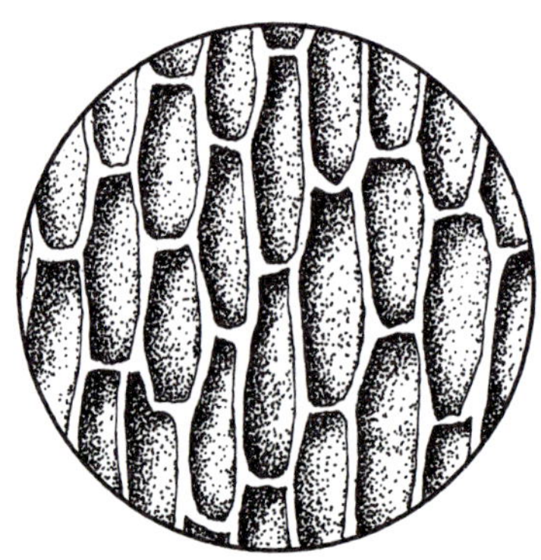

Devil's Boletus
Boletus satanas Lenz

Boletus calopus Fr.

The true Devil's Boletus (1) is a sturdy, thick-fleshed mushroom with a pale grey or silvery brown, 10–20 cm wide cap; the pores of the yellow tubes are vivid carmine-red. The stipe is 5–12 cm long and 3–6 cm thick, reddish in its central part, and decorated with a fine reticulum. The pale yellowish flesh turns slightly bluish when cut, but this colouration disappears again later. It has a mushroom-like smell soon becoming unpleasant, reminiscent of sweat; old fruit bodies emit a vile odour of decomposing meat.

It is confined to deciduous forests, mostly to oak-hornbeam stands frequently including lime and hazel. It appears in July and August almost exclusively on calcareous substrates, accompanying communities of thermophilous plants. The Devil's Boletus is extremely poisonous; a small bit of flesh taken from a fresh fruit body is enough to cause intensive vomiting.

Boletus calopus (2) has a light grey or ochre-brown, dry cap 6–12 cm in width, and pale yellow tubes with yellow pores. The stipe is yellow below the apex, red and reticulate at the base and in the middle, 3–8 cm long and 2–5 cm thick. The pale yellow flesh stains blue when cut and later discolours to a dirty grey-yellow. The taste of the flesh in the whole fruit body is strongly bitter.

B. calopus grows in summer and in autumn in coniferous, more rarely in deciduous forests, being more common at lower-mountain elevations.

Spore of *Boletus satanas*:
10–15 × 6–7 μm, spindle-shaped,
yellowish olive-green

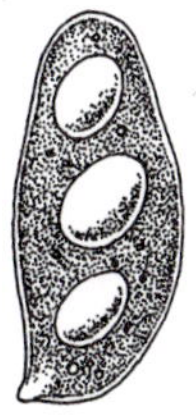

Spore of *Boletus calopus*:
10–13 × 4–5 μm, spindle-shaped,
pale yellowish

Boletus satanas

Boletus calopus

Boletus impolitus Fr.

Some Boletaceae (predominantly representatives of the genus *Boletus*) belong to the significant thermophilous species of fungi accompanying forests in regions inhabited by the thermophilic flora. *Boletus impolitus* can be included in this group. It is strictly confined to regions with prevailing deciduous forests, where it likes to grow in sunny places and warm woodland margins, but it also occurs in old parks under oaks, beeches, hornbeams, limes, and other deciduous trees. It prefers calcareous soils. Its main vegetation period is June and July, but it can also be found in autumn. It is readily recognized by its robust stature. The cap may attain as much as 25 cm in diameter; it is pale yellowish to light brownish, the tubes are pale lemon-yellow to golden-yellow, with a greenish tint in age, not changing colour when handled. The stipe is 2.5–8 cm thick, oblong-clavate or cylindrical, yellowish, always lighter-coloured under the tubes, shading to deeper brown or reddish at the base. This reddish colouring is sometimes apparent only in the youngest fruit bodies but soon disappears. The stipe surface is fibrillose-scaly. The flesh is whitish or lemon-yellowish, unchanging when exposed to air, and sometimes reddish in the stipe base. It has a mild taste and a characteristic smell of phenol, often only faint in raw fruit bodies. The odour becomes most conspicuous when the fruit bodies are being cooked. It is for this reason that mushroom pickers usually avoid collecting *B. impolitus,* though it is an edible mushroom.

Spores: 10–15 × 4–5 μm, ellipsoid-fusiform, yellowish

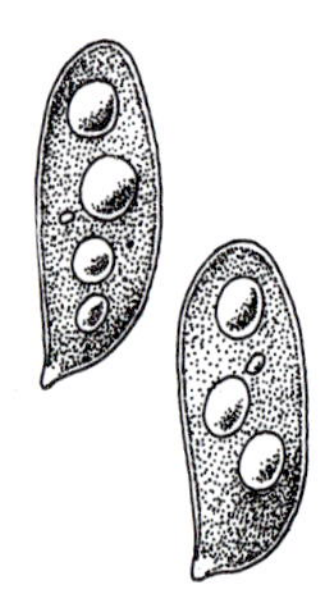

Boletus aereus Bull. ex Fr.

This beautiful bolete is an explicitly thermophilous species. It accompanies old oak and other deciduous forests situated without exception in protected, warm localities with thermophilous flora. It is more common in southern and southeastern Europe and in the southeastern parts of North America than in central Europe. It is characterized by a dark chocolate- to black-brown, 5–20 cm wide cap bearing a dry, finely velvety cuticle becoming later glabrous and sometimes breaking up into irregular patches. In sharp contrast with the dark colour of the cap are the white tube mouths turning green-yellow with an olive tinge upon maturity. The stipe is 5–10 cm long and 2–4 cm thick, substantially lighter-coloured than the cap, covered with a fine reticulum on the surface. The flesh is white, only under the cap cuticle is it light flesh-brownish, unchanging, sometimes staining slightly pink when cut. It is relatively firm and softens only with age. It has a mild taste and almost no odour when fresh, but when dried it emits a pleasant mushroom-like smell.

B. pinophilus is similar to *B. aereus* in colouring and appearance but for its cap which is dark red-brown with a pinkish margin. It appears as early as May in pine forests (rarely also under oaks). These two species are among the best edible mushrooms.

Spores of *Boletus aereus*:
11–17 × 4.5–6 μm, spindle-shaped elliptical, smooth, brown-yellow

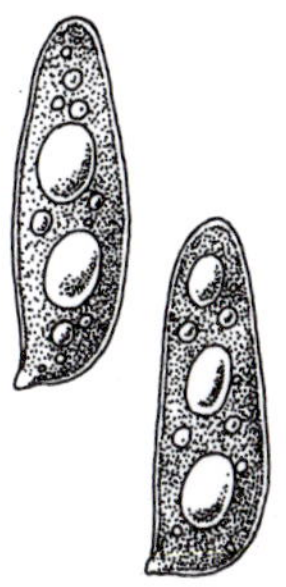

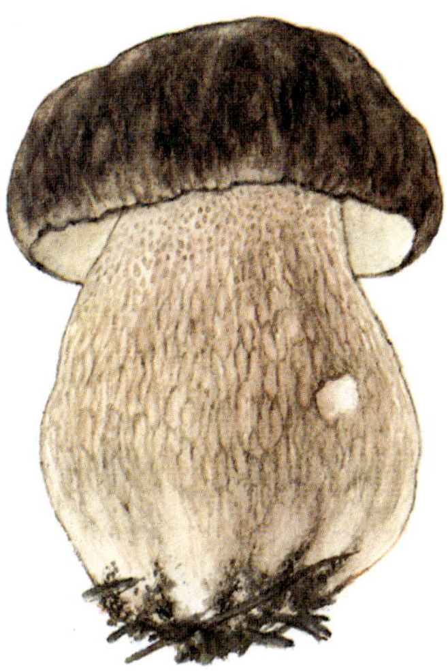

Boletus pinophilus

Boletus aereus

Boletus aestivalis

(Paulet) ex Fr.

Besides the Edible Boletus, *Boletus aestivalis* is the second best-known and most popular member of this genus. It is widespread in the whole of western and central Europe, and also occurs in North America and north Africa. Its favourite habitat are deciduous forests; it is far less common in mixed and coniferous forests. It can be found mainly under oaks and beeches on whose roots it lives in mycorrhiza, but it is capable of establishing such a relationship with other deciduous trees as well. In Europe it can also form mycorrhizal associations – though rather exceptionally – with exotic trees kept in parks or planted in woods; thus, for instance, it was found under the North American oaks *Quercus rubra* and *Q. palustris*. However, finds have been reported even from established coniferous monocultures, from spruce, fir and pine forests where deciduous trees are entirely absent.

B. aestivalis grows from May until autumn. It differs from the related and very similar Edible Boletus by the structure and appearance of the cap cuticle, as well as by the surface of the stipe. The cuticle of *B. aestivalis* is matt, finely velvety to tomentose, lighter coloured, pale grey-brown, light yellowish grey to leathery brown, often cracking in age. The stipe is uniformly pale brownish, marked with a coarse brownish reticulum. This reticulum either covers the whole stipe or reaches to more than half the length of the stipe.

Spores: 14–16 × 4–5 μm, spindle-shaped, brown-yellow

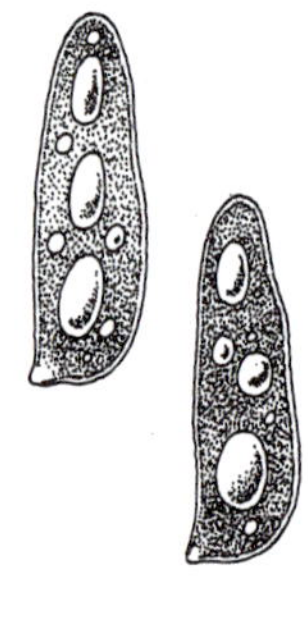

Edible Boletus, Cèpe

Boletus edulis Bull. ex Fr.

This is the most popular mushroom growing wild, and is collected both for table use and for the purposes of large-scale industrial production. As a mycorrhizal fungus, the Edible Boletus is associated primarily with spruces but occurs also in deciduous forests, though far more rarely. Under specific conditions its mycelium is capable of forming mycorrhizal relationships also with oaks and beeches, eventually with other deciduous trees. This is in fact no exceptional phenomenon, as some species live in mycorrhiza with both deciduous and coniferous trees (e. g. *Xerocomus chrysenteron* and *X. subtomentosus*).

The range of the Edible Boletus is extremely variable, and there are different views about the classification of individual variations – from mere forms and varieties to subspecies and independent species. In its typical form the Edible Boletus has a deep brown to black-brown, smooth and glossy cap cuticle, slightly felted only in youth; in adult specimens it is often slimy in wet weather. It is always somewhat darker than in the related *Boletus aestivalis* – of course with the exception of the youngest fruit bodies still covered by needle leaves, whose caps are entirely white. At maturity the stipe is white only near the apex, while in its lower parts it is brownish; the reticulum reaches no higher than half the length of the stipe.

The Edible Boletus is distributed throughout the north temperate zone, though unevenly. It is rare in North America, where it is replaced by the related *B. clavipes.*

Spores: 15–17 × 4–15 μm, fusiform, olive-brown

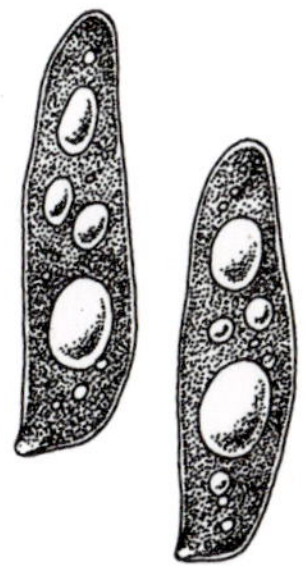

Bitter Boletus

Tylopilus felleus (Bull. ex Fr.) P. Karst.

The greyish pink spore print is one of the main diagnostic features differentiating the genus *Tylopilus* from the so-called true boleti of the genus *Boletus*. The 'true' boleti have a brown or olive-brown spore print. Most of the species included in the genus *Tylopilus* (about 10 of which are known) do not form any mycorrhizal associations but grow as saprophytes on forest humus and very putrescent wood. In Europe this genus is represented by one species only, i. e. by the Bitter Boletus – most of the others are widespread in North America.

As a rule, the Bitter Boletus grows in coniferous (mainly spruce and pine) forests on acid soils, both in lowlands and in the mountains. It often grows on decaying stumps overgrown with moss. In the past decade it has been expanding its range, frequently flooding the forests as a weed fungus. Its neat fruit bodies strongly resemble those of the Edible Boletus but their offensive taste makes them uneatable. Careless or inexperienced mushroom pickers are disappointed by the food prepared with these fungi: their distasteful bitterness cannot be eliminated by any processing. Nonetheless, the Bitter Boletus may readily be distinguished from true boleti when picking them – not only by their bitter taste but, even without tasting them, primarily by their greyish pink or flesh-pink tubes, mostly conspicuously pulvinate (this applies especially to older fruit bodies). Also the reticulum covering the stipe is substantially coarser, with meshes larger and deeper than in the Edible Boletus.

Shed spore print

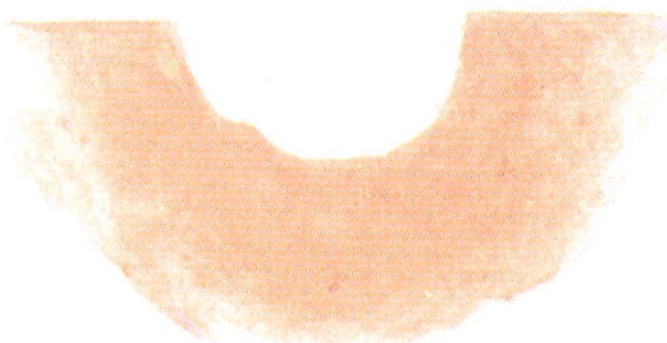

Spores of *Tylopilus felleus*:
12–15 (to 18) × 3–4.5 µm,
fusiform, almost colourless

Detail of the stipe surface

Tylopilus felleus

Fruit bodies of *Boletus edulis* can be mistaken for those of *Tylopilus felleus*

Krombholziella aurantiacа

(Bull. ex St. Amans) R. Maire

Boleti that are very popular are those whose conspicuous red-orange caps give colour to dark forest stands of aspen or birch. *Krombholziella aurantiaca* is associated with aspens, under which mushroom pickers frequently search for it. The stipe is 6–15 cm long and 1–3 cm thick, covered in youth with whitish, in age with red-brown to brown-orange scales. The cap is 4–15 cm wide, dark brown-orange to red-brown, pulvinate. The tubes are whitish. The flesh is white; when cut, it turns greyish pink at first, then black. These are the essential features for distinguishing this species from the similar *K. rufescens*.

K. aurantiaca is an excellent and pleasant-looking edible mushroom; the fact that it is rarely infested by insect larvae is one of its advantages. It grows in summer (sometimes as early as May) and in autumn from lowlands to the mountains in the whole north temperate zone.

Spores: 13–16 × 4–5 μm, fusiform, ochre-brown

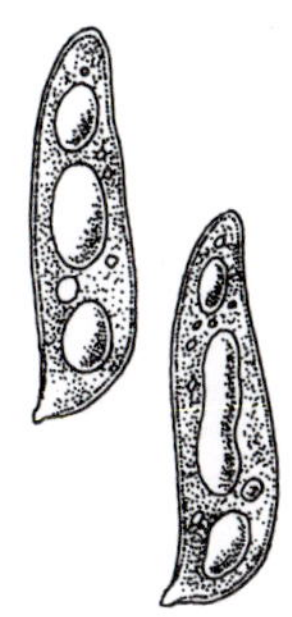

Detail of the stipe cuticle

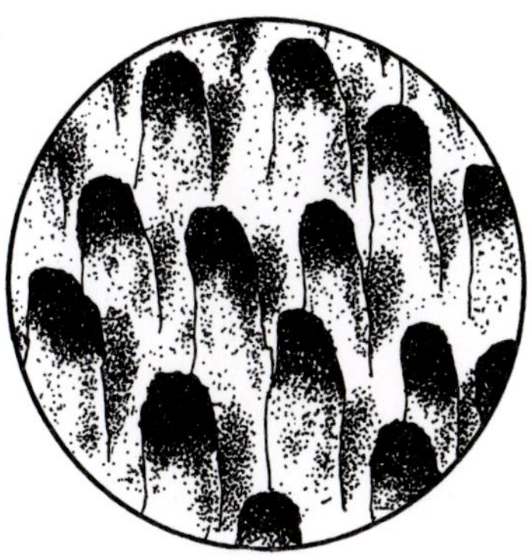

Krombholziella rufescens

(Konr.) Šut.

The second of the couple of boleti with a reddish orange cap is *Krombholziella rufescens,* which grows exclusively under or near birches. In contrast to *K. aurantiaca,* it has a lighter-coloured cap that is deep orange-brown to yellow-brown. The cap is 5–15 cm wide, pulvinate, usually with a membranous border. The stipe is 6–15 cm long and 1–3 cm thick, the minute scales covering it are black or brown-black. The tubes are tinged grey already when young. When injured or cut, the originally whitish flesh slowly turns grey-violet with a pink flush, and greenish blue in the basal portion of the stipe. This colouring, however, is not an exclusive characteristic, since it also sometimes appears in *K. aurantiaca.*

Like *K. aurantiaca,* this species is also edible, very tasty, and suitable for all culinary purposes. It grows in summer and autumn in most countries of the north temperate zone where it shares the habitat of the birch.

Some closely related species grow under other trees, e. g. *Leccinum vulpinum* under pines and *L. piceinum* under spruces. Characteristic of both these species is a rusty brownish orange cap whose colouring resembles that of *Lactarius rufus.* The cap of *Leccinum quercinum,* growing under oaks, has a more pronounced whitish shade.

Spores: 13–16 × 4–5 μm, fusiform, yellow-brown

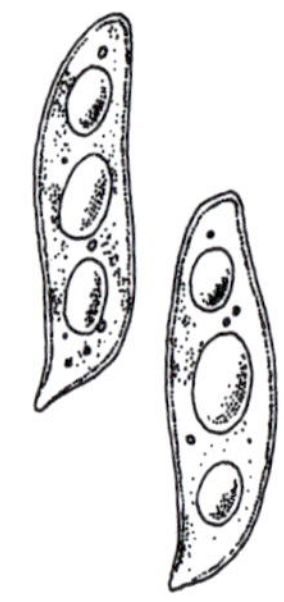

Detail of the stipe surface

Krombholziella oxydabilis (Sing.) Šut.

This mushroom strongly resembles *Krombholziella rufescens.* Its cap is dark brown, sometimes grey-brown with a blackish tinge, occasionally ochre to pale brown. The stipe is grey to blackish scaly on a white background. The originally white flesh stains pink to red when cut, which applies either to all of it or at least to the parts adjacent to the cap cuticle. The reddened places never turn violet or black. The flesh in the base of the stipe is often of a dingy pale yellow or only yellow, staining blue or blue-green when cut. The cap cuticle is slightly dark fibrillose, almost cream-coloured, but not felted; it is dry, turning viscid only in long-lasting rains but soon drying again.

K. oxydabilis occurs under birches in colder regions and in the mountains (up to the altitude of 1,500 m) in the temperate zone of the northern hemisphere. It is common particularly in northern and northeastern Europe, in Siberia, in the Far East and in North America. Data concerning its occurrence in central Europe are most probably incorrect, as they evidently refer to *K. thalassina. K. thalassina* has an ash-green cap, the bottom part of its stipe is green. It also grows under birches.

The flesh of *K. duriuscula* also bruises reddish but is grey-violet to bluish near the apex of the stipe and at its base. It grows exclusively under poplars. All these species are edible and tasty.

Spores of *Krombholziella oxydabilis*:
13–21 × 5–6.7 µm, fusiform, honey-brown

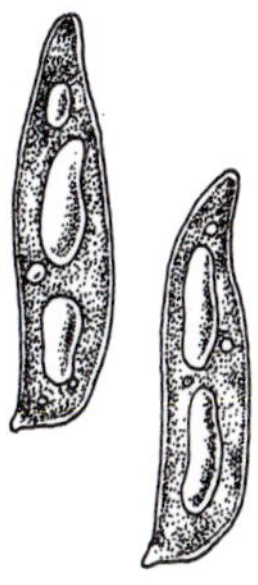

Section through the fruit body of *Krombholziella thalassina*

Krombholziella oxydabilis

Brown Birch Boletus

Krombholziella scabra (Bull. ex Fr.) R. Maire

In forests and their outskirts, it is birches that often hold the attention of mushroom pickers. Underneath, they most frequently seek members of the genera *Krombholziella* and *Leccinum.* The Brown Birch Boletus is in fact the best-known representative of Boletaceae whose mycelium lives in a symbiotic relationship with birch roots. Fruit bodies of the Brown Birch Boletus appear in summer and autumn both under old birches and under young trees in clearings and copses all over the north temperate zone. Its grey to brownish, 5–15 cm wide cap is seated on a relatively thin and long (6–15 × 1–1.5 cm), white stipe covered with almost black scales. The flesh is white or whitish, almost unchanging when cut, drying black. It has a pleasant mushroom-like taste and smell.

The Brown Birch Boletus is a tasty edible mushroom, but has one disadvantage: its cap soon becomes soft. On the other hand, its stipe is excessively tough to fibrous-woody. This is why young mushrooms are most suitable for collection. Even though the flesh turns black in the process of cooking, this does not affect the taste.

Closely related to the Brown Birch Boletus are several similar species. These differ in the species of woody plant they depend on, as well as in the colour reaction of the bruised context. *K. holopoda* is found – though rather rarely – under birches on peaty soils. It used to be considered an albino form of the Brown Birch Boletus. Most similar to the latter in appearance is *Leccinum carpini* with its dark brown to nearly black, often pitted cap; the whole fruit body is rather tough, the flesh turns grey-black on injury. It grows sporadically in hornbeam woods.

Spores of *Krombholziella scabra*:
13–18 × 5–6 μm, fusiform, yellowish

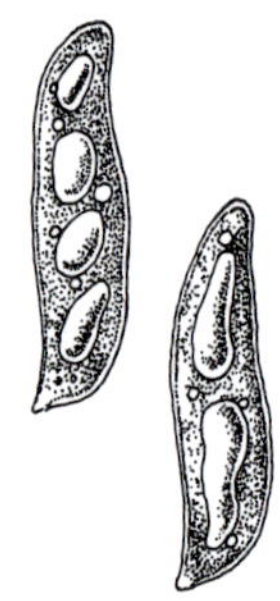

Krombholziella scabra

Leccinum melaneum grows under birches, mostly on damp soil.
It is rare and distributed probably only in Europe

Paxillus involutus (Batsch ex Fr.) Fr.

Paxillus atrotomentosus (Batsch ex Fr.) Fr.

The relatively small genus *Paxillus* includes both larger- and smaller-sized fleshy fungi with a short central or eccentric stipe, or they may be stipeless altogether, whose cap margin is involute at least in youth, but usually throughout their lifetime. The decurrent gills are readily separable from the cap context. The spore print of all members of the genus *Paxillus* is brown.

One of the most abundant species is *Paxillus involutus* (1) whose 5–15 cm wide cap, viscid at the centre and felted at the margin, is the same colour as the short stipe. The yellowish, juicy flesh has a faintly acid taste and smell. When handled, the entire fruit body becomes rusty and ultimately turns brown. *P. involutus* occurs from June until late autumn not only in all types of forest, but also under single trees in hedgerows, parks, etc., from lowlands up to high mountain elevations.

This fungus was long considered edible. Nowadays, however, *P. involutus* has been proved to be poisonous to man. Repeated ingestion forces the human body to form antidotes that create an allergic reaction accompanied by a simultaneous decomposition of erythrocytes. This may sometimes result in the death of the poisoned person. Hence it is necessary to warn most strongly of the serious danger involved in gathering *P. involutus*.

P. atrotomentosus (2) is an explicitly lignatile fungus. It is readily distinguished by its rusty brown, velvety, 6–20 cm wide cap and its short, eccentric to lateral, conspicuously black-velvety stipe. In summer and in autumn it may be found growing profusely on stumps and decayed conifer roots. It is an edible fungus but of a rather poor quality. The taste and smell of its flesh are bitter and acidic.

1

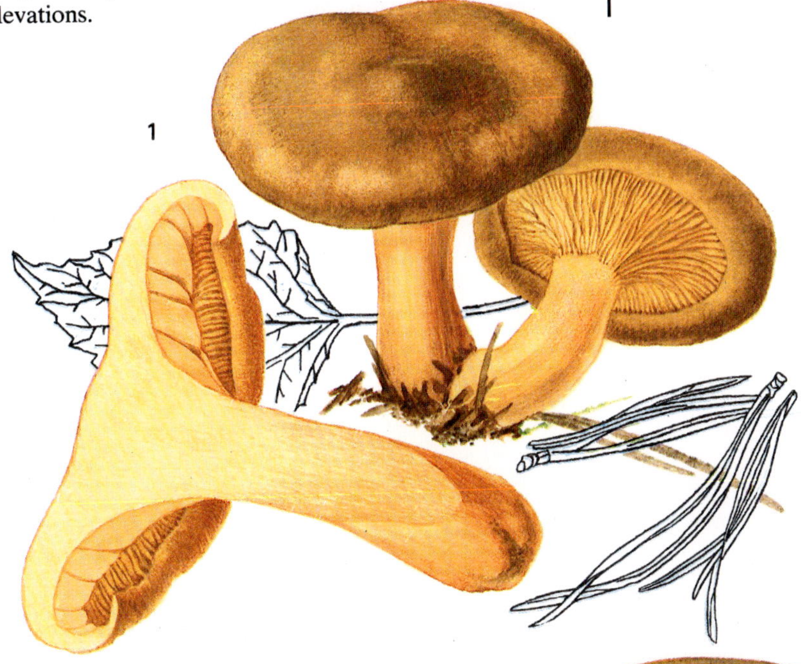

Spore of *Paxillus atrotomentosus*:
5–6 × 3–4 μm, ellipsoid, yellowish brown

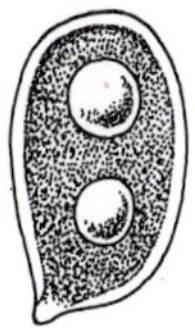

Spore of *Paxillus involutus*:
8–10 × 4–6 μm, ellipsoid, yellowish brown

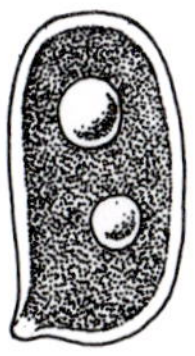

2

Paxillus involutus

Paxillus atrotomentosus

False Chanterelle

Hygrophoropsis aurantiaca (Wulf. ex Fr.) R. Maire

The False Chanterelle is a conspicuously coloured fungus resembling the Chanterelle in appearance. For some time it was thought to be deadly poisonous, later on this view was refuted and the fungus was declared to be edible. However, most recent experience has shown it to be less innocent than was assumed, as the ingestion of a larger amount of fruit bodies causes digestive troubles. It is therefore recommended to avoid it altogether.

The False Chanterelle has a 2–6 cm wide cap with relatively thin and dry flesh, elastic, with a margin remaining involuted for a long time, apricot or bright orange-coloured, growing paler in older specimens. Some forms, however, possess a whitish or white cap from the very beginning. The gills are narrow, crowded, forked, and deeply decurrent on a thin stipe. The flesh has a faint pleasant smell and a mild taste. The spore print is white.

The False Chanterelle occurs towards the end of summer and especially in autumn in moist coniferous (pine and spruce) or mixed forests. Often it grows in moss or passes over into putrescent branches and stumps.

In the past mycologists used to classify it as a member of the family Cantharellaceae, but its appearance is misleading. It is actually related to the genus *Paxillus* from which it differs by its white spore print and orange gills.

Spore of *Hygrophoropsis aurantiaca*: 4–7 × 2–4 μm, ovoid-ellipsoid, colourless, smooth

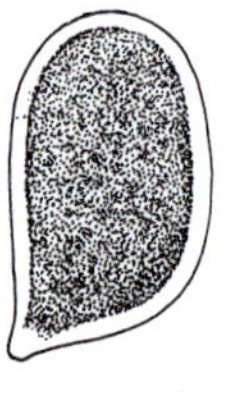

Hygrophoropsis aurantiaca

Cantharellus cibarius

Omphalotus olearius
(DC. ex Fr.) Sing.

Omphalotus olearius was for a long time classified as a member of the genus *Pleurotus*. The Swiss mycologist Fayod, who was one of the first to study the anatomy of gill-fungi fructifications in detail, noticed the difference in the structure of the fruit bodies and separated the genus *Omphalotus* from the genus *Pleurotus*. The German mycologist R. Singer subsequently excluded *O. olearius* from the genus *Pleurotus* and reclassed it with the genus *Omphalotus*. In the present narrow conception, all true *Pleurotus* species typically have two types of hyphae in at least a part of the fruit body, while species included in the genus *Omphalotus* are monomitic (i.e. formed by hyphae of a single type).

O. olearius usually forms clusters consisting of several fruit bodies. Their caps are 4–15 cm wide, vivid orange or brown-orange, infundibuliform, with a wavy-lobed margin. The gills are deeply decurrent, golden-yellow to orange, the stipe is often eccentric to lateral. Also the context is golden-yellow or reddish, lacking a distinctive taste and smell. The spore print is slightly yellowish.

O. olearius is a markedly thermophilous species, widespread particularly in regions bordering the Mediterranean. In central Europe it shares the habitats of the thermophilous fauna. The further to the north, the rarer is its occurrence. It usually grows from roots hidden in the ground, or directly on stumps of deciduous trees. While in the Mediterranean region it grows most frequently on olives, in the other parts of Europe it occurs on oak, chestnut, hornbeam, etc. It is poisonous. Poisoning by this fungus manifests itself as an irritation of the stomach and the intestines.

Spores: 5–7 × 4–6 μm, subglobose, smooth, colourless

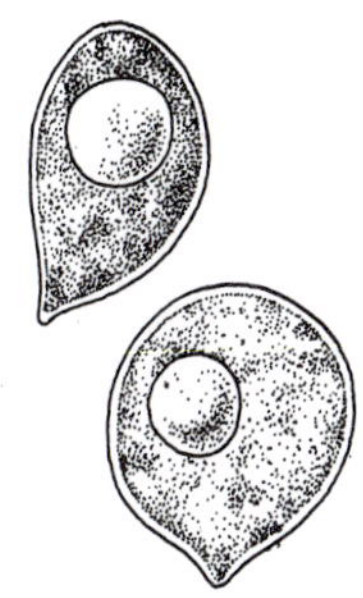

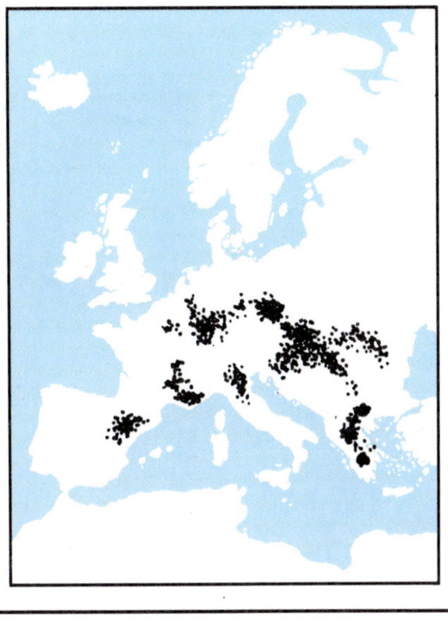

Gomphidius roseus

(Fr.) P. Karst.

This is the smallest member of the genus *Gomphidius* which can hardly be confused with any other species. Its cap is 3–6 cm wide, and of a beautifully light pink or greyish pink; more rarely it is brick-reddish in colour. This colouring weathers in age to some shade of brown, and black stains appear on the cap surface. When moist, the cap cuticle is slightly slimy, in young specimens it is attached to the stipe by a white veil. Young gills are white, then grey-brownish to almost black, distant, thick, and decurrent. The cylindrical white stipe, narrowing downwards, is tinged with brown or black at the base. The slimy ring soon disappears from its surface. The context is white, staining slightly pink where cut, yellowish pink to brownish in the stipe base, with a faintly acidulous taste and scarcely any smell. Numerous cylindrical cystidia are present on the gills.

Gomphidius roseus lives in mycorrhizal dependence on the pine and spruce, occurring mainly in pine woods on sandy substrates, almost always solitarily. It appears from August to October, most often on woodland paths among grass and moss, and usually in company with *Suillus bovinus,* a mycorrhizal fungus associated with the pine. Not infrequently the close vicinity in which the fruit bodies of both species grow makes their stipes coalesce.

G. roseus is widespread in Europe and Asia, but is rather scarce everywhere, and absent from some regions altogether. It is edible, yet it should rather be protected because of its rarity.

Spores: 16–22 × 5–6.5 μm, cylindric spindle-shaped, smooth, dark olive-green

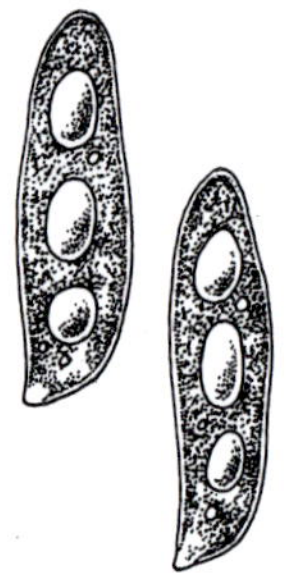

Spore print

Gomphidius glutinosus
(Schaeff. ex Fr.) Fr.

Groups of conspicuously slimy fungi appear in coniferous forests after rains in late summer and in autumn. At first sight they resemble grey-coloured members of the genus *Suillus,* coated with a thick layer of gelatinous slime. In fact they share many of their properties and are, moreover, closely related to the family Boletaceae. In the genus *Gomphidius,* however, the hymenphore is gill-shaped.

Gomphidius glutinosus has a 5–12 cm wide cap coated with a readily separable gelatinous layer. At first it is slightly convex, grey or chocolate-coloured, then flesh-grey and expanded. The gills are whitish at first, later they are greyish to blackish, relatively narrow, elastic and deeply decurrent. The stipe is 4–10 cm long and 1–1.5 cm thick. The youngest fruit bodies are covered with a transparent gelatinous veil whose remnants are discernible in mature fruit bodies in the form of an elevated ridge on the stipe right below the gills. Dry fruit bodies are shiny.

G. glutinosus belongs among the most common species of this genus. Owing to its white, nonamyloid flesh, some mycologists classify it together with several other species as a member of the genus *Leucogomphidius.* Fungi of the genus *Gomphidius* (like those of the genus *Suillus*) live in mycorrhiza with forest trees, usually with conifers. Hence it follows that these fungi often share the same habitat.

G. glutinosus is edible and very tasty, which also applies to all the other *Gomphidius* species. It is distributed throughout the north temperate zone, wherever spruces or pines have their home.

Spores of *Gomphidius glutinosus:*
16–22 × 5–7.5 μm, cylindric, spindle-shaped, brown

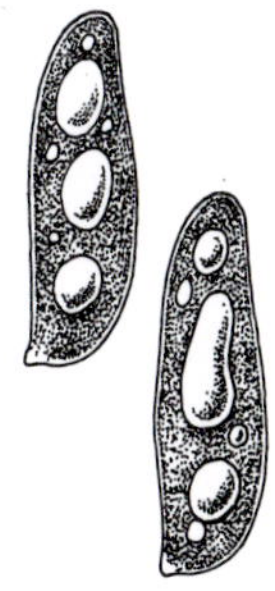

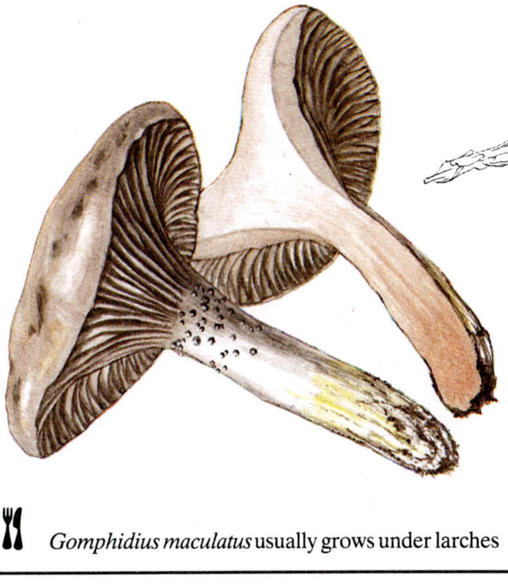

Gomphidius maculatus usually grows under larches

Gomphidius glutinosus

Chroogomphus rutilus

(Schaeff. ex Fr.) O. K. Miller

Chroogomphus rutilus is another commonly occurring member of this group. It grows in summer and autumn in coniferous forests, particularly in pine woods. Unlike *Gomphidius glutinosus,* it is only slightly viscid or only sticky when moist. It has a 5–13 cm wide, yellow-brown to orange-yellow umbonate cap and deeply decurrent yellowish to yellow-orange gills. When mature, the gills blacken by the spore mass. The stipe is 5–10 cm high and 0.5–1 cm thick, the same colour as the cap, with a fugacious superior ring. The flesh is soft, orange-yellow. An interesting microchemical reaction can be observed on the context of fresh fruit bodies: a drop of soda solution instantly changes the colour of the context to violet, whereas when touched with green-vitriol solution it stains vivid green, and in an aqueous ammonia solution it stains carmine. The cuticle of both cap and stipe change to pink, together with the flesh, when the fruit body is drying up.

Like *Gomphidius glutinosus, C. rutilus* is also an excellent edible mushroom suitable for many culinary purposes. It turns violet when cooked and almost black when pickled in vinegar – but this does not lower its quality.

Spores: 18–24 × 6–7 μm, oblong spindle-shaped, brownish

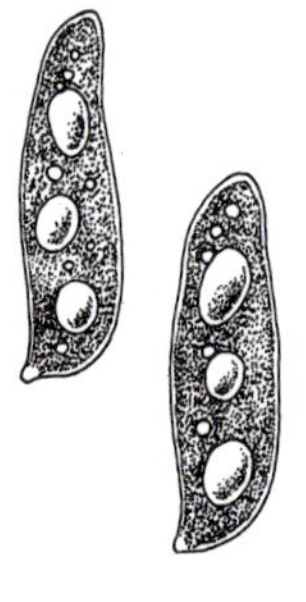

Ivory Wax Cap

Hygrophorus eburneus (Bull. ex Fr.) Fr.

The family Hygrophoraceae comprises variously coloured, medium- to smaller-sized fungi whose common feature are very thick, distant, decurrent or broadly adnate gills. Often the entire fruit-body surface is covered with slime, especially in fungi of the subgenus *Limacium* (formerly treated as an independent genus).

The Ivory Wax Cap, which also belongs to this subgenus, is a medium-sized mushroom with a white cap, stipe and gills. The cap is 4–8 cm wide, fleshy, at first convex, later almost flat, with a strongly narrowed and involuted margin. In wet weather it is coated with a thick layer of colourless slime; when dry, it is shiny. The stipe is cylindrical, long, narrowing and often hooked near the base, firm, 1–1.5 cm thick, viscid, floccose-granular only under the gills. The gills are distant, broad, deeply decurrent. The flesh is white, either odourless or with an odour reminding of Goat-moth caterpillars (*Cossus ligniperda*), its taste is mild. The spore print is white.

For the most part, the Ivory Wax Cap occurs in groups among leaves and needles in both deciduous and coniferous forests. It is a relatively abundant, edible autumn mushroom.

Fruit bodies smelling of Goat-moth caterpillars but otherwise not differing from odour-free fruit bodies were erroneously regarded by some mycologists as the Goat Moth Wax Cap (*H. cossus*).

Spores: 8–9 × 5–6 μm,
cylindric-ellipsoid, colourless

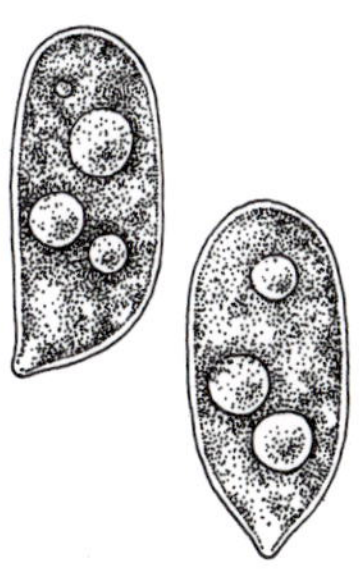

Goat Moth Wax Cap

Hygrophorus cossus (Sow. ex Fr.) Fr.

In mycological literature, this *Hygrophorus* has also been described under the name *H. chrysaspis* or *H. melizeus*. It is related to the Ivory Wax Cap. However, while the latter's fruit bodies do not change their white colour, the cap and the gills of the Goat Moth Wax Cap very obviously stain yellow or rust-coloured.

The 3–5 cm wide cap is convex at first, rounded, with a slightly felted and incurved margin, later expanded, often wavy, thin-fleshed, slimy when moist, and at first whitish. Sooner or later it starts changing colour, to become finally honey-yellow all over. The stipe is 4–8 cm long, 8–10 cm thick, cylindrical, attenuated, white at first and then rusty-yellowish, almost entirely granular-pruinose, and minutely scaly only near the apex. The gills are rather thick, broad, deeply decurrent, distant, pallid in youth, and cream-coloured with an ochraceous tinge in age. Towards the cap margin they acquire a rich rusty colour, and blacken when dried. The flesh is whitish, straw- or rusty-yellow under the cuticle, and reacts to potash-lye solution by staining yellow. It is odourless and its taste is mild. The spore print is white. The Goat Moth Wax Cap grows in autumn in deciduous forests, mostly under beeches, but rather sporadically. It is edible.

Also the more robust *H. penarius* has its home in beech forests, particularly on calcareous soils. It is white all over; only the cap centre is of a pale ochre buff. It has a dry stipe, often short, thick and obtusely angular, scaly all along its length. It is also edible.

Spores: 7–10 × 4–6 µm, cylindric-ellipsoid, smooth, colourless

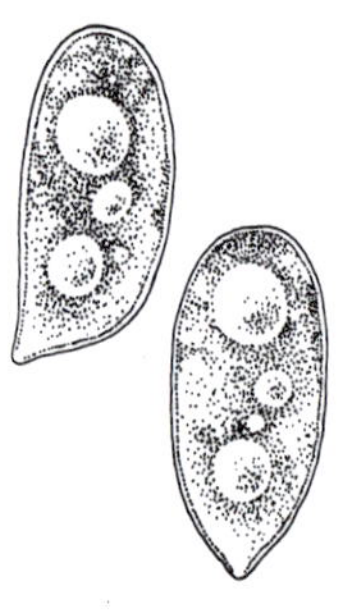

Pinewood Wax Cap
Hygrophorus hypothejus (Fr.) Fr.

One of the last mushrooms to appear only after the first autumn frosts on the needle carpet of pine forests is the Pinewood Wax Cap. It frequently occurs in great profusion under pine trees (particularly under the Scots Pine). It likes to grow in places exposed to sunlight, in woodland glades and along forest paths. It is smaller in size, with a 3–5 cm wide cap and a 5–10 cm long, 3–7 cm thick stipe. The cap is convex at first, then expanded, depressed at the centre later on, with an involute margin, and is relatively thin-fleshed. The thick cuticle, covered with colourless slime, is readily separable, its colour is cocoa-brown with a cloudy olive tinge. It is darkest towards the centre of the cap. The distant, relatively thick, elastic, decurrent gills are pale yolk-yellow. The stipe is long and thin, cylindrical, often distorted, coated with colourless slime on a yellowish background, with remnants of the viscid veil in the apical part. The flesh has no specific smell and taste. The spore print is white.

The Pinewood Wax Cap is a relatively tasty edible mushroom – all the more welcome since it grows at a time when larger species of edible mushrooms are rapidly disappearing from the wood. It cannot be confused with any other species. When cleaning the fruit bodies, the viscid cuticle is to be peeled off; this is best done immediately on finding them.

Late autumn is also the time when *H. lucorum* occurs in abundance. It is approximately the same size as the Pinewood Wax Cap, but its predominant colour is yellow. It is found exclusively under larches.

Spores of *Hygrophorus hypothejus*:
7–9 × 4–5 μm, ellipsoid, smooth, colourless

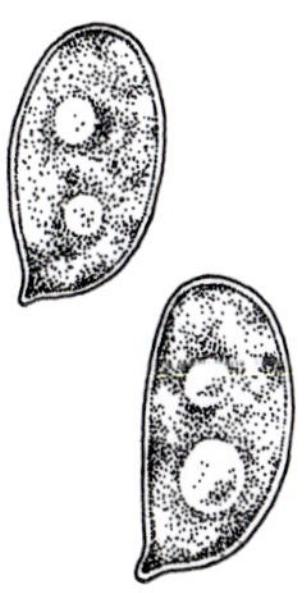

Hygrophorus lucorum

Hygrophorus hypothejus

Hygrophorus marzuolus
(Fr.) Bres.

Hygrophorus marzuolus is the opposite of the Pinewood Wax Cap. Its robust fruit bodies start pushing themselves through the forest humus in early spring, as soon as the first rays of sunlight begin to warm up the earth. Sometimes they make their appearance at a time when there are still patches of snow. The first fruit bodies grow as early as February, yet the main period of growth sets in in April, exceptionally – after long-lasting and severe winters – in May and June. The fruit bodies may reach the size of 12 cm in diameter and have a thick layer of firm flesh; at first they are white all over but soon the cap surface turns pearl-grey or black-grey, the cuticle is matt, very finely radially fibrous. The fruit bodies are often rather deformed and contaminated by soil, since they grow from a greater depth. Groups of fruit bodies develop under the surface of the earth which they heave up like mole hills, thus betraying the place of their growth. The short and thick stipe tapers downwards, white with a greyish tinge, fibrous, the gills are thick, distant, shortly decurrent, white, later slightly bluish grey to pale grey. The firm white flesh has a sweetish smell and a mild taste. The whole surface of the fruit body is dry. The spore print is white.

Particularly interesting is the geographical distribution of *H. marzuolus:* it has been reported from Europe only, being most abundant in the Alpine region, the northernmost limit of its range is probably in Bohemia. It is most profuse in established coniferous or mixed stands, being rather scarce in deciduous forests (here it particularly favours oak stands). It is an edible, nutritious mushroom.

Spores: 6–8 × 4–5 µm, ellipsoid, smooth, colourless

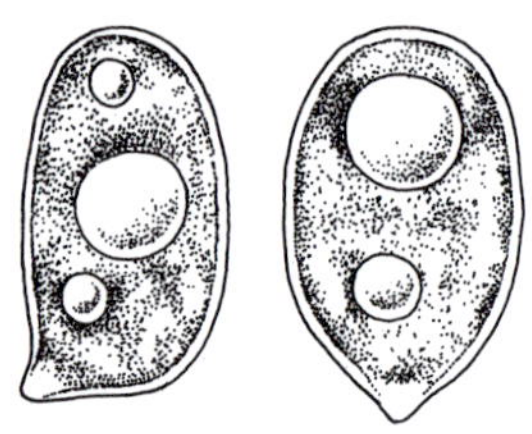

Camarophyllus pratensis

(Pers. ex Fr.) Kumm.

There are many members of the family Hygrophoraceae found not in but outside the forest: in lawns, heaths, pasturelands, meadows, and on grassy slopes. One of them is *Camarophyllus pratensis.* Its cap is 3–5 cm wide, slightly convex, soon expanded, and relatively fleshy but with an attenuated margin; the cuticle is dry, smooth, pale buff or beige. The stipe is 3–7 cm long, 3–7 mm thick, cylindrical, tapered downwards, pallid, dry and glabrous. The gills are thick and distant, deeply decurrent, pale beige, often rib-like near the base. The flesh is white or cream, unchanging on injury, odourless and tasteless. The spore print is white.

C. pratensis is an edible mushroom growing from August to October, sometimes gregariously. It is often found in moss on the outskirts of young spruce stands, but also in pastures and similar places among grass. Not infrequently it coexists with other white fungi of the genus *Camarophyllus.* One of these is *C. niveus,* which is somewhat smaller and less fleshy, with a 1.5–3 cm wide cap, slightly viscid when moist, pellucid-striate. Its stipe is thin, 5–6 cm long and 2–4 mm thick. Its spores are 8–10 × 5–6 mm in size. Another related species is the more fleshy and larger *C. virgineus* whose older fruit bodies sometimes have a reddish-spotted cap surface. Both of these species are edible.

The genus *Camarophyllus,* like the genera *Limacium* and *Hygrocybe,* are regarded by some authors as being mere subgenera of the genus *Hygrophorus.*

Spores: 5–7 × 4–5 µm,
cylindric-ellipsoid, smooth, colourless

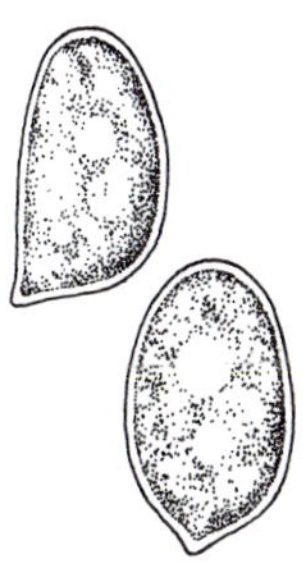

Hygrocybe nigrescens

(Quél.) Kühner

In the colouring of the genus *Hygrocybe* the predominant colour shades are bright yellow, orange and red; in some species these are mutually combined and complemented by still other colours. Fungi belonging to this genus are readily distinguished by their colouring and a peculiar, almost waxy, consistency of their fruit bodies. These wonderful little fungi are usually found outside the forest, in grass and moss – mostly in natural localities substantially unaffected by man's interference. However, because such localities are disappearing very rapidly, the species of *Hygrocybe* are increasingly becoming a rarity. The fruit bodies appear in summer or in autumn after heavy rainfalls. Their vitality is low owing to their exposure to sunshine, which is usually intense outside the forest.

Hygrocybe nigrescens and its double, *H. conica,* are among the most common and, due to their peculiar colour change, most conspicuous of *Hygrocybe* species. These two species have one characteristic in common: they gradually blacken on injury or with age. Young specimens have vivid colours and a remarkable shape. The cap is 2–6 cm across, acutely conical, tapering to a point, orange-yellow or scarlet-red, with a radially fibrous cuticle; the gills are yellow, the stipe is yellow or orange, longitudinally fibrillose-striate. The differences existing between these two species are negligible. *H. conica* is smaller, its cap is only 2–4 cm wide and sharply conical, its stipe is orange rather than lemon-yellow, its basidia are bisporous. *H. nigrescens* is more robust, with a more pronouncedly lemon-yellow stipe and tetrasporous basidia. Both species are slightly poisonous.

Spores of *Hygrocybe nigrescens*:
8–12 × 5–6 µm, cylindric-ellipsoid, smooth, colourless

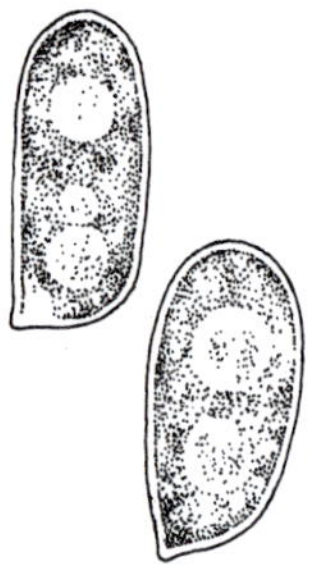

☠ *Hygrocybe nigrescens*

Hygrocybe punicea
(Fr.) Kumm.

This is one of the largest members of the genus *Hygrocybe.* The cap grows up to 12 cm in diameter; it is fleshy, campanulate-convex, and viscid in wet weather. Its colour is that of deep red ripe cherries. The thick (8–20 mm) stipe is cylindrical, firm-fleshed, orange-yellow, white at the base, covered with relatively coarse, purple-coloured fibres, dry. The gills are thick, subdistant, deep yellow, later orange to orange-red, emarginate and adnexed. The flesh is white in the stipe, and orange under the cap cuticle; it does not change colour on injury or with age. It is also odourless and without any distinctive taste.

Hygrocybe punicea occurs in the grass of dry woodland meadows or in similar habitats outside the forest. Its collection for table use is not advisable. Its sturdy build, its longitudinally coarsely fibrillose stipe, non-viscid even in wet weather, and its never-blackening flesh clearly distinguish it from other species of this genus. *H. coccinea* is similar in colour but is smaller, with a semiglobular, 2–6 cm wide cap. The stipe is deep red, yellowish at the base, the context is red, the gills are adnate to decurrent. It grows in moist meadows, pastures and grassy forest margins, and is inedible.

Another orange-red species, *H. quieta,* may be found in sparse deciduous forests. It is also inedible.

Spores of *Hygrocybe punicea*:
8.5–11 × 5–6 μm, cylindric-ellipsoid, smooth, colourless

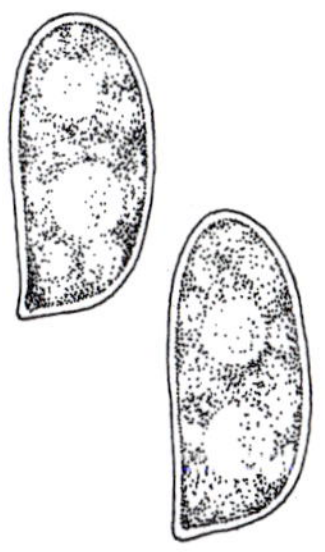

Hygrocybe quieta

Hygrocybe punicea

Omphalina epichysium

(Pers. ex Fr.) Quél.

The genus *Omphalina* is formed by small gill-bearing fungi, either thinly coriaceous or thin-fleshed, with a cap ranging from several millimetres to a few centimetres in diameter. The cap, which is convex or expanded, is mostly rather deeply depressed round the centre. The arcuate-decurrent gills show through the thin flesh of the cap, so that its cuticle appears as if it were radially striate. The thin, tubular stipe is cartilaginous in consistency. In general, *Omphalina* is largely grey, greyish brown or brownish with a pink flush. The spore print is pure white, or rarely may be pink. The genus *Omphalina* is heterogeneous and, to a large extent, artificial. The fungi belonging here are similar in appearance to the small species of the genus *Clitocybe* or even *Mycena*.

Omphalina epichysium has a 1–3 cm wide cap, deeply depressed to infundibuliform, radially fibrous to finely scaly in wet weather, almost glossy when dry, smoky grey-brown or dirty ash-brown. The similarly coloured stipe is 2–4 cm long, 2–3 mm thick, coated at the base with a white, matted-tomentose mycelium. The gills are subdistant, and are whitish to light grey. The flesh has no distinctive smell or taste. *O. epichysium* grows on rotten stumps often overgrown with moss, and on uprooted conifer trunks. It is widespread mainly in mountain virgin forests, sporadically it also descends to lower elevations. It is inedible.

Spores: 6–10 × 3.5–5 μm, ovoid-ellipsoid, smooth, colourless

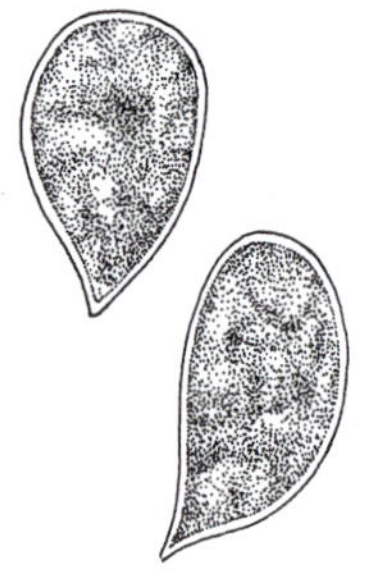

Section through the fruit body

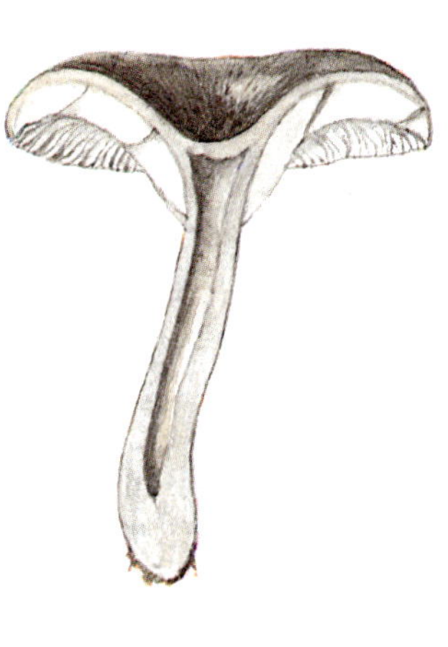

Gerronema chrysophyllum
(Fr.) Sing.

R. Singer devised the independent genus *Gerronema* to involve some fungi formerly classified as members of the genera *Omphalina* or *Mycena*. Even in its present delimitation, however, the genus *Gerronema* is rather problematical: it can be defined with difficulty, only on the basis of microcharacteristics.

Gerronema chrysophyllum, still frequently referred to under the name *Omphalina chrysophylla,* is a most conspicuous, easily recognizable fungus. The 2–6 cm wide cap is yellow-brown, in dry weather greyish brown, deeply funnel-shaped in the centre. The broad and rather distant gills, deeply decurrent, are orange- or yolk-yellow, as is the 4–5 mm thick, cartilaginous stipe. The spore print is also yellowish. The flesh has no specific odour or smell.

This species usually develops clusters on strongly putrescent stumps or fallen spruce or fir trunks in mountain forests and virgin forests. It is edible.

It should not be mistaken for *Xeromphalina campanella* which also grows on the stumps of conifers. It is in fact a related species but belonging to a different genus. It is smaller in every respect. Its cap is only 0.5–1 cm across, the slender stipe is 1–2 mm thick, rusty strigose at the base. It is rusty yellow to rusty brown. The gills are yellow and vein-like. It is much more common than *G. chrysophyllum* and occurs at low elevations as well. It is inedible.

Spores of *Gerronema chrysophyllum*:
10–12 × 5–6 μm, ellipsoid, smooth, almost colourless

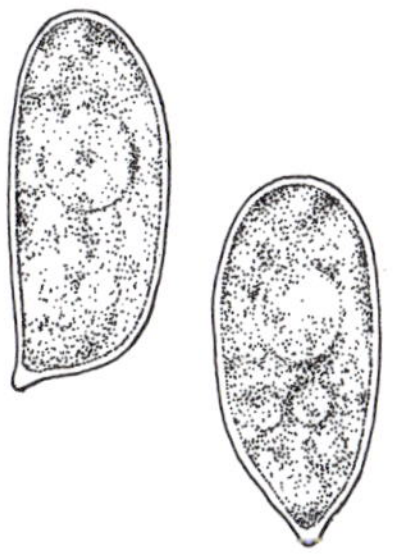

A group of *Xeromphalina campanella* fruit bodies

Gerronema chrysophyllum

Laccaria amethystina
(Huds. ex Hook.) Cooke

The genus *Laccaria* is related to the genus *Clitocybe*, differing from the latter in its relatively thick gills, broadly adnate to subdecurrent, whose surface is covered at maturity with a coating of powdery, white spore-mass. Microscopic examination reveals typical globose or subglobose spores whose surface is ornamented with minute warts or spines.

Laccaria amethystina (also referred to in some handbooks under the name *L. amethystea*) is violet-coloured throughout. Fresh fruit bodies are of a deep amethyst colour, drying paler, finally becoming violet-grey to whitish – hence they are strongly hygrophanous. The 2–6 cm wide cap is often depressed at the centre, with a matt to finely squamulose surface and distant gills. The stipe is narrowly and longly cylindrical, longitudinally fibrous, white felted at the base. The flesh has no specific odour nor taste.

L. amethystina usually forms colonies in rather damp deciduous and coniferous forests, growing either directly on the moist ground in the fallen foliage or from decaying twigs and wood. It appears from July to October and is edible, though of little nutritive value. It would be difficult to confuse it with any other species: similarly violet-coloured gill fungi are scarce (e. g. some *Lepista* and *Cortinarius* species) but all of them differ in shape, fleshiness, size and spores.

Spores: 8–10 μm, globose, shortly echinulate

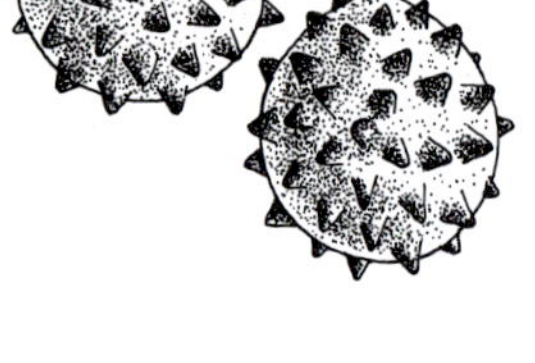

Laccaria laccata
(Scop. ex Fr.) Cooke

Laccaria laccata occurs still more abundantly than *L. amethystina* – in fact it belongs among the most common gill fungi in general. It posesses all the characteristic features of the genus *Laccaria,* i.e. thick, distant, broad and broadly adnate, subdeccurent gills strewn with white spore powder when mature, and globose, echinulate, colourless spores, 7–10 μm in size. It resembles *L. amethystina* in size but differs from it in colour. *L. laccata* is entirely flesh-reddish or pink, sometimes more pronouncedly flushed pink, sometimes mixed with brown or rusty brown. The cap is also hygrophanous, rather faded in dry weather, the stipe is longitudinally fibrous. The context has a mild taste and practically no smell.

L. laccata grows throughout the summer until late autumn in moist places in all types of forests. It can very often be found among grass and moss in the vicinity of forest brooks or at the edge of woodland tracks.

It is closely related to several other species of *Laccaria,* similar in colour but distinguished e.g. by a scaly cap surface and a coarsely fibrous stipe – *L. proxima,* or by a small size of fruit bodies – *L. tortilis,* no more than 1 cm long, mostly growing on the muddy ground of forest paths. All *Laccaria* species are edible, but mushroom pickers mostly ignore them because of their exceedingly small size and negligible nutritional value.

Spores of *Laccaria laccata*:
7–10 μm, globose, echinulate

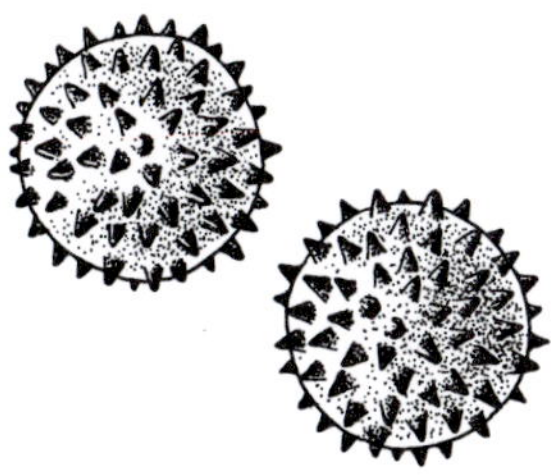

Spore of *Laccaria proxima*
is densely covered with spines

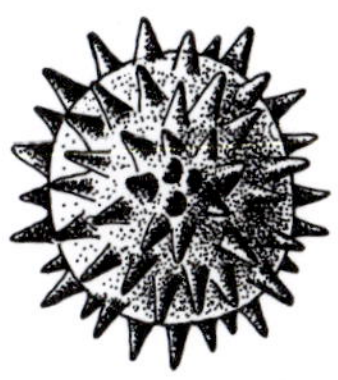

Fruit bodies of *Laccaria proxima*

Laccaria laccata

Clitocybe odora

(Bull. ex Fr.) Kumm.

The colours prevailing in fungi of the genus *Clitocybe* are white, whitish grey, greyish brown and brown. Only a very few species are coloured differently, and *Clitocybe odora* is one of them. Not only the verdigris blue-green to green-grey colouring of the cap, fading to off-white, and the green-tinged gills and stipe, but also the pleasant sweetish aniseed scent of the whole fruit body make the confusion of this fungus with another species practically impossible. Its smell can also be compared to fennel. There are two other *Clitocybe* species emitting a similar scent – *C. suaveolens* and *C. fragrans*. Both of them, however, are quite differently coloured: their cap is pale greyish to ochre-brownish when moist, white when dry (i.e. the cap is typically hygrophanous).

C. odora has a 3–10 cm wide cap, umbonate at first, then broadly funnel-shaped, smooth and silky. The stipe is 3–8 cm high and 0.6–1.2 cm thick. In calm weather the smell of *C. odora* spreads to a distance of several metres from the fruit bodies, particularly if more of them grow close together. It is found in autumn, mostly in spruce woods among decaying needles. It is edible, and is best suited for flavouring less aromatic mushroom mixtures. Drying makes it lose its typical odour.

Spores: 6–7 × 3–4 μm, ellipsoid, colourless

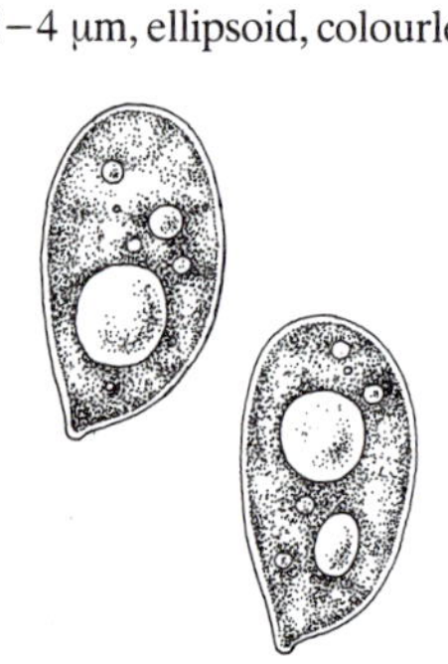

Clitocybe clavipes
(Pers. ex Fr.) Kumm.

A characteristic of this fungus is a peculiar shape of young fruit bodies, suggestive of skittles. Mature mushrooms can easily be distinguished by a bitter-almond scent, as well as by the shape of their stipe. The 4–6 cm wide cap is slightly convex, prominently obtusely umbonate; the cap margin remains incurved for a long time, the cuticle is of a matt grey-brown or olivaceous grey. The thick stipe, conically thickened in its lower part, is clavately inflated at the base and firmly attached to the substrate, so that this (mostly needles) adheres to the stipe of a drawn-out fruit body. The stipe surface is finely silky fibrous, greyish, the flesh is watery-soft. The gills are crowded, subdecurrent, visibly yellow-tinged. The cap context is softly spongy and fleshy, white, faintly smelling of bitter almonds, with a mild taste. The spore print is white.

The fruit bodies occur from August to October in coniferous or mixed forests – especially under larches where they sometimes form large communities. They also grow under pines and spruces. *Clitocybe clavipes* is edible but not particularly tasty, hence it is best used in combination with other mushrooms. Due to its soft consistency, the whole fruit body becomes saturated with water when it rains. This water can easily be squeezed out, especially from the stipe.

Spores: 5–6 × 4 µm, subglobose-ellipsoid, smooth, colourless

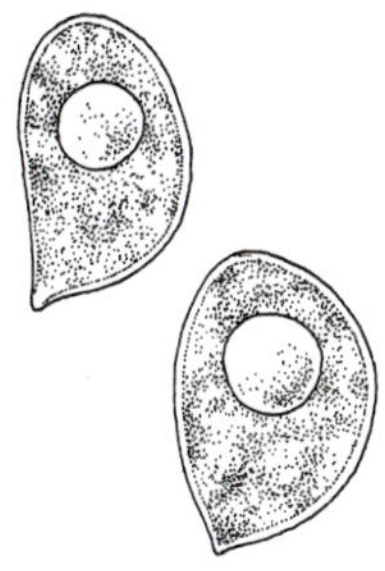

Clitocybe geotropa

(Bull. ex St. Amans) Quél.

This species is one of the largest of this genus; its fruit bodies have caps as much as 25 cm across. The cap is almost flat, subumbonate at the centre when young, later it becomes funnel-shaped with the umbo remaining at the bottom of the hollow. The cap margin is distinctly involute, the cuticle covering the whole surface is smooth, dry, matted-tomentose round the centre, and tan or ochre-brownish. The stipe is whitish, slightly brownish with age, longitudinally fibrous striate, up to 30 cm long and 1–4 cm thick, vertically cylindrical, slowly enlarging downwards. The gills are rather crowded, decurrent, and pale yellowish. The flesh is white, with a faint pleasant smell and a mild taste. The spore print is white.

As a rule, *Clitocybe geotropa* grows in groups on the ground in deciduous forests, preferring warmer situations, and sometimes is also found in woodland meadows. It is edible. Young fruit bodies may be mistaken for the Common Funnel Cap (*C. gibba*), but this is substantially smaller, with a cap at most 8 cm wide, a stipe only 8–12 cm thick, and lacrimiform pores 5–7 × 3–5 μm in size.

Spores of *Clitocybe geotropa*:
5–9 × 6.5 μm, subglobose, smooth, colourless

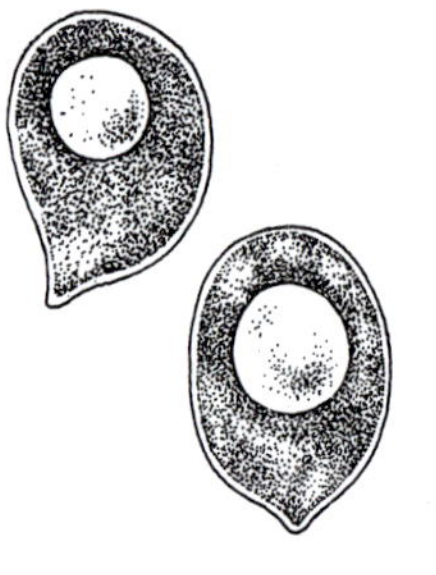

Part of a longitudinal section through the cap of *Clitocybe geotropa*

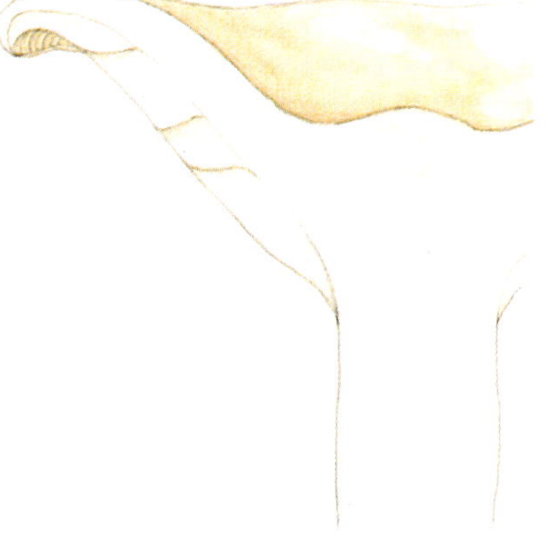

Clitocybe maxima
(F. Wett. ex Fr.) Kumm.

Clitocybe maxima strongly resembles *C. geotropa,* and is usually treated as its subspecies. In the latter the stipe is always longer than the diameter of its cap, while the stipe of *C. maxima* is, on the contrary, substantially shorter, being only 5–10 cm long and 1.5–4 cm thick, whereas the diameter of the cap may exceed 30 cm. Thus *C. maxima* is a real giant among fungi. However, its fruit bodies are not particularly fleshy, they are softer and differ from those of *C. geotropa* also in shape: though the cap in the latter is also funnel-shaped, the umbo in its centre is usually absent or at most vestigial. The cap cuticle is finely silky, sometimes flocculose-scaly, with a slightly felted involute margin. The cream-coloured gills taper towards both the cap margin and the stipe, and are deeply decurrent. The almost white flesh pleasantly smells of lavender, while the odour emitted by the gills resembles that of bitter almonds.

C. maxima frequently grows gregariously or in 'fairy rings'. It can be found in autumn in both coniferous (mainly fir) and deciduous forests. It is more rare than *C. geotropa,* and is also edible.

Spores: 6–8.5 (10) × 4–5.5 (7) μm, shortly ellipsoid or broadly ovoid, smooth, colourless

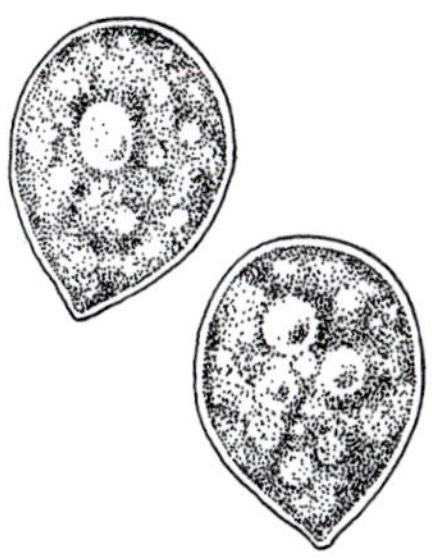

Part of a longitudinal section through the cap

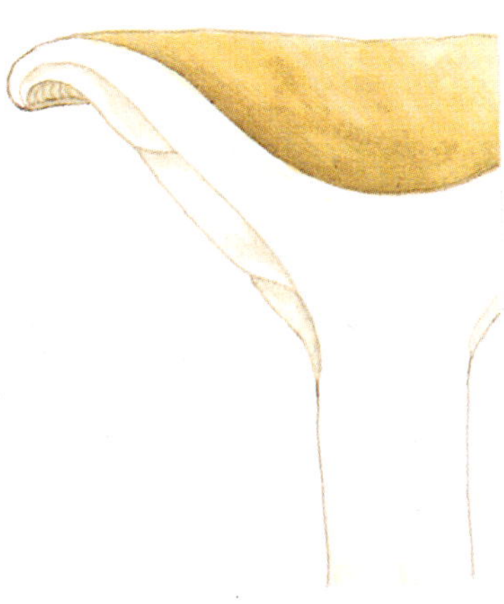

Common Funnel Cap

Clitocybe gibba (Pers. ex Fr.) Kumm.

In a number of manuals this *Clitocybe* is introduced and described under the name *C. infundibuliformis*. It has a 3–8 cm wide, funnel-shaped cap, bluntly subumbonate in the centre, relatively very thin-fleshed and rather elastic, with a quite typically scalloped-striate margin. The cap cuticle is fibrous, finely felted, almost unicoloured – pale ochre-yellow, light buff or creamy. The stipe is slender, clavate, approximately of the same length as the diameter of the cap, 0.5–1 cm thick, whitish, enveloped at the base in a felted coating of white mycelium. The gills are crowded, deeply decurrent, and white. The context is creamy, with a pleasant but faint smell of bitter almonds and a mild taste. The spore print is white.

The Common Funnel Cap grows profusely in coniferous forests, most often in moss and grass, but also among shed needles, usually in small groups. It is very similar to and is still confused with *C. incilis,* distinguished by a non-umbonate cap usually with a wavy and smooth, non-striate margin, greyish cinnamon gills, a slightly urinous smell, and also by somewhat larger spores. The question remains open whether these two species are actually independent: whether in fact they do not constitute a single species. These *Clitocybe* species are edible and collected in some countries as 'forest Fairy-ring Champignons'.

Spores of *Clitocybe gibba*: 5–7 × 3–4 µm, ovoid-ellipsoid, smooth, colourless

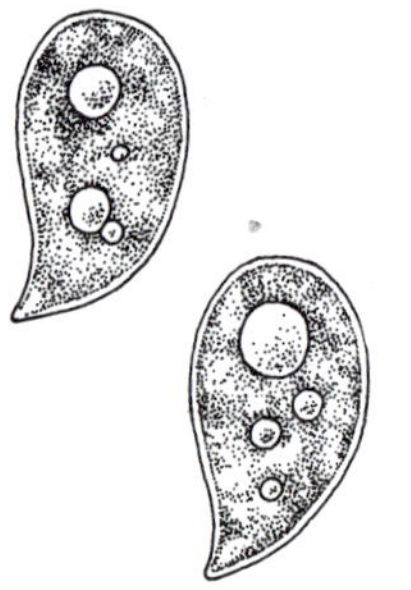

Clitocybe gibba

Clitocybe incilis

Clitocybe cerussata

(Fr.) Kumm.

The genus *Amanita* is not the only one to include deadly poisonous fungi: these may belong to genera fairly remote from the amanitas. This concerns particularly the large group of white *Clitocybe* species related to *C. cerussata.*

C. cerussata has a 4–12 cm wide cap, soon broadly expanded, obtusely subumbonate in the centre, then broadly depressed, circular, with an involute margin when young, often lobed at maturity. The cap surface is either matt white, or it looks as if smeared with lime or lacquered. This thin pruinose layer disappears with age or is washed away by rain; old fruit bodies have a pale yellowish tan cap, often finely cracked into concentric circles. The stipe is usually relatively short, rather elastic and tough, white and then cream-yellowish, cylindrical, and sometimes with a swollen and white-felted base. The gills are crowded, subdecurrent, thin and narrow. The context is white, with a mild taste and a faint, pleasant smell. The spore print is white.

C. cerussata occurs most abundantly in autumn, in both deciduous and coniferous forests. It often forms large groups or 'fairy rings', and tends to remain in its habitat for a long time. It is extremely poisonous. However, a still greater amount of muscarine is contained in *C. dealbata* and *C. phyllophila.* Hence the collection of white *Clitocybe* species for table use is definitely not advisable!

Spores: 4–6 × 3–4 µm, ovoid-ellipsoid, smooth, colourless, nonamyloid

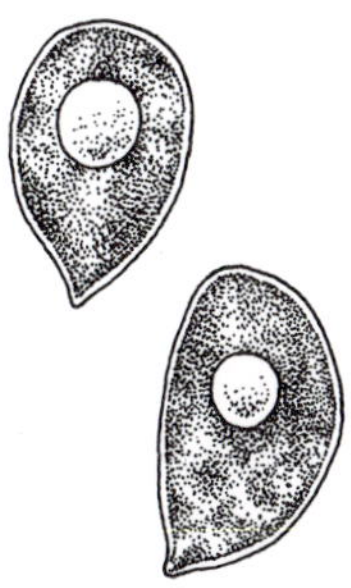

Marasmius oreades sometimes grows even in the forest – then it can easily be confused with small fruit bodies of *C. cerussata*

Clitocybe cerussata

Clitocybe candicans
(Pers. ex Fr.) Kumm.

Clitocybe candicans belongs to the same group of white *Clitocybe* species as the poisonous *C. cerussata.* It is substantially smaller in size, its cap is only 1–3 cm across, rarely larger, more convex, later depressed, non-umbonate, with a strongly involute margin, dirty whitish and white-pruinose when moist, white when dry. The relatively thin, 1.5–4 mm thick stipe is white, and attached to decaying leaves or needles by a profuse white mycelium covering its base with a hairy coating. The gills are only subdecurrent and are white or slightly yellowish. The flesh has no distinctive taste, and either no smell at all, or a very faint farinaceous smell. The spore print is white.

C. candicans is usually solitary and grows in relatively damp situations in deciduous, rarely coniferous, forests. It is also poisonous, as are the majority of the related species of *Clitocybe* (*C. dealbata, C. phyllophila* and *C. cerussata*), all of which greatly resemble each other and are hard to distinguish. *C. dealbata* is very similar to *C. candicans* both in appearance and colour, and has the highest muscarine content of all the species mentioned here. It is differentiated only by possessing a somewhat more distinctly greyish or yellowish cap, narrower spores (4–6 × 2.5–3.5 μm), and particularly by its habitats; it grows outside the forest, among grass in meadows and gardens.

Spores: 4–5 × 3.5 μm, ellipsoid, smooth, colourless

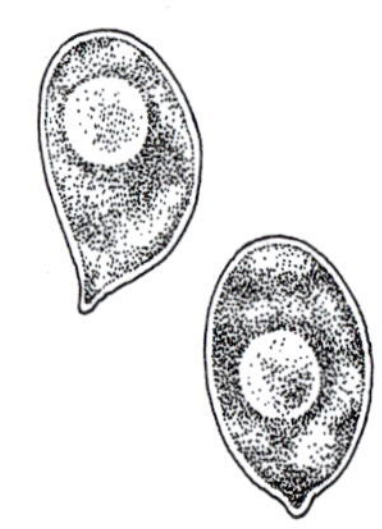

Clitocybe candicans

Clitocybe dealbata

Clitocybe brumalis
(Fr. ex Fr.) Kumm.

An obvious characteristic of some species of *Clitocybe* is a strongly hygrophanous cap which, in wet and rainy weather, is strongly saturated with water and becomes darker-coloured and pellucid, so that the darker striae of gills are often visible up to the cap centre. After drying, the cap is always lighter-coloured and the gills are no more discernible. Such strongly hygrophanous species exist in large quantities and can be distinguished only with difficulty. *Clitocybe brumalis* is one of them. Its cap is 2–5 cm across, flatly expanded, with a broadly depressed centre, thin-fleshed, in wet weather light grey to yellow-grey, glabrous and smooth. In the course of drying up from the centre the cap becomes whitish. The 3–4 mm thick stipe is usually a little longer than the diameter of the cap; it is slightly tinged with yellow, finely longitudinally white fibrous, relatively tough. The gills are crowded, narrow, attenuated towards both the cap margin and the stipe, subdecurrent, white at first, but greyish yellow later. The context is white, has almost no smell and has a mild taste. The spore print is white.

C. brumalis grows in moss or needles in spruce and pine forests. It occurs from the end of summer until late autumn when the woods are abounding in most various species of uniformly coloured, hygrophanous members of the genus *Clitocybe*. Let us mention at random *C. langei*. The differences prevailing between individual species are often negligible and their variability has not been satisfactorily evaluated. They should not be collected for table use.

Spores: $4-5 \times 3-4$ µm,
broadly ellipsoid, smooth, colourless

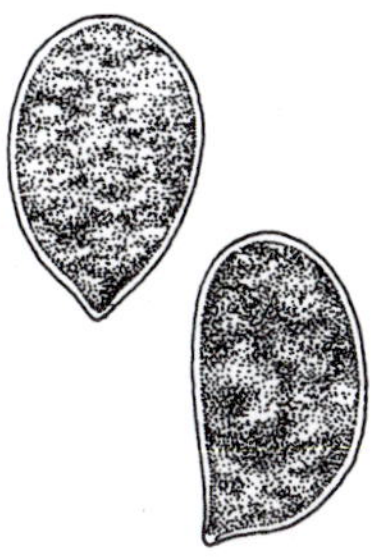

Clitocybe langei

Clitocybe brumalis

Lepista nebularis

(Batsch ex Fr.) Harmaja

Lepista nebularis is one of the most easily identifiable of gill fungi. Its robust stature, appearance, colouring and specific odour are properties characterizing it so strongly that it cannot be mistaken for any other species. Also its relatively late occurrence in autumn is typical. It appears – in clumps as a rule – from September until the first frosts, usually in rather deep forest humus among fallen leaves and needles, but sometimes also in parks and gardens. The fruit bodies last for a long time in their habitat. The cap sometimes exceeds 20 cm in width (usually measuring 8–12 cm); it is ash-grey or greyish brown, whitish pruinose when young, dry, fleshy, and convex. The stipe is markedly clavately expanded towards the base, fibrous, greyish, and firm-fleshed. The originally white gills gradually shade to yellow: this is called forth by the colour of the spore mass. The flesh is white, unchanging, sweetish-acid, with a quite specific aroma – according to some authors it has a farinaceous smell, others compare it to that of orange blossoms, but what is involved here is most probably a mixture of both these scents with a mouldy tinge.

Although *L. nebularis* is edible and popular with a number of mushroom pickers, it is much too aromatic and, in some cases, causes vomiting or diarrhoea. Recently it has been found to contain organic substances of the antibiotic type. Until lately it was currently classed into the genus *Clitocybe* from which it was excluded only a short time ago.

Spores: 6–8 × 3–4 μm, ellipsoid, smooth

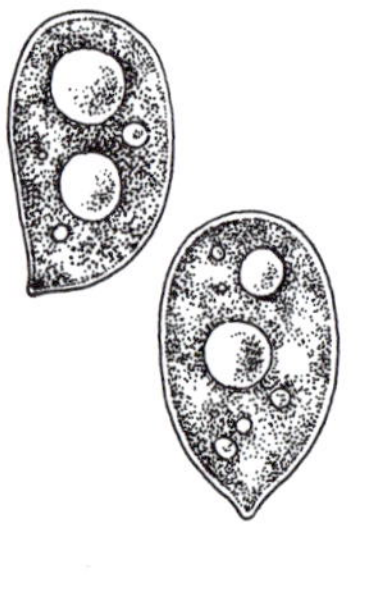

Wood Blewitt, Bluette, Blue Leg
Lepista nuda (Bull. ex Fr.) W. G. Smith

The Wood Blewitt is almost the double of the Blewitt (*Lepista saeva*) from which it differs in that it grows exclusively under trees. The entire fruit body is amethyst-violet when young. This colouring disappears with age, passing into cloudy violet to beige-brownish both on the cap and on the gills. Also the flesh changes to whitish or greyish with age. It is the stipe that retains its violet colour for the longest time. The cap is 6–15 cm wide, fleshy, slightly convex, with an attenuated, involute margin. The stipe is 5–10 cm high, 1–2,5 cm thick, firm, swollen at the base. The gills are crowded and relatively narrow. The spore print is pale pinkish. The flesh has a pleasant smell and taste.

The Wood Blewitt occurs from September to December in deciduous and coniferous forests, orchards, parks and hedgerows. It prefers places with a high layer of humus through which its mycelium makes its way. As a rule, it grows in large groups: this is particularly attractive for mushroom pickers at a time when other edible mushrooms are scarce. One of the peculiarities of the Wood Blewitt is that it occasionally appears as early as spring – of course only solitarily. Fresh fruit bodies of both the Blewitt and the Wood Blewitt contain a substance contributing to the decomposition of erythrocytes, which is neutralized by cooking. Well-cooked fruit bodies are therefore harmless.

The Wood Blewitt can be confused at most with some violet-coloured species of *Cortinarius*. All of these, however, differ in the brownish-rusty spore print, the presence of a cobwebby cortina, and a usually unpleasant smell. The Wood Blewitt is an excellent edible mushroom.

Spores: 6–8 × 4–5 μm, ellipsoid, verrucose, pale pink

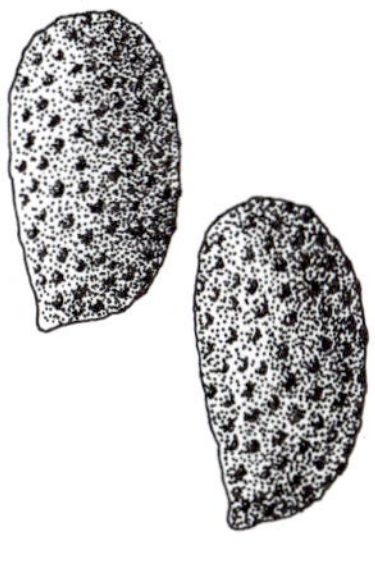

Blewitt, Bluette, Blue Leg

Lepista saeva (Fr.) P. D. Orton

In its appearance, size and partly also in colouring it closely resembles the Wood Blewitt. Nevertheless, it can be quite reliably distinguished by the colour combination of cap and stipe. The cap and the gills bear inconspicuous shades of dirty yellow or grey-ochre without any violet tints. Far more remarkable is the shortly cylindrical, sturdy stipe, usually thickened below; it is pale violet and coated with coarse longitudinal fibres of a lovely blue-violet. The flesh is creamy and pleasantly smelling. The spore print is grey-pink.

The ecology of the Blewitt differs from that of the Wood Blewitt. The Blewitt occurs outside the forest, in the grass of meadows and pastures, and under fruit trees. It never appears before September at the earliest; if the weather is favourable, it continues to grow until December, or until the onset of the first frosts. It is frequently gregarious and often forms 'fairy rings'. Its presence in these places manifests itself even outside its period of growth by zones of deep-green vegetation (mostly grasses), conspicuously differing from the environment. The same applies to *Marasmius oreades.*

The Blewitt is an edible mushroom with a pleasant taste. According to most recent findings, it is expanding its range and spreading into areas from which it has so far never been reported.

Spores of *Lepista saeva*:
6–8 × 4–5 μm, cylindrical-ellipsoid, finely verrucose, pale pink

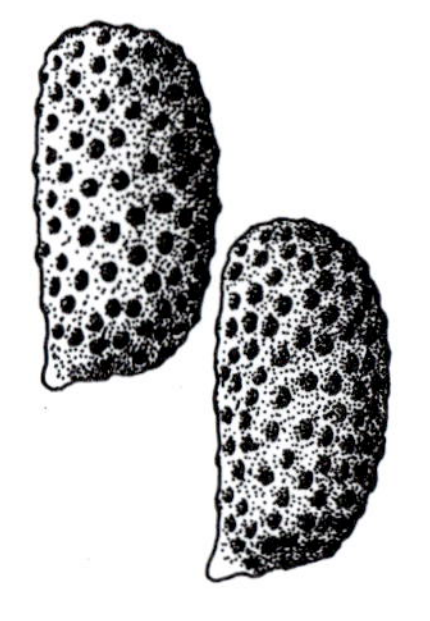

Lepista saeva

Lepista sordida grows in summer and in autumn, often sharing the habitats of *L. saeva*

Tricholomopsis rutilans
(Schaeff. ex Fr.) Sing.

The genus *Tricholomopsis* was separated from *Tricholoma* on the basis of a combination of the following characteristics: it includes lignicolous fungi with a central stipe and a yellow ground colour which becomes most apparent in the gills and in the cortex; innate reddish, green, olive, blackish or reddish brown scales are present not only in the cap cuticle but often also on the stipe. The flesh is rather tough, the spore print is white, the spores are smooth and nonamyloid. Large cheilocystidia are present on the gill edges.

The leading representative of the genus is *Tricholomopsis rutilans,* a neat fungus found on the stumps of conifers from July to October. Occasionally it grows out of dead roots or wood logs. It is particularly abundant in spruce and pine forests on acid substrates. The fruit bodies appear either solitarily or in smaller clumps. They have a 5–15 cm wide cap, campaniform at first, soon flatly expanded, slightly obtusely umbonate at the centre; the cuticle is purple-red over a yellow ground colour, finely felted, with appressed fibrous scales. The broad gills are golden-yellow, emarginate, decurrent by a tooth. The stipe is cylindrical, 1–1.5 cm thick, golden-yellow with reddish velvety patches. The flesh is pale yellow, with a faint resinous smell. Young fruit bodies are suitable for eating in mushroom mixtures. Older fruit bodies, when cooked, smell unpleasantly of earth or mice but their taste remains unimpaired.

The rare *T. decora* may occasionally be found growing in mountain forests on fallen timber of coniferous trees. It attains half the size of the species described here, and is inedible.

Spores: 6–8 × 4.5–5.5 μm, broadly ellipsoid, smooth, colourless

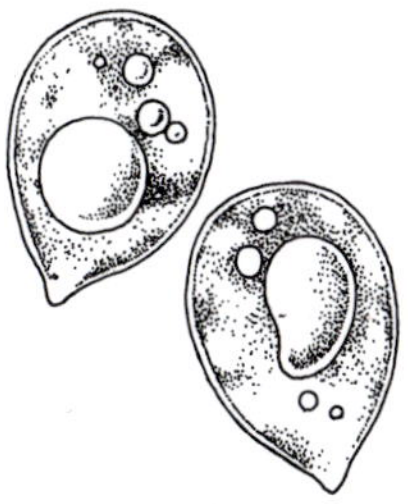

Tricholomopsis decora

Tricholomopsis rutilans

Tricholoma caligatum
(Viv.) Ricken

This fungus is much better known in Japan than in Europe, being the most popular edible mushroom there, where it is called *matsu-take,* i.e. 'pine mushroom'. In Japanese mycological literature it is most frequently referred to as *Armillaria matsu-take.* In Japan it mostly grows in *Pinus densiflora* woods, less frequently under spruces or firs, rarely also under *Tsuga sieboldii.* It is highly esteemed for its taste and smell. It grows from October to November, yet in a rainy spring it may occur as early as May and June. Pine-mushroom hunting is a Japanese national sport, particularly for city dwellers with pine woods in their neighbourhood.

T. caligatum is widespread throughout the north temperate zone, yet in Europe it is extremely rare. It occurs more abundantly in warmer regions – the more northwards, the more sporadic is its occurrence. Robust, thick- and firm-fleshed fruit bodies usually grow solitarily. The greater part of the 10–15 cm wide cap is covered with large, appressed, fibrous scales, rusty to sepia-brown, the whitish ground colour being visible among the scales. A thick veil joins the cap margin to the stipe where it leaves a broad, membranous annulus that later withers. The gills are crowded, white, then cream, and brown-spotted at the edge. The flesh is white or cream-coloured, with a sweetish or fruity smell and a mild taste.

Spores: 5.5–8 × 4.5–5 μm, broadly ellipsoid, smooth, colourless

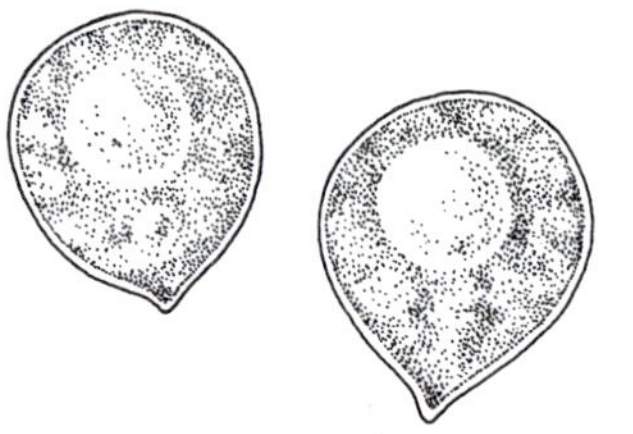

Tricholoma colossus
(Fr.) Quél.

Tricholoma colossus is one of the largest gill fungi: its fruit bodies are truly gigantic and the impression they produce is further enhanced by their frequent occurrence in clumps. The cap is as much as 25 cm in diameter; it is thick-fleshed, semiglobular with a thickly involute margin when young, expanded-convex in age, with a finely felted cuticle, sticky to moderately slimy in wet weather, and is of a cloudy flesh- to brick-red colour. The 10–15 cm long stipe is 5–10 cm thick at the base, at first ovoid-bulbous, later almost cylindrical, with its base inflated so as to resemble a turnip root. It is white and floccose near the apex, the lower part being covered with a reddish brown, soon slightly lacerated coating whose upper part is only weakly developed, so that no perceptible ring is formed. The gills are emarginate, decurrent by a tooth, rather crowded, whitish, and sprinkled with reddish spots. The flesh is thick and tough, white, later pinkish – especially in the stipe, slowly staining salmon-pink to red when cut. It has no specific smell or taste. The spore print is white.

T. colossus is a rare mushroom. It grows on the ground in sandy pine woods from September to October, and has been reported from most European countries. It is not poisonous but its excessively tough flesh makes it unsuitable for table use.

Spores: 8–10 × 5–6 µm,
broadly ellipsoid, smooth, colourless

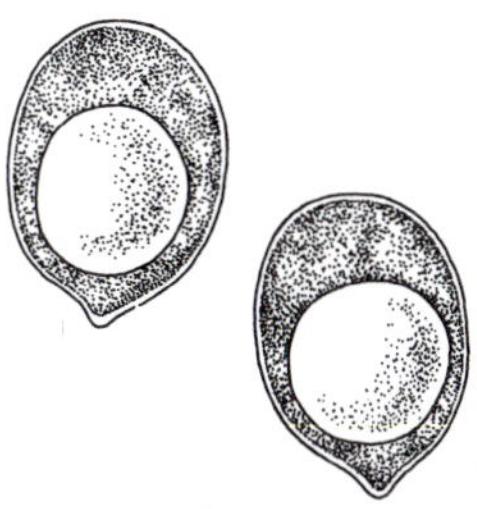

Tricholoma fulvum
(DC. ex Fr.) Sacc.

Many species of fungi are associated with the birch or have a preference for birch wood. This is certainly true of *Tricholoma fulvum,* although it may occur under other woody plants as well. Its cap is 5–12 cm in diameter, broadly conical-campanulate, later convex to flat, broadly and obtusely umbonate at the centre. The cuticle is slimy when wet, rusty brown or brown. It is darkest in the centre, gradually shading to rusty yellow towards the margin. The cylindrical, relatively long and slender stipe is 1–12 cm thick, always narrowing downwards, pale brown or red-brown, glabrous at the apex, dark brown, fibrous, and slimy at the base. The gills are rather crowded, at first pale yellow, then yellow, changing to russet with age; their edges are particularly marked with rusty stains. The flesh is creamy in the cap, yellow in the stipe, rusty brown in the stipe base. It has a rather unpleasant smell of freshly ground meal with an admixture of radish and a taste of urine. The spore print is white.

T. fulvum grows from summer until late autumn in lighter forest habitats, often in grass bordering tracks, in woodland margins and meadows, and preferably in foothills.

The prevailing opinion is that this and the related *T. albobrunneum* are poisonous, causing diarrhoea and vomiting. *T. albobrunneum* has persistently white gills and a markedly red cap; its white flesh has a cucumber-mealy smell and taste. It grows in pine woods.

Spores: 6–7 × 4.5 –6 μm, broadly ellipsoid, smooth, colourless

Tricholoma fulvum

Tricholoma albobrunneum

Tricholoma vaccinum

(Pers. ex Fr.) Kumm.

Tricholoma vaccinum is a small- to medium-sized fungus with a typical reddish colouring, scaly cap surface and bitter taste. The cap is 3–9 cm wide, rarely larger, relatively thin-fleshed, and of a red-brown or reddish rusty colour, covered with fibrous erect scales all over the surface. The cuticle between the scales is lighter and fibrous-felted. The stipe is up to 10 cm long and up to 1.5 cm thick, cylindrical, sometimes slightly inflated at the base, always hollow. The stipe surface is fibrous scaly, and the same colour as the cap. Below the apex of the stipe, under the gills, there is a sharp colour divide, the stipe apex being lighter-coloured than the rest. The fibrillose veil which in the young fungus connects the cap margin with the stipe soon disappers. The gills are emarginate and decurrent by a tooth, dirty whitish, later dingy reddish, and up to 15 mm broad. The flesh is whitish, then reddish or with a rusty tinge; it has an earthy smell and a bitter-sour taste. The spore print is white.

T. vaccinum grows from July to October in groups in the needle carpet covering the ground of coniferous forests. It occurs particularly often in younger, dense spruce stands, primarily on a calcareous substrate. It is unsuitable for eating because of its bitter taste.

Spores: 4–6 × 4.5 μm,
shortly ellipsoid, smooth, colourless

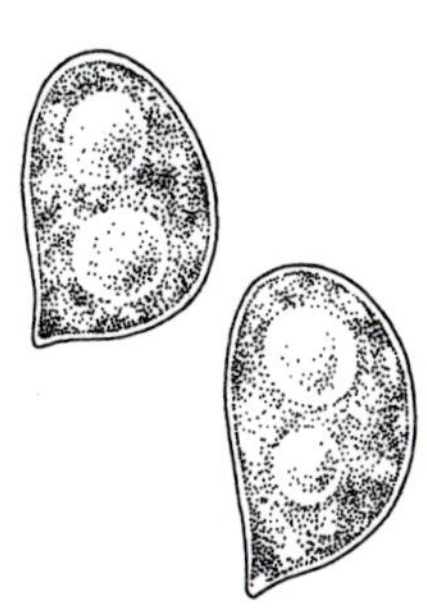

Tricholoma portentosum

(Fr.) Quél.

Two species of the genus *Tricholoma* occupy a special position among mushrooms collected for culinary purposes, namely *T. portentosum* and *T. flavovirens*. Both these species are excellent edible mushroom.

T. portentosum is a fleshy mushrooms with a greyish to grey-black cap streaked with blackish fibres. The cap is 3–10 cm wide, umbonate, slightly viscid when moist, without scales, and often with an irregularly wavy margin. The stipe and gills are white but with quite an apparent lemon-yellow tinge. The flesh has a pleasant farinaceous smell and taste.

The favourite habitat of this species are coniferous, mostly pine, forests on a sandy substrate. It appears in clumps and never occurs before late autumn (from September to December). It can be prepared for the table in many ways.

T. portentosum may sometimes be mistaken for the edible but far less palatable *T. argyraceum* which has a fibrillose cap and yellowing gills and stipe. Its smell is similar to that of *T. portentosum,* and it also grows in clumps in autumn in coniferous forests, especially in the outskirts of spruce stands.

Very rarely indeed, *T. portentosum* is confused with the inedible *T. virgatum.* The latter has an acutely conical, ash-grey, shiny cap with ingrown radial fibres. The whole fruit body shows no trace of lemon tint – on the contrary, it is predominantly grey. The acrid-tasting flesh of this species is capable of spoiling any mushroom dish to which *T. virgatum* has been added by mistake.

The only truly poisonous grey-coloured species of *Tricholoma* with which all the above-mentioned species might be confused through utter carelessness is *T. tigrinum,* a large fleshy fungus growing on calcareous forest soils in hilly and mountainous regions; its cap is coarsely scaly from the break-up of the cuticle and the stipe stains red where handled.

Tricholoma portentosum

Spores of *Tricholoma portentosum*:
5–6 × 3.5–5 μm, shortly ellipsoid, colourless

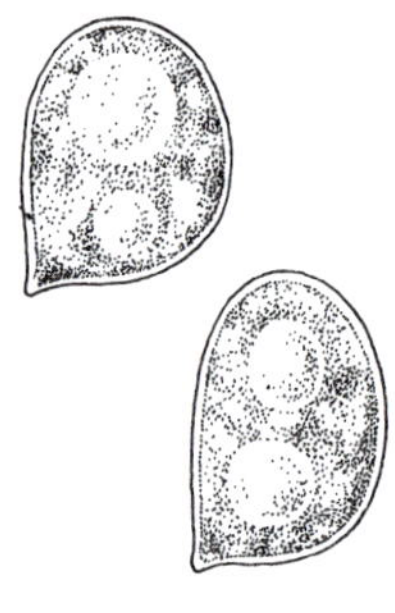

Tricholoma terreum resembles *T. portentosum* but is more slender, brittle, lacking the yellow tint on the stipe as well as the farinaceous taste and smell

Tricholoma flavovirens
(Pers. ex Fr.) Lund.

The conspicuously coloured *Tricholoma flavovirens* occupies the foremost place among the edible species of *Tricholoma.* It attracts attention not only through its predominantly green-yellow colouring but also by being one of the last larger-sized edible mushrooms profusely growing in pine woods in late autumn.

The cap measuring up to 10 cm across is at first bell-shaped, then flattened, slightly umbonate at the centre, entirely greenish yellow or olive-toned, darker radially fibrous, slimy in damp weather. The stipe is usually shorter than the diameter of the cap, cylindrical, 1–1.5 cm thick, tough-fleshed, fibrose on the surface, greenish yellow. The gills are emarginate, attached to the stipe by a tooth, bright sulphur-yellow, and subcrowded. The flesh is white, yellowish only under the cuticle of both cap and stipe, unchanging when cut, with a pleasant mealy smell and taste. The spore print is white.

In older mycological literature *T. flavovirens* is usually called *T. equestre.* It is a mushroom peculiar to dry pine woods on a sandy substrate, where it occurs gregariously from the end of September until November, practically until the first frosts. Occasionally it appears even in mixed forests. In recent years, however, it has almost completely disappeared from some regions, or has become a rarity. It is an excellent edible mushroom. When it is collected, care must be taken not to confuse it with the poisonous *T. sejunctum* or with *T. sulphureum.*

Spores: 6–8 × 3.5–5 μm,
ellipsoid-ovoid, smooth, colourless

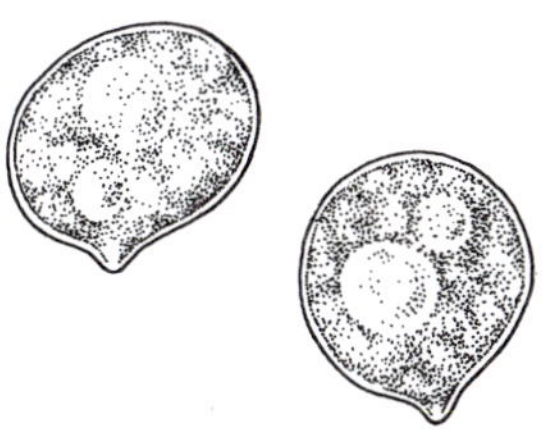

☠ *Tricholoma sulphureum*

Tricholoma flavovirens

Tricholoma sejunctum

(Sow. ex Fr.) Quél.

It is urgently recommended that mushroom pickers should not collect this fungus for table use as it is poisonous. It is relatively variable, at least in the coloration and sculpture of the cap. This is 3–10 cm wide, yellowish green to yellow-brown, fuscous and deeper brown in the centre, lighter and bright yellow or yellowish green towards the margin. The cuticle, mainly around the centre, is streaked with fine innate dark brown or blackish brown fibrils, in places it may be slightly scaly. The stipe is up to 10 cm long and 1–3 cm thick, cylindrical, white or yellow-toned, finely fibrous, and scaly near the apex. The gills are fairly distant, deeply emarginate, relatively broad, white when young and later tinged whitish green or yellowish, brownish in age, and frequently have an uneven to dentate edge. The flesh is brittle, white or creamy, lemon-yellowish under the cap cuticle, sometimes with grey stains, the smell resembles freshly ground flour and so does the taste – this may also be bitter and sometimes astringent. The spore print is white.

The typical *Tricholoma sejunctum* occurs usually solitarily from August to November in warm and dry mixed or deciduous forests, particularly in oak stands, but also in coniferous forests. Inexperienced mushroom pickers might confuse the specimens growing in coniferous forests with *T. flavovirens*. *T. sejunctum* is poisonous.

Spores: 5–7 × 5–5.5 μm, globose-ovoid, smooth, colourless

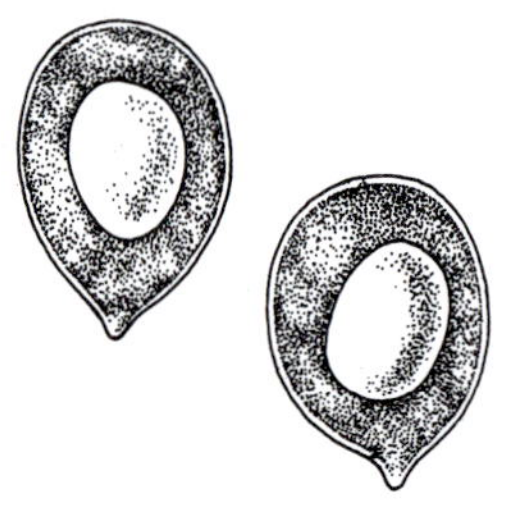

Sulphurous Tricholoma

Tricholoma sulphureum (Bull. ex Fr.) Kumm.

The Sulphurous Tricholoma readily betrays its presence by its penetrating, unpleasant odour strongly similar to coal gas. The fruit body is sulphur-yellow, and more or less olive-toned on the cap. It is smaller in size, the cap is usually 3–5 cm in diameter, rarely somewhat larger, the cuticle is dull, very finely fibrous. The gills are distant, broad (ventricose), readily breakable, deeply emarginate, adnate-subdecurrent. The stipe is usually greater than the diameter of the cap in length; it is 0.5–1 cm thick, cylindrical, attenauted and hooked at the base, often compressed all along its length, with a finely fibrous surface, full or hollow. The flesh of the entire fruit body is sulphur-yellow and unchanging. The spore print is white.

The Sulphurous Tricholoma grows solitarily in dry deciduous forests (particularly in oak and oak-hornbeam stands) as well as in mixed forests from July till September. It is a poisonous fungus. Its nauseous smell should ensure that nobody would care to pick it for table use. There is a possibility of confusing it with similarly coloured but edible species of *Tricholoma* (mainly with *T. flavovirens*). However, the consistency of *T. flavovirens'* fruit bodies, their noticeably different colouring and especially their white context, always with a yellowish tinge in the margin and pleasantly smelling of flour, are sufficiently distinctive characteristics to make confusion highly improbable.

Spores: 8–10 × 5–6 µm, ellipsoid, smooth, colourless

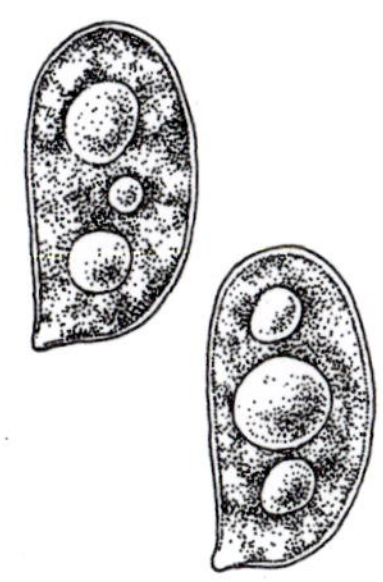

Fruit bodies of *Tricholoma flavovirens*

Tricholoma sulphureum

Tricholoma columbetta
(Fr.) Kumm.

This species of *Tricholoma* is easily identified by its snow-white colouring, the silky sheen of its cap surface sometimes scattered with carmine patches, and its pleasant smell. The 4–10 cm wide cap is very fleshy, at first convex, then expanded, with a wavy-lobed, involute, finely matted-tomentose margin. The cuticle is smooth, silky-shiny, often irregularly sprinkled with violet stains. The stipe is cylindrical, uneven, often contorted, 1–2 cm thick, mostly attenuated and covered with earth at the base. Just above this layer of earth it is tinged blue to greenish blue, otherwise it is entirely white, fibrous and shiny. The gills are rather broad, distant, deeply emarginate, white, then cream-yellowish, with uneven or crinkled edges. The flesh is white, not liable to change, juicy, with no specific taste and an agreeable scent like that of the Bird Cherry. The spore print is white.

Tricholoma columbetta is a typical but rare fungus of sparse deciduous forests growing on noncalcareous soils. It occurs, usually under birches, from August to October, and is edible. This fungus could be mistaken for *T. album* which is also white, but its cap is cream-coloured or straw-yellow; the context soon has a sharply acrid taste and smells unpleasantly of coal gas, in which it resembles the Sulphurous Tricholoma. *T. album* is an inedible fungus occurring in deciduous forests.

Spores: 5–6 × 4–5 μm,
ovally globose, smooth, colourless

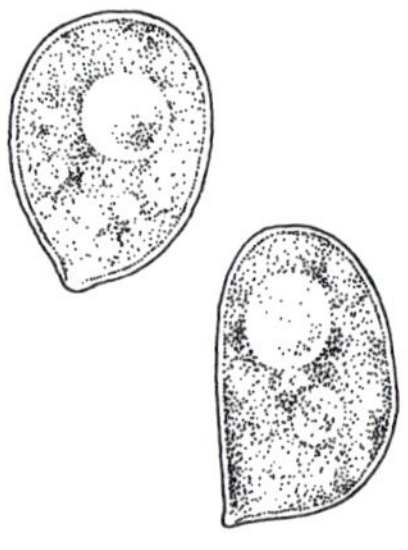

Tricholoma terreum

(Schaeff. ex Fr.) Kumm.

Tricholoma terreum is a remarkably hardy fungus growing mostly after the cooler autumn weather sets in, often even after the first frosts – insofar as they are followed by warm spells. Its grey or greyish brown colouring makes it quite inconspicuous. The 4–7 cm wide cap is softly and finely scaly-felted, dry, thin-fleshed and brittle. The stipe, rarely exceeding the diameter of the cap in length, is cylindrical, slender, shining white, and longitudinally fibrous. The gills are subcrowded, emarginate and attached by a tooth, white when young and greyish when older. The flesh in white, unchanging, with a taste and smell markedly like freshly ground flour. The spore print is white.

T. terreum appears in clumps in all kinds of forests, but mainly in dry pine woods on calcareous soils. It favours habitats under the European Black Pine. It is edible and savoury enough, yet its fruit bodies are friable and cannot be transported without damage. It is often collected because it grows at a time when other edible mushrooms are scarce. Some mushroom pickers mistake it for *T. portentosum* which, however, is very different as regards both the fleshiness of its fruit bodies and the yellow-toned stipe and gills. The deadly poisonous *T. tigrinum* is distinguished by robust fruit bodies, by an ash-brown cap covered with tectiform, originally silvery grey, darkening scales, and finally by a stipe rufescent in its inflated lower portion after handling.

Spores: 5–7 × 4–5 μm,
ellipsoid, smooth, colourless

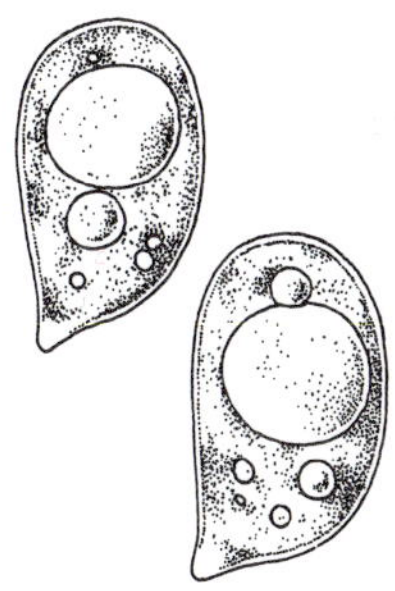

Tricholoma terreum

Honey Fungus, Honey Agaric, Shoestring Mushroom

Armillaria mellea (Vahl. ex Fr.) Kumm.

The generally known Honey Fungus is in fact a complex of several species differing from each other in a number of characteristics of secondary importance, whose taxonomic evaluation has hitherto not been finalized. Therefore the state of knowledge of this species and the distinctions among individual varieties differ from one author to another. As an edible mushroom, the Honey Fungus has been widely collected for culinary purposes for a long time. Yet the ingestion of quite a small part of a raw fruit body causes indigestion. Similar troubles may sometimes arise even after sufficient heat processing. The probability may not be excluded that one of the several closely related species making up this complex is poisonous.

From the point of view of mycological phytopathology, *A. mellea* is a much-feared and generally widespread tree disease, particularly dangerous in its mycelial stage.

Clumps of Honey-Fungus fructifications, more rarely single fruit bodies, grow predominantly on stumps but also on roots and trunks of both living and dead woody plants. The main vegetation period of Honey Fungi is in September and October, but in cooler summers they may appear as early as July. The Honey Fungus is distinguished from caespitose species of the genera *Pholiota* and *Gymnopilus* by the pure white spore print, among other factors.

The related *Armillaria tabescens* is more plentiful in warmer regions where it grows particularly on oaks.

Spores of *Armillaria mellea*:
7–9 × 5–6 µm, ellipsoid-ovoid, colourless

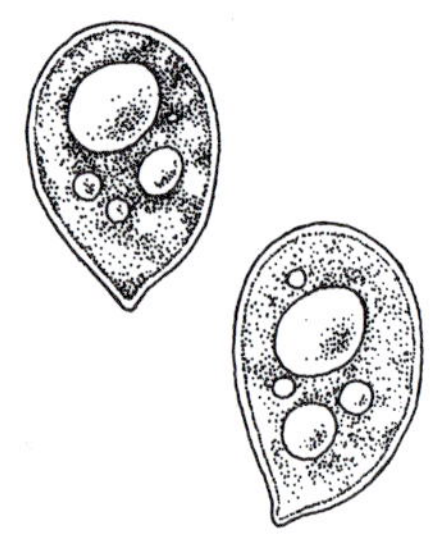

Armillaria mellea

Armillaria tabescens

Lyophyllum connatum
(Schum. ex Fr.) Sing.

The genus *Lyophyllum* includes white-spored fungi of the family Tricholomataceae, and is approximately halfway between the genera *Tricholoma* and *Clitocybe.* They are characterized by a particular combination of macro- and micro-features the most important of which are the 'siderophilous basidia'. These are basidia whose plasma contains carminophilous granules (i. e. granules becoming dark-coloured through the operation of acetocarmine). On the whole, however, both *Lyophyllum connatum* and *L. fumosum* can reliably be identified without using a microscope.

L. connatum has a 3–15 cm wide, fleshy, obtusely convex cap, almost entirely white or whitish, sometimes olive-greyish to light bluish when moist, with an involute margin and a smooth, glabrous, finely pruinose cuticle. The gills are subdecurrent, white, and yellowish in age. Fruit bodies grow in dense clusters with their stipe bases mutually fusing to form a tuberiform structure. The context has a cucumber-mealy taste and smell, it is white and shows a colour reaction when touched with a 10 per cent green-vitriol solution, at first becoming bluish violet and then pink. The spore print is white.

L. connatum may be found in summer and in autumn on bare, damp ground or in grass in deciduous and coniferous forests, sometimes also on the remnants of rotten wood, e. g. on sawdust. It is edible.

Spores: 6–8 × 3.5–4.5 µm, subglobose, smooth, nonamyloid, colourless

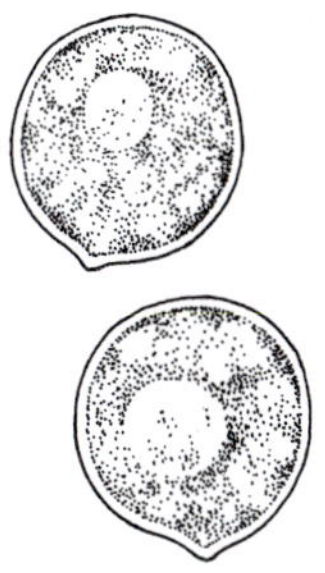

Lyophyllum fumosum

(Pers. ex Fr.) Orton

This mushroom has also been known and described in literature as *Lyophyllum conglobatum,* or still earlier as *Tricholoma conglobatum.* It resembles *L. connatum* in its general appearance, as well as in that its whitish stipes grow out of a common tuberiform base in large numbers. It is distinguished from it by a dark grey, greyish brown to blackish brown cap and whitish gills, which ultimately turn grey. Fruit bodies growing in the dark, e. g. in cellars or other subterranean spaces, are usually white or very light-coloured. The white flesh tastes and smells of cucumber and flour. Quite different is the shape of spores which are subglobose and extremely small.

L. fumosum occurs predominantly in places associated with human activity – in yards, along fences, in roadside ditches, rubbish heaps, orchards, gardens, but also in cellars, on piles of excavated earth, or in street pavements. Its occurence in nature – especially in woods – is rare.

Powerful clumps of *L. fumosum* sometimes contain as many as 100–200 fruit bodies, and the tuberiform structure concealed in the ground, from which the fruit bodies grow, measures approximately 5–10 cm in diameter. The force developed by growing fruit bodies is remarkable. Reports of pedestrian pavements being uplifted by fruit-body clusters serve to support this fact. *L. fumosum* is an edible mushroom with a pleasing taste.

Spores: 5–6 μm, subglobose, smooth, colourless

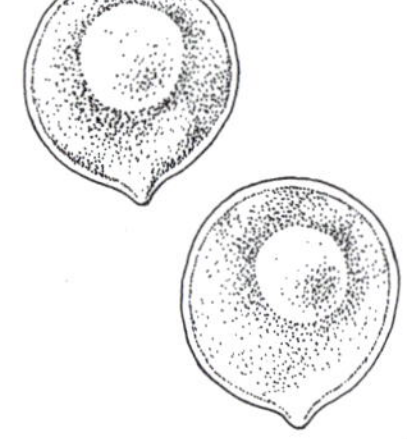

Tephrocybe atrata

(Fr. ex Fr.) Donk

Nowadays the genus *Tephrocybe* includes fungi whose common feature are basidia with siderophilous granulation. In the past they were classified as members of the genus *Collybia.* They are mostly smaller fungi with caps rarely exceeding 5 cm in diameter, coloured in darker shades of grey, greyish brown to blackish. Also the gills are more or less grey or off-white. A number of species have an intense cucumber-mealy smell and a similar taste.

Tephrocybe atrata is one of the characteristic representatives of an ecologically interesting group of fungi whose occurrence is confined to burned ground only. It occurs predominantly on burned-over areas on man-made sites and in forests. Its cap is 2–4 cm across, with relatively elastic and thin flesh, depressed at the centre, blackish brown to black in wet weather, lighter in dry weather, and glabrous. The stipe is thinly cylindrical, unequal, the same colour as the cap, whitish at the base, glabrous, and cartilaginous. The greyish gills are subdistant, broadly adnate, and subdecurrent. The crushed flesh smells strongly of cucumbers and flour with a tinge of cod-liver oil. The spore print is pure white.

Another, much rarer, species is *T. ambusta.* It greatly resembles *T. atrata* in appearance but for a wartlike excrescence situated in the centre of the cap. It can be safely recognized by its verrucose spores, 5–8 × 5–6.5 μm in size.

Spores of *Tephrocybe atrata*:
5–6 × 3–4 μm, broadly ellipsoid, smooth, colourless

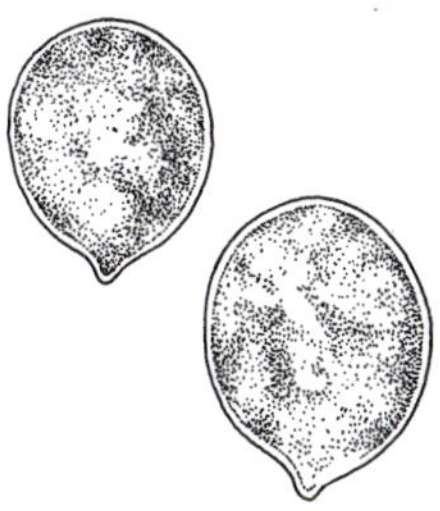

Tephrocybe atrata

Geopetalum carbonarium also populates burned-over areas, but is a rarity

St. George's Mushroom
Calocybe gambosa (Fr.) Donk

St. George's Mushroom is one of the well-known and very popular edible species. It is an excellent mushroom which can be prepared and cooked in very many ways, dried or otherwise preserved. St. George's Mushrooms appear in nature with the arrival of spring, perhaps as early as the end of April but more often in May. They grow mostly outside the forest – usually on warm, sun-bathed slopes overgrown with grass and shrubs, in sheltered woodland margins, under shrubs, in gardens and pasturelands. If they are occasionally found in woods, it is in forest clearings. The fruit bodies usually grow in circles; they often remain hidden in tufts of larger grasses, sometimes covered by their last year's leaves, and consequently are easily overlooked. At higher elevations they tend to occur somewhat later, in high mountains they grow in July.

The colour of St. George's Mushroom is extremely varied. The cap is usually whitish but can also be pale ochre-yellowish, buff, brownish and greyish brown; the gills are conspicuously narrow and crowded, whitish, yellow-toned, pale ochre, but also greyish; the stipe is whitish to yellowish. Quite specific and persistent is the intense farinaceous smell and taste of the white, fleshy cortex. Cases of poisoning are caused by its confusion with the poisonous *Inocybe patouillardii* which is distinguished, among other things, by olive-greyish brown gills and a rufescent cortex.

Spores of *Calocybe gambosa*:
4–7 × 2–4 μm, ellipsoid, smooth, colourless

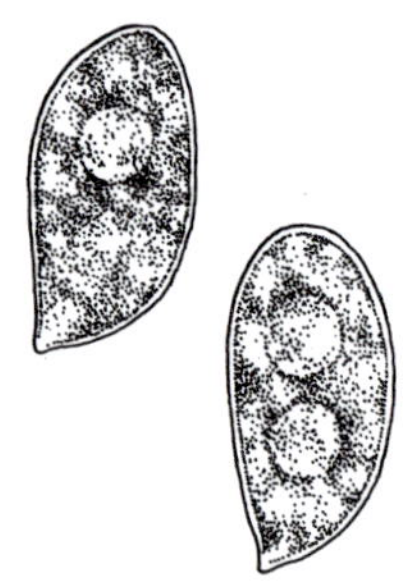

Calocybe gambosa

Inocybe patouillardii

Giant Clitocybe

Leucopaxillus giganteus (Sibth. ex Fr.) Sing.

This giant among gill fungi is in ract one of the largest of any fungi. The cap attains as much as 25 cm in diameter and soon becomes deeply funnel-shaped in the centre, clearly involute and striate in the margin, with a smooth, finely sericeous surface; the originally white colouring gradually changes into leathery yellow. The deeply decurrent gills are also white, discolouring to leathery yellow with age. The stipe, 5–8 cm long and 2–5 cm thick, is remarkably short, tough-fleshed, solid, whitish. Also the flesh is white, unchanging, with an unpleasant spermatic odour and no distinctive taste. The spore print is white.

The Giant Clitocybe grows in groups or circles in grass in pastures, gardens, forest outskirts and woodland meadows. It is edible, though relatively tough. The species included in the genus *Leucopaxillus* were originally classified as members of the genus *Clitocybe.* They typically possess amyloid spores usually sculptured with warts which distinguish this genus from *Clitocybe* on the one hand, and *Tricholoma* on the other. The fruit bodies of all *Leucopaxillus* species are large and fleshy; the Giant Clitocybe, belonging to the most common ones, is the largest of them.

Leucopaxillus candidus closely resembles the species referred to above but is persistently white, with a smooth, felted cap margin. It grows in subalpine meadows.

Spores: 6–7 × 4–5 μm, ovoid-ellipsoid, smooth, colourless, amyloid

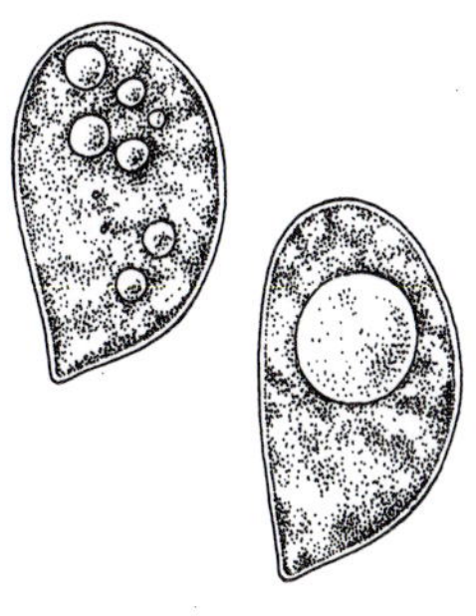

Section through a part of the fruit body of *Leucopaxillus giganteus*

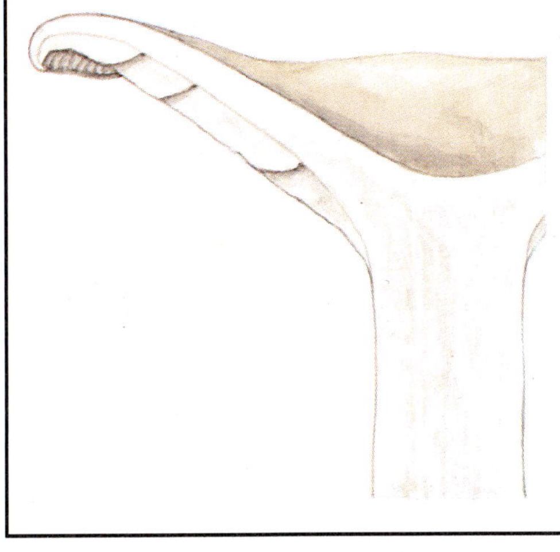

Melanoleuca brevipes

(Bull. ex Fr.) Pat.

Fungi of the genus *Melanoleuca* are in fact *Tricholoma* species with amyloid, minutely verrucose, finely ornamented spores and characteristic cheilocystidia. They are, however, distinguishable at first sight even without a microscope by their slender, upright stipe with a fibrous surface, and a very regularly circular, relatively thin-fleshed cap that gives the impression of having been turned on a lathe; the cap may be grey, brown, or less often ochre or white. The cap often bears an obtuse umbo at the centre, the gills are always crowded and regular, white or yellowish. Individual species, about fifty of which have been described, are extremely similar and can be distinguished only with difficulty.

Melanoleuca brevipes occasionally makes its appearance in grassy places beside field paths, in meadows or in gardens. Its cap measures 3–6 cm in diameter; it is greyish brown, umber or porphyritic-brown, innately radially fibrous, and depressed-umbonate in the centre. The gills are persistently white, the stipe is concolorous with the cap or somewhat paler, claviform, 2–4 cm long, 4–8 mm thick. The flesh is whitish in the cap, brownish in the basal part of the stipe, tasteless and odourless. The spore print is white.

Noteworthy among the other species, edible just like *M. brevipes,* is *M. cognata* with its brownish cap measuring up to 10 cm in diameter and bright ochre-yellowish gills. It occurs from April to May, and then again in autumn, in both coniferous and mixed forests at path edges, but also in the decaying foliage in old gardens, parks, and on compost heaps.

Spores of *Melanoleuca brevipes*: 7–8 × 4.5–6 μm, ellipsoid, verrucose, colourless, amyloid

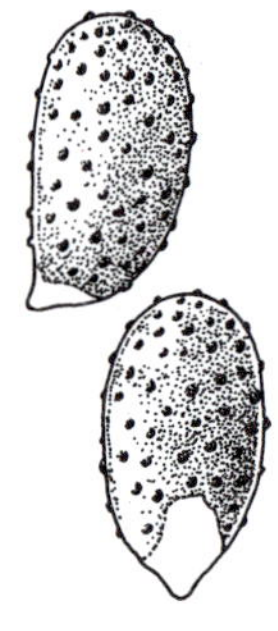

Cheilocystidia

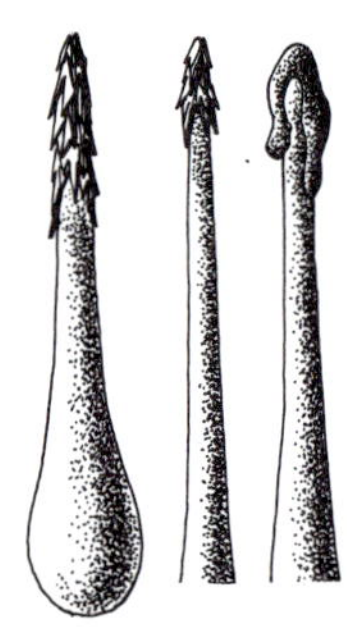

Catathelasma imperiale
(Fr.) Sing.

This is a robust fleshy fungus of the Tricholomataceae group, resembling the genus *Tricholoma* also in its general appearance. It is distinguished from the typical representatives of the genus *Tricholoma* by a double annulus on the stipe, as well as by clearly decurrent gills. The genus *Catathelasma* is microscopically differentiated from the true *Tricholoma* by amyloid spores and a bilateral gill trama. It is a monotypic genus; its only species, *C. imperiale,* is referred to in older mycological literature as *Armillaria imperialis.* The cap is 10–15 cm broad (sometimes even broader), at first strongly convex, whitish, later slightly convex and broadly depressed, reddish brown, streaked with brown to mottled, appressedly scaly in the centre, later glabrous, sometimes cracked, with a strongly involute margin, and often lobed or wavy. The gills are dirty white to pale yellowish. The stipe is up to 15 cm long and 3–4 cm thick, tough-fleshed, pale ochre, usually attenuated downwards, with a double membranous, flaring, whitish annulus situated right below the gills. As a rule, the stipe is deeply submerged in forest soil. The flesh is white, very tough, of a pleasant mealy smell and a mild taste. The spore print is white.

C. imperiale grows in August and September on calcareous soils in coniferous, mainly pine and spruce forests, and also in mixed forests including oaks. In general it is a rare species, occurring more profusely in some regions only – e.g. in the Carpathian Mountains. It is edible.

Spores: 11–15 × 5–6 μm, ellipsoid, smooth, colourless

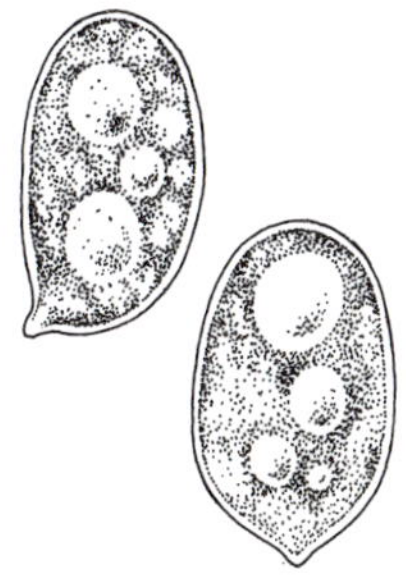

Wood Woolly-foot

Collybia peronata (Bolt. ex Fr.) Kumm.

Not all species in the relatively large genus *Collybia* resemble the widely known Russet Shank (*Collybia dryophila*). The Wood Woolly-foot is dissimilar both in colour and – particularly – in its markedly distant gills. The 2–5 cm wide cap is planoconvex, later expanded, with a slightly furrowed margin and thin, elastic context, light flesh-brown when moist, pale buff when dry, glabrous. The gills are at first pale yellow to yellow-brown, then pale brown. The stipe is relatively long, thinly cylindrical, 3–5 mm thick, slightly inflated at the base, strigose-felted, yellowish to reddish brown, elastic. The flesh is pale yellow, with a burning acrid taste and an acidulous smell. The spore print is white.

The Wood Woolly-foot occurs profusely throughout the summer and early autumn. It grows either singly or in sparse clusters in rotting leaves heaped up in higher layers in deciduous and mixed forests; occasionally it can be found also in conifer forests. Its acrid taste makes it unsuitable for eating.

Not uncommon in similar habitats is *C. confluens*. It often forms dense clusters consisting of many dozens of specimens. This species has a pale tan or brownish, sometimes whitish, cap, and very crowded, narrow, whitish, later brownish gills. The context is not acrid. The stipe base is densely overgrown with a whitish mycelium enveloping the leaves, needles or twigs from which the fruit bodies grow. *C. confluens* is inedible.

Spores of *Collybia peronata*:
6–7 × 3–4 μm, spindle-shaped, smooth, colourless

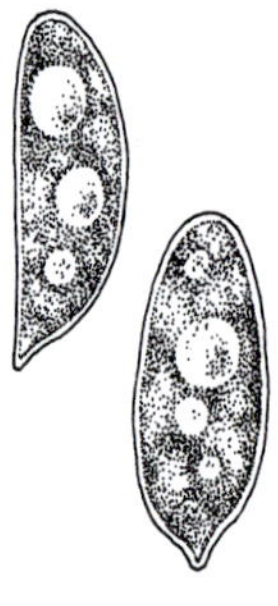

Collybia peronata

Fruit-body cluster of *Collybia confluens*

Russet Shank

Collybia dryophila (Bull. ex Fr.) Quél.

The Russet Shank is an ecologically extraordinarily adaptable species not depending exclusively on the oak, as its name would suggest, but occurring under both deciduous and coniferous trees. Neither is it choosey as regards the substrate: it can grow on extremely acid substrates – e. g. in peat soils – as well as on basic calcareous soils. It ranges from low elevations high up into the mountains where it accompanies communities of low, decumbent willow shrubs. In spite of its colour variability it can be fairly easily recognized by some of its persistent properties, especially by the markedly dense, white, whitish to pale yellow gills, and also by the tubular, thin and elastic, ochre-yellow stipe which is glabrous and smooth, with the exception of the white felted base. The typical variety of *Collybia dryophila* has a 2–6 cm wide cap, soon flatly expanded, with thin and elastic flesh, pale ochre and fading to whitish when dry. In other varieties the cap is yellowish brown, flesh-reddish or chestnut-brown. The white or yellowish context has a pleasant smell not unlike the Edible Boletus, and a mild taste. The spore print is pure white.

The Russet Shank is an edible and savoury mushroom, although of no great nutritive value due to the thin flesh of the cap (for it is only the caps that are used, the stipes being too tough). The most marked colour variation has sulphur-yellow gills, a yellowish stipe and a red-brown cap; it is regarded by some mycologists as an independent species, *C. exsculpta*. It is also edible but much less common, and grows like the typical Russet Shank from May until the autumn.

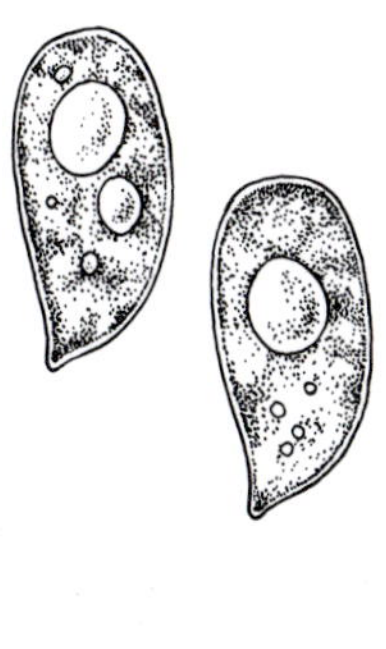

Spores: 4–6 × 2–3 μm, ellipsoid, smooth, colourless

Greasy Tough Shank

Collybia butyracea (Bull. ex Fr.) Quél.

The Greasy Tough Shank has a 4–8 cm wide cap, bell-shaped when young, later expanded, sometimes slightly and obtusely umbonate in the centre, deep red-brown, chestnut-brown in wet weather, pale cocoa-brown when dry. The cap cuticle is glabrous and smooth. The stipe is 4–8 cm long, 5–20 mm thick, cylindrical, markedly clavately enlarged towards the base, soft, coarsely longitudinally fibrous and sulcate. The apical part of the stipe below the gills is lighter to whitish, the rest is red-brown. The gills are deeply emarginate and adnexed, crowded, rather broad, whitish. The flesh is white, sometimes faintly smelling of rancid butter, with a mild taste. The spore print is pure white. The Greasy Tough Shank is a common species inhabiting deciduous, mixed and coniferous forests. It grows in leaves and needles, usually in groups, from July to November, practically till the first frosts. It is edible; only caps are gathered.

Collybia asema is a closely related species considered by some mycologists to be a variety of the Greasy Tough Shank. Its similarity to the latter in both size and appearance is striking, the only difference being that *C. asema* has an ash-grey or greenish grey cap with an almost dark brown central umbo. The strongly hygrophanous cap fades to a whitish shade in dry weather. Also the stipe is light grey or brownish grey. *C. asema* grows mainly in coniferous and mixed forests, and, in some regions, it is more common than the Greasy Tough Shank. It is also edible.

Spores of *Collybia. butyracea*:
6–8 × 3–3.5 μm, ellipsoid, smooth, colourless

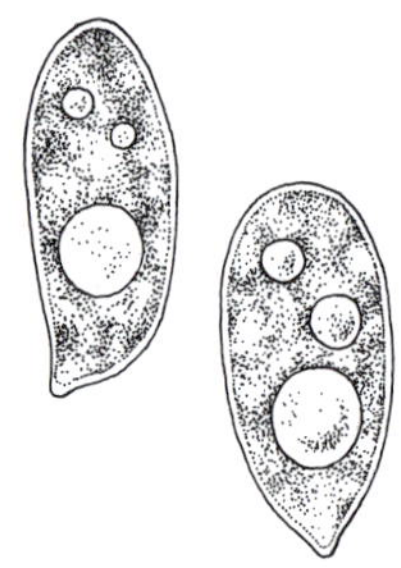

Collybia asema

Collybia butyracea

Spotted Tough Shank

Collybia maculata (Alb. et Schw. ex Fr.) Kumm.

The Spotted Tough Shank is distinguished from the other species of *Collybia* by the size and fleshiness of its fruit bodies. The 5–12 cm wide cap is semiglobular, convex, then expanded, with a narrowly involute margin; its surface is smooth, glabrous, originally white or slightly yellow-toned, sooner or later scattered with irregular brownish red or rusty brown spots. The stipe is often longer than the cap diameter, 1–2 cm thick, cylindrical, often flexible, longitudinally finely fibrous, tough, contorted, and with an abrupt root that looks as if it had been bitten off at the base. It is white but, later on, strewn with reddish brown patches, just like the cap – particularly at the base. The gills are very crowded, narrow, emarginate, attached by a tooth, white, with finely serrate or minutely dentate edges. The spore print is yellowish pink. The entire fruit body changes to reddish brown with age or on handling. The flesh is white, tough, with a slightly sweetish smell and a tart, bitter taste.

The Spotted Tough Shank grows on rotten wood below ground, i. e. seemingly from the ground, sometimes directly on stumps and roots. It occurs exclusively in coniferous forests, especially in pine woods and in mountain spruce forests. It appears mostly in late summer and in autumn, growing until the onset of frosts.

Being ecologically and morphologically considerably different from other *Collybia* species, it is treated by some mycologists as a member of the independent genus *Rhodocollybia*. It is inedible.

Spores: 5–6 × 4–5 μm, subglobose, smooth, colourless

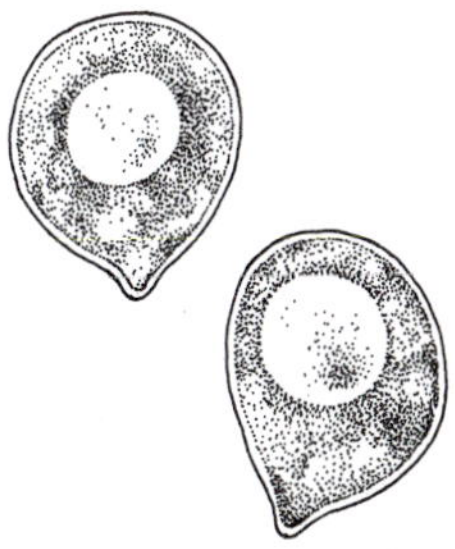

Hohenbuehelia petaloides

(Bull. ex Fr.) Schulz.

Hohenbuehelia petaloides has fleshy fruit bodies, usually either stipeless or with a lateral stipe; a gelatinous layer of hyphae is present in the cap tissue. Under the microscope it is readily distinguished by fairly thick-walled hymenial cystidia, the so-called 'metuloids'. *H. petaloides* has a 3–10 cm wide and 3–6 cm long cap, either tan-coloured or only pale brownish, but it may also be ochre-yellow to brownish yellow. The cap is spatulate or fan-shaped, sometimes passing over into a lateral pallid stipe. The cap margin is even or wavy-lobed, in larger specimens rolled up into a funnel, with a coarse flocculose-felted surface, particularly near the stipe. Young mushrooms are almost white. The gills are deeply decurrent, white or with an ochre tinge. The stipe is 5–12 cm long and 1–2 cm thick. The flesh is white, odourless and tasteless. The spore print is white.

H. petaloides grows in summer and in autumn on rotten wood, mainly on stumps, usually in damp mountain forests. Its range extends over the temperate zones of both the northern and the southern hemisphere.

It is extremely difficult to make a distinction between the species discussed here and *H. geogenia.* This is of approximately the same size, but its cap is a darker yellowish brown. It grows on the grassy ground of deciduous and coniferous forests. Both species are edible.

Spores of *Hohenbuehelia petaloides*:
5–8 × 4–5 μm, broadly ovoid, smooth, colourless, sometimes slightly scabridulous, nonamyloid

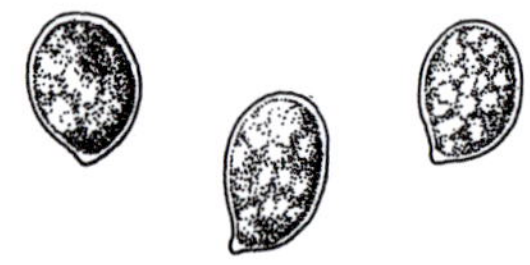

Metuloids of *Hohenbuehelia petaloides*

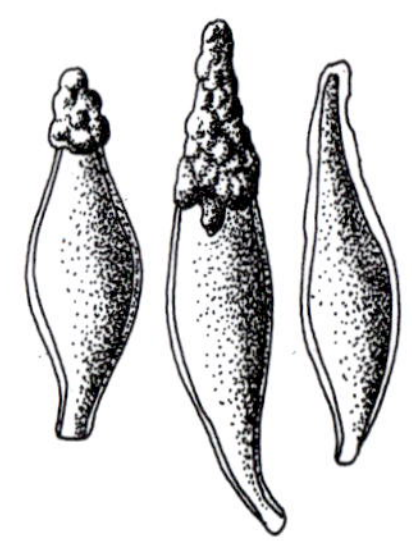

Longitudinal section through the fruit body

Megacollybia platyphylla

(Pers. ex Fr.) Kotl. et Pouz.

This robust, fleshy mushroom grows solitarily in summer and in autumn in deep, damp, especially coniferous forests, on stumps or in the humus arisen from decomposing branches and roots. It is particularly widespread in foothill and mountain elevations. The cap is 5–15 cm wide, rather thin-fleshed and almost watery, expanded-convex, sometimes slightly obtusely umbonate in the centre, with a long incurved, sharp, attenuated, membranously pellucid margin exceeding the gills. Its surface is dark ash-grey, smooth, radially darker fibrous, in dry weather fibrously lacerated over a white ground colour. The stipe is often shorter than the diameter of the cap, 1–2 cm thick, cartilaginously tough, elastic, coarsely fibrose, grooved, cylindrical, light grey to whitish; its base is overgrown with numerous tough, white mycelial threads penetrating through rotten wood. The gills are very distant, remarkably broad (1.5–3 cm), whitish, with often uneven, brown-rimmed edges, deeply sinuate near the stipe, with a transversely wrinkled surface. The spore print is pure white. The flesh has neither smell nor taste.

The gill edges bear vesicular cheilocystidia, up to 60 × 15 μm in size.

Megacollybia platyphylla has so little in common with other fungi of the genus *Collybia* that it can be classed as an independent species. In some books it is treated as a member of the genus *Oudemansiella* – yet this involves species with a copiously slimy cap cuticle, or of the genus *Tricholomopsis,* which again includes pigmented fungi. It is edible.

Spores: 7–10 × 6–8 μm, broadly ovoid, smooth, colourless

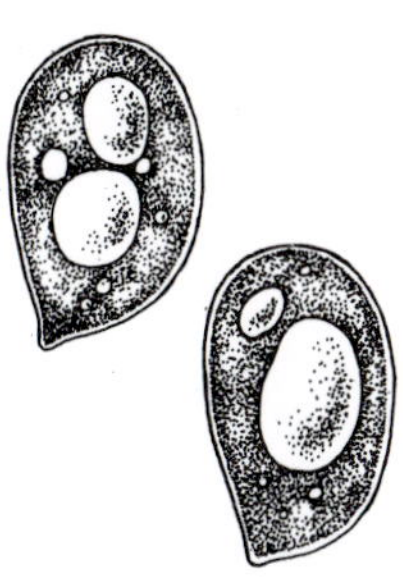

Slimy Beech Tuft

Oudemansiella mucida (Schrad. ex Fr.) Hoehn.

Old beech forests harbour a large number of fungus species: the remarkable Slimy Beech Tuft grows on dying or already dead, but still standing beech trunks. Its dazzling porcelain white fruit bodies, coated with colourless slime in wet weather, sometimes are scattered in large clumps over the moss-overgrown trunks of ancient beech giants in mountain virgin forests. In some regions with a relatively damp climate, the Slimy Beech Tuft occurs at lower elevations as well.

The 3–10 cm wide cap is broadly bell-shaped, thin-fleshed, and hyaline. The thinly cylindrical stipe is approximately the same length as the diameter of the cap or somewhat shorter, 0.5–1 cm thick, tough, with a broad, glutinous superior annulus. The gills are subdecurrent, distant, and ventricose. The context has no distinctive smell nor taste. The spore print is pure white. Large, thin-walled, colourless, lageniform cystidia, 80–90 µm long and 15–30 µm broad, develop on the gills.

The Slimy Beech Tuft grows from July to October. This remarkable fungus is not only aesthetically impressive: it is also of primary importance in biochemistry. Its mycelium produces the antibiotic mucidin, which is effectively applied in treating some skin diseases, especially mycoses. The Slimy Beech Tuft is an edible fungus. Nevertheless, the excessive sliminess of its small fruit bodies and their negligible fleshiness render it unsuitable for table use. On the contrary, it deserves protection, as the rapid decline of its habitats is accompanied by the disappearance of this fungus.

Spores: 15–18 × 12–16 µm, subglobose, smooth, colourless

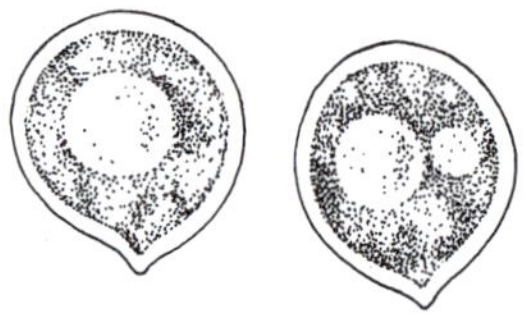

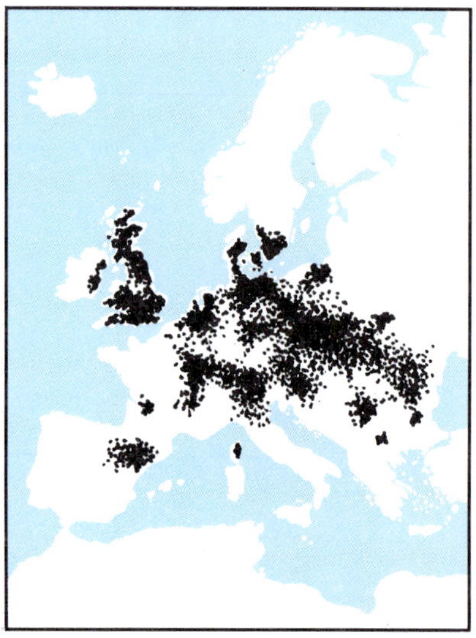

Rooting Shank

Oudemansiella radicata (Relhan ex Fr.) Sing.

From July to September, especially in deciduous forests, we may come across a conspicuous fungus on a tall, slender stipe, whose cap is strongly glutinous in moist weather (particularly when raining); moreover, it attracts attention by its prominent radial wrinkles. The cap is 4–10 cm in diameter and only rarely a little larger, and is light ochre-brown to yellowish brown in colour. The gills are white, deeply emarginate, subdecurrent, broad, and distant. Most remarkable is the 5–10 mm thick stipe, whose total length may amount up to 20 cm or more. A great part of it is hidden in the ground and can be inspected only after a very careful extraction of the whole stipe from the soil – of course the stipe usually breaks. The lowermost part of the stipe, fusiform at first, suddenly passes over into a long, gradually attenuating rooting structure which is white and terminates in a white, thin point. Above the surface the stipe is light brown, glabrous, and often slightly crooked. The flesh has no specific smell nor taste. The spore print is white. Broad vesicular cystidia are situated on the gill edge and face.

The Rooting Shank grows solitarily or in smaller groups from very decomposed stumps, from putrescent wood logs or roots concealed in the ground; thus the impression often arises that it is growing straight out of the ground.

Its double is *Oudemansiella longipes*. This also has an elongated rooting section but possesses a brown velvety stipe and a dry velvety cap. Both mushrooms are edible but their stipes are much too tough.

Cystidia and spore of *Oudemansiella radicata*:
12–16 × 9–11 µm, broadly ellipsoid, smooth, colourless

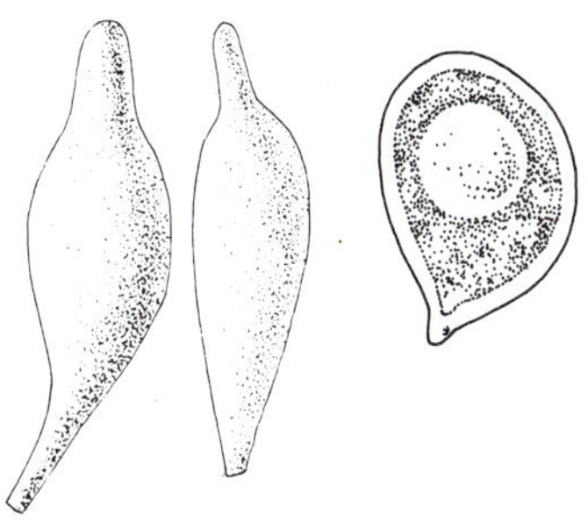

Oudemansiella longipes

Oudemansiella radicata

Strobilurus esculentus
(Wulf. ex Fr.) Sing.

The genus *Strobilurus* was devised to contain fungi similar in appearance to those of the genus *Collybia,* whose mycelium grows upon the cones of conifers – mainly of spruces and pines – which have been lying about on the ground for some time. Yet it is not only its biology that characterizes this genus. It differs morphologically from similar fungi of the Tricholomataceae family in having a 'hymeniform cap cuticle', i. e. a cuticle made up of globular cells. In fungi belonging to the genus *Strobilurus,* numerous cystidia of a characteristic shape are inserted among the hymenial basidia. They differ from the species of *Marasmius* – which they resemble in appearance – in that the dried and again moistened *Strobilurus* fruit bodies do not revive. Almost all species belonging to the genus *Strobilurus* are edible, and since they appear in early spring when mushrooms are scarce, their caps (the stipes being too tough) can adequately be used for flavouring spring soups. Three species occur in Europe.

Strobilurus esculentus grows from old spruce cones – usually a larger number of little fruit bodies from a single cone. Its caps, up to 2 cm in width, range from pale grey to almost chocolate-brown, rarely whitish; they are thin-fleshed, soon flatly expanded; the gills are white or greyish and are fairly crowded. The stipe is thin, long, smooth, glabrous, and ochre-yellowish, coated with long white hairs in its basal part, and if the cone is deeply buried in the humus, this part is proportionally extended to resemble a long string. The other two species, the inedible *S. tenacellus* and the edible *S. stephanocystis,* grow on pine cones.

Cystidium and spores of *Strobilurus esculentus*: 4–6 × 2.5–4 μm, colourless, nonamyloid

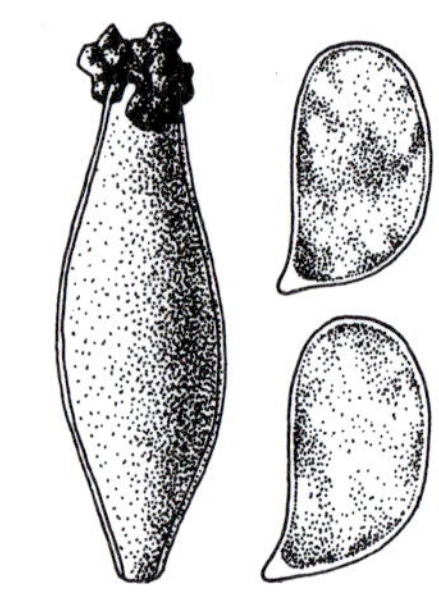

Cystidium and spores of *Strobilurus stephanocystis*

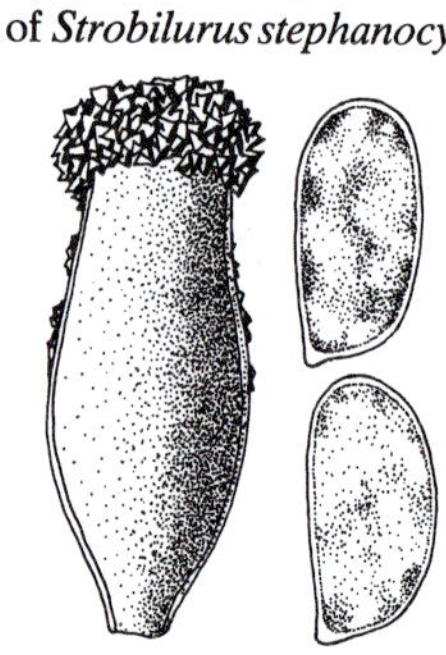

Two cystidia and a spore of *Strobilurus tenacellus*

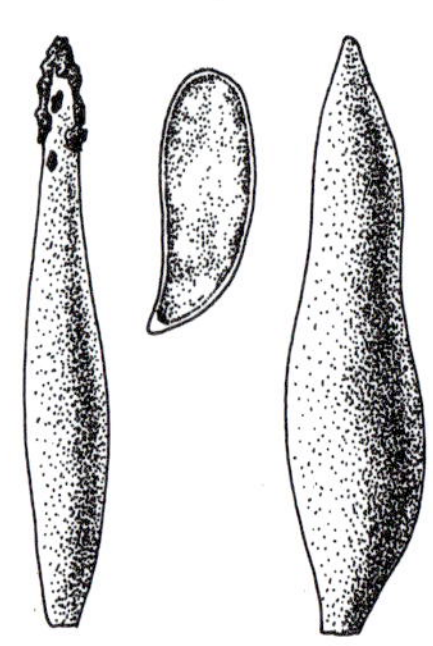

Strobilurus esculentus and *Strobilurus stephanocystis*

Strobilurus tenacellus

Little Wheel Toadstool

Marasmius rotula (Scop. ex Fr.) Fr.

Nature has created an immense variety of remarkable forms in the kingdom of fungi. The caps of the Little Wheel Toadstool look like miniature filigree mud-pies, flooding whole areas in their thousands and enlivening the forest twilight by their dazzling whiteness. It prefers damp and dark localities along forest brooks, mainly in alder growths. Here, in summer and in autumn, it occupies a great many fallen twigs, needles, stumps, and sometimes also decaying leaves. This species is noteworthy for the form, striation and colour of the cap contrasting with the bristly, dark stipe. Most remarkable, however, are the gills, coalescing into a 'collarium' along the circumference of the stipe. This attribute serves to distinguish the Little Wheel Toadstool with no difficulty.

The genus *Marasmius* is rich in species. Several hundreds of them have been described; they are widespread particularly in the tropics. One of their significant characteristics is the reviving of their thin, membranous caps. The caps can be completely dried up, but when moistened with water, they are capable of absorbing it and resuming their former shape. Many exotic species are beautifully coloured, whereas in the temperate zone it is the inconspicuous colours that are prevalent. *Marasmius graminum* is an exception in this respect. Its almost brick-red caps, turning dark with age and fading in dry conditions, no more than $2-5$ mm wide, can be found with some patience on rotten grass remains during summer. More often, however, they grow directly from the lower parts of dead leaves still attached to living grasses. Thus they may be hunted for in lawns, gardens, pastures and unmown meadows after summer rains.

Cheilocystidia and spore of *Marasmius rotula*:
$5-7 \times 2-3$ µm, longish-ellipsoid, colourless

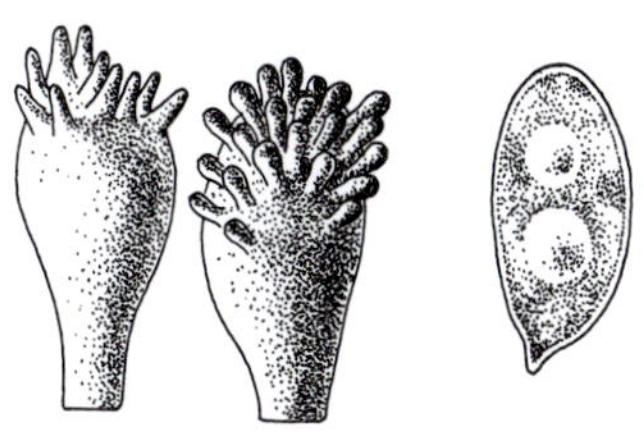

Little fruit bodies of *Marasmius graminum*

Marasmius rotula

Marasmius scorodonius (Fr.) Fr.

Many fungus species can be identified by a specific persistent smell or aroma that typifies the species in question. This attribute is consequently of paramount importance in identification, and a keen sense of smell is invaluable to any mushroom collector. The odour of garlic is characteristic of *Marasmius scorodonius;* it becomes apparent after rubbing dry fruit bodies between the fingers, but is of course most intense in fresh fungi. This odour has inspired some mushroom lovers into adding the species to their food as a substitute for garlic; unfortunately the aroma almost entirely disappears in cooking.

M. scorodonius is most commonly found in sparse coniferous forests, in their outskirts and in heather moors – that is, mainly on acid soils. It grows on dead twigs, roots, but also on needles and stumps. The cap is 1–2 cm across (rarely larger), thinly leathery, light flesh-brown or buff pinkish to off-white, often sulcate-striate, flatly expanded. When desiccated, it can be revived by moistening. The tough and elastic, only 1–2 mm thick stipe is completely glabrous, shiny red-brown. The gills are quite dense, pure white, adnate. The spore print is white.

In similar habitats, *M. androsaceus* and *Micromphale perforans* grow out of the decaying needle carpet. The former is smaller and odourless, similar in colour to *M. scorodonius* except for its black and glossy, horsehair-like stipe. *M. perforans* is approximately the same size but has a pubescent stipe and an offensive odour of old rotting cabbage.

Spores of *Marasmius scorodonius*:
8–9 × 4–5 μm, ovoid, smooth, colourless

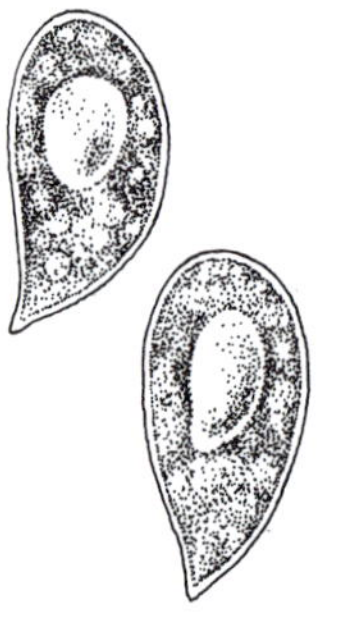

Fruit bodies of *Marasmius androsaceus*

Marasmius scorodonius

Marasmius androsaceus and *Micromphale perforans*

Fairy Ring Fungus, Fairy Ring Champignon, Scotch Bonnet

Marasmius oreades (Bolt. ex Fr.) Fr.

The Fairy Ring Fungus is the best-known species of *Marasmius.* It grows profusely from May until autumn in meadows and pastureland, along field tracks, and sometimes in woodland clearings, particularly after long-lasting rainfalls. In the past the soil in these habitats used to be regularly enriched by the dung of grazing cattle. At that time the Fairy Ring Fungus was one of the most common fungi growing in groups in deep green grass, often in stripes or circles. A darker green vegetation, whose more lavish growth contributes to setting it off from its environment, indicates a higher nitrate content in the soil and usually betrays the presence of this fungus. Fruit bodies of the Fairy Ring Fungus appear in swarms soon after rainfalls. With the arrival of dry weather they desiccate but the next rain helps them resume their natural shape.

The cap of the Fairy Ring Fungus measures 2–5 cm in diameter; at first it is bell-shaped, obtusely umbonate in the centre, slightly striate in the margin, and pale flesh-coloured or buff all over. It is glabrous and elastic, the same as the stipe which can be bent without being broken. The gills are deeply emarginate, attached by a tooth, distant, broad, whitish. The spore print is pure white. The flesh smells pleasantly of bitter almonds.

The Fairy Ring Fungus is a good edible mushroom, particularly suitable for flavouring soups. Only caps are collected, the stipes being exceedingly tough. In collecting it, care must be taken not to confuse it with some poisonous *Clitocybe* species growing in similar habitats, e.g. with *Clitocybe dealbata.*

Spores: 7–9 × 4–5 µm,
ellipsoid, smooth, colourless

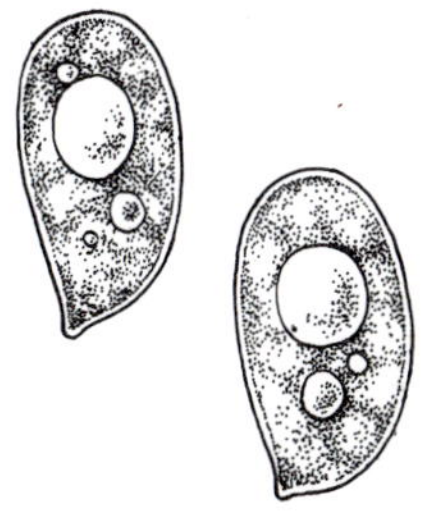

The 'fairy ring' in grass

Lilac Mycena

Mycena pura (Pers. ex Fr.) Kumm.

Some *Mycena* species can be recognized by their smell. This applies also to the Lilac Mycena with its strong smell of radish. This species varies greatly in size and particularly in colour. In its typical form the cap is pale to rosy violet but there are also bluish, brown and white varieties. In a drying fruit body the intensity of colouring will change: it is always paler than when moist. The tubular stipe is brittle, covered with long white hairs in the basal part, 3–7 cm long and 0.3–0.5 cm thick. The distant, broad, deeply emarginate gills are interveined at the base, and are pale violet.

The Lilac Mycena grows in most various types of forests from May until October. Both solitary and groups of fruit bodies develop in humus and detritus, rotting foliage and needles, always favouring damp situations. Older data concerning the toxicity of the Lilac Mycena have recently been revised: today it is considered definitely as poisonous. Since the symptoms of poisoning following the ingestion of a large amount of fruit bodies are not unlike those caused by the Fly Agaric, the Lilac Mycena presumably contains the poisonous alkaloid muscarine.

It is practically impossible to confuse it with any edible violet-coloured gill fungi. For instance, the Wood Blewitt is a fleshy, robust mushroom of quite a different appearance, with a pale pink spore print. *Laccaria amethystina* is recognizable by its tough stipe and thickened gills strewn with white powdery spores.

Spores: 5–6 × 2.5–3 μm, cylindrical, amyloid, colourless

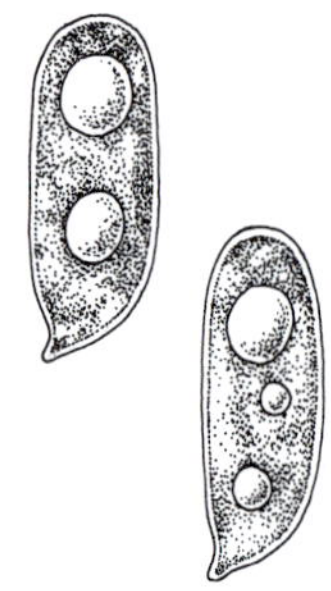

Mycena pura

Laccaria amethystina can resemble only exceptionally the more intensely violet fruit bodies of *Mycena pura*

Mycena rosea
(Bull.) ex Sacc. et Dalla Costa

In the past, *Mycena rosea* was regarded by some mycologists as a mere variety of the Lilac Mycena, whereas now it is treated as an independent species. It resembles the Lilac Mycena in shape and size, but is distinguished from it by the beautifully light rosy colour of the cap in wet weather. The stipe and gills are usually paler. The gills are sometimes only whitish; sometimes they have a slight pink flush; this also applies to the stipe which is always yellowish at the base. The brittle flesh is white to pinkish; it smells and tastes of radish, resembling in this respect the Lilac Mycena. The spores are somewhat broader than in the Lilac Mycena.

M. rosea grows exclusively in deciduous or mixed forests, especially under oaks and beeches. It is poisonous. The symptoms of poisoning are of the muscarine type – i.e. excessive sweating, nausea, vomiting, diarrhoea, contraction of the pupils and sight disorders. However, *M. rosea* is an easily recognizable fungus which can hardly be confused with an edible mushroom. In any case it is much rarer than the very abundant Lilac Mycena.

Spores: 6–9 × 3–4 μm, cylindrical,
with an apiculus at the base, smooth, colourless, amyloid

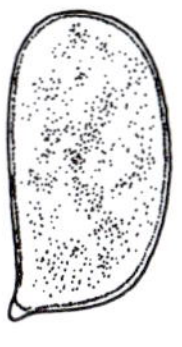

Cystidium

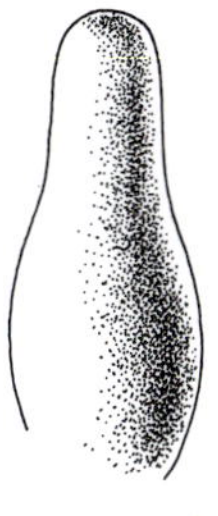

Mycena fagetorum

(Fr.) Gill.

Mycena fagetorum is a rare species whose fruit bodies do not appear before late autumn, in October and November, in the rotting foliage covering the floor of beech woods. Its specific name was derived from its association with the beech, which also determines the type of its habitat. It may grow solitarily but usually is found in larger communities. The 1–3 cm wide cap is at first semiglobular or conical, then very slightly convex, sometimes almost flat, in wet weather distinctly striate, pallid or whitish, pale grey-brown round the centre and in the striate parts, with a frequently pellucid and colourless central part, whitish all over when dry. The gills are distant, whitish or slightly grey-brown, adnate to shortly decurrent, and relatively elastic. The stipe is 3–8 cm long, 1.5–2.5 cm thick, dark or olive-grey, later grey-brown, hyaline, hollow, attached to the leaves by its white, hairy base. The spore print is white. The cheilocystidia have branched excrescences at the top. The flesh has a farinaceous smell and a mild taste.

Like the majority of *Mycena* species, *M. fagetorum* is inedible. In spite of their profuse occurrence, members of the genus *Mycena* are of no importance for practical mushroom pickers because of their small size. Many of them, however, occur in such great numbers that they become conspicuous towards the end of summer and in autumn.

Spores: 6.5–10 × 2.5–4.5 μm,
long, cylindrical, smooth, colourless, amyloid

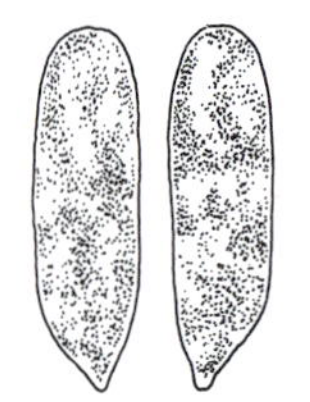

Cheilocystidia

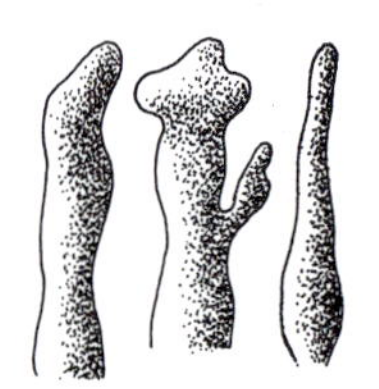

Xeromphalina campanella

(Batsch ex Fr.) R. Maire

In mountain forests, on old spruce stumps overgrown with moss, we often have the opportunity to see a small, conspicuously coloured lignicolous gill fungus – *Xeromphalina campanella.* Its relatively small fruit bodies form dense growths consisting of from several dozens to hundreds of specimens, and they may attract widespread attention by their deep brown-orange or orange-yellow colouring. The campaniform caps are 1–2 cm in diameter. They are seated on short (1–2 cm) and thin (1–2 mm) stipes which are curved and yellow-brown to rusty brown with a strigose base. The gills are deeply decurrent, distant, densely intertwined at the base, and pale yellow. The flesh has no distinctive odour nor taste. The spore print is white.

X. campanella sporadically occurs also at lower elevations, but only in microclimatically favourable habitats with a higher aerial humidity – i.e. mostly in deep valleys or brook and river ravines. Here, too, it grows on the rotting wood of old spruce, more rarely on pine or fir stumps.

X. campanella resembles *Rickenella fibula* which is even smaller. It is differentiated by its orange, 0.5–1 cm wide cap and a long, thin stipe. It grows solitarily, usually in moss on forest soil. Both species are inedible.

Cystidia and a spore of *Xeromphalina campanella*:
5–6 × 2–3 μm, ellipsoid, smooth, colourless, amyloid

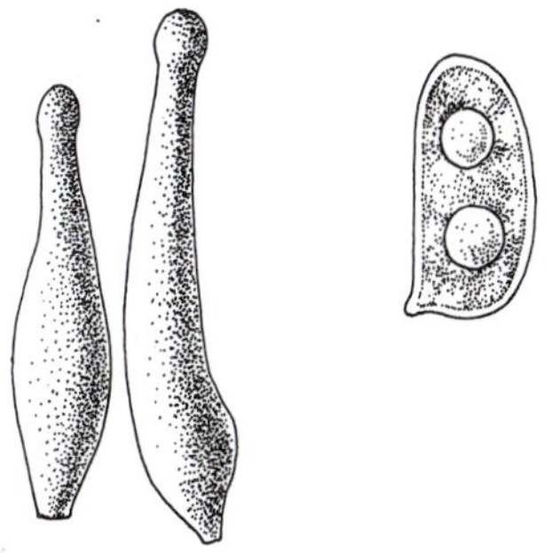

A group of *Rickenella fibula* fruit bodies

Xeromphalina campanella

Velvet Shank, Winter Fungus
Flammulina velutipes (Curt. ex Fr.) Sing.

Fresh fungus fruit bodies can be gathered even during a mild winter. The Velvet Shank is one of the few species that grow at low temperatures and are capable of tolerating a fall to below freezing point. Its clumps can often be seen growing on live trees in insufficiently healed scars left by detached branches and on stumps. They also grow on dead trunks of various deciduous trees, but rarely on conifers.

The cap attracts attention by its ochre-yellow colouring, almost chestnut-brown at the apex. Exceptionally it can attain as much as 10 cm in diameter, but its usual width is 2–5 cm. It is expanded-convex, with thin and elastic flesh, sticky in wet weather. The gills are emarginate, crowded, white, then yellowish. The stipe, narrowing downwards, is sometimes tapering to a rootlike extension; it is yellow above, black-brown below, entirely covered with velvety tomentum. The spore print is white. The tasteless flesh smells faintly of raw fish meat.

It is only the caps of the Velvet Shank that are gathered, the stipes being much too tough. Recent research has revealed the extract of raw fruit bodies to be poisonous. Cooked fruit bodies, however, can be eaten. The Velvet Shank is particularly well-known to mushroom enthusiasts living in large cities: they see it in winter in parks and gardens.

Clumps of the poisonous Sulphur Tuft (*Hypholoma fasciculare*) very commonly appear on stumps. Its gills are yellowish green, the same colour as the flesh which is, moreover, intensely bitter. Hence only a great deal of carelessness or ignorance might bring about the confusion of the two species.

Cystidia and spores of *Flammulina velutipes*: 7–9 × 4.5–6 µm, ellipsoid, smooth, colourless

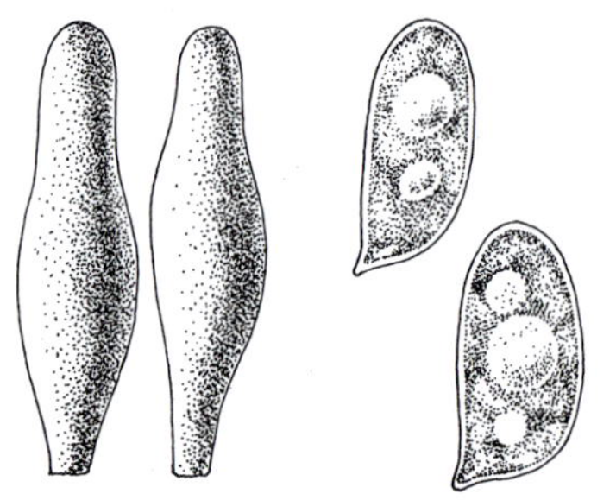

Flammulina velutipes

A clump of *Hypholoma fasciculare* fruit bodies

The Miller

Clitopilus prunulus (Scop. ex Fr.) Kumm.

Woodland tracks overgrown with grass, especially where damp, are noteworthy for a rather characteristic and interesting mycoflora – be it small subterranean fungi or species developing larger fruit bodies. These fungi are either symbiotically related to the nearby trees and shrubs, or grow independently of them – e.g. in deep ruts hollowed out by the wheels of vehicles, where they find adequate living conditions.

One of the gill fungi very frequently occurring on woodland tracks in spruce forests is the Miller. It is less common in mixed and dedicuous forests.

The Miller's fruit bodies have 10 cm wide caps, soon slightly convex to expanded, depressed in the centre, with a wavy margin remaining incurved for a long time; their cuticle is smooth, finely pruinose. The deeply decurrent gills are crowded, whitish, later flesh-pink from the spore mass. The stipe is short – usually 3–6 cm long and 0.7–2 cm thick, and sometimes eccentric. It is broadest below the cap, white-felted at the base. The cut flesh strongly smells of raw cucumbers and freshly ground flour, its taste is similar.

The Miller is an edible mushroom characterized by white fruit bodies, pink gills and a strongly cucumber-mealy smell and taste. Its frequent presence in the company of Edible Boleti is interesting.

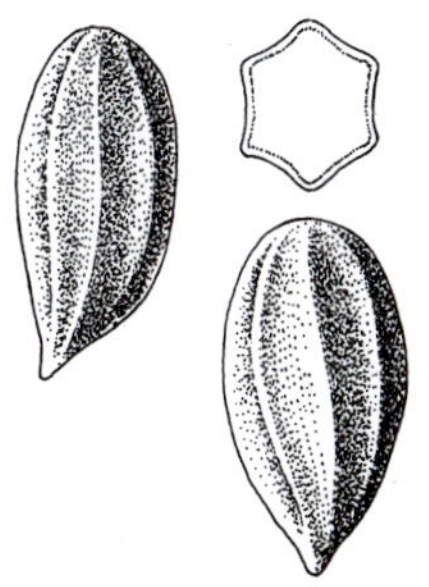

Spores: 8–14 × 5–6 μm, fusiform, with six longitudinal ribs, pale pink; the ornamentation is well visible under the microscope on an optical cross section

Spore print

Nolanea verna

(Lundell) Kotl. et Pouz.

When the weather is favourable, the first fruit bodies of *Nolanea verna* appear in early spring in sunlit, grassy woodland sites. Characteristic is their dark colour and greyish pink gills. The 3–6 cm wide cap is conical or bell-shaped, later slightly convex, umbonate in the centre, fragile, brittle, strongly hygrophanous, deep dark brown to black-brown when moist, pale grey-brown with a silky sheen when dry. The gills are distant, broad, grey when young, grey-pink and covered with pink spore powder at maturity. The stipe, sometimes exceeding the diameter of the cap in length and 0.5 cm thick, is laterally depressed, brittle, hollow, and grey. The flesh is greyish, almost odourless and tasteless.

N. verna is an extremely poisonous fungus whose ingestion is followed by poisoning with diarrhoea as its main symptom. Careless or inexperienced mushroom pickers usually take *N. verna* instead of the Fairy Ring Fungus because it also grows in grass. Yet it does not resemble in any way the Fairy Ring Fungus, being absolutely dissimilar not only in its colouring and fragility, but particularly in the pink or fleshy red spore mass and angular spores. There is a multitude of gill fungi with spores of this colour, and many of them are demonstrably poisonous.

Another vernal species is the Roman Shield Entoloma (*Entoloma clypeatum*). It also grows in grass under some fruit trees, mostly under plums. It is much larger and more fleshy than *N. verna* and has a white stipe; its flesh emits a farinaceous smell. It is edible.

Spores of *Nolanea verna*:
8–11 × 8 μm, angular, pale pink

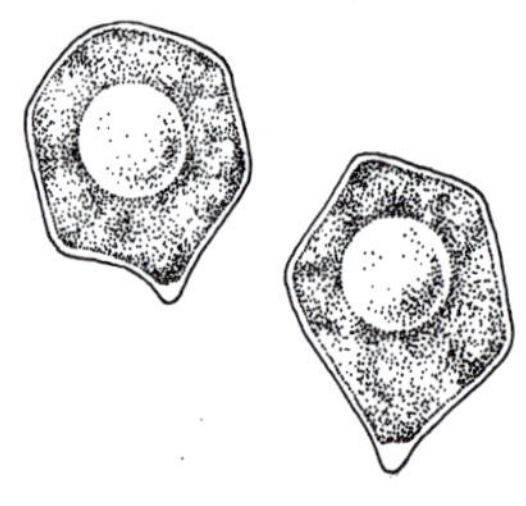

A section through *Entoloma clypeatum*

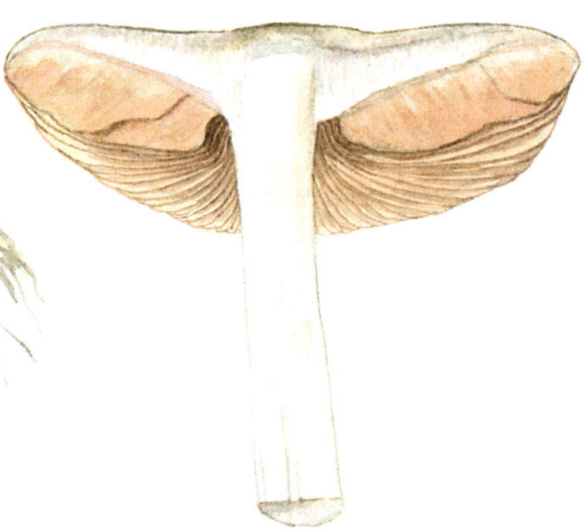

Spore print

Nolanea verna *Entoloma clypeatum*

Livid Entoloma

Entoloma lividum (Bull. ex St. Amans) Quél.

Fruit bodies of this attractive fungus develop at the beginning of July (occasionally as early as the end of May) in oak forests on calcareous soils, and continue to grow until September. They may occur also outside the forest under solitary oaks, e.g. on pond dams or in tree alleys. A thermophilous species, it avoids cool and mountainous areas and never grows on acid substrates. Sometimes it occurs together with *Boletus aestivalis,* and the young fruit bodies, resembling young boleti in shape, can be gathered together with them by inexperienced mushroom pickers. The fruit bodies growing in early summer can be mistaken for belated St. George's Mushrooms (*Calocybe gambosa*). The ingestion of the extremely poisonous Livid Entoloma causes vomiting and diarrhoea in about 2–4 hours; this condition may last for several days. The toxic principle of a hitherto unknown composition can be destroyed neither by boiling nor by the use of vinegar in preservation.

The caps of the robust, fleshy fruit bodies are 5–15 cm (sometimes up to 20 cm) wide, at first semiglobular, with their margin pressed against the stipe and involute for a long time, later broadly expanded, with a rounded central umbo. The separable cuticle has a silky sheen; ingrown fibres form a reticular pattern. It is whitish in youth, then ash-yellow and finally light brownish. The gills are relatively narrow, crowded, yellowish, then pinkish to flesh-red. The stipe is clavately enlarged towards the base, up to 20 cm long and 8 cm thick at the base, solid, white, later yellowish, fibrous. The flesh is white, with a cucumber-mealy smell and taste. The spore print is reddish.

Spores: 9–11 × 9–10 μm, subglobose and obtusely hexagonal, pale pink

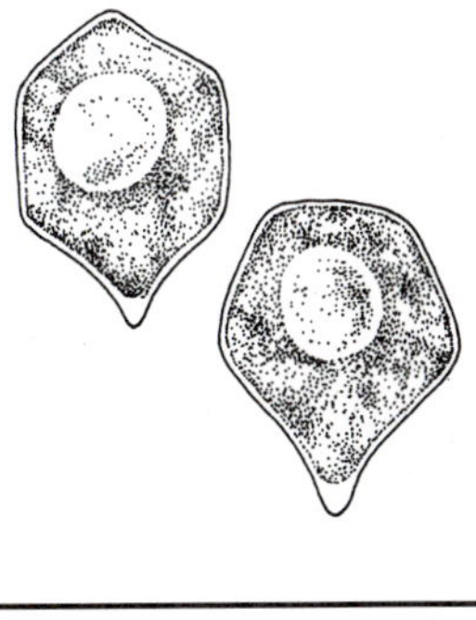

Entoloma nidorosum
(Fr.) Quél.

The numerous species of the genus *Entoloma* greatly resemble each other, and this makes distinguishing between them rather difficult. Only a few of them possess characteristics so conspicuous that they can be identified on the spot, without a long search in literature and microscopic study. One of these is *Entoloma nidorosum* whose specific smell, reminiscent of ammonia fumes, helps distinguish it from other species. Its cap is 5–8 cm wide, with relatively thin and brittle flesh, easily breakable, soon flatly convex, with a very thin, pellucid margin, often wavy-lobed, hygrophanous, dark grey-brown in moist conditions, greyish buff when dry, smooth, and with a silky sheen. The gills are broad, distant, deeply emarginate with a tooth to subdecurrent, pale greyish to brownish, finally brownish pink. The stipe is cylindrical, often rather elongate and narrowing downwards, flexuose, 0.5–1 cm thick, white with a silky sheen, turning grey with age, hollow and brittle. The spore print is pink.

This *Entoloma* is relatively common in damp deciduous forests, often accompanying aspens, poplars, hornbeams and limes. Its occurrence in coniferous forests is rare. It might be mistaken for *E. clypeatum;* this, however, has a cucumber-mealy smell and grows outside the forest under prunus trees, mostly in gardens and orchards.

Spores: 8–10 × 7–9 μm, obtusely angular, pale pink

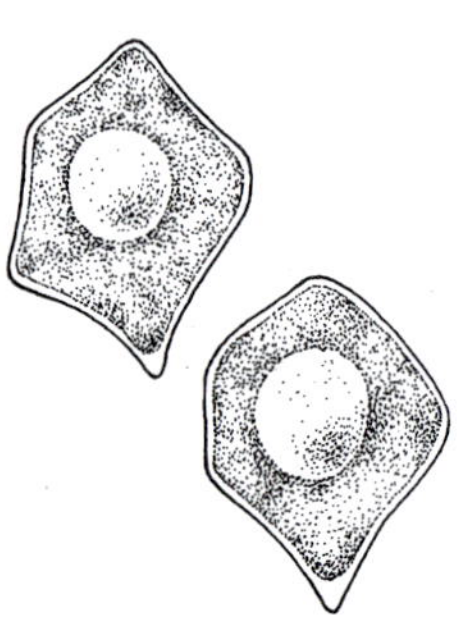

Entoloma hirtipes
(Schum. ex Fr.) Moser

Entoloma hirtipes is a rare species sometimes also classified under the generic name *Nolanea.* Its cap is 3–5 cm wide, rarely larger, campanulate-conical, grey-brown, with gills slightly showing through in wet weather. The stipe is 7–16 cm long, 4–6 mm thick, with a white tomentose base swollen to a thickness of about 1 cm, the same colour as the cap, very brittle. The gills are ventricose, broad, at first whitish and finally grey. The flesh, particularly after handling, emits an intensive and penetrating smell of codliver oil. The spore print is pink.

From April onwards, *E. hirtipes* grows on the ground in grass, mostly in coniferous forests. It is inedible.

This fungus is closely related to *E. mammosum* which grows in summer and in autumn and also prefers grassy habitats, but more often outside the forest. *E. mammosum* is smaller, its cap is usually umbonate, sometimes with a sharp point; the stipe is thin, only 1–3 mm thick, not thickened at the base.

Similar grassy places are inhabited in spring by the poisonous *Nolanea verna.* This fungus, however, becomes very dark in wet weather and its flesh has a slight and indistinct smell.

All these pink-spored or red-spored gill fungi are distinguished with difficulty; since they can so easily be confused, the practical mushroom picker had better avoid them altogether.

Cystidia and spores of *Entoloma hirtipes*:
10–14 (16) × 7–9 μm, oblong, angular, pale pink

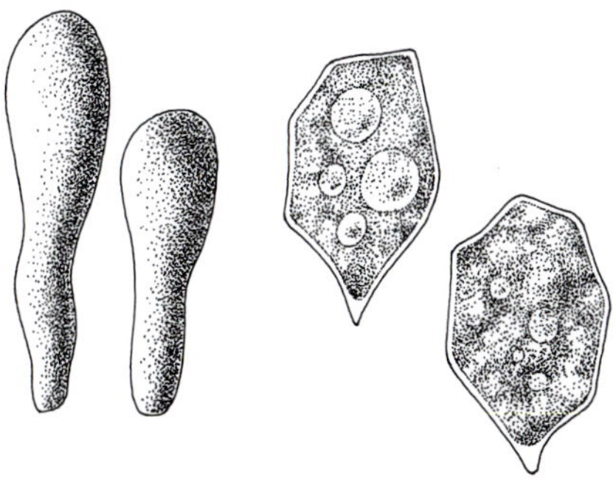

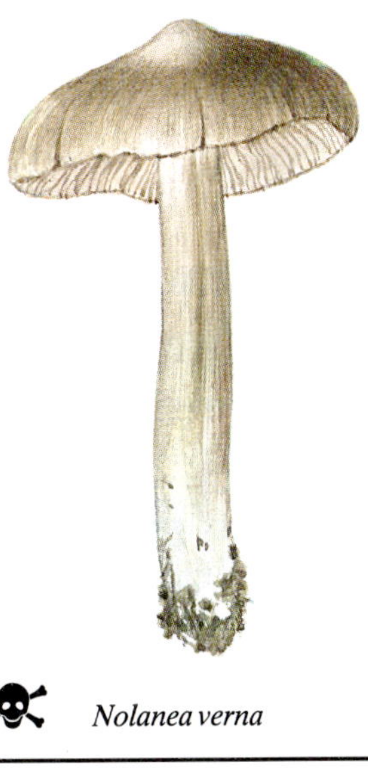

Nolanea verna

Entoloma hirtipes

Volvariella speciosa
(Fr.) Sing.

The genus *Volvariella* consists of medium- to large-sized fungi with soft to watery flesh whose young fruit bodies are enveloped in a firm membrane; this breaks open as the stipe develops, leaving a clearly discernible, high sheath (volva) which often splits into lobes. The stipe is ringless, neither are there any visible remains of the veil on the cap surface in most cases. The broad, ventricose gills are free (as in the amanitas). The colour of the spore print substantiates the classification of *Volvariella* among red-spored gill fungi belonging – together with the genus *Pluteus* – to the family Pluteaceae. They somewhat resemble members of the genus *Amanita* in appearance.

Volvariella speciosa is one of the best-known representatives of its genus. It is a high and robust fungus having a 6–12 cm wide, relatively fleshy cap with a thin margin, at first obtusely conico-campanulate, later expanded, slimy when moist, shiny, grey-whitish. If the colour of the cap is grey or blackish brown, especially in the centre, then this means that the variety *gloiocephala* is involved. The gills are crowded, whitish, and flesh-reddish when mature. The 20 cm long and 1–1.5 cm thick stipe is solid, white, slightly thickened to bulbous at the base, with a volva almost disappearing in older fruit bodies and remaining in the ground after the removal of the stipe. The flesh smells of rotten fruit.

V. speciosa is a typical fungus of gardens, parks, fields, urban rubbish heaps, occurring mostly on manured soils. It is inedible but not poisonous, as was previously thought.

Spores: 16–18 × 8–10 μm, ellipsoid, smooth

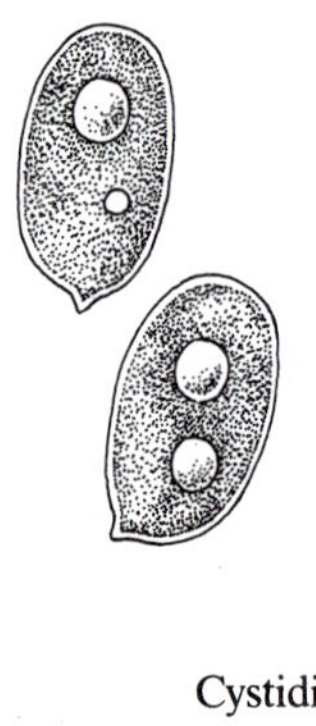

Cystidia

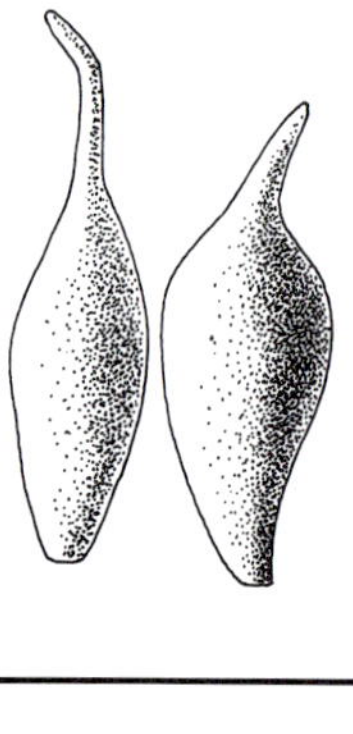

Pluteus cervinus

(Schaeff. ex Fr.) Kumm.

Pluteus cervinus is one of the very common red-spored fungi that grow on stumps and decaying wood logs. Its relatively large fruit bodies consist of a light to dark grey or grey-brown cap and a rather thin, white, dark-fibrous stipe. The cap is 5–12 cm wide, bell-shaped when young and expanded at maturity, radially filamentous, glossy, sometimes cracked when dry. The stipe is 6–12 cm long and 0.8–1.5 cm thick, and firm. A distinguishing feature – shared by all *Pluteus* species – are remote gills, whitish at first but soon becoming pale pink and ultimately flesh-reddish as the spores mature. Their edges are the same colour as the gill surface, unlike the closely related *P. atromarginatus* whose gill edges are rimmed with black. *P. cervinus* prefers the wood of deciduous trees (being particularly abundant on birches, hornbeams, oaks and beeches), whereas *P. atromarginatus* is found exclusively on conifers – usually on pine stumps, but also on spruces; it is less abundant than *P. cervinus*. Both species can be found from May to October. Both are edible, but are of little nutritional value and of inferior quality. Their flesh is very brittle and watery, so that they damage easily during transport. Hence fungi belonging to the genus *Pluteus* are only sporadically collected by mushroom pickers. They can be used for flavouring soups and in fried mushroom mixtures.

The family Pluteaceae also includes the genus *Volvariella* whose basal portion is enveloped by a membranous volva.

Spores of *Pluteus cervinus*:
8–9 × 5–6 μm, broadly ellipsoid, pink

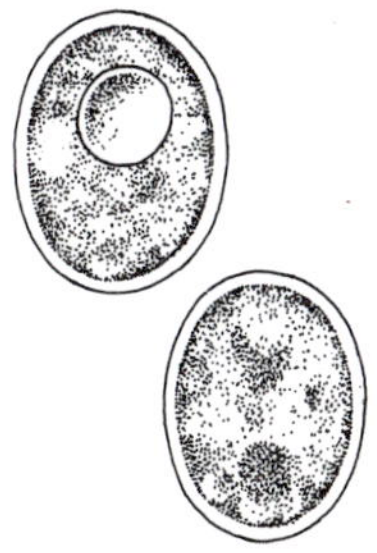

Variable cystidia of *Pluteus cervinus*

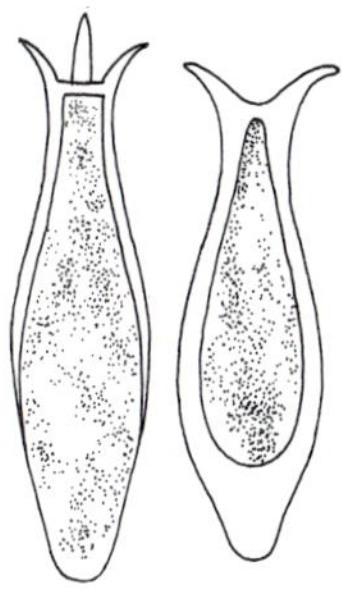

Shed spore print

Grisette

Amanita vaginata (Bull. ex Fr.) Vitt.

Not all species of *Amanita* have a ringed stipe – in many of them the membranous universal veil (*velum universale*) persists in the form of a volva, i.e. a sheath which envelops the base of the stipe and roughly resembles half of an egg-shell. In the past, these ringless *Amanita* species possessing a volva were classified as members of the genus *Amanitopsis,* yet the present mycological system treats them as a mere section (*Vaginaria*) of the genus *Amanita.*

The Grisette and several other closely related species are the most common ones. The typical form has a brittle, thin-fleshed cap, light or dark grey, frequently fading to off-white. It is usually 3–12 cm wide, soon flatly expanded, slightly and obtusely umbonate, with a markedly grooved margin. The stipe and the volva are whitish, the gills are pure white, crowded, and free. The spore print is white.

The Grisette occurs throughout the summer until the autumn in all types of forests. It is mostly found on damp soils overgrown with grass and moss, often under birches growing on acid substrates. It is poisonous when raw (as are all the species of this family) and is easily confused with the extremely poisonous Death Cap.

The related *A. fulva* closely resembles the Grisette in appearance and size, except for its reddish brown cap and an orange-yellow volva. A common and quite abundant species, it favours spruce stands rich in moss but also grows under deciduous trees.

Spores of *Amanita vaginata*: 9–12 μm in diameter, globose, colourless, nonamyloid

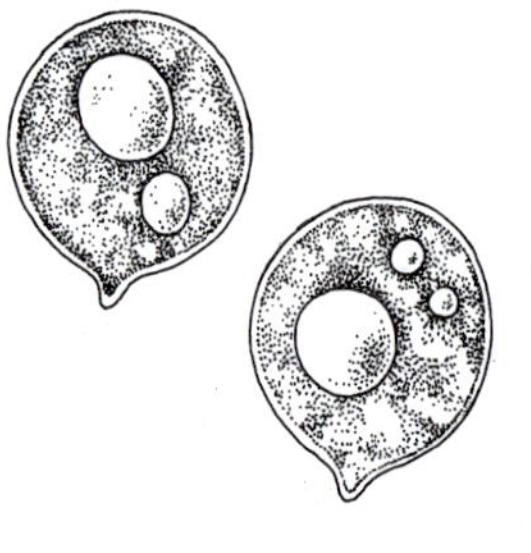

Amanita umbrinolutea Secr.

Amanita umbrinolutea is closely related and similar to the Grisette whose variety it is sometimes considered to be. It is distinguished from the latter by its colour and larger spores. The 5 – 12 cm wide cap is at first ovoid and enclosed in a firm membranous veil, later it becomes slightly convex to flatly expanded, with an attenuated and distinctly grooved margin. The universal veil adheres to the apex of the young fruit body's cap but sloughs off later, leaving the cap surface of older specimens glabrous. The cuticle is slimy at first, then dry, shiny, yellow-brown or grey-brown to olive-brown, and whitish at the grooved margin. The gills are free, loosely packed, thin and white. The cylindrical stipe is white, typically streaked with grey to yellowish grey, slightly thickened at the base which is embedded in an ample, membranous, white volva. The ring is absent, as is the case in all *Vaginaria.* The spore print is white.

The favourite habitat of *A. umbrinolutea* are upland spruce monocultures. Its colouring sometimes resembles that of *A. fulva* whose cap is reddish brown, paler towards the margin, rarely with an olivaceous tinge; the stipe is whitish to red-brown, not streaked; the volva is rusty or orange-brown. Another similar species, *A. lividopallescens,* has an ochre-grey cap, often with rusty stains and a whitish, flocculose-pruinose stipe. It grows in the grass of woodland meadows.

All these amanita species are poisonous.

Spores of *Amanita umbrinolutea*:
11 – 16 × 9 – 13 μm, globose,
smooth, colourless, nonamyloid

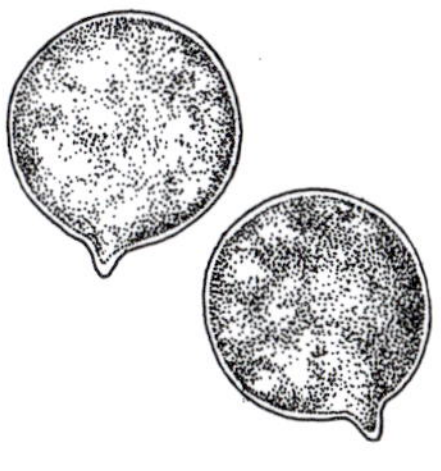

Amanita fulva

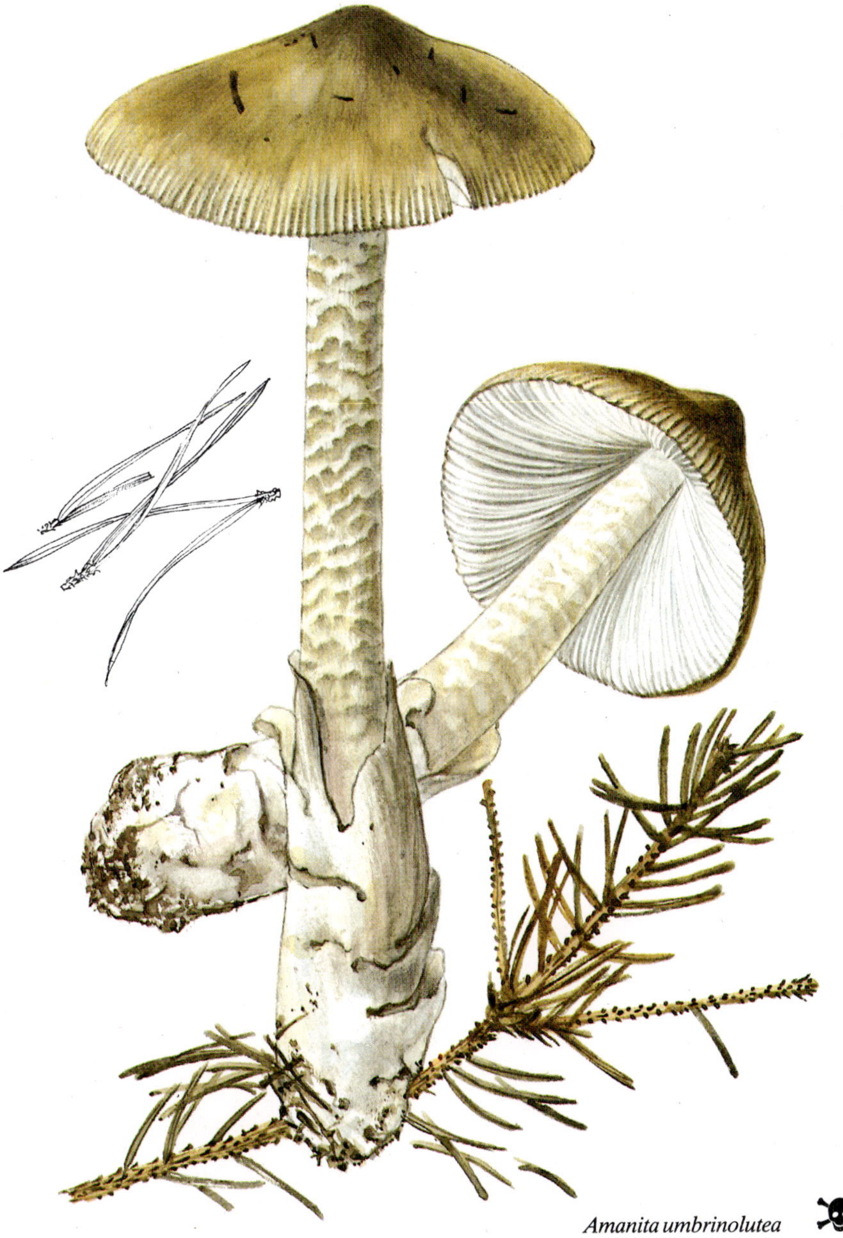

Amanita umbrinolutea

Fly Agaric
Amanita muscaria
(L. ex-Fr.) Hook.

Amanita regalis
(Fr.) Michael

The Fly Agaric (1) has been known as a poisonous species since ancient times. Its toxicity is mainly due to the presence of mycoatropine which causes disorders of mental activity. The content of another poisonous principle, muscarine, is relatively small. Recently the identity of the Fly Agaric with the drug called 'soma', venerated by the most ancient Aryan tribes in the time of migrating to and settling in the mountains of Afghanistan, has been established. The migration of peoples contributed to the further spreading of the Fly-Agaric cult. Particularly remarkable is the Siberian cult of the Fly Agaric: people were drinking fruit-body decoctions, chewing dry toadstools and washing them down with cold water; or they would prepare a beverage from a mixture of the toadstool and leaves of the Bog Whortleberry nad *Salix angustifolia*. Since the effective substance is secreted with urine, they even drank the urine of intoxicated persons.

The symptoms of poisoning include vomiting, headache, accelerated heartbeat, dilatation of pupils; often a state similar to alcoholic intoxication and hallucinations set in, and finally the poisoned person falls into a deep sleep and usually awakes in the morning in a normal condition, without remembering his or her previous behaviour.

Amanita regalis (2), growing in upland spruce stands, is distinguished by a yellowish brown cap, a yellowish stipe and similarly coloured remnants of the outer veil on the cap, and by a ring. It seems to be as poisonous as the Fly Agaric.

Spores of *Amanita muscaria:*
10–12 × 7–10 μm, subglobose, colourless, nonamyloid

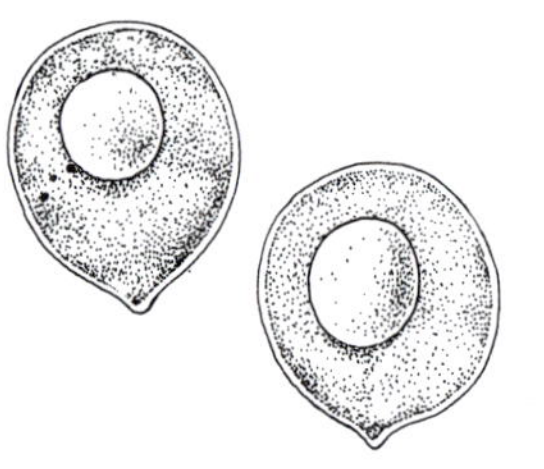

Amanita muscaria　　*Amanita regalis*

Caesar's Mushroom, Imperial Mushroom
Amanita caesarea (Scop. ex Fr.) Grev.

Caesar's Mushroom is a strictly thermophilous species whose range coincides with that of the warmth-loving flora. In the countries of southern Europe, it is one of the most popular amanitas. In central Europe it occurs very rarely indeed, and is absent from Britain and north-western Europe. It prefers oak and oak-hornbeam woods on calcareous substrates, yet in southern Europe it occurs even under pines. It grows from July to September.

The wonderfully brilliant-orange to red cap, measuring 8–20 cm in diameter, is fleshy, smooth and glabrous, or strewn with sporadic white fragments of the universal veil. In youth the universal veil envelops the entire fruit body in the form of a relatively thick white membrane, persisting at maturity as a high, free volva at the base of the stipe. The cap margin is more yellow and finely grooved. The colouring of the cap is variable, forms ranging from white to honey-brown and deep red may occur. Attached to the deep yellow to golden-yellow stipe is a concolorous, grooved, thinly membranous ring. The gills are free, fairly crowded, broad, golden-yellow, covered by a yellow veil in youth. Also the flesh under the cap cuticle and at the apex of the stipe is yellow, sometimes only tinged with yellow to almost white. When submerged in water, it releases a yellow pigment. It has an inconspicuous odour and a pleasant taste. The spore print is yellowish.

Caesar's Mushroom is considered to be one of the most appetizing mushrooms. It was also highly thought of in antiquity, and in Ancient Rome it was regarded as a select delicacy.

Spores: 10–12 × 6–7 μm, subglobose, smooth, colourless

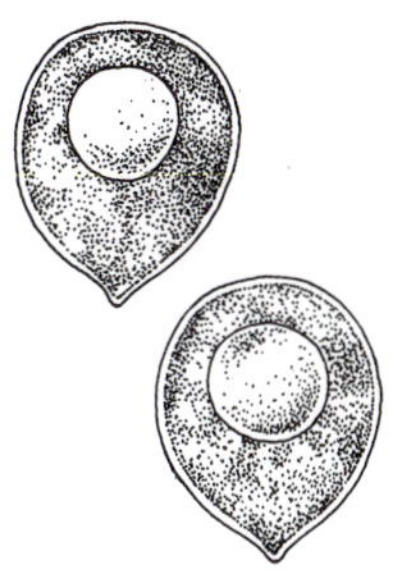

Panther Cap

Amanita pantherina (DC. ex Fr.) Krombh.

After the Death Cap, the second most frequent cause of poisoning is the Panther Cap. The symptoms of poisoning resemble those of alcoholic intoxication and more poisonings now occur than in the past, the reason being its confusion with the edible Blusher (*Amanita rubescens*) or *Amanita spissa.* Cases of poisoning are particularly frequent in the vicinity of big cities and in recreational areas where people are accustomed to picking Blushers and *A. spissa* for table use, and where the possibility of confusion is consequently enhanced.

The Panther Cap is not difficult to identify. Its cap is 4–12 cm in diameter, soon expanded. Its colour variability is remarkable – usually it is yellowish brown but it may also be beige, greyish or grey-brown. Its surface is slimy when moist, shiny when dry, with a distinctly grooved margin, usually strewn with small fragments of the universal veil. These fragments are white and often concentrically arranged, thus vaguely resembling a panther's skin: hence the name of the toadstool. The gills are crowded and cream-yellowish. The stipe, up to 15 cm long and 2 cm thick, is white, soon hollow, with a white, smooth, narrow, ungrooved, often fugacious superior ring; it is slightly tuberously enlarged at the base. The tuberous base has a shallow ridge on the upper angle; above this, 1–3 slanting rings are often situated. The white, unchanging flesh has an odour and taste of raw potatoes and smells sweet when drying. The Panther Cap grows in summer and in autumn mostly in deciduous forests, usually under oaks. The ungrooved ring and the context exhibiting no colour change are characteristic attributes of the Panther Cap.

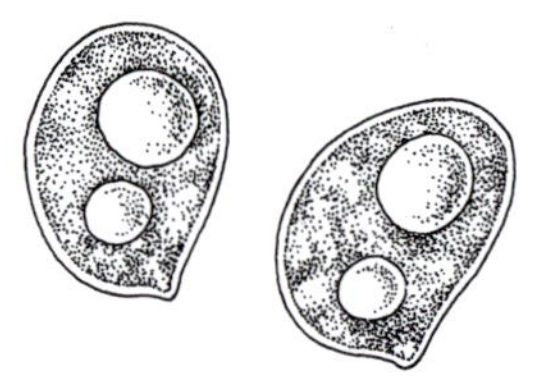

Spores of *Amanita pantherina*: 10–12 × 7–8 μm, ellipsoid, colourless

Amanita pantherina can be mistaken for *Amanita rubescens* (a) and for *Amanita spissa* (b)

Amanita pantherina

Amanita rubescens and *Amanita spissa*

Amanita gemmata

(Fr.) Gill.

If *Amanita gemmata* appears in its typical form, it is recognizable by a straw- or wax-yellow, sometimes almost lemon- or ochre-yellow cap cuticle growing paler with age and in dry conditions. The cap is 3–10 cm wide, with a grooved margin. The universal veil leaves on its surface white scab-like patches of an irregular shape. The stipe is white, with a slightly onion-shaped to clavately dilated base sheathed with a minute adnate volva which forms a low, often indistinct collar along the upper edge of the soft, easily detachable bulb. The surface of the stipe is sinuose-flocculose, sometimes almost smooth. The ring below the stipe apex is fine, easily detachable, and white like the stipe. The gills are crowded and white. The consistency of the context is soft (especially in the basal part of the stipe); it is white, yellowish only under the cuticle, unchanging, slightly smelling of radish, and with a mild taste. The spore print is white.

A. gemmata grows in sparse deciduous and coniferous forests, often in pine stands, particularly in drier situations on sandy soils. As a general rule, it grows solitarily. It is one of the first *Amanita* species to be seen in the woods at the beginning of the season: it appears as early as May and grows until late autumn. It is poisonous.

Very closely related to *A. gemmata* is *A. eliae,* distinguished by a pinkish or wine-brownish cap; this, however, may also be pale ochre to pure white.

Spores of *Amanita gemmata*: 10–12 × 7–8 μm, broadly ellipsoid, smooth, colourless, nonamyloid

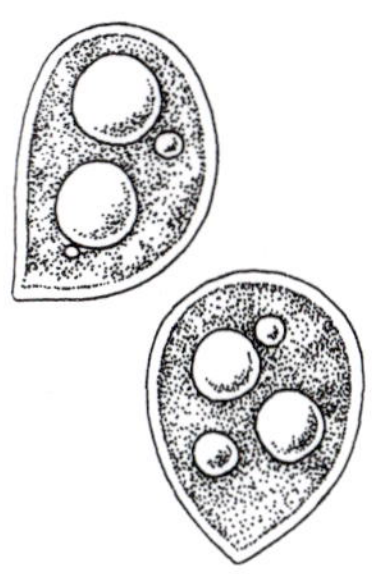

Central part of the stipe with the ring and the basal part of the stipe

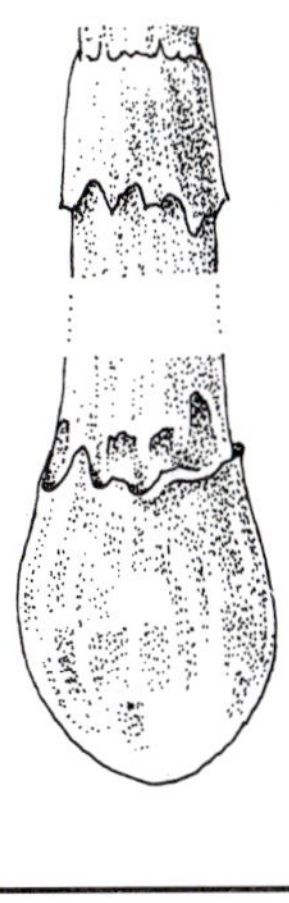

Death Cap

Amanita phalloides (Fr.) Link

Everyone who wants to pick edible mushrooms yet guard against fatal poisoning must thoroughly acquaint himself with the Death Cap. In its typical form it is readily distinguished on the basis of the following characteristics of major importance.

Its cap is either some shade of green: olive-green, yellow-green, brown-green, or, on the other hand, pallid to white – but mostly there is at least a trace of green. The cap is 5–15 cm in diameter, its cuticle is radially striate with ingrown dark fibrils. The gills are persistently white. The high membranous volva enveloping the basal, tuberous, up to 4 cm thick part of the stipe disrupts into several lobes and is sometimes called the 'death cup'. The ring situated on the stipe has a smooth (exceptionally slightly grooved) upper surface. The stipe surface below the ring is often streaked with fine greenish scales. The pure white, unchanging flesh faintly smells of raw potatoes. Its taste is indistinctive but quite pleasant. The spore print is white. It grows in deciduous forests, mainly in oak and beech woods, also under solitary deciduous trees and exceptionally in pine stands (in situations once probably overgrown with deciduous forests), from summer to autumn – usually in September.

Young fruit bodies are embedded in the ground and enclosed in the universal veil, which makes them resemble an egg. The Death Cap is the most poisonous European fungus. It causes what is known as phalloid poisoning accompanied by liver damage, which is usually fatal. It contains amatoxins and phalotoxins which, with a view to their effects, belong to the most insidious fungal poisons.

Spores of *Amanita phalloides*: 8–10 × 7–9 μm, subglobose, smooth, colourless, slightly amyloid

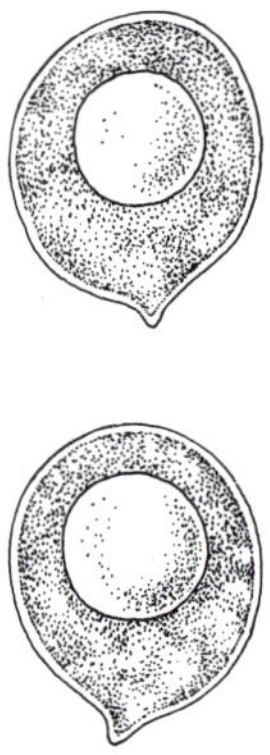

Carelessness may result in a confusion of the Death Cap with the Horse Mushroom (*Agaricus arvensis*)

Agaricus arvensis

Amanita phalloides

Distribution of *Amanita phalloides* in Europe

Destroying Angel

Amanita virosa (Fr.) Bertillon

This is another poisonous species. In many respects, it takes after *A. phalloides*. In youth it also resembles a white egg, the disrupted universal veil also gives rise to a membranous sheath at the stipe base which remains hidden in the ground. Even the cap is equal in size, but it is usually more pronouncedly bell-shaped to pointed, its surface is glabrous, usually without traces of the universal veil, slimy when young, then dry, with a silky sheen, white, occasionally tinged with yellow or brown in the centre. The crowded white gills, at first covered with a white partial veil, are free. The stipe is slowly distending towards the base where it terminates in a bulb inserted in the volva. It is hollow inside, white all over, with a white, non-striated, superior ring; below this, the stipe surface is conspicuously flocculose-scaly. The flesh is unchanging, white, with an inconspicuous odour and taste. The spore print is white.

Unlike the Death Cap, the Destroying Angel is a species of coniferous forests, accompanying mostly pine forests at lower elevations, spruce forests at higher elevations. Its occurrence, however, is only sporadic, and from some regions it is absent altogether. It grows from August to October. Its ingestion causes poisoning with liver damage. It is usually confused with Field Agarics which, however, are distinguished by their grey, pink or black-coloured gills and by having no volva.

The similar, also deadly poisonous *A. verna* grows exclusively in warm oak and oak-hornbeam woods, predominantly in southern and southeastern Europe. It has a glabrous stipe and rather small fruit bodies.

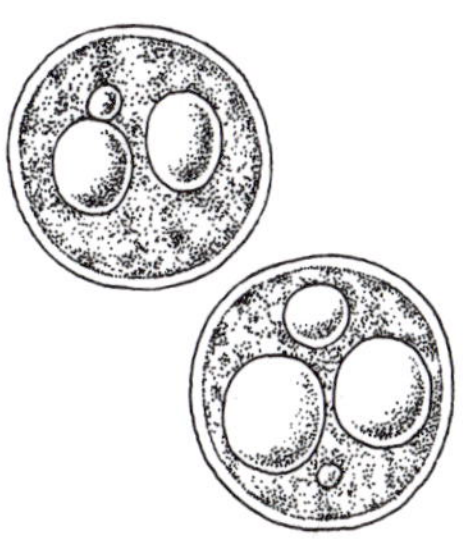

Spores of *Amanita virosa*: 8–10 μm in diameter, globose, smooth, colourless, amyloid

Amanita verna

Amanita virosa

False Death Cap
Amanita citrina (Schaeff.) ex Roques

The False Death Cap resembles the deadly poisonous Death Cap in colour, and is also toxic. It contains the toad poison bufotenin and serotonin-related indole derivates. In the past it was not considered poisonous, yet research results have disproved this view and it should not be collected.

The False Death Cap has a 4–10 cm wide, lemon- to greenish yellow cap, irregularly scattered with brownish wartlike projections. A cap perfectly white all over is an uncommon sight. The gills are broad, free, persistently white. The stipe expands at the base into a conspicuous semiglobular bulb which looks as if it were sharply cut off at its upper angle. The membranous volva is only a little developed; at the stipe base it is firmly attached to the bulb, from which it is flaring away in its upper part like a low collar. The stipe surface is glabrous, pale lemon-yellow, its upper part bears an identically coloured membranous ring which is smooth and more or less appressed to the stipe. The smell and taste of the white flesh is rather like raw potatoes. The spore print is white.

The False Death Cap is one of the most abundant toadstools. Towards the end of summer and in autumn it often appears in large communities in all forests. It is a typical species of spruce stands on rather acid substrates. The characteristic attributes for easy identification are the shape of the bulb, the lemon-yellow colouring and the scab-like veil remnants on the cap.

Spores of *Amanita citrina*:
8–10 µm, globose, smooth, colourless, amyloid

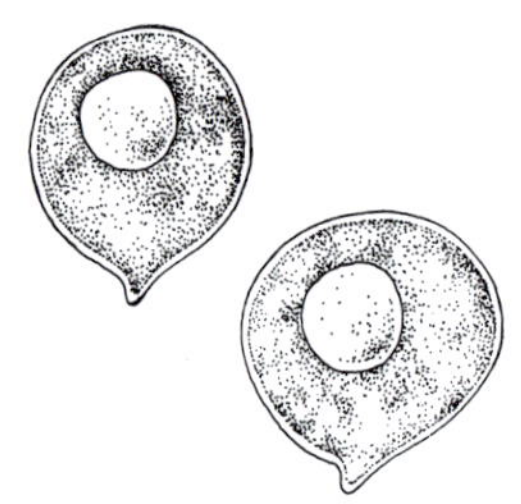

Some specimens of *Amanita citrina* can be mistaken for fruit bodies of *Amanita phalloides*

Amanita citrina

Amanita phalloides

Amanita porphyrea

(Alb. et Schw. ex Fr.) Schummel

The inconspicuously coloured *Amanita porphyrea* is not abundant and is usually solitary – it is therefore often overlooked by mushroom pickers. This is probably why, in spite of its toxicity, no cases of poisoning have so far been reported. Recent research has shown it to contain bufotenin and indole compounds (as does *A. citrina*).

The cap of *A. porphyrea* has a peculiar grey-violet or brown-grey colouring (the violet colour gave rise to its specific name). It is 4–8 cm wide, the cuticle is smooth and scattered with sparse, readily detachable fragments of the violet-grey universal veil. The gills are free, crowded and white. The stipe is relatively long and slender, whitish with a violet tinge, with a thin, limp, grooved ring pressed tightly to the stipe whose basal part suddenly swells into a globular bulb bearing the remnants of the volva. The white unchanging flesh has a rather unpleasant taste and smell of old raw potatoes or of radish. The spore print is white.

A. porphyrea grows in the rotting needle carpet of spruce and pine forests. It appears either solitarily or only in small groups from July to October. Its colouring is so specific that it cannot be confused with any other amanita. The grey-coloured *A. spissa* is distinguished by a differently shaped stipe base, and the same applies to the grey-coloured Grisette (*A. vaginata*) which, moreover, is always ringless.

Spores: 7–10 μm, globose, smooth, colourless, amyloid
One spore is densely filled with oil droplets,
while the other contains a single droplet only.

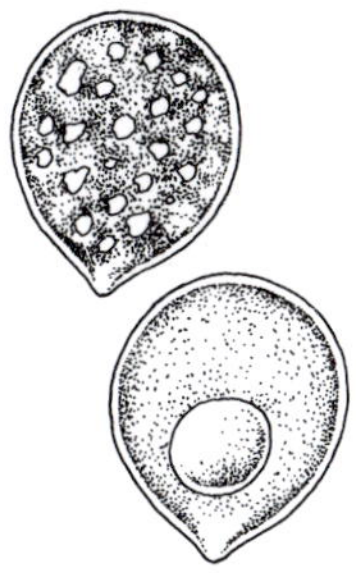

Characteristic termination of the stipe

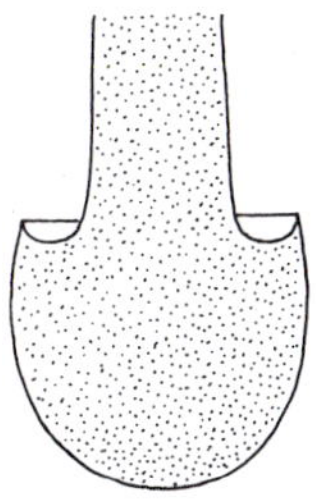

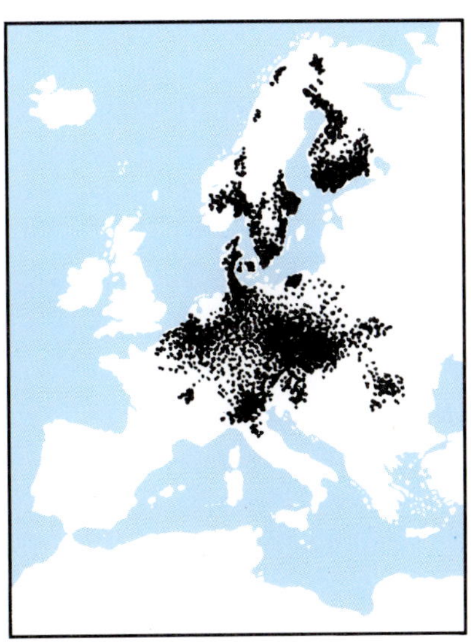

Amanita spissa (Fr.) Opiz

Amanita spissa it not poisonous, and many people collect is for table use at times when other edible mushrooms are scarce. However, it is a mushroom of inferior quality; moreover, careless and superficial identification in nature can easily lead to confusion with the deadly poisonous Panther Cap – which in fact is frequently the case. It occurs, sometimes in clumps, in summer and autumn, in both deciduous and coniferous forests, especially on lighter sandy soils. It grows even in long-lasting drought. Its cap is 5–10 cm (sometimes as much as 20 cm) wide, smooth and ungrooved at the margin, entirely grey or ashy brown-grey, lighter-coloured and sometimes whitish in wet weather. When dry it is shiny, scattered with many scab-like, whitish or pale grey remnants of the universal veil, often arranged into incomplete concentric rings. The clavate white stipe swells at the base into a conical or turnip-shaped bulb, ending in a hooked and attenuated to pointed excrescence. It has no volva but one or two scarcely discernible rings of wartlike projections. The ring is large, flaring, membranous, distinctly longitudinally grooved, white. The gills are free, broad, crowded and white. The flesh is also white, occasionally greyish under the cap cuticle, smelling of raw potatoes, with a mild taste. The spore print is white.

Both *A. spissa* and *A. rubescens* are distinguished from the poisonous Panther Cap by the colour of the cap and by a distinctly grooved ring; in *A. rubescens* also by the reddening flesh.

Spores: 9–10 × 7–8 µm,
broadly ellipsoid, smooth, colourless, amyloid

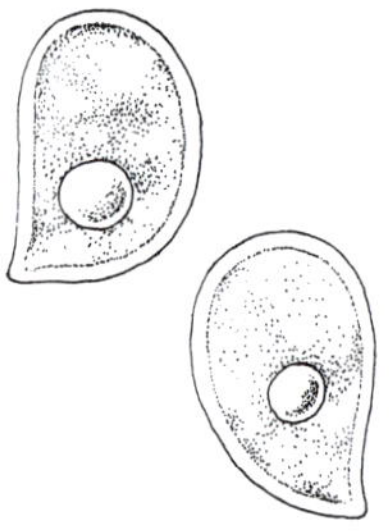

Blusher

Amanita rubescens (Pers. ex Fr.) S. F. Gray

The Blusher, especially in the last few decades, has attained so great a popularity that in the vicinity of big cities it has become almost as uncommon as the true boleti. Even though the Blusher is clearly and unambiguously characterized first of all by the reddening of its flesh, most marked in the basal portion of the stipe which is almost always bored through by insect larvae, cases of poisoning are still reported each year. Their cause lies in mistaking the Blusher for the poisonous Panther Cap. The latter species differs from the former not only in the colouring of the cap but also in its unchanging flesh. Also the shape of the enlarged stipe base is different: in the Panther Cap the basal part of the stipe is provided with a shallow ridge and 2–3 additional ringlets, while the Blusher has no ridge but only several circularly arranged rows of wart-like excrescences. Also the ring on the Panther Cap's stipe is narrow, limp, and lacking longitudinal furrows which are quite clearly apparent on the thick, membranous and flaring annulus of the Blusher.

As a rule, the Blusher is a mushroom of a robust habit. Its cap is pale red-brown or flesh-pink, strewn with whitish to brownish warts, 5–15 cm in width. The stipe is 5–12 cm long, 1–3.5 cm thick, with a conical bulb and several ringlets of wart-like projections at the base.

The Blusher is common in summer and autumn in woods of all types. It is often found in clumps, mainly in spruce forests, and occurs mainly when the weather is dry. The Panther Cap, on the other hand, is usually found under oaks. It prefers warmer situations and is more a solitary species.

The Blusher is an excellent edible mushroom which tastes best in soups or fried. It is not suitable for drying.

Spores: 8–9 × 7 µm, broadly ellipsoid, colourless, amyloid

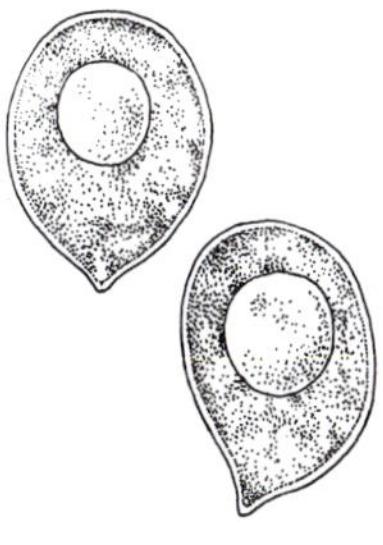

Central part of the stipe with ring and the stipe's base

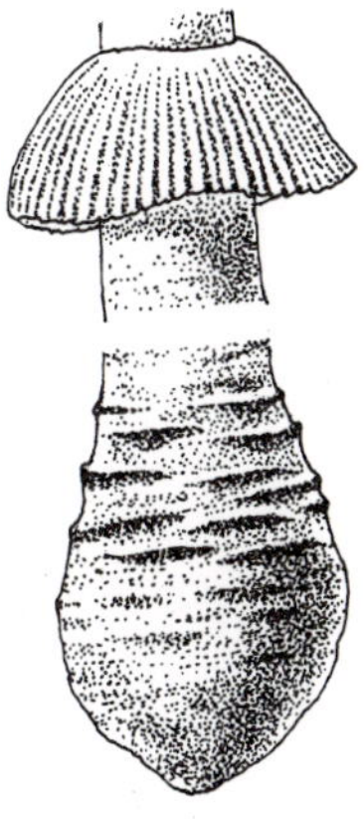

Agaricus brunnescens Peck

This agaric is better known as *A. bisporus*. It is medium-sized, with a cap rarely exceeding 10 cm in width, firm in texture and thick-fleshed, globular at first, then flatly bell-shaped, with a central navel-like depression, expanded in older specimens. The cap cuticle is dingy brownish to deep dark brown, smooth in the centre, with ingrown radially arranged brown fibres near the margin, eventually cracking into appressed brown scales. The cap's margin usually bears soft, wool-like veil remnants. The originally white gills soon turn a vivid pink, then reddish chocolate, finally almost black with whitish edges. The stipe is cylindrical, 3–6 cm long, 1–2 cm thick, glabrous, white. The membranous white veil leaves behind a ring; this, however, is not attached to the apex of the stipe but to its lower part – hence it is detachable in the downward direction. The flesh is white, pale flesh-red where cut, then becoming rusty, without a distinctive odour and taste. Microscopically this species is characterized by bisporous basidia.

It usually occurs on manured soil outside forests, along roadsides, in tree rows, gardens, on composts. Today it has become a habit to produce this agaric artificially – both on a small scale and in large growing establishments. It is nowadays identified with *A. hortensis* which is regarded only as its white-capped variety. It grows in similar habitats and is also bisporous. Both are edible.

Spores: 6.5–7.5 × 5–6 μm, broadly ovoid to subglobose, brown

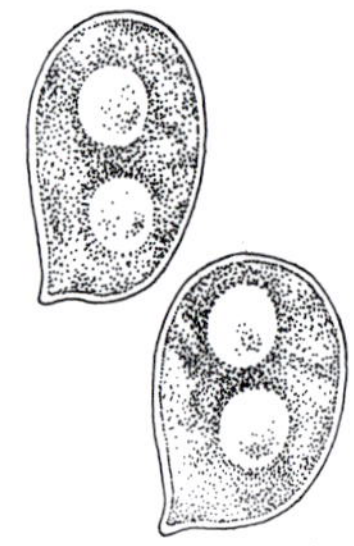

Spore print

Red-staining Agaric, Wood Mushroom

Agaricus silvaticus (Schaeff. ex Krombh.) Kumm.

An important distinguishing feature in identifying individual species of agarics is the colour change taking place in the injured, bruised or cut flesh. In a number of species the original white flesh stains pink or red. These include the Red-staining Agaric in which this reaction becomes particularly distinctive in young fruit bodies, though it is fairly evident in mature fruit bodies as well.

The cap of the Red-staining Agaric is 4 – 10 cm wide, pale ochre when young, soon dingy cinnamon-brown, usually covered with dark fibrous scales. The gills are pale greyish red at first, then brown, mature gills are dark chocolate-brown. The cylindrical and relatively slender stipe, usually exceeding the cap diameter in length, bears a membranous superior ring; at the base it is tuberously expanded and glabrous. When damaged the fruit body rapidly turns carmine red, then brown. The flesh has a pleasant spicy odour and a sweetish taste.

The Red-staining Agaric grows relatively profusely from July to October in spruce forests, mostly on calcareous soils. It is an edible, tasty species.

A. haemorrhoidarius, inhabiting deciduous woods, has a similarly rubescent flesh. Its cap is darker, almost umber-brown, with appressed scales of the same colour. The other rubescent species are uncommon. They include e.g. *A. benesii* and *A. squamulifer*. These are white species with whitish or pale brownish scales or flakes strewn over the cap surface.

Spores of *Agaricus silvaticus*: 5 – 6 × 3 – 3.5 μm, ellipsoid, brown

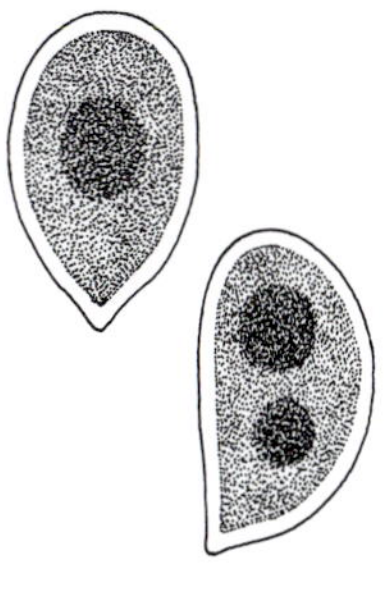

A cut fruit body of *Agaricus silvaticus*

Common Field Agaric, Meadow Mushroom
Agaricus campestris L. ex Fr.

The Common Field Agaric is the best known and most commonly collected of all the agarics growing in the wild. Its cap is 5–12 cm wide, at first globularly closed, then semiglobular, finally flatly expanded with a silky-fibrous surface, sometimes cracking into scales, white, in old fruit bodies tinged slightly with yellow to brown after handling. The gills remain pink for a long time, gradually discolouring to red; when old they range in shades from chocolate to black-brown. The stipe is 5–10 cm long, stoutly cylindrical, 2–4 cm thick, white or slightly pinkish and rusty or brownish in the lower part, tapering to a point at the base. The membranous ring is white and readily detachable. The flesh is white, either turning pale pink or remaining unchanged on injury, with a pleasant, somewhat fruity smell and taste.

The Common Field Agaric occurs outside the woodlands in manured soils, e.g. in meadows, fields, ditches and compost heaps. It grows in summer and autumn; large numbers of fruit bodies usually emerge after heavy rainfalls. Due to its strong variability within the species, it forms numerous varieties.

The similar Horse Agaric (*A. arvensis*), in spite of the fact that its Latin specific name means 'of the field', is a forest species favouring the forest humus of drier woods and shrub growths along forest edges. It is distinguished mainly by the cap and stipe cuticle rapidly becoming bright yellow on injury, as well as by an intense and pleasant scent rather like aniseed. When young the Horse Agaric has only pale flesh-coloured to grey-reddish gills.

Spores of *Agaricus campestris*: 7–8 × 4–5 μm, ellipsoid, brown

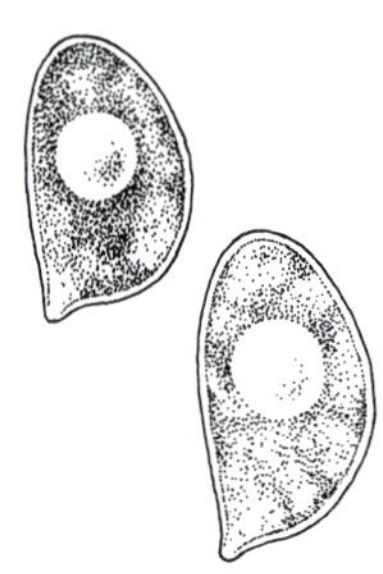

Agaricus augustus Fr.

Agaricus augustus belongs to the largest *Agaricus* species. Its cap attains 10–20 cm in diameter, in youth it is subglobular, later broadly convex, finally flat. Rusty brown appressed scales are concentrically arranged on a straw-yellow cuticle, the cap centre is brown. The robust, stoutly cylindrical, 10–25 cm long and 2–5 cm thick stipe is slightly enlarged at the base, sometimes swollen into a broad bulb. It is solid and firm at first, later hollow, bearing a remarkably large, softly membranous, white superior ring. The stipe below the ring is covered with large, protruding, woolly, recurved scales, disappearing with age. The gills are white at first, then greyish pink, grey-brown, and ultimately chocolate-brown. The flesh is white, when handled or cut it turns pale yellow at first, then brown; it smells pleasantly of aniseed and has a mild taste.

This edible and very tasty agaric grows from July to September in the needle carpet of spruce and pine forests, mainly on calcareous substrates. It has a particular liking for dry, sunny places, often also in forest outskirts.

The closely related *A. perrarus* differs from *A. augustus* in having ochre-yellow scales on the stipe and on the underside of the ring, and lighter-coloured (more yellow) scales on the cap. These two species often remain undifferentiated, because the colouring of scales is extremely variable, and hence an unreliable characteristic.

Spores: 8–10 × 5 μm, ellipsoid, brown

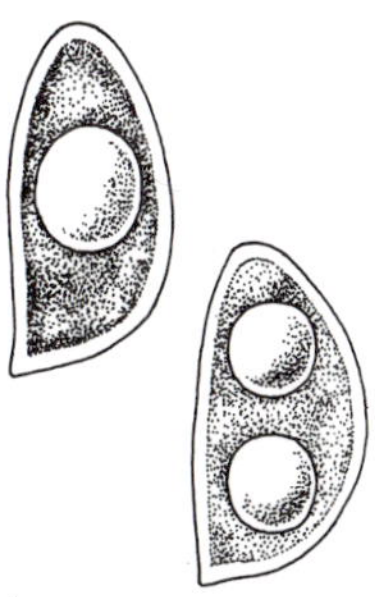

Agaricus abruptibulbus Peck

This species belongs to the group of agarics with yellowing flesh. It looks very like the Horse Agaric, and in fact it is only in the basal portion of the stipe that the two species differ. The base expands into a characteristic bulb whose upper side is marginate-depressed, i.e. as if cut off almost circularly around and having a distinctly marked border. The cap is 8–12 cm wide, convex, thimble-shaped in youth, flatly expanded when older, with a white, finely fibrous-scaly to glabrous cuticle. The gills are greyish pink when young, grey-brown to chocolate-brown when old. The stipe is 10–12 cm long, 1–2 cm thick, cylindrical, the bulb at its base is up to 3 cm broad; a thin membranous double ring is attached to the upper part of the stipe. The flesh has a pleasant taste and smell reminiscent of aniseed. The surface of the whole fruit body as well as the flesh turn much more intensely yellow on injury than does the Horse Agaric.

This agaric grows almost exclusively in the fallen needles of spruce forests, usually in late summer and autumn. It is edible and tasty.

In some mycological literature *A. abruptibulbus* is erroneously described as *Agaricus* or *Psalliota silvicola*. The true *A. silvicola* differs from *A. abruptibulbus* in having a thin-fleshed, cream-white cap (in *A. abruptibulbus* this is pure white), flesh turning brown or black with age, and smaller spores (5–6 × 3–4 μm).

The rare *A. macrocarpus* has a stipe only slightly thickened at the base, and a fleshy cap up to 15 cm wide. It grows both in woods and in meadows.

Spores: 6–8 × 4–5 μm, ellipsoid, brown

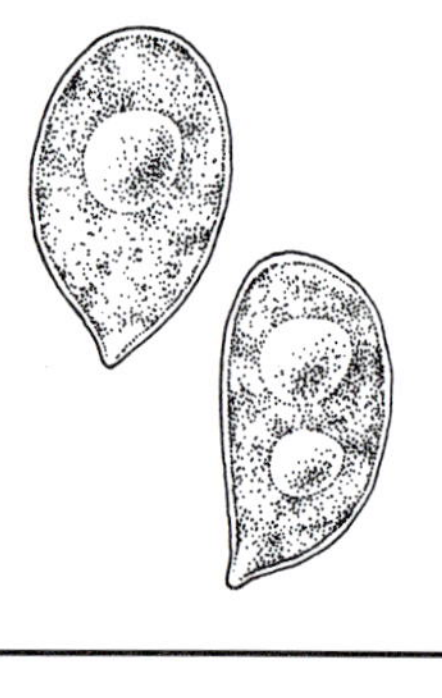

Horse Agaric, Horse Mushroom

Agaricus arvensis Schaeff. ex Fr.

The Horse Agaric is one of the most common forest agarics. It is easily recognized by its white fruit bodies rapidly staining yellow on injury, and by its pleasant aniseed smell. The cap is 5–12 cm wide and sometimes even wider, at first globular or thimble-shaped, later semiglobular to flatly expanded, with a glabrous, smooth and dry silky-shiny surface and a partly separable cuticle. The cap is white, mostly with a yellowish tinge, drying lemon- to orange-yellowish. The gills are greyish pink when young, gradually turning grey-brown, chocolate-brown to blackish brown. They are never a vivid pink. The cylindrical stipe sometimes exceeds the cap diameter in length; it is 1–2 cm thick, abrupt or slightly pointed at the base, with a membranous (sometimes double) superior ring bearing a ringlet of flaky scales on its underside. The spore print is violet-brown.

This excellent edible aromatic mushroom is abundant in summer and autumn in grassland as well as in all types of forests. It is most commonly found in the rich humus of spruce stands on calcareous ground.

When collecting it, care must be taken to avoid confusion especially of young fruit bodies with the deadly poisonous Death Cap (*Amanita phalloides*) – particularly its white form – and the poisonous Yellow Stainer (*Agaricus xanthoderma*). The Death Cap is readily identified by its high volva at the stipe base and persistently white gills, and the Yellow Stainer by a distinctive odour of phenol, deep pink gills, and the bright chromium-yellow flesh in the base of its stipe.

Spores: 6–8 × 4–5 μm, ellipsoid, brown

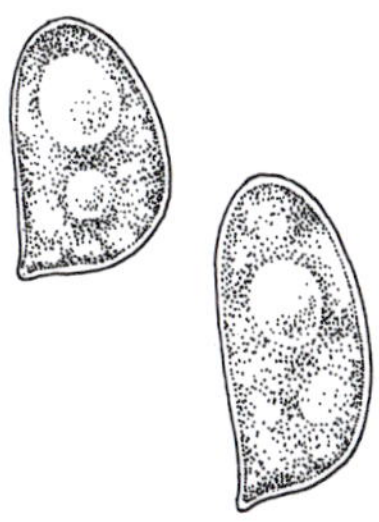

The white form of *Amanita phalloides*

Agaricus arvensis

Yellow Stainer

Agaricus xanthoderma Genev.

At first glance this fungus strongly resembles the Horse Agaric – its fruit body, however, is strikingly chalk-white and lacks the typical, pleasant smell of aniseed which is particularly characteristic of the Horse Agaric. The 5–15 cm wide cap is globular at first, later convex, staining yellow when handled, but this yellow colouring soon fades to some shade of grey-brown. The gills are whitish when young, soon turning vivid pink, becoming chocolate-brown to black with age. The white cylindrical stipe is 5–15 cm long, 1–2 cm thick, bearing a membranous superior ring; it is tuberously enlarged at the base, its surface turns chromium-yellow where handled. The flesh is white, chromium-yellow in the stipe base (which is best revealed on a longitudinal section through the fruit body), gradually turning yellow also in the other parts of the fruit body. It smells of phenol, faintly when fresh, intensely later.

The Yellow Stainer is poisonous. It is fairly abundant in deciduous woods, parks and gardens but occurs also in spruce forests on a calcareous substrate. It follows from some observations that fruit bodies growing in spruce forests are less poisonous, but this fungus should, for safety's sake, not be collected.

Besides the Yellow Stainer there are several other species possessing similar properties, yet all of them are rare. They are assigned to the independent section *Xanthodermatei*, characterized by a chromium-yellowing flesh in the stipe base and an odour of phenol or iodoform.

Spores: 5–7 × 3–4 μm, ovoid-ellipsoid, purplish brown

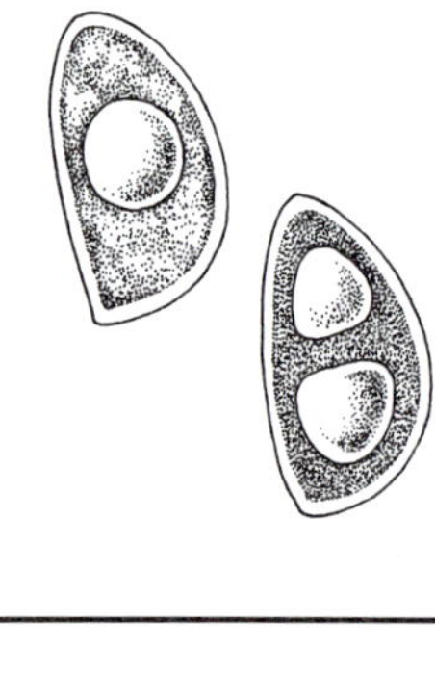

Lepiota cristata
(Alb. et Schw. ex Fr.) Kumm.

The genus *Lepiota,* rich in species, has several representatives in the European mycoflora. These are commonly found in our forests in late summer and early autumn. One of them is *Lepiota cristata.* A relatively small fungus, it has a cap only 2–5 cm wide, slightly convex, flatly expanded, obtusely umbonate at the centre. The cuticle of the cap is rusty brown or red-brown all over the surface, at first continuous and smooth but soon splitting up (with the exception of the umbo) into fine scales scattered over a white, glossy, fibrous background. The scales are more sparse towards the edge of the cap. The cap margin is connected with the stipe by a veil leaving behind only modest traces and a disappearing, easily detachable membranous ring on the stipe. The stipe is very long but only 3–5 mm thick, shiny silky white fibrous, often with a pinkish flush. The gills are crowded, ventricose, free, and white. The spore print is white. The intense smell of the flesh resembles that of the *Scleroderma* species.

L. cristata occurs in clumps in summer and in autumn both in the needles covering the floor of spruce and pine forests and in the fallen foliage and grass in mixed and deciduous forests, but also outside the woods in gardens and meadows. It is inedible and believed to be slightly poisonous. It is clearly distinguished from similar small *Lepiota* species by the colouring and coating of its cap, by a frequently pinkish stipe, and especially by its specific odour.

Spores: 6–7.5 × 3–3.5 μm, ellipsoid, with a characteristic spurlike projection at the base

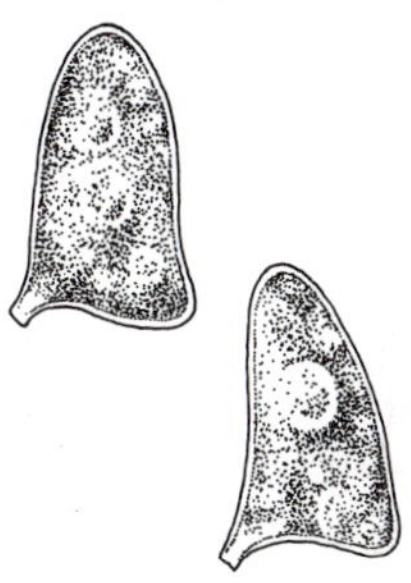

Lepiota clypeolaria
(Bull. ex Fr.) Kumm.

Lepiota clypeolaria is a generally widespread fungus. It can be found in both coniferous and deciduous forests throughout the summer until autumn. The cap is 5–10 cm wide, at first campanulate-convex, then flatly expanded with an obtuse, smooth, brown-coloured umbo at the centre and a cuticle broken up into ochre-yellow, brown-yellow or brown, woolly scales lying on a white background. The colouring of the scales is extremely variable. When young, the cap margin is connected to the stipe by a white or whitish cobweb-like veil, later leaving the margin fringed with irregular appendiculate fragments or scraps. The stipe is 5–10 cm long, 4–10 mm thick, cylindrical, tubular, rather brittle, breakable, with a disappearing woolly or only cobwebby ring below which it is thickly and softly yellowish or brownish woolly to scaly. The gills are free, crowded, ventricose, attenuated towards the margin, white, turning brown when handled. The flesh is white, unchanging, with a specific, hardly definable smell and a mild taste. The spore print is white. *L. clypeolaria* is an inedible fungus.

In coniferous forests, the closely related *L. ventriosospora* (or *L. metulaespora*) is not uncommon. It is distinguished by a yellowish-coloured veil, an ochre cap with bright yellow to brown scales, a yellowish stipe and larger spores, 14–18 × 4–6 μm in size. This species is also inedible.

Spores: 12–16 × 5.5–6.5 μm,
longly spindle-shaped,
without a spur at the base, colourless

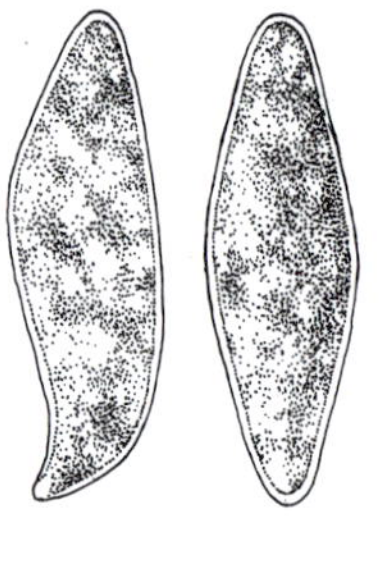

Lepiota clypeolaria

Lepiota ventriosospora

Parasol Mushroom

Macrolepiota procera (Scop. ex Fr.) Sing.

On or about midsummer, robust fruit bodies of the Parasol Mushroom make their appearance in the drier parts of deciduous forests, particularly in their sunny margins and woodland clearings. It usually grows in groups and tends to occur in the same places for several years. When young, this conspicuous mushroom, one of the largest gill fungi, has the cap closed into the shape of a claviform mallet, while at maturity it becomes expanded, 10–25 cm wide, always with a darker umbo in the centre. On its surface are very dark scales which decrease in size towards the cap margin. The stipe is 15–40 cm high, 2–4 cm thick, firm, almost cylindrical, narrowing towards the cap, inflated at the base into a conspicuous bulb covered with a white, felt-like mycelium. The surface of the stipe is transversely streaked in brown and bears a loose, collar-like, double-edged annulus. The gills are white and very broad. The flesh is white and unchanging; in older fruit bodies the cap is fluffy and dry, the stipe woody and fibrous.

The Shaggy Parasol (*M. rhacodes*) is readily distinguished from the Parasol Mushroom by its glabrous, unstreaked stipe and a marked colour reaction of the flesh: when scratched, the stipe surface – especially in its basal portion – rapidly turns saffron-yellow at first and reddish brown later. This is most clearly observable in fresh fruit bodies.

Both species are edible, yet it is advisable to collect only young fruit bodies. They are best while the cap is still closed.

The Parasol Mushroom and the Shaggy Parasol grow in similar habitats and their range extends throughout the north temperate zone.

Spores: 16–20 × 10– 13 μm, broadly ellipsoid, colourless

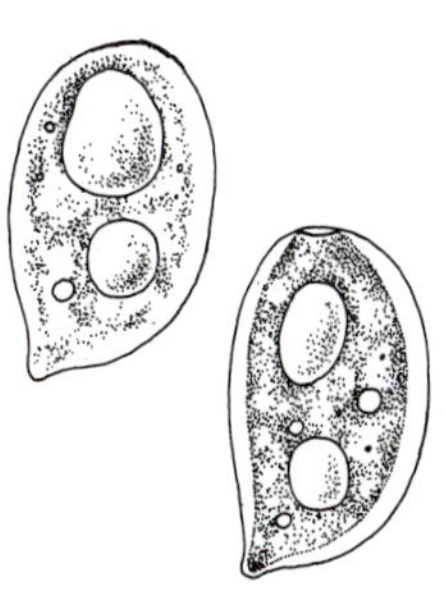

Shaggy Parasol
Macrolepiota rhacodes (Vitt.) Sing.

The Shaggy Parasol resembles the Parasol Mushroom but never attains its height. The cap is at first globularly closed, then conically bell-shaped, and finally flatly expanded, 10–15 cm wide. Its cuticle breaks up into large, overlapping scales which are larger and more recurved than in the Parasol Mushroom, pale brown at first, darker-hued later. Only the umbo in the cap centre remains persistently smooth. The gills are white, turning in old age orange or red on injury; they are broad, crowded, and free. The stipe is 10–20 cm high, up to 1.5 cm thick, cylindrical, tuberously enlarged at the base to a thickness of 4.5 cm, white, hollow, bearing a powerful superior double ring which is freely movable and thus can easily be shifted along the stipe. The injured stipe surface becomes at first saffron-yellow, then red, and finally brown. The flesh is white, fibrous, also staining orange at first and then red when injured; its smell and taste are pleasant.

The Shaggy Parasol grows very profusely in woods of all types, especially in warmer and drier situations. It is edible but only the cap is suitable for eating. It is easily distinguished from the Parasol Mushroom by the remarkable colour change in the cut flesh. In contrast to the Parasol Mushroom, its stipe surface is not striated. A very light-coloured variety of *M. rhacodes,* var. *hortensis,* may be found growing on compost heaps and manured garden soil. Just like in the Parasol Mushroom, the mycelium of the Shaggy Parasol tends to remain in the same spot for a number of years. Thus it is possible repeatedly to gather the Shaggy Parasol in regular places.

Spores: 9–12 × 6–7 μm, broadly ellipsoid, smooth, colourless

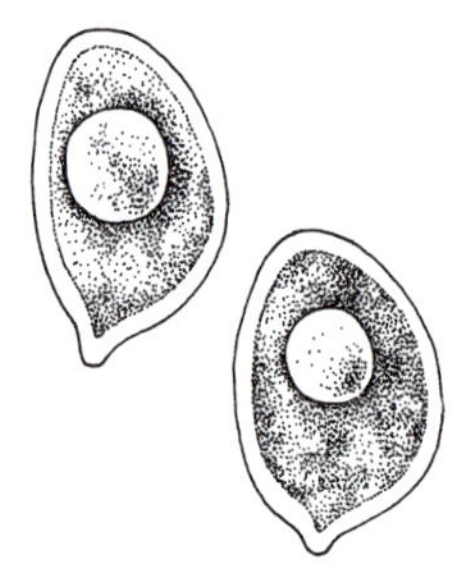

Macrolepiota excoriata
(Schaeff. ex Fr.) Acker-Sch.

Towards the end of summer and in autumn, whole colonies of this white mushroom often appear in stubble-fields, ploughed fields, potato-fields, or even in meadows and on grassy slopes. The 6–12 cm wide cap is only occasionally tinged with brown in the centre, at first smooth, then covered with minute pale ochre to brownish scales. The stipe is 5–12 cm long, 1–1.5 cm thick, gradually expanding downwards into a globular bulb, glabrous, bearing a movable, broad, membranous ring. The gills are free, broad, thin, crowded, white, unchanging or slightly staining brown where handled. Also the flesh is white, unchanging, odourless, with a mild taste. The spore print is white. *Macrolepiota excoriata* is edible.

Lepiota naucina (or *L. pudica*) shares the habitats with *M. excoriata*. It is also entirely white – with the exception of the gills which turn pink with age, when they become covered with a pink spore mass. Pink gills are characteristic of this species. Its cap is up to 10 cm wide, smooth, scaleless; a narrow, sometimes fugacious, immovable ring is attached to the cylindrical stipe. The flesh is white, unchanging, of a rather unpleasant fruity smell. *L. naucina* has more recently been classed with the genus *Leucoagaricus* differing from the genus *Macrolepiota* in some microcharacteristics. For example, it has clampless hyphae and spores smaller than 12 μm.

Spores of *Macrolepiota excoriata*:
12–15 × 8–9 μm, broadly ellipsoid, colourless

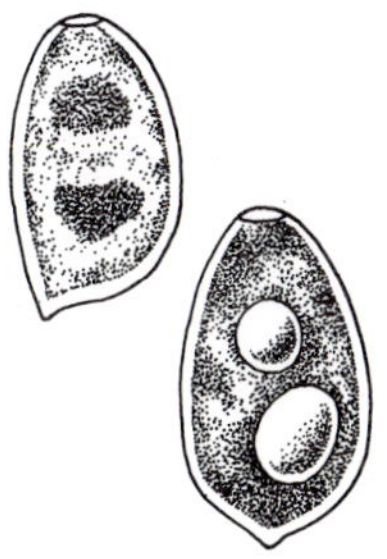

Cystoderma amianthinum
(Scop. ex Fr.) Maubl.

The species included in the genus *Cystoderma* are usually small fungi with a 2–6 cm wide cap. In the past they were classified as members of the genus *Lepiota.* From these, however, they are distinguished by a granulose coating of both cap and stipe consisting of small conical warts, and by having gills adnate with tooth.

Cystoderma amianthinum has a slightly convex cap, ochre to deep golden-yellow, often wrinkled, densely granular. The gills are white when young, later ochre-yellowish, and crowded. The stipe is longer than the cap diameter, 2–5 mm thick, cylindrical, with a slight clavate swelling at the base, ochre-yellow, bearing a scaly ring, with ochre-coloured scales below the ring. The flesh is yellowish, giving a faint rancid smell, its taste is mild. The spore print is pure white.

C. amianthinum grows from the end of summer until the first frosts in grassy habitats and in moss, particularly in damp coniferous forests, pine woods and heather moors, greatly favouring acid soils. It is inedible.

C. longisporum was distinguished from *C. amianthinum* as an independent species. Its cap and stipe are somewhat darker, reddish to rusty ochre, the gills are cream-yellow, sometimes pinkish. It is almost odourless. It is found in both coniferous and deciduous forests. Both species have amyloid spores. In the genus *Cystoderma,* examination of the amyloidity of spores is necessary before individual species can be exactly identified.

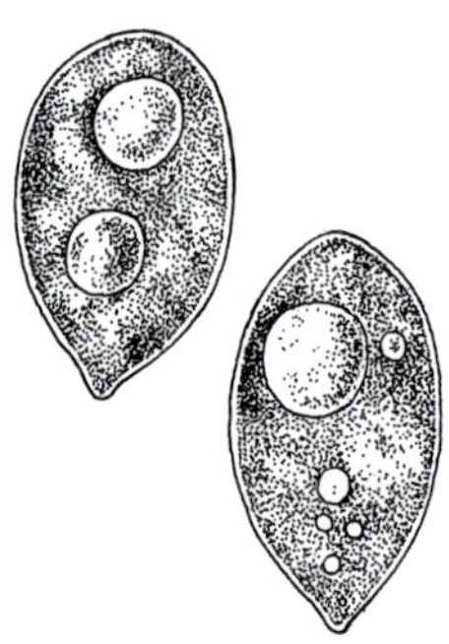

Spores of *Cystoderma amianthinum*:
5–6 × 3–4 μm, broadly ellipsoid, colourless

Cystoderma cinnabarinum
(Alb. et Schw. ex Fr.) Maubl.

Cystoderma cinnabarinum greatly resembles *C. amianthinum,* but has a different colouring and is larger. The cap may attain 8 cm in width and is a wonderful cinnabar-red, only occasionally fading to yellow. Also the stipe, often ascending slantwise, bent and usually inflated at the base, is vermilion, scaly below the narrow ring, and glabrous above it. The gills are crowded, white, bearing developed cystidia. The flesh is white, unchanging, almost odourless, and of a mild taste. The spore print is white.

C. cinnabarinum occurs mainly in coniferous forests, but in no great abundance. Occasionally it may be found growing on very rotten wood.

C. granulosum and *C. carcharias* are more common. *C. granulosum* has a red-brown, rusty, cinnamon to orange-brown cap, its spores are nonamyloid. There are no cystidia on the gills. It grows in autumn in mossy forests. In *C. carcharias* the cap is beige or pale buff, the stipe is covered with a detachable granulose layer forming flaring, funnel-shaped rings below the apex. The context emits an intense rancid (i. e. earthy) smell, spores are amyloid. *C. carcharias* often grows in autumn in mossy coniferous forests. All *Cystoderma* species are considered inedible and cannot be recommended for table use.

Spores of *Cystoderma cinnabarinum*:
4–5 × 2.5–3 μm, ellipsoid, colourless, nonamyloid

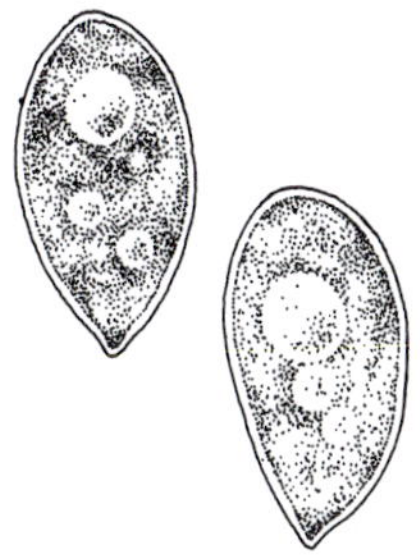

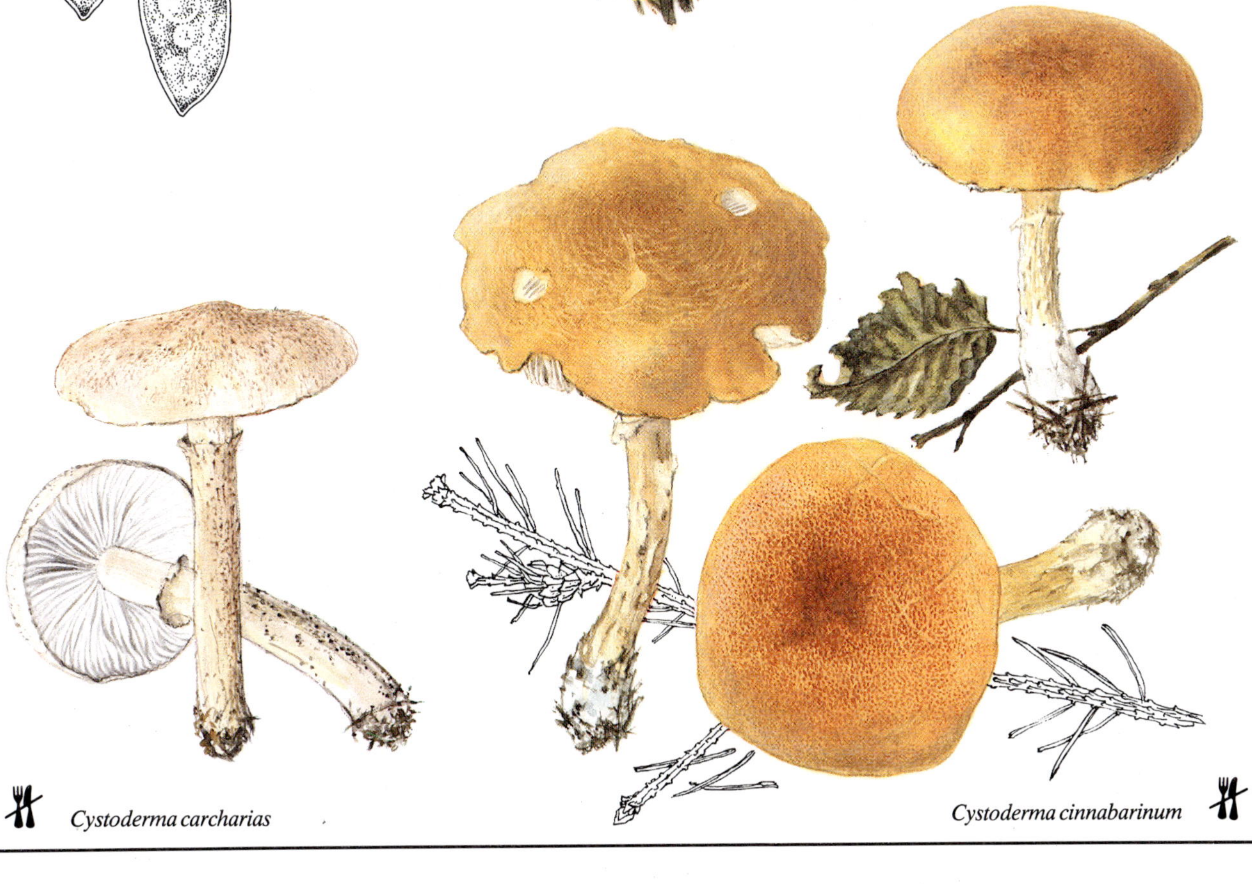

Cystoderma carcharias

Cystoderma cinnabarinum

Shaggy Mane, Shaggy Cap, Lawyer's Wig

Coprinus comatus (Müll. ex Fr.) S. F. Gray

The fruit bodies of most ink caps develop at an amazingly rapid rate: some species need only a few hours to proceed from the germ past the ripening of spores to the deliquescence of mature fruit bodies.

Of the large-sized and more fleshy ink caps, it is the Shaggy Mane that occurs in greatest abundance. It can be found in manured soil, in garden grass, along roadsides and on the edge of woods. The cap varies considerably in shape; the typical form is at first longly cylindrical but occasionally may be subglobular, 5–10 cm high, 3–6 cm wide, later conically convex, white when young, later with an ochre-hued apex, its entire surface being subtomentose-scaly. Mature fruit bodies colour brown from the margin, the overlapping scales are in part concentrically arranged. The caps of mature specimens turn entirely black and dissolve. In the mature fruit body it is the gills that are first subjected to autolysis, and because the spore print is dark brown to black, the caps of the Shaggy Mane are transformed, together with the gills, into an ink-black pulpy matter. The cylindrical stipe may be as much as 15 cm long and 1–1.5 cm thick, white, with a slightly thickened base, tubularly hollow, with a narrow, free, almost movable ring which soon falls off and sometimes persists at the stipe base. The crowded, remote gills are at first white, then rapidly turning pink from the cap margin, later they become red-brown and finally black. Young fruit bodies are edible and tasty, but it is not recommended to accompany any meals containing them with alcoholic drinks.

Spore: 10–14 × 6–8 μm, ellipsoid almond-shaped, with a discernible germ pore, black-brown

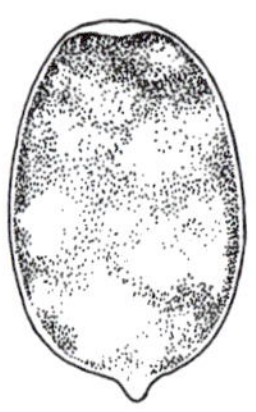

Common Ink Cap

Coprinus atramentarius (Bull. ex Fr.) Fr.

Fruit bodies of the Common Ink Cap usually grow in clumps from rotten wood concealed in the ground, and thus seem to be growing directly from the soil. They mostly occur in fields, on rubbish heaps, in gardens, along roads, sometimes on compost heaps, and may be found from spring until autumn, especially after heavy rains.

The cap is egg-shaped at first, 3–7 cm high, later bell-shaped or conical, 4–10 cm wide, with a wavy-lobed margin, upturned when old. The original ash-grey or greyish brown colouring of the cap turns black as the spores gradually mature. The colour change proceeds from the margin to the cap centre. Ripe fruit bodies dissolve into a black pulp. The cap cuticle is brownish and scaly, later glabrous, brown and cottony at the apex only. The gills are crowded, free, whitish when young, greyish, then brown, finally black and deliquescent. The stipe is 7–18 cm long, 1–1.5 cm thick, cylindrical, white, finely fibrous, with a silky sheen, at first full, then hollow, ringless, often with a circularly or annularly swollen, spindle-shaped, narrowing base. The flesh is odourless, with a mild taste. The spore print is dark brown. Young fruit bodies are edible and tasty. It is necessary to warn against taking alcoholic drinks with or following any meal containing the Common Ink Cap (and any other species of *Coprinus*), otherwise symptoms of poisoning might occur from 20 minutes to 2 hours after the ingestion, mostly as very unpleasant psychical states.

Spore: 8–11 × 5–6 μm, ellipsoid or ellipsoid almond-shaped, with a germ pore, dark date-brown

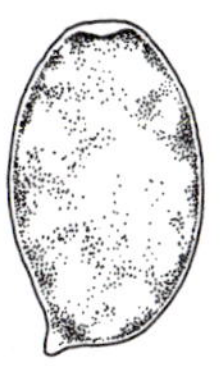

Glistening Ink Cap

Coprinus micaceus (Bull. ex Fr.) Fr.

Large clumps of Glistening Ink Caps appear usually after summer rains around the stumps of deciduous trees or directly attached to them. These clumps consist of a great number of fruit bodies whose caps are 1–4 cm high, 1–2.5 cm wide, thin-fleshed, brittle, pale ochre-brown, buff or red-brown. The caps, initially cylindrical or egg-shaped, become bell-shaped or flatly expanded later, up to 4 cm wide, with an at first grooved, then radially cracking surface. Like the majority of ink caps, mature fruit bodies dissolve into a pulpy matter. The cap surface of young fruit bodies is densely covered with glistening, white or ochre-hued granules; as these are readily deciduous, the caps eventually turn glabrous. The gills are free, crowded, whitish at first, then greyish, mature gills are black and deliquescent. The 4–10 cm long and 2–5 cm thick stipe is white, ringless, brittle and hollow, white pruinose to pubescent at first, then glabrous. The context has no specific odour or taste. The spore print is umber- or date-brown.

The Glistening Ink Cap grows from stumps, and often also from the foot of older live trunks of deciduous trees. Young fruit bodies are edible, but after their ingestion it is necessary to avoid alcohol.

Still other similar ink caps may be found on stumps and tree trunks. Their exact identification requires microscopic study.

Spores: 7–10 × 4–5 × 4.5 –6 μm, lenticularly flattened, almond- or spindle-shaped in the lateral view, egg-shaped or almost mitriform in the front view, with a clearly discernible germ pore, red-brown

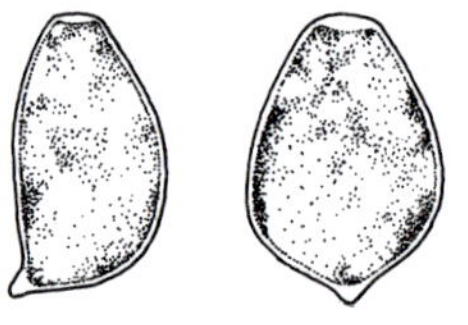

Three cells of the veil from the cap surface

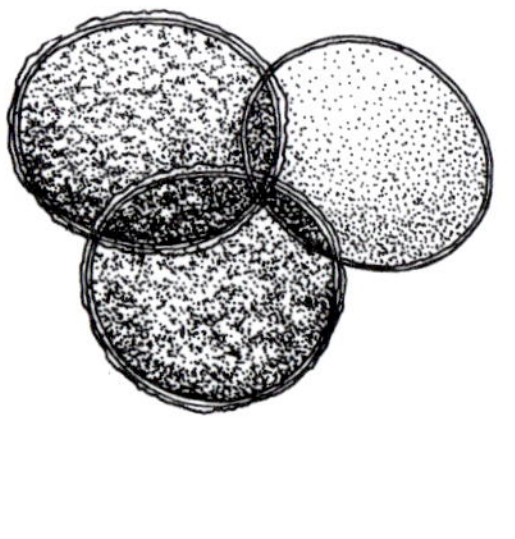

Panaeolus papilionaceus

(Bull. ex Fr.) Quél.

Cow dung accommodates a peculiar mycoflora. Once small-scale agricultural production was common in most European countries and huge amounts of cow dung were widespread on grassy field tracks, providing adequate living conditions for an exuberant, variegated community of specialized coprophilous fungi. Noteworthy among these were small semiglobular or conical caps seated on long, thin stipes – members of the genus *Panaeolus*. At that time they were incomparably more abundant than nowadays when cattle are often permanently lodged in stalls.

The genus *Panaeolus* includes a large number of species whose exact identification is far from easy. They have, however, one feature in common: their gill faces are spotted with unevenly maturing basidia. The paler spots of immature basidia alternate with almost black patches harbouring fully developed spores.

Panaeolus papilionaceus has a 2–4 cm wide, thin-fleshed, almost non-hygrophanous cap: irrespective of whether it is moist or dry, it is dirty white or greyish, sometimes with an ochre tint. A cobwebby veil connects the cap margin with the stipe but soon disappears without leaving any notable traces. A very long, only 2–4 cm thick stipe is tough, breaking with a snapping sound, brownish, smooth and glabrous, grooved and pruinose only below the apex. The gills are broad, ventricose, fairly crowded, broadly adnate, grey, then grey-black, with white edges and unevenly spotted surfaces. The flesh has no specific odour nor taste. The spore print is black. *P. papilionaceus* is inedible.

Spores and cystidia of *Panaeolus papilionaceus*:
11–16 × 9–1 μm, almond-shaped, smooth, black

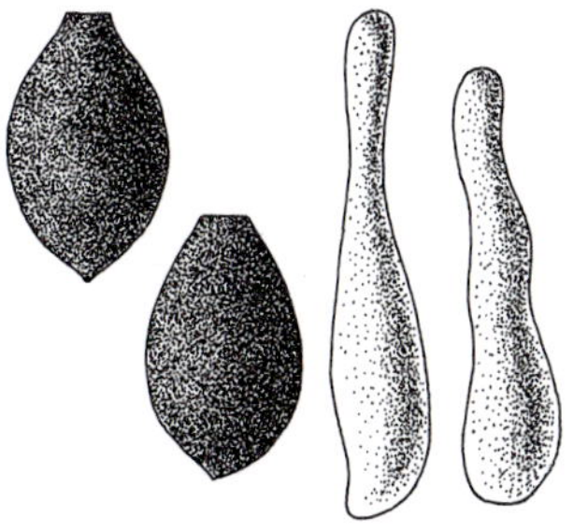

Spores of *Panaeolus sphinctrinus*:
14–18 × 9–12 μm, lemon-shaped, black

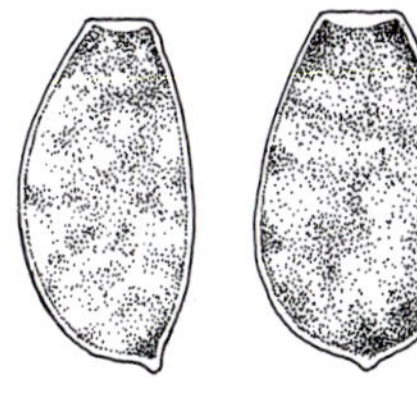

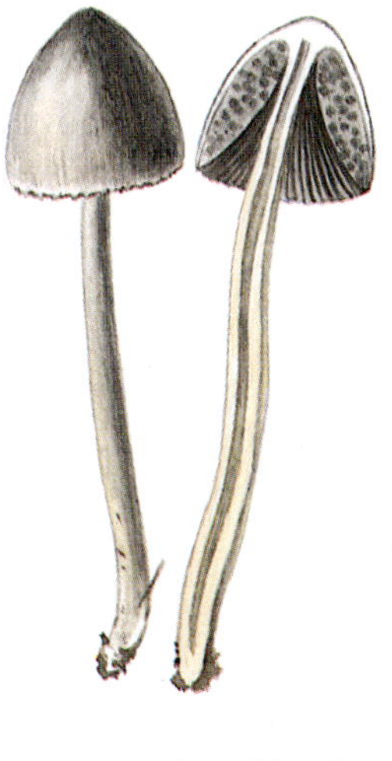

Panaeolus sphinctrinus grows abundantly in summer and in autumn on horse and cattle dung

Panaeolus papilionaceus

Psathyrella candolleana

(Fr. ex Fr.) R. Maire

As presently defined, the genus *Psathyrella* includes a large number of black-spored gill fungi, often small and inconspicuous, growing solitarily in grass, under shrubs, and on the damp forest ground. Some species become more conspicuous by growing in groups on stumps and at the foot of tree trunks. The most commonly found of these is *Psathyrella candolleana.* It is very variable but its typical form can be distinguished by its brittle, conically bell-shaped, thin-fleshed, 3–8 cm wide cap, in youth with numerous white veil fragments hanging from the margin and disappearing with age. The cap cuticle is radially wrinkled, almost white, whitish or pale beige to buff-yellowish, later becoming dingy violet near the margin of the cap from maturing gills. The gills are at first whitish, soon turning violet, later purple-brown, with white edges, crowded, relatively narrow, adnexed. The gill edges are strewn with large, colourless, almost cylindrical, thin-walled cheilocystidia. The stipe is 3–8 cm long, 2–5 mm thick, hollow, white, smooth and shiny. The flesh is almost odourless, with a mild taste. The spore print is purple-brown.

P. candolleana usually grows in larger groups in the vicinity of old stumps or at the foot of live trees; it is particularly abundant on false acacias but can also occur solitarily on decaying twigs and wood detritus. It grows from May until autumn. It is edible but of little importance because of its brittleness.

Spores: 7–8 × 3–4 μm, almond-shaped, smooth, red-brown

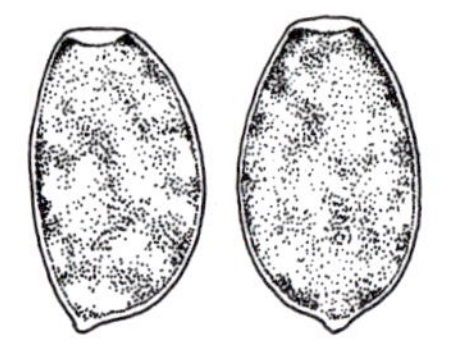

Cheilocystidia

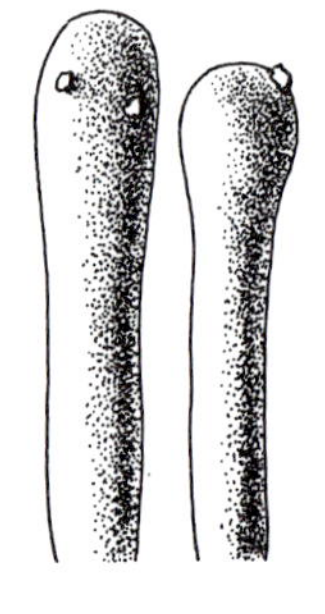

Psathyrella velutina
(Pers. ex S. F. Gray) Sing.

Psathyrella velutina is a relatively large fungus. Its cap is 6–10 cm wide, hygrophanous, pale rusty brown or rusty yellow, in dry weather almost yellow-grey, fibrous-scaly, often slightly wrinkled. The cap margin of young fruit bodies is connected with the stipe by a light-coloured veil, leaving remains on the stipe in the form of lacerate flaps and a woolly fugacious ring. The stipe is almost cylindrical, 15 cm long and 7–10 cm thick, hollow, dirty pallid, rusty brown scaly-fibrous, pruinose at the apex. The gills are considerably crowded, emarginate or roundly adnate, dark brownish, blackish rusty to spotted chocolate-brown, then almost black. The gill edge is white, ciliate, with conspicuous droplets ('weeping'), and is formed by colourless, broadly clavate or cylindrical cheilocystidia. The flesh is yellowish, brownish in the basal part of the stipe, with a faint earthy smell and an astringent taste. The spore print is brown-black.

P. velutina grows either solitarily or in small clumps mostly outside the wood, in grass, often along tracks, and profusely in parks, in late summer and in autumn. It is poisonous. *P. velutina* has wart-like spores and is therefore excluded by some mycologists from the genus *Psathyrella* and classed in the independent genus *Lacrymaria.*

P. hydrophila is a clump-forming lignicolous fungus whose cap is coffee- to chestnut-brown when moist, buff when dry; the stipe is white. It is edible.

Spores of *Psathyrella velutina*:
10–12 × 6–7 μm, almond-shaped, verrucose, black-brown, with a colourless germ pore and apiculus

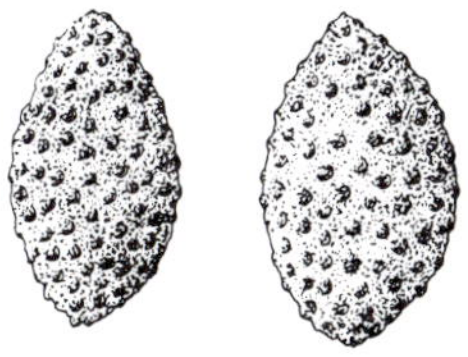

Cheilocystidia

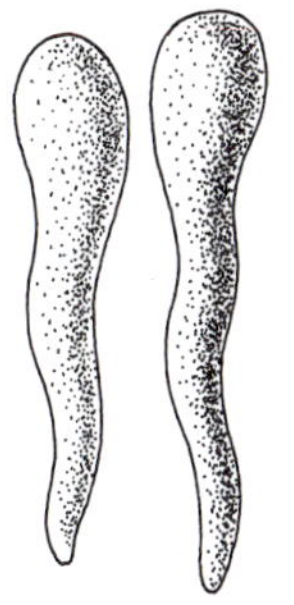

Water droplets on the gills

Psathyrella hydrophila

Psathyrella velutina

Yellow Cow-pat Toadstool

Bolbitius vitellinus (Pers. ex Fr.) Fr.

On decaying straw, overgrown tracks and in grass we may come across small, bright yolk- or lemon-yellow fungi, often as early as in spring. The cap is egg-shaped at first, then conically bell-shaped and finally expanded, 2–6 cm wide, very thin-fleshed, almost membranous. The cap surface is radially grooved up to the centre, sticky slimy when moist, fading with age. The stipe is up to 10 cm long, 2–5 mm thick, soft, hollow, narrowing towards the apex, white, pruinose all along its length. The gills are fairly crowded, thin, narrow, pale earth-brown, then light rusty yellow to ochre-brown. The flesh is odourless and has a mild taste. The spore print is rusty brown.

The Yellow Cow-pat Toadstool is inedible. Its overall appearance is suggestive of ink caps but besides other differentiating characteristics it has a rusty brown spore print, while the spore print of ink caps is dark brown to black. It occurs throughout the summer soon after rainfalls, develops rapidly, and disappears in 1–2 days without leaving any trace at all. It grows solitarily as a rule, or in small groups. It prefers an environment rich in nitrogenous substances and sometimes grows directly on old excrement, dung or freshly manured soils of fields and meadows, or on compost heaps. It is a representative of the family Bolbitiaceae which also includes the genera *Agrocybe* and *Conocybe*. Their common features are yellow-brown spores and the cap cuticle consisting of globular, vesicular or pyriform cells.

A part of the hymenium with basidioles and a cheilocystidium

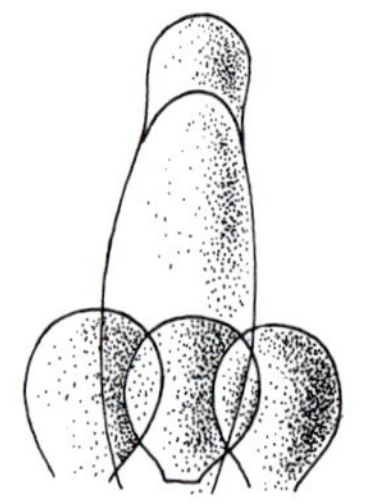

Spores of *Bolbitius vitellinus*: 12–13 × 6–7 μm, almond-shaped, smooth, with a germ pore, rusty brown

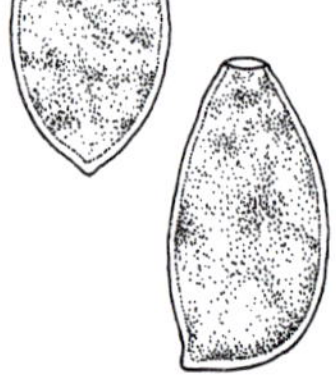

Bolbitius vitellinus

Bolbitius aleuriatus is a small lignicolous fungus with a slimy cap, growing mainly on beech stumps

Agrocybe dura
(Bolt. ex Fr.) Sing.

Agrocybe dura is closely related to and often confused with *A. praecox*. Some mycologists even refuse to regard it as an independent species, treating it as a variety of *A. praecox*. *A. dura* has fleshier and tougher fruit bodies, a non-hygrophanous, dry, brownish or ivory-whitish cap, at maturity sometimes cracking into irregular patches. The stipe bears a flaky ring which disappears in time (*A. praecox* has a membranous ring). The gills are pallid, then violaceous grey, ultimately light coffee-brown, with white ciliate edges. Unlike *A. praecox*, the flesh has no mealy smell and is faintly bitter. Microscopically it can be distinguished by larger spores which, however, are similar in shape.

A. dura occurs predominantly on cultivated soils, in gardens and fields, mainly on lime-rich substrates; sometimes it also grows in summer and autumn – later than *A. praecox*.

Another species that is very similar to *A. praecox* is *A. paludosa*. It is a slender, small fungus with a hygrophanous, only 1–4 cm wide cap and a thin (2–4 mm), strongly elongated stipe. It is confined to swampy meadows overgrown with moisture-loving vegetation and grows mostly in sphagnum. All species of *Agrocybe* are edible.

Cystidia

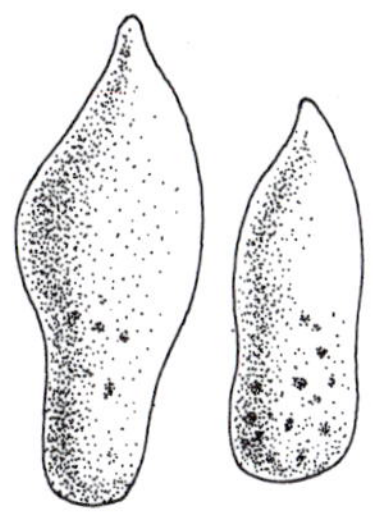

Spores of *Agrocybe dura:*
10–12.5 × 6–8 μam,
almond-shaped, honey-brown

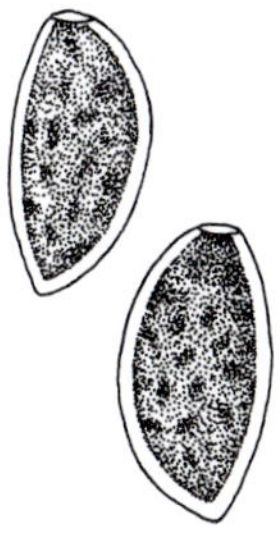

Agrocybe paludosa

Agrocybe dura

Agrocybe praecox

(Pers. ex Fr.) Sing.

If the weather is favourable, *Agrocybe praecox* can sometimes be found as early as April – as a rule, however, it appears in May and June. Its favourite habitats are grassy places, pastures and the borders of woodlands, as well as gardens and parks. Being an edible and relatively tasty mushroom, it is a welcome contribution to the springtime diet. It is easily recognizable and could hardly be mistaken for any poisonous species. When young, the 2–8 (exceptionally 10) cm wide cap is hemispherical or campanulate-convex, soon flatly expanded, light coffee-coloured when moist, weathering to pale ochre or cream-yellow on drying up and in aging. In wet weather, the cuticle is liable to crack. The gills are adnate and shortly decurrent by a tooth, fairly crowded, whitish at first, then brown. The relatively thin stipe may grow up to 12 cm in length; at the base it is either equal or slightly inflated, entirely white or cream-yellowish, with a membranous disappearing ring. This ring is a remnant of the veil covering the gills of the youngest fruit bodies. The flesh is white or yellowish, with a markedly farinaceous smell and taste. The spore print is brown.

The genus *Agrocybe* now contains several species formerly treated as members of the genus *Pholiota,* having a hymeniform cap cuticle and a tobacco-brown spore print.

Cystidium and spore: 9–12 × 5–6 μm, almond-shaped, grey-yellowish, smooth, with a germ pore

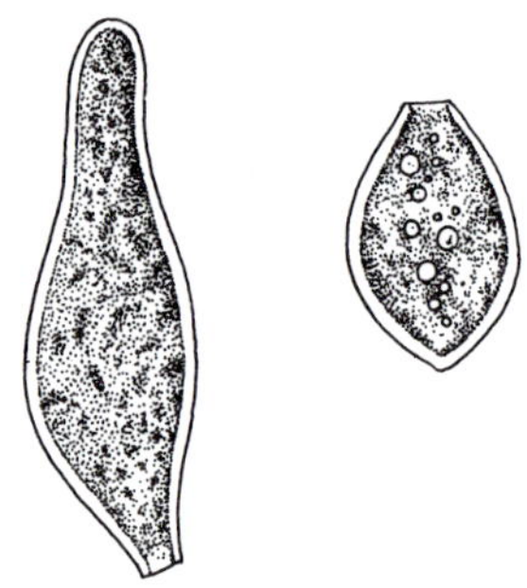

Spore print

Stropharia rugosoannulata

Farlow in Murrill

For the time being, this is the only mushroom that can successfully be grown in one's own garden. Its cultivation is much simpler than that of field agarics. Straw of various cereals or flax stems are used as a living substrate. This corresponds to its natural substrate, since in the wild it occurs on rotten straw. It grows from June to November.

Originally it was described from North America and later from Italy (under the name of *S. ferrii*), but the idea that both might be just two geographical races of the same species cannot be ruled out. In the course of cultivation, strains with diversely coloured caps were obtained; of these, the highly productive cultivar 'Vinnetou' with a pale red-brown cap, grey-blue gills and yellowish white stipe is raised most commonly.

The typical form occurring in the wild has a cap 8 – 15 cm – rarely 25 cm – in width, at first grey-brown, dingy yellow-brown, at maturity red-brown or chestnut-brown with a violaceous tinge, growing paler later on and very sticky. The stipe bears a double ring, white and grooved above, yellowish white below. The flesh has a faint radish-like smell and a mild taste, and is relatively tough. The spore print is purple-brown to violet black-brown.

Spores of *Stropharia rugosoannulata*:
10 – 13 × 7 – 8 μm, almond-shaped,
smooth, lilac-violet

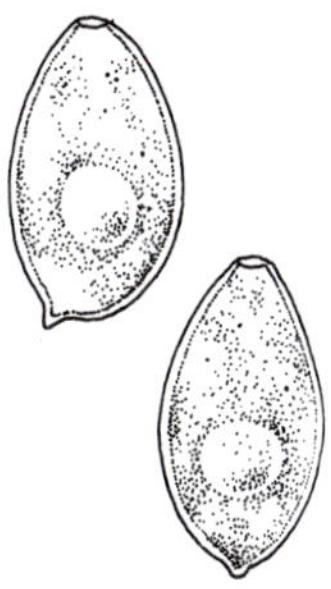

Spores of *Stropharia semiglobata*
15 – 19 × 7 – 10 μm, violet-brown

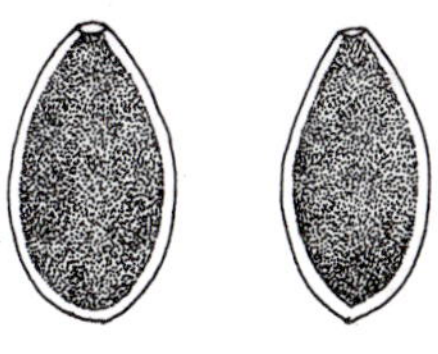

In free nature we frequently come across *Stropharia semiglobata,* growing on older excrements of herbivores

Stropharia rugosoannulata

Verdigris Agaric

Stropharia aeruginosa (Curt. ex Fr.) Quél.

Some *Stropharia* species resemble small field agarics, since they have in common the colour of the spore print (brown or violet-black) and a veil leaving a ring on the stipe.

The most commonly occurring species of *Stropharia* is *S. coronilla.* Its cap is up to 6 cm in diameter, yellowish white to pale ochre. The gills are chocolate-brown, the stipe is relatively short and bears a grooved ring. It occurs after rainfall in dry lawns, pastures and along field margins.

One of the strikingly coloured species is the Verdigris Agaric whose 3–10 cm wide, green cap, weathering to ochraceous later, is covered with a layer of slime. The green or green-blue stipe is also slimy, 4–8 cm long and 0.3–0.6 cm thick, white scaly, bearing a collar-shaped ring below the apex. The blue-greenish flesh emits a peculiar tannin-like smell, or one rather like rotting radish, which – together with the slimy cuticle – does not make the Verdigris Agaric particularly attractive for mushroom pickers. Until recently it had been considered edible; now, however, it is classed as poisonous and should be avoided.

Fruit bodies of the Verdigris Agaric grow from August to November on the remains of wood logs and branches lying on the ground or hidden immediately beneath the surface. Sometimes they also grow on rotten stumps of deciduous and coniferous trees, especially in mixed forests, gardens, fields, parks, shrub growths, etc.; they may even occur on rotting straw.

Blue-green is also the characteristic colour of the *Clitocybe odora*; this, however, has no veil, smells of aniseed, and its spore print is white.

Spores: 7–8 × 4–5 μm, ellipsoid, black-brown

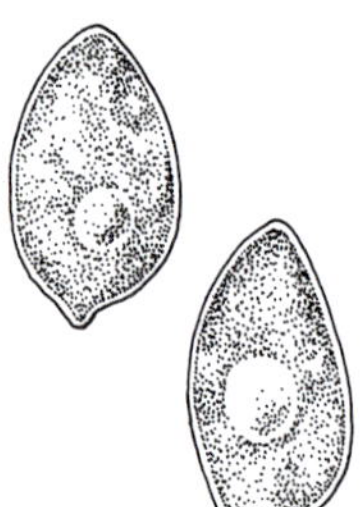

Stropharia albonitens
(Fr.) P. Karst.

It is clearly distinguishable from the other yellow- or green-coloured species of *Stropharia* by its white colouring. The cap is 1.5–4 cm wide, sometimes even wider, obtusely conically campanulate when young, soon flatly expanded, with a prominent central umbo, markedly viscid when moist, in dry conditions smooth and glabrous, white, sometimes yellowish only at the apex, thin-fleshed. At maturity a lilac-violet tinge from the gills shows through. The long stipe is 3–5 mm thick, often crooked, firm and elastic, white or slightly tinged yellowish, granular-pruinose, bearing a membranous, ungrooved superior ring. The gills are crowded, rather narrow, emarginate, at first white, then lilac, violet grey-brown, later blackish grey, with white edges. The spore print is purplish dark brown. The gill edge consists of numerous shortly lageniform, sinuous cheilocystidia. The flesh is almost odourless and tasteless. *Stropharia albonitens* grows in moist, grassy places in woods, e. g. in alder growths, but also outside woods.

S. melasperma has a similarly coloured cap, slimy when young but soon drying up, frequently cracking into patches. The ring is at least partly grooved. It occurs in similar grassy places, in meadows and pastures. Both species are inedible.

Cheilocystidium and spores of *Stropharia albonitens*:
8–9 × 4–5 µm, ellipsoid, smooth, violet-brown

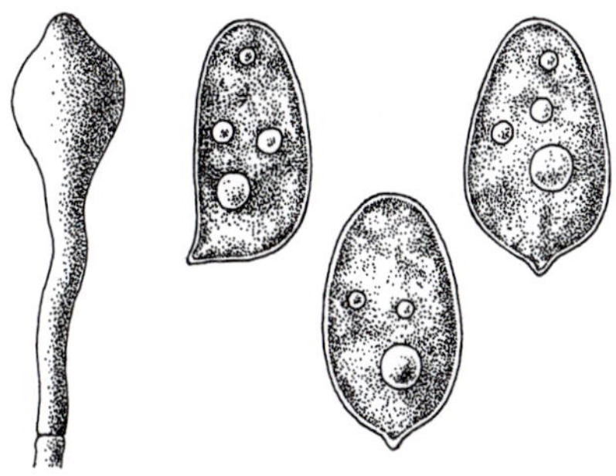

Brick Red Hypholoma, Bricktop, Bricktop Mushroom

Hypholoma sublateritium (Fr.) Quél.

The Brick Red Hypholoma usually grows in larger or smaller clumps, but solitary fruit bodies may occasionally be found – these, as a rule, are very robust. From the beginning of summer until the first frosts it can be seen growing out of rotten stumps mainly of deciduous trees. Its taste is bitter, but is not so offensive as in the Sulphur Tuft. The flesh in the stipe apex is whitish, while in the Sulphur Tuft it is sulphur-yellow in the whole stipe. The cap of the Brick Red Hypholoma is yellowish red in the centre, sometimes almost brick-red, lighter coloured at the margin where it changes to orange or yellow. It is 3–10 cm wide and, when young, is covered with scaly or fibrous cobwebby remnants of a whitish or yellowish veil connecting the cap margin with the stipe in very young fruit bodies. The remnants of the veil are subsequently washed away by rain or disappear in the course of the fruit bodies' development; thus the cap surface of mature fungi is glabrous. The 7–12 mm thick stipe is usually firm-fleshed, later hollow, yellowish, rusty brown at the base, fibrous scaly, with veil remnants in the form of whitish or yellowish filaments finely powdered with loosened blackish grey spores. The gills are crowded, adnate with a tooth, at first yellowish, then yellowish brown, mature gills are olive- to blackish brown. The spore print is olive dark brown.

The Brick Red Hypholoma is not recommended for table use, not only because of its bitter taste but also because of possible confusion with the Sulphur Tuft.

Cystidia and spores of *Hypholoma sublateritium*: 6–8 × 3–4 μm, ellipsoid, with a germ pore, violet-grey

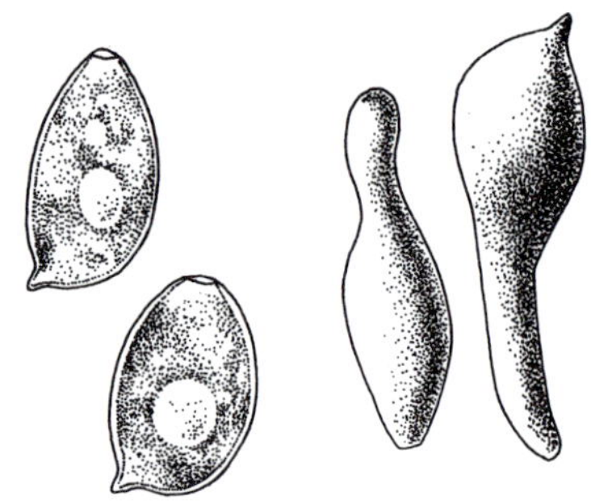

Hypholoma sublateritium

Hypholoma fasciculare

Sulphur Tuft

Hypholoma fasciculare (Huds. ex Fr.) Kumm.

This is one of the commonest lignicolous gill fungi, growing almost throughout the year from lowlands up to the mountains, both in and out of the forest. It can be found on the stumps and dead roots of most various trees and shrubs, as well as on the remains of decaying wood in the ground. The cap is up to 6 cm wide, glabrous and smooth except for the remnants of a cobwebby veil near the margin; its colour is orange red-brown to orange-yellow in the centre, changing to an almost sulphur-yellow towards the margin. The gills are crowded, narrow, attached by a tooth, at first sulphur-yellow, then green, deep olive-grey, ultimately chocolate-brown to almost black. The stipe is usually longer than the diameter of the cap, 3–5 mm thick, firm-fleshed, smooth, later hollow, with fugacious remnants of a yellow-coloured veil. The flesh of the whole fruit body is a vivid sulphur-yellow, brownish only at the stipe base, intensely bitter. The spore print is violet black-brown.

The Sulphur Tuft is a poisonous fungus which careless or inexperienced mushroom pickers may confuse with the edible *Kuehneromyces mutabilis,* or even with the Honey Fungus (*Armilaria mellea*). It can easily be distinguished from both these species by the sulphur- or greenish yellow, repulsively bitter flesh. If eaten, symptoms may resemble those caused by the Death Cap, even though the European variety of the Sulphur Tuft is less poisonous than, for instance, the Japanese variety.

Spores: 6–8 × 4–5 μm, ellipsoid, with a germ pore, smooth, dirty yellow-brown

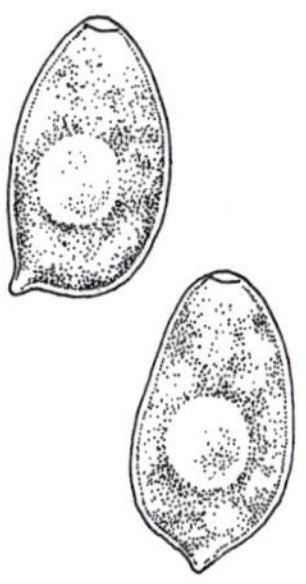

Chrysocystidia

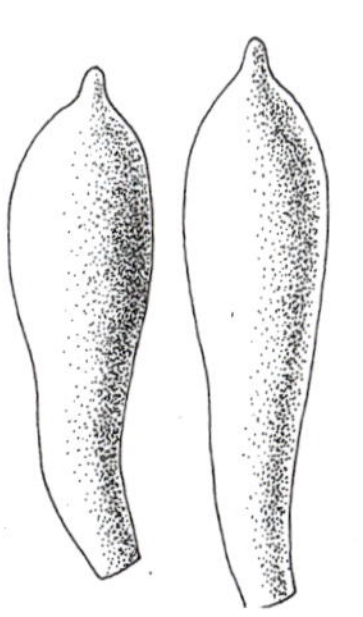

Hypholoma capnoides
(Fr. ex Fr.) Kumm.

Hypholoma capnoides belongs to common *Hypholoma* species, though it is far less common than the Sulphur Tuft and the Brick Red Hypholoma. It forms tufts on stumps and dead roots of some conifers, mainly spruces and pines, mostly in upland forests. Since the fruit bodies develop in the cooler seasons of the year, they may regularly be found both in late autumn and in early spring. *H. capnoides* resembles the Sulphur Tuft in general appearance, size and colouring, but is distinguished by having a differently coloured flesh – it is white or whitish in the stipe as well as in the cap, rusty yellowish only in the stipe base, but never sulphur-yellow. Its taste is not bitter but mild. The flesh is almost odourless or smells slightly of iodoform. In youth the gills are poppyseed grey-blue and later lilac. The stipe is often sinuous, whitish above, otherwise yellowish, rusty-hued in its lower part, finely silky fibrous with white filamentous remnants of the veil. The cap is up to 5 cm wide, yellowish orange-ochre, darker at the apex, later weathering to paler, with temporary fibres left by the veil in the margin. The spore print is brownish purple-violet. Chrysocystidia are present in the hymenium, which is a common feature of all species of *Hypholoma.*

H. capnoides is edible, some mushroom pickers consider it a good mushroom with a pleasant flavour, especially when pickled in vinegar. Of course, care must be taken not to confuse it with the Sulphur Tuft or the Brick Red Hypholoma.

Spores: 7–9 × 4–5 μm, ellipsoid, violet-brown, with a germ pore

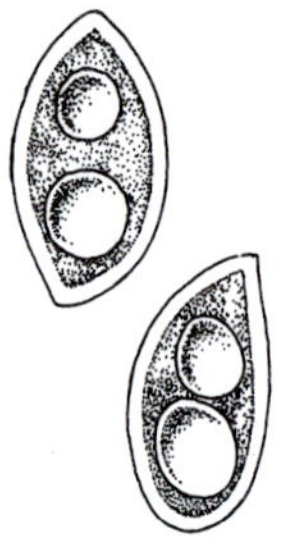

Chrysocystidia

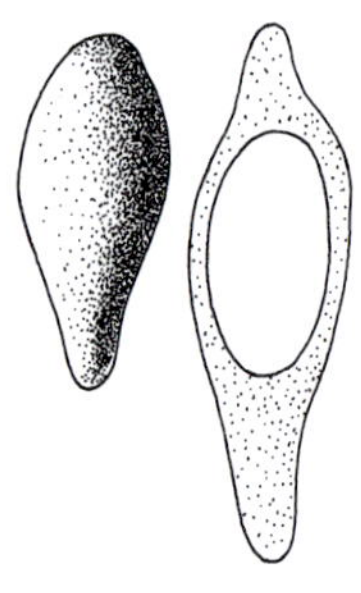

Hypholoma capnoides

Section through the fruit body of *Hypholoma fasciculare*

Psilocybe semilanceata
(Fr. ex Weinm.) Kumm.

The genus *Psilocybe,* as well as the related genera *Panaeolus* and *Stropharia,* have become better known – and especially more popular – following the discovery of hallucinogenic substances obtained from numerous Mexican species of *Psilocybe.* Further analyses have shown that some European species of the genus *Psilocybe* also contain substances with hallucinogenic effects, even though in substantially smaller quantities so that the symptoms following their ingestion are much milder.

Psilocybe semilanceata is a very small fungus which easily escapes attention. Its cap is 1–2 cm high, always higher than it is wide, markedly and persistently lanceolate-pointed or narrowly conical, often with an abruptly projecting point, thin-fleshed, hygrophanous, slimy or sticky, dark olive grey-brown or yellow-brown when moist, in dry conditions leathery yellow, smooth, glabrous, with greenish spots. The stipe is very long, only 2–3 mm thick, firm and tough, tortuous, pallid or brownish, with a silky sheen, often blue-green at the base, attached to the substrate by a bluish green mycelium. The gills are broadly adnate, olive-grey or brownish with a lilac tinge, then red-brown to black-brown, with white ciliate edges. The gill edges harbour numerous cheilocystidia. The flesh has no specific odour nor taste. The spore print is dark brown.

P. semilanceata grows in grass tufts in pasturelands and forest tracks from August to October. It is not particularly abundant and appears more commonly in upland regions. It is inedible because of the hallucinogenic substances it contains.

Spores: 12–16 × 6–8 μm, ellipsoid, with a germ pore, smooth, brown

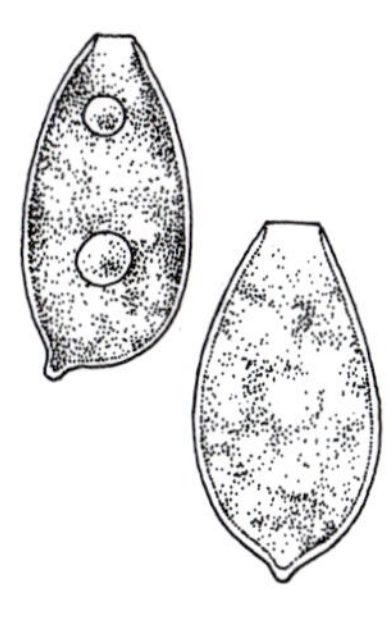

Section through the fruit body

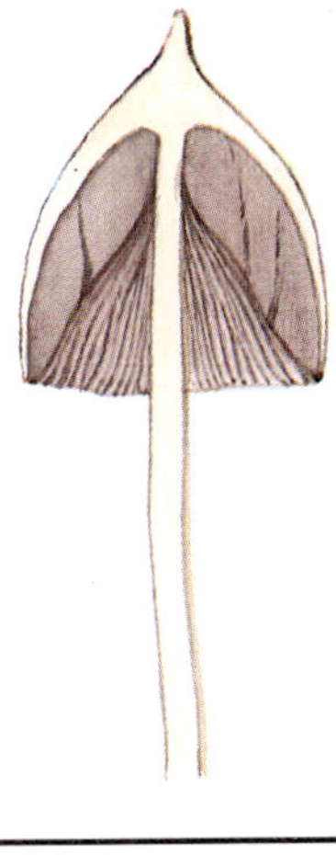

Cheilocystidia

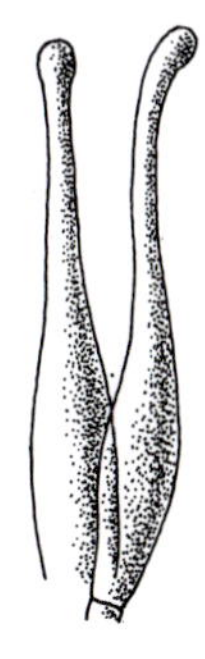

Pholiota destruens

(Brond.) Gill.

Huge clumps of *Pholiota destruens* often appear on felled poplar trunks that remain lying on the ground for a long time. This is a very sturdy, firm-fleshed fungus; one of the largest in its genus. Its 5–20 cm wide, dirty buff to pale brownish caps, convex in youth, later flat, are scattered with white scales. They are sticky when moist. The cap margin of young fruit bodies is joined to the stipe by a whitish veil, later fringed with its appendiculate fragments of irregular shape. The veil also leaves a fugacious ring on the stipe. The stipe is stout, pallid, scaly, 5–15 cm long and 1–3 cm thick, often inflated and rooting at the base. The brownish gills have a sinuate, irregularly denticulate edge.

P. destruens is inedible. Its bitter, rather tough flesh emits an unpleasant fungussy smell. Clumps of this *Pholiota* appear from August to November not only on dead trunks and stumps, but fairly often also directly on live trees, mainly on poplars and willows.

In the contemporary mycological system, the genus *Pholiota* is connected with the genus *Flammula,* which was once treated as independent. The only feature substantiating its separation from the genus *Pholiota* was its weakly developed, fugacious ring. Furthermore, the fruit bodies of most *Flammula* species are less fleshy and form smaller tufts than members of the genus *Pholiota.*

Spores: 7.5–9 × 5–5.5 μm, ellipsoid, rusty brown

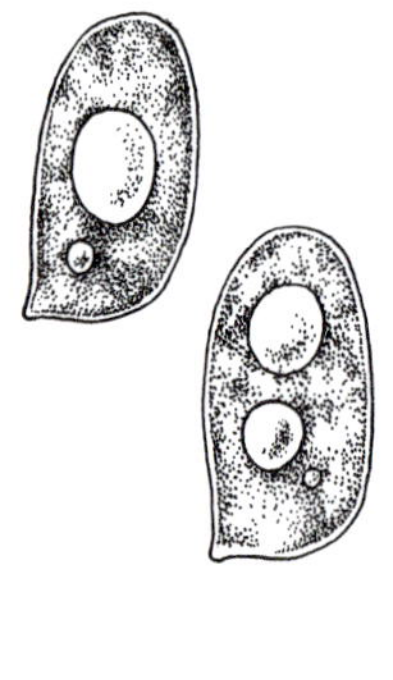

Shaggy Pholiota

Pholiota squarrosa (Pers. ex Fr.) Kumm.

The Shaggy Pholiota is readily recognized by the conspicuous scales covering both cap and stipe. It forms dense tufts on dead wood, mainly on stumps and fallen trunks of both deciduous and coniferous trees. It is frequently parasitic, damaging live tree trunks or roots into which it penetrates through frost-cracks or wounds caused by mechanical injury, e. g. by cutting or scratching. It grows mostly in autumn. Some mushroom pickers mistake it for the Honey Fungus whose white spore print represents a substantial difference between the two species.

The cap of the Shaggy Pholiota grows to a size of 12–15 cm in diameter and is coloured in various shades of yellow. The scales covering its surface are rusty brown, with upturned or even recurved tips, usually arranged in dense circles. The tough stipe also has rusty brown scales on a pale yellowish background. In young specimens it is connected to the cap margin by a thick coriaceous veil, persisting on the stipe in the form of a woolly tomentose ring. The gills are adnate to shortly decurrent, fairly crowded, relatively narrow, at first pale olive-yellowish, then brownish yellow, ultimately rusty brown. The flesh is yellowish, with a rather pleasant spicy smell and a mild or even harshly astringent to bitterish taste. The spore print is rusty brown. The Shaggy Pholiota is particularly suitable for pickling in vinegar, but most mushroom pickers refuse to collect it because of its tough flesh.

Spores: 6–8 × 3.5–4 μm, ellipsoid, smooth, yellow-brown

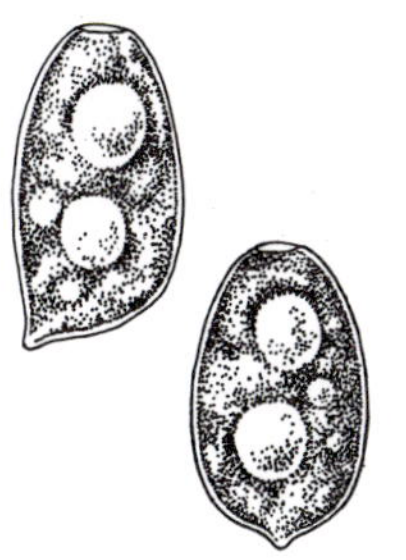

Section through the fruit body

Pholiota carbonaria

(Fr.) Sing.

On burned ground both within and outside the forest we may come across a great number of interesting anthracophilous fungi whose occurrence is strictly confined to such an environment. One of the most common is *Pholiota carbonaria* which often covers the entire burned-over area with dozens of its fruit bodies.

The 1.5–6 cm wide cap is at first semiglobular, then flat, with a narrowly incurved margin, thin-fleshed. The cuticle is sticky when moist, shiny when dry, smooth and glabrous, brown-yellow to cloudy reddish orange or rusty yellow. It is often contaminated with incrusting soil and charcoal particles. The stipe is usually equal to the cap diameter in length, relatively thin (2–5 mm), pale yellow, whitish below the apex, finely scaly all along its length, covered in younger fruit bodies with fugacious white filaments of the cortina. The gills are moderately crowded, emarginate with tooth, pale or ochre-yellow when young, olive-brown in age, white ciliate at the edge. Numerous cylindrical, colourless cheilocystidia occur on the gill edges. The flesh is pale yellow, with a bitter taste and a faint acidulous smell. The spore print is rusty brown.

P. carbonaria is inedible. The fruit bodies grow singly or in sparse clusters, either upon burned wood or directly upon burned-over soil. *P. carbonaria* used to be classed into the genus *Flammula,* which no longer exists; the greater part of its species has been reclassified within the genus *Pholiota.*

Spores: 6–7 × 3–4 μm, ellipsoid, smooth, pale yellow

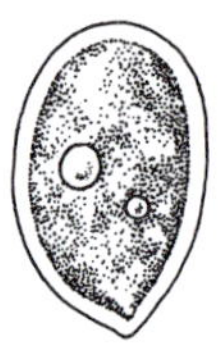

Cheilocystidia

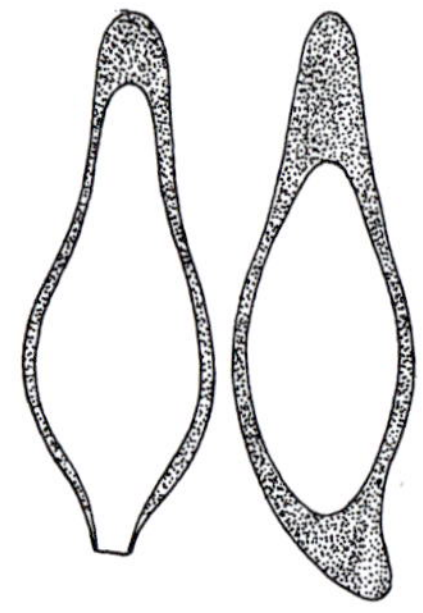

Pholiota carbonaria

Pholiota spumosa grows on the ground in coniferous forests, mainly in pine stands. It never occurs in burned-over areas.

Gymnopilus spectabilis
(Fr.) Sing.

The genus *Gymnopilus* includes several larger-sized and relatively fleshy ochre, golden-yellow to orange-yellow fungi. They all have a somewhat slimy cap when moist, a cuticle turning black in lyes, a rusty brown spore print, verrucose spores, and cystidia turning green when touched with cotton blue. They are, for the most part, lignicolous fungi.

Gymnopilus spectabilis is one of the sturdiest among them: its cap is as much as 10 cm wide, exceptionally even larger. It is almost velvety felted, neither shiny nor viscid, semiglobularly convex, later expanded, with no umbo or only lightly and obtusely umbonate, later cracking into patches, with a slight purple flush here and there. The stipe is pale yellow, cylindrical, often clavately thickened towards the base, terminating in a rootlike extension, up to 20 cm long, 1–3 cm thick, solid, dark fibrous and flocculose, red-brown at the base. A membranous, yellowish and persistent ring is located in its apical part, and the stipe above the ring is whitish. The gills are pale yellow-brown, later almost golden-yellow brownish, crowded, rather narrow, roundly adnate or emarginate and slightly decurrent. The flesh is yellow, very bitter, and with an intense fungussy, almost radish-like odour.

G. spectabilis is a striking, beautifully coloured fungus growing in autumn usually in tufts from stumps, roots or bases of deciduous trees, especially oaks. Sometimes it seems to grow directly from the ground, yet in fact it is attached to decaying submerged wood. Large clumps consist of 30 or more fruit bodies coalescing at the base into a fleshy structure. It is more common in warmer regions, more often outside the wood, along tracks, in parks, etc. It is inedible.

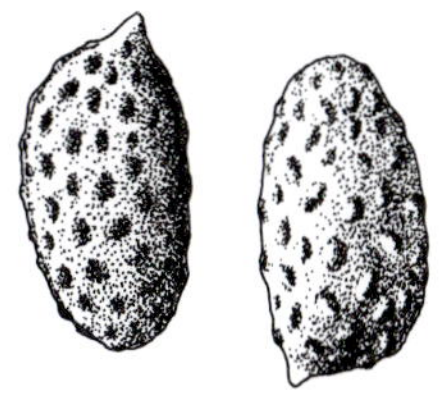

Spores: 7.5–10 × 5–7 μm, ellipsoid almond-shaped, densely verrucose, yellow-rusty

This species may sometimes be confused with older or rain-washed fruit bodies of *Pholiota squarrosa*

Pholiota squarrosa

Gymnopilus spectabilis

Gymnopilus sapineus
(Fr.) R. Maire

In summer and in autumn, clumps (rarely individual specimens) of conspicuous, mostly rusty brown gill-fungi fruit bodies may be found growing on putrescent stumps or dead trunks of conifers. These fungi usually belong to the genus *Gymnopilus* which was also separated from the no more valid genus *Flammula*. Fungi of the genus *Gymnopilus* have rusty, often bright yellow or orange brown colours turning black when exposed to alkalic solutions. Their stipe usually bears a ring.

Gymnopilus sapineus is substantially smaller than the robust *G. spectabilis*. The cap is no more than 3–5 cm wide, at first hemispherically convex, soon flatly expanded, with a dry cuticle, fibrous to finely brownish scaly on a golden-yellow background. The stipe is 4–7 cm long, 5–10 mm thick, cylindrical, often terminating in a rooting and whitish matted-tomentose base embedded in rotten wood. The stipe surface is silky shiny fibrous, pale yellow or only yellow-tinged. The gills are fairly crowded, adnate with tooth, at first pale yellow, then golden-yellow to vivid yellow, powdered with a rusty brown spore mass, slowly staining rusty where handled. The yellowish flesh has a bitter taste.

Several species closely related to *G. sapineus* have been described. Distinguishing between them is difficult, in fact it is possible only after detailed microscopic examination. None of these species is edible.

Spores: 7–10 × 4–5 μm, ellipsoid, almond-shaped, minutely verrucose, yellow-brown

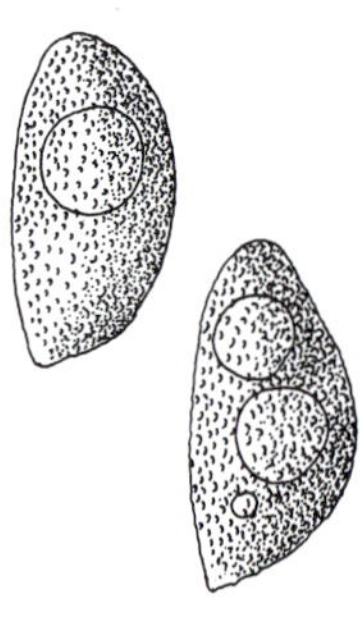

Cystidia

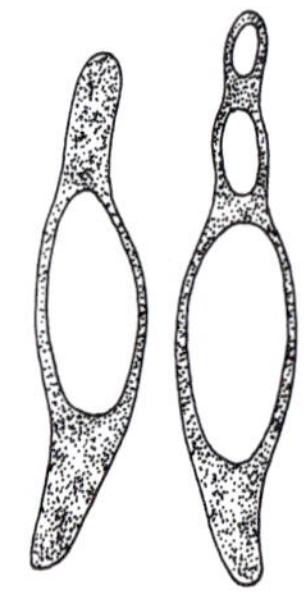

Kuehneromyces mutabilis

(Schaeff. ex Fr.) Sing. et Smith

Kuehneromyces mutabilis is one of the most popular edible lignicolous fungi. Its clumps, sometimes consisting of dozens of fruit bodies, may be found growing from spring till autumn – but mostly during cooler periods – on stumps, fallen timber, or at the base or even in the hollows of trunks of living deciduous trees, mostly limes and birches. Only caps of young fruit bodies are collected,the flesh of stipes being too tough. A distinguishing feature of *K. mutabilis* is the strongly hygrophanous cap. When moist it is rusty cinnamon-brown with gills showing through as darker striae, while in dry weather it is substantially lighter-coloured, pale honey-yellowish. After wet weather, it is the marginal zone that remains dark the longest. The cap grows to 7 cm in width. Its cuticle is glabrous and smooth, as if greasy. The gills are adnate or shortly decurrent, crowded, pale brownish to cinnamon-brown. The membranous veil covering them in youth is whitish. The stipe is up to 10 cm long, 5–8 cm thick, hollow but tough, brown, almost black-brown at the base, with a fugacious, scaly, brown ring near the apex; below it the stipe surface is dark brown scaly. The flesh in the cap is whitish, soft to watery fleshy, rusty brown in the stipe; it has a pleasant spicy smell similar to that of fresh moist wood, its taste is mild. The spore print is rusty brown. Inexperienced mushroom pickers may confuse *K. mutabilis* with some fungi of the genus *Hypholoma* – these, however, are more brightly yellow and usually have a bitter flesh and blackish spore print.

Spores: 6–7 × 4–4.5 µm, ellipsoid, almond-shaped, smooth, rusty brown, with a large germ pore

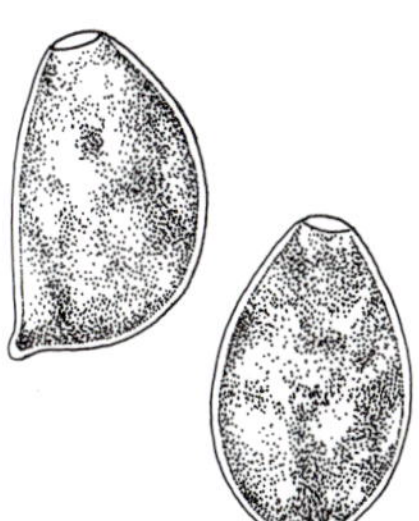

Tubaria conspersa

(Pers. ex Fr.) Fayod

Small, inconspicuous and mostly uniformly cinnamon-brown fungi, attracting attention by their occurrence in clusters, make their appearance in summer and in autumn on bare, moist ground shaded by trees or shrubs, sometimes also on decaying plant remains. They usually belong to some species of the genus *Tubaria*. Only a closer acquaintance with their microcharacteristics makes their exact identification possible.

Tubaria conspersa belongs to the most abundant members of this group. The deep cinnamon-brown ground colour of the cap cuticle is covered in a fine greyish white felt, splitting into a fibrous-scaly pattern later on; in very young fruit bodies the cap margin is connected with the stipe by a cobwebby veil. The cap is only 8–25 mm wide, almost semiglobular in youth, then slightly and roundly convex, somewhat depressed in the centre, with a sparsely grooved margin, thin-fleshed throughout. The stipe is 2–3.5 cm long, 1.5–3 mm thick, paler than the cap, enveloped at the base by a white felted mycelium. The gills are broadly adnate and shortly decurrent, broad, distant, deep cinnamon-brown. The flesh is odourless and has a mild taste. The spore print is brown. The cheilocystidia are cylindrical to clavate, often irregularly sinuous. *T. conspersa* is inedible.

During a mild winter and in early spring, very similar *Tubaria* species – *T. pellucida* and *T. furfuracea* – may often be found in grassy patches in fields and along roadsides, outside the wood as a rule. Yet these species cannot be safely distinguished from each other without a microscope.

Spores: 6.5–9 × 4.5–5.5 μm,
asymmetrically ovoid-ellipsoid,
pale yellowish, smooth, markedly thin-walled

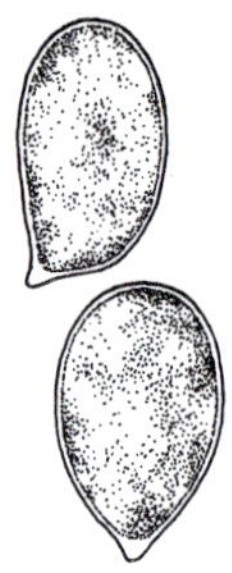

Cheilocystidia

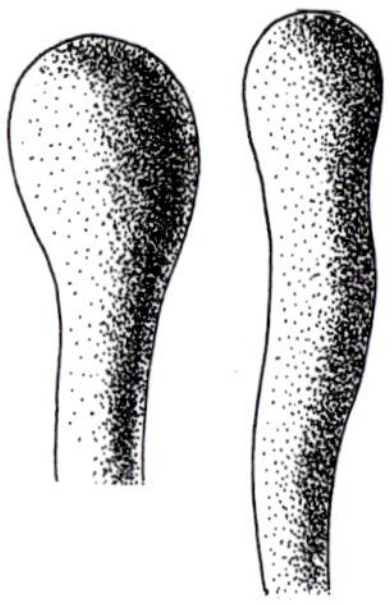

Crepidotus variabilis

(Pers. ex Fr.) Kumm.

In observing small twigs lying about in damp and shady places in deciduous and mixed forests after summer rainfalls, we may discover small, white, only 0.5–3 cm wide, stipeless caps attached directly to the substrate, usually occurring in large groups. They are rounded or kidney-shaped, and their lobes encircle the point of attachment. Their surface is snow-white and finely felted to woolly pubescent. The gills situated on the underside of the caps are whitish at first, but the maturing spores soon colour them grey-pink, more pronouncedly brown when older. The gills are subdistant, thin, meeting at a single, usually eccentric, point. The spore print is brown.

Crepidotus variabilis is the most frequently occurring representative of its genus. Under favourable conditions it is capable of covering an area of several square metres with its caps, and passes over from twigs to nearby fallen leaves, dead grasses and herb stems. Other species of *Crepidotus,* mostly similar in shape and size, occur on dead wood and tree trunks, but also on herbs, grasses and various moss species. Most of them belong to rare fungi whose correct identification necessarily requires microscopic study. Being so small, they are of no great importance to the practical mushroom gatherer.

Very similar to *C. variabilis* in appearance is *Pleurotellus chioneus.* This, however, is distinguished by its white, only slightly yellowish gills and by smooth, somewhat larger spores.

Cheilocystidia

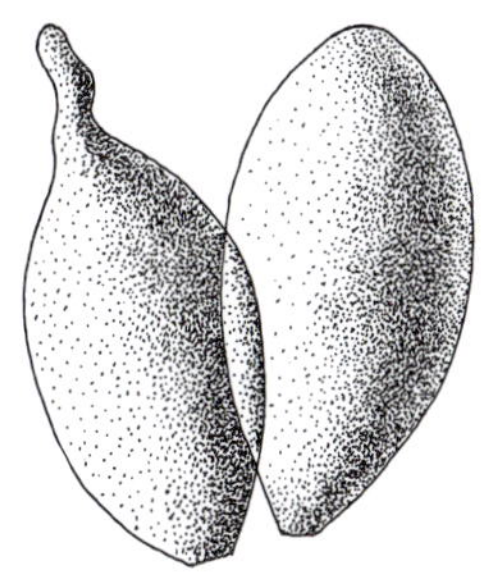

Spore: 5.5–7 × 2.8–3.5 µm, cylindrical-ellipsoid, very finely spiny-warty, pale brownish

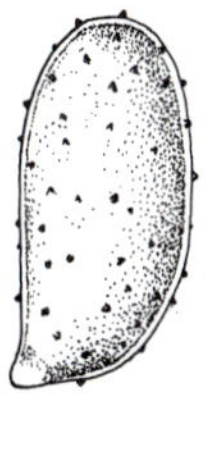

Inocybe patouillardii Bres.

With regard to the number of species included, the genus *Inocybe* is one of the richest genera of gill fungi. Well over a hundred species grow in Europe. They are of considerable practical importance; many of the species are poisonous fungi – some of them are highly toxic. This also applies to *Inocybe patouillardii* which is all the more dangerous as its large, fleshy fruit bodies make a pleasant sight and attract mushroom pickers at a time when the edible St. George's Mushroom (*Calocybe gambosa*) appears in similar localities. Consequently cases of poisoning are reported every year.

The fruit bodies of *I. patouillardii* have caps up to 10 cm wide, conically bell-shaped at first, later flatly expanded, umbonate in the centre, with a usually wavy-lobed margin. The silky fibrous cap cuticle is at first white or whitish, but fairly soon – especially when handled – develops brick-red stains. This rubescence is very characteristic of *I. patouillardii:* it can be seen not only on the cap but also on the stipe and gills. Also the originally white flesh, when cut, turns red in the stipe and pink in the cap. Older fruit bodies are entirely brown-red to brown. The stipe is cylindrical, up to 12 cm long, 1–1.5 cm thick, swollen at the base. The gills are at first white, then olive-brownish. The spore print is brown. Cylindrical to claviform, glabrous cheilocystidia are situated at the gill edges. The flesh has a faint fruity smell and a mild taste.

I. patouillardii grows from May onward, but especially in June and July under deciduous trees, often in parks and hedgerows, on lime-rich soils. It is deadly poisonous, containing five hundred times more muscarine than the Fly Agaric.

☠ ☠ *Inocybe patouillardii*

Spores of *Inocybe patouillardii*:
9–14 × 5–8 μm, ovoid bean-shaped, light brown

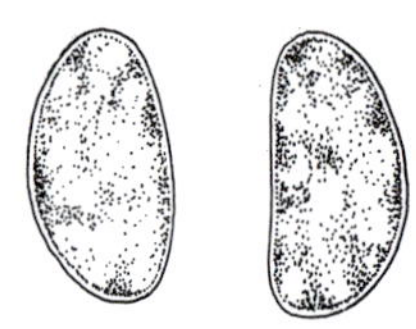

Cheilocystidia

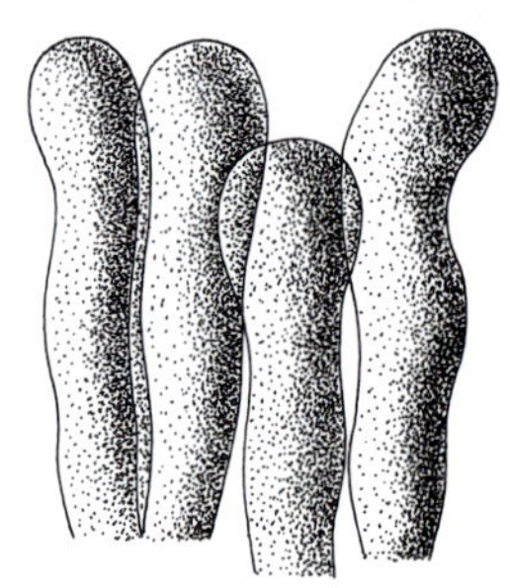

Inocybe godeyi grows in summer,
mainly on calcareous soils in deciduous forests.
Its cuticle and flesh also turn red on injury and in aging.

Inocybe godeyi ☠

Inocybe fastigiata

(Schaeff. ex Fr.) Quél.

This is one of the most abundant species of *Inocybe.* It is extremely variable in colour. One of its distinguishing features is an acutely conical cap, 2–8 cm wide, with a conical umbo persisting even later, after the cap has become flatly expanded. The cuticle is markedly radially cracked, ochre-yellow, yellow-brown to dark brown. The gills are free, ventricose, light olive-yellowish, gradually turning brown, whitish in the edges. The cylindrical, often considerably elongate, 3–8 mm thick stipe is whitish or pale yellow, pruinose at the apex. The flesh is white, unchanging, with a spermatic smell and an unpleasant taste. The spore print is ochre-brown. Colourless vesicular cheilocystidia develop on the gill edges (there are no lageniform cystidia in this species).

Inocybe fastigiata grows in both deciduous and coniferous forests, especially on bare ground by tracks or on ditch banks, from summer until autumn. It is poisonous, the fruit bodies contain a large amount of muscarine. Its variety, designated as var. *umbrinella,* has a dark greyish brown to umber-brown coloured cap. It is less common but equally poisonous as the type.

Spores: 10–18 × 5–7.5 µm, ellipsoid, smooth, pale ochre-brown

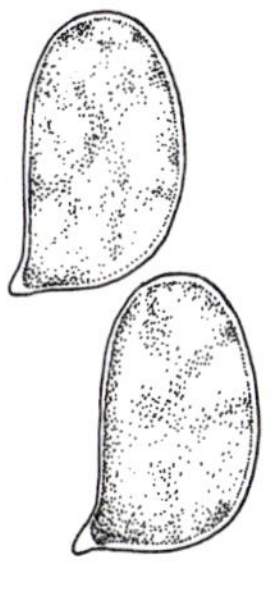

Cheilocystidia

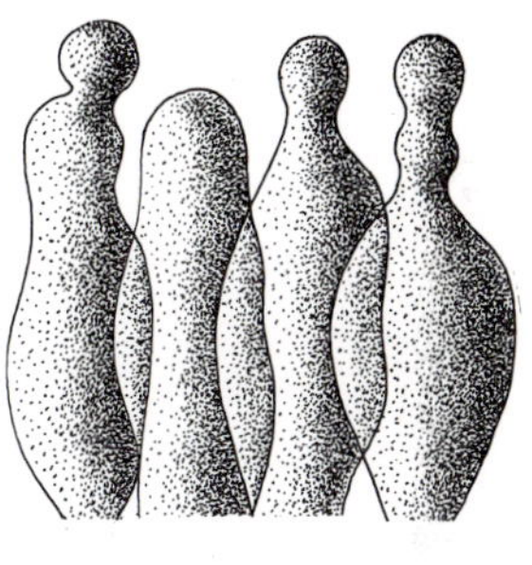

Inocybe argillacea
(Pers. ex Pers.) Sing.

Inocybe argillacea is a very common sight in summer and in autumn in forests of all types, especially on damp, bare ground, but also in the needle carpet where whole swarms of this fungus frequently make their appearance. The 2–4 cm wide cap is at first ovoid and connected to the stipe by a white cobwebby veil, then conical, at maturity expanded, slightly centrally umbonate. The cuticle is silky fibrous, in rainy weather somewhat viscid, white or whitish, weathering to yellow at the apex only with age. The gills are free, crowded, white, turning brown at maturity, white ciliate at the edge. The gill edges typically bear lageniform, thick-walled cystidia with crystals in the upper portion, which is also characteristic of a number of other *Inocybe* species. The stipe is up to 6 cm long, 2–7 mm thick, usually bulb-like, expanded at the base, white, finely fibrous all along its length, pruinose under the lens. The flesh is white, with an unpleasant smell and taste. The spore print is greyish brown.

A very closely related species is *I. geophylla,* previously considered as a mere colour variation (var. *violacea*) of *I. argillacea.* It greatly resembles *I. argillacea* both in appearance and in size, except for its cap which is lilac to dark violet. The cap weathers to paler shades with age and becomes yellow at the apex only. The stipe is pale violet, the flesh is violet-white. *I. geophylla* is equally abundant as *I. argillacea* and is distributed mainly in deciduous forests. Both the above species contain muscarine and are deadly poisonous. However, cases of poisoning have rarely been reported, because hardly anybody would think of collecting these small, disagreeably smelling fungi for table purposes.

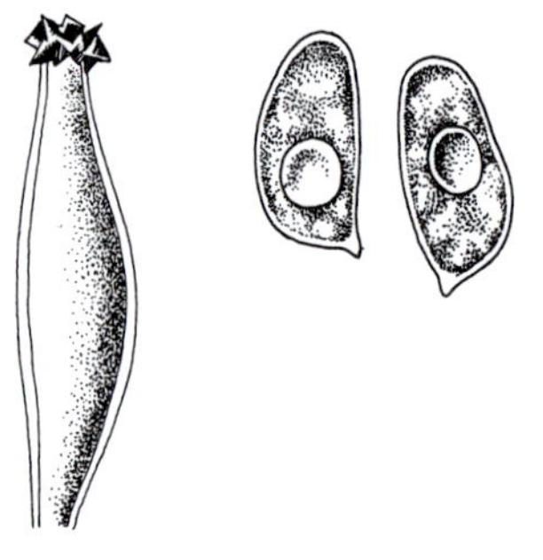

Cystidium and spores of *Inocybe argillacea*: 8–12 × 5–7 μm, ellipsoid, smooth, pale brown-yellow

Inocybe argillacea

Inocybe geophylla

Inocybe lacera
(Fr.) Kumm.

This is the earliest species of *Inocybe* appearing as early as May on bare forest ground, along roadsides, in woodland glades and in clearings, in rather dry, sun-exposed places, mostly in coniferous forests on acid substrates. It is most abundantly found in heather moors or in sandy pine woods where it can be quite common until autumn. The uniform, rather dark brown colour of its cap and stipe serves as a satisfactory diagnostic feature. The cap is 2–5 cm wide, with a soft fibrous-felted surface, scaly around the apex. The stipe is rather long and slender, 2–4 mm thick, relatively firm, fibrous all over its earthy grey-brown surface. The gills are crowded, almost free, ventricose, whitish at first, then pale earthy, finally brown, with white ciliate edges. Lageniform cystidia capped with colourless, sharp-edged crystals develop in great numbers on the edge and face of gills. The flesh is whitish, thin in the cap, brownish in the stipe, with a rather unpleasant odour. The spore print is pale brown.

Inocybe lacera is deadly poisonous; like the greater part of this genus it contains muscarine. Though greatly variable, it can always be safely recognized by characteristic spores. Only complete ignorance and carelessness may lead to its confusion with the Fairy Ring Fungus (*Marasmius oreades*).

Cystidium and spores of *Inocybe lacera*:
10–18 × 4.5–7 μm, conspicuously large, longish cylindrical, smooth, light brownish

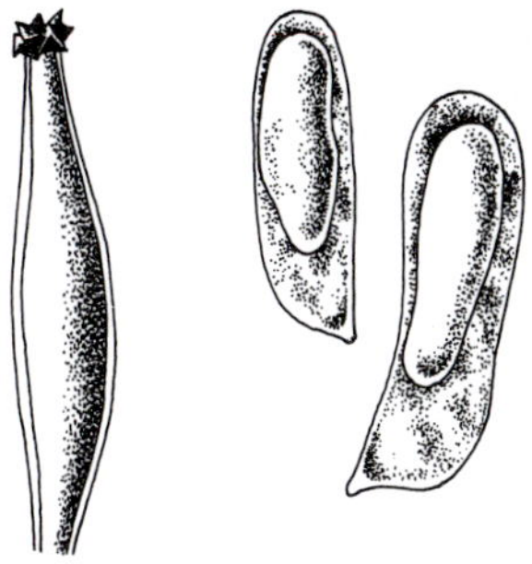

Inocybe dulcamara grows both under deciduous trees and under conifers. It is more robust and prevalently yellow-coloured

Inocybe lacera

Hebeloma radicosum
(Bull. ex Fr.) Ricken

Though fungi of the genus *Hebeloma* can easily be recognized at first glance, their assignment to individual species implies a perplexing mental challenge even for an expert. A great many species have been described, but only a few of them possess truly characteristic features or properties facilitating their immediate identification. *Hebeloma radicosum* is one such exception. It is a large fungus having a 12 cm wide, slightly and broadly convex, firm-fleshed cap. The cap cuticle is sticky when moist, smooth when dry, glabrous, pale earth-coloured, with fine fibrous remnants of the white veil at the margin. The gills are adnate, emarginate with tooth, pallid at first, then earth-brown, almost red-brown as the spores mature. Its most important diagnostic feature is a stout, firm-fleshed to tough stipe, with a swollen base rapidly tapering into a long root-like extension in the soil. At the stem apex there is a flaring superior ring below which the whitish surface is sparsely strewn with scales. The flesh is whitish, rusty brown in the stipe, and pleasantly smelling of bitter almonds. The spore print is a pale earth-brown.

Usually, *H. radicosum* grows solitarily out of rotten sıumps or tree roots in deciduous forests. In taking the fruit body out of the substrate, the long root-like part of the stipe is usually torn off. *H. radicosum* is inedible. It must not be mistaken for *Hypholoma radicosum* which also has a rooting stipe but is more slender and strongly smells of iodoform.

Spores of *Hebeloma radicosum*:
8–10 × 5–6 μm, almond-shaped,
minutely warty, ochre-yellow

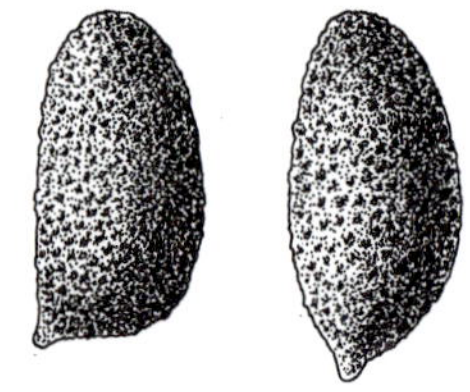

Hypholoma radicosum

Hebeloma radicosum

Distribution of
Hebeloma radicosum in Europe

Jew's Ear, Judas' Ear

Hirneola auricula-judae (Bull. ex St. Amans) Berk.

The gelatinous consistency of fungi of the Auriculariales group makes them resemble the Jelly Fungi (Tremellales), the only substantial difference between them being the shape of basidia. The basidia in this case are long and cylindrical, transversely septate, the spores usually arise in fours on sterigmata growing out on one side of single cells. This order is only poorly represented in the temperate zone, while in the subtropics and tropics it has developed numerous species. In Europe there are only two genera with relatively large fruit bodies: *Hirneola* and *Auricularia.*

The first of these is generally widespread mainly on the Common Elder and False Acacia but also occurs on other deciduous trees. In youth the Jew's Ear fruit bodies are cup-shaped, later roundly lamellate, irregularly wavy and lobed, 3–12 cm wide. Their outer surface is pubescent, velvety, olive-grey, while their underside, covered by the hymenium, is very venously wrinkled and brown. The entire fruit body is gelatinously pliant, darker in dry weather, black-brown or grey-brown, hard and strongly convolute. The spore print is white.

The Jew's Ear may be collected all the year round on dead trunks and branches, sometimes even in frost cracks on live trees. It is usually added to mushroom mixtures. In China and Japan, some related species belong to the popular and currently used edible mushrooms. Our European species, however, has no particularly appetizing flavour.

Spores: 17–23 × 5–8 μm, cylindrically curved, colourless

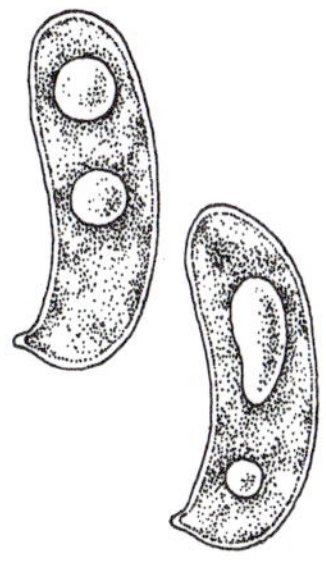

Transversely septate basidia with sterigmata

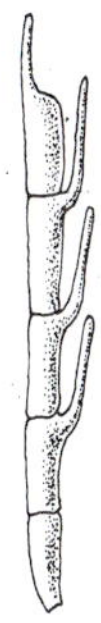

Yellow Brain Fungus, Witches' Butter
Tremella mesenterica Retz. ex Hook.

The jelly fungi have fruit bodies of various forms, ranging from semiglobular protuberances or resupinate coatings up to discoid, cup-shaped, cerebrally convolute or lamellarly lobed structures. Newly grown fruit bodies usually have an elastic, gelatinously soft consistency. They are often bright coloured, usually yellow, and change greatly when drying; shrivelling up into a shapeless, unsightly membrane or crust firmly attached to the substrate. When moistened they rapidly absorb water and swell up to almost their original shape and size. Microscopically they are characterized by globose or oval basidia, longitudinally divided by two planes perpendicular to each other into four (or two) parts giving rise to long sterigmata with basidiospores. The basidia form the hymenium which in the *Tremella* covers the entire surface of the fruit body.

The Yellow Brain Fungus is 2–4 cm wide, rounded, cerebrally convolute, golden-yellow or pale orange. It grows on dead branches of deciduous trees, mostly on hornbeams, in the cooler and damper seasons of the year.

Another species in this group is *Tremella foliacea,* occurring mainly on the wood of oaks and beeches. It is as much as 15 cm wide, pale brown, sometimes violaceous, consisting of large, crinkled lobes.

Exidia plana has 3–10 cm wide, almost black fruit bodies with brain-like folds, sparsely scattered with minute warts; the hymenium is developed in the upper part only. In dry weather it resembles a thin, hyaline, breakable varnish. It is common on oaks and beeches. It is inedible.

Basidium and spores of *Tremella mesenterica*:
7–12 × 6–10 µm, ovoid-globose, colourless

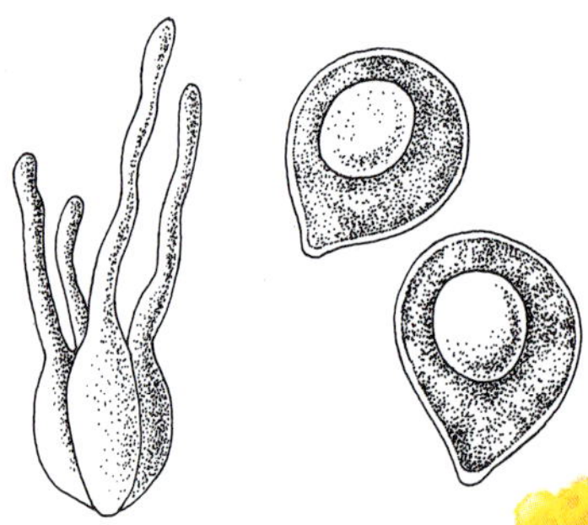

Tremella foliacea

a b

Tremella mesenterica

Exidia plana when dry (a) and when moistened again (b)

Yellow Chanterelle, Pixie Stool
Cantharellus cibarius Fr. ex Fr.

The Yellow Chanterelle belongs to popular edible mushrooms. It is so typical and generally known that its confusion with any other species would be difficult. The whole fruit body is coloured yolk yellow, its cap is 1–7 cm wide (occasionally larger), fleshy, sometimes fading to paler, glabrous, matt, slightly convex at first, later plane to funnel-shaped. The cap margin is lobed and wavy to crinkled. The hymenophore on the underside of the cap assumes the form of veins or of thick, relatively very narrow gill folds, bifurcating and transversely anastomosing, running deep down the stipe. The stipe, broadest at the top, gradually widens into the cap. The stipe is sometimes relatively short and thick, sometimes, on the contrary, elongated. The flesh is paler than the cap, firm-fleshed, with an agreeable fruity smell and a slightly peppery taste. The spore print is pale yellow.

The Yellow Chanterelle appears in clumps in summer and in autumn. Not long ago it was, at least in some European countries, one of the commonest mushrooms forming huge colonies especially in mossy spruce stands without undergrowth, but also in pine and mixed forests. At present it is disappearing from the woods and has become almost rare in some regions. Its range extends throughout the north temperate zone. It is a good edible mushroom in spite of its relatively tough consistency which makes it less digestible. Two of its advantages are that it is never infested with insect larvae and may be transported easily.

In deciduous forests it is possible to find the more fleshy but pale to almost white *Cantharellus pallens*.

Spores of *Cantharellus cibarius*: 8–11 × 5.5–6.5 μm, ellipsoid, with one or more oil droplets, smooth, colourless

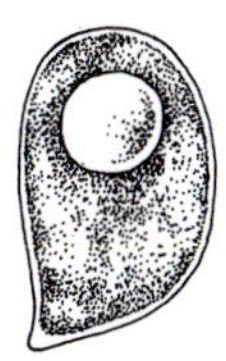

The fruit bodies of *Cantharellus aurantiacus* are similar to the Yellow Chanterelle in appearance and in size

Cantharellus cibarius

Cantharellus tubaeformis

Bull. ex Fr.

This chanterelle has a 2–6 cm wide cap, irregularly deeply funnel-shaped, at maturity with a strongly lobed and scalloped margin, ochre-brown to yellowish smoky-grey, darker when moist, sparsely dark innately scaly, mostly wrinkled-striate. The gill folds are grey, yellowish grey, sometimes yellowish, entirely hoary-pruinose when old. They are running down the stipe like wrinkles. The stipe is 4–6 cm long, 0.5–1 cm thick, yellow, greyish above, mostly compressed and rugose. The whole fruit body is hollow (down to the stipe base). The flesh is relatively thin, greyish yellow, odourless, with a mild taste. The spore print is white.

Cantharellus tubaeformis favours damp soils in conifer forests, mainly in spruce and pine stands. Fairly often it grows from rotting stumps overgrowing with moss. It can be found from the end of summer until late autumn, practically until the first frosts. Having a special liking for acid substrates, it is less abundant on calcareous soils. It is an edible, relatively tasty mushroom.

In professional mycological literature and in mushroom-collectors' manuals we often come across the name *C. infundibuliformis,* by which most authors understand *C. tubaeformis.* Other authors, however, assign the designation *C. tubaeformis* to a different species identical with *C. lutescens,* having bright orange, lamelliform gill folds and a golden-yellow orange stipe. It is much rarer and occurs in wet conifer forests.

Spores: 9–10 × 7.5–8 μm, broadly ovoid to subglobose, smooth, colourless

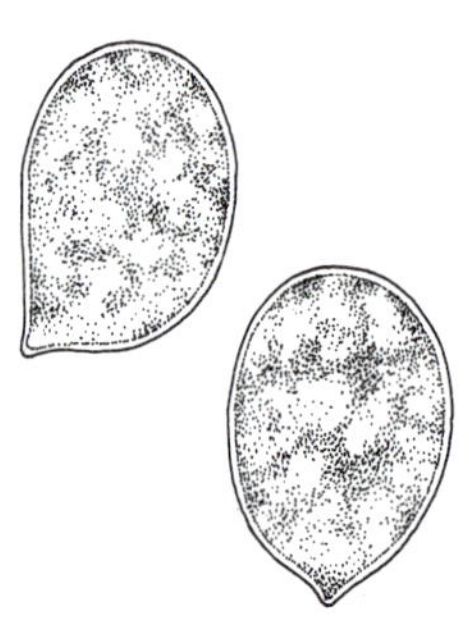

Oyster Fungus, Oyster-cap Fungus, Oyster Mushroom

Pleurotus ostreatus (Jacq. ex Fr.) Kumm.

In some European countries, efforts are being made to produce the Oyster Fungus commercially. In the wild it is found on the trunks or stumps of various trees and shrubs, mainly of deciduous trees. On the basis of genetic experiments, variations in shape and mainly in colour have been promoted to four independent species: *Pleurotus columbinus, P. cornucopiae, P. ostreatus* and *P. pulmonarius.*

The typical Oyster Fungus forms clusters of caps situated one above the other. They are most frequently bluish violet but may also have a brown to blackish tint, and become paler with age. The gills are white, brownish to lilac, rarely forked. The stipe is strongly eccentric to lateral. The flesh has a mild taste and sometimes an unpleasant spicy smell. The spore print is brownish or lilac. The Oyster Fungus ranges from lowlands to the mountains and grows from October to February.

The very similar *P. pulmonarius* grows only at higher temperatures from May to October; it has a whitish or cream-yellow cap with a tendency to turn yellow. *P. columbinus* is bluish grey or bluish and grows from October until the onset of frosts. *P. cornucopiae* has an almost central or eccentric, short or long stipe with gills descending on it in the form of an irregular reticulum. It grows from July until the beginning of autumn. All the above *Pleurotus* species are edible and savoury, older fruit bodies are rather tough.

Spores of *Pleurotus ostreatus*:
7.5–8.5 × 3–3.5 μm,
subcylindrical, smooth, colourless

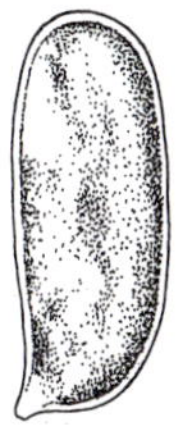

Clump of *Pleurotus pulmonarius* fruit bodies

Pleurotus ostreatus

Lentinus lepideus

(Fr. ex Fr.) Fr.

Lentinus lepideus is one of the commonest fungi of the northern hemisphere growing on worked wood: beams, piles and railway sleepers. It prefers to grow on spruce, pine, fir and larch wood. The 5–15 cm wide cap is at first convex, then expanded, depressed at the centre, in youth with an involute and matted-tomentose margin, with thick and elastic flesh, bestrewn with large, at first ochraceous, later brown scales. The stipe is up to 7 cm long, 1–1.5 cm thick, solid, tough and elastic, concolorous with the cap, usually attenuated downwards into a blackish rootlike extension. It is covered with a large number of recurved, brownish, fibrous scales but often grows glabrous. The stipe apex is glabrous and smooth. The annulus is scaly, retrocurved, sulcate on the outside; usually it is only indicated. The gills are broadly adnate, subdecurrent, broad and distant, white at first, then straw-yellowish, almost lemon-yellow near the cap margin, with irregularly dentate edges. The flesh is white and relatively soft in youth, but firm and coriaceous when old, as hard as bone when dry; it has a pleasant fungussy or aniseed smell and an inconspicuous taste. The spore print is white.

L. lepideus is a considerably versiform fungus. The caps of fruit bodies growing in darkness (e. g. in mines) is either underdeveloped or absent altogether – thus they form only an abnormally elongated, often deformed stipe branching like antlers. *L. lepideus* is inedible.

Spore of *Lentinus lepideus*: 8–15 × 3.5–5.5 μm, cylindrical or cylindrical-ellipsoid, smooth, colourless, nonamyloid

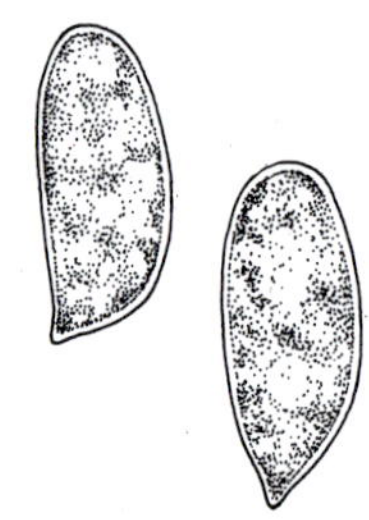

Lentinus lepideus

Lentinus tigrinus is a rare fungus. It grows predominantly on willow and poplar stumps in riparian forests.

Bibliography

Note: The selection of titles is oriented to the basic literature concerned primarily with higher fungi, and complemented by several titles of more recent comprehensive mycological textbooks.

Ainsworth G. C., Bisby G. R.: *Dictionary of the Fungi.* 7th ed. 1971

Alexopoulos C. J.: *Einführung in die Mykologie.* 1966

Bourdot H., Galzin A.: *Hymenomycètes de France.* 1928

Bresadola G.: *Iconographia mycologica.* 1–26. 1927–1933

Dennis R. W. G.: *British Ascomycetes.* 1978

Gasteromycetes – Houby břichatky. Flora ČSR. 1. 1958

Hawksworth D. L.: *Mycologist's Handbook.* 1974

Kavina K., Pilát A.: *Atlas hub evropských (Atlas of European Fungi).* 1–6. 1934–1948

Klán, J.: *Mushrooms and Fungi.* 1981

Konrad P., Maublanc A.: *Icones selectae fungorum.* 1–6. 1924–1937

Kuehner R., Romagnesi H.: *Flore analytique des champignons supérieurs.* 1953

Lange J.: *Flora agaricina danica.* 1–5. 1935–1940

Moser M.: Basidiomyceten. 2. In Gams H., *Kleine Kryptogamenflora.* 2/2. 4th ed. 1978

Mueller E., Loeffler W.: *Mykologie. Grundriss für Naturwissenschaftler und Mediziner.* 2nd ed. 1971

Pilát A., Ušák O.: *Naše houby (Our Fungi).* 1–2. 1952, 1959

Rayner, R.: *Mushrooms and Toadstools.* 1979

Saccardo P. A.: *Sylloge fungorum omnium hucusque cognitorium.* 1–26. 1882–1972

Svrček M., Kubička J., Erhart M., J.: *Pilzführer.* 1979

Singer R.: *The Agaricales (Mushrooms) in Modern Taxonomy.* 3rd ed. 1975

Webstre J.: *Introduction to Fungi.* 2nd ed. 1980

Important mycological reviews and periodicals:

Bulletin trimestriel de la Société mycologique de France (1885–)

Česká mykologie (1947–)

Index of Fungi (1920–)

Mycologia (1904–)

Revue de Mycologie (1936–)

Sydowia. Annales mycologici II. (1946–)

Transactions of the British Mycological Society (1917–)

Westfälische Pilzbriefe (1963–)

Zeitschrift für Pilzkunde (1934–)

Persoonia (1965–)

INDEX